BOOK 1

Broken Hill

A story about a first-generation Irish immigrant growing up in 1950's and 60s Britain.

Bernie J Butler

A note from the author

When I was a child, the first book I read was Treasure Island by Robert Louis Stevenson. I read that book in a dark bedroom under the blankets with a torch. It wasn't necessary to use the torch as our house had a perfectly good electricity supply. However, the night I met Blind Pew, the effect would not have been the same in a brightly lit room. Under the blankets, the wind howling outside and rain lashing the window, which was probably when the seed was sown. Life in a quiet country village would never be enough from then on.

Years later, at four o'clock on a humid tropical morning, I stepped off a plane at Santa Cruise airport in Bombay, India. I was twenty-one years old. Over seven thousand kilometres from home, alone with a single five-pound note safety-pinned into the inside pocket of my jacket, I was about to start a new job as an engineer on a tramp steamer. It was a far cry from a factory in Dunstable.

I always intended to write about life sailing the tropics in old hulks before they were consigned to the scrap heap of history by container ships, bulk carriers, and supertankers.

However, I realised that reading Treasure Island alone was not why I ended up in Bombay. It was just the starting point. There were hundreds of conversations with sailors, old soldiers and other travellers. Plus, summer holidays with my grandfathers in Rosslare Harbour, Ireland. There were the times spent sitting on the harbour wall waiting for my uncle's trawler to come in from a night's fishing. There were thousands of seemingly unrelated incidents. All these things led to that adventure.

In the end we are all ordinary people who sometimes get to do extraordinary things.

Life is a journey. We are all connected, and one thing leads inexorably to another. Before I go on to Ocean Tramp, I may as well start at the beginning.

Every life has a story, welcome to mine. I hope you enjoy it.

Published in The United Kingdom by
Roberto Sendoya Escobar Trading Co
Registered in London Trade Mark 00003619143
5, Brayford Square
London. E1 0SG
United Kingdom
ISBN : 978-1-7391581-0-1

www.robertosendoyaescobar.com

Interior photos of the book by the author.
Covers designed by Rohan James Productions. (Mallorca)

Legal notice

This book is based on real facts and people. It has been written, in part, as a memoir and therefore, some places, dates, and events may have changed. In order to preserve anonymity and ensure compliance with data protection laws, some names may also have been changed. Although every effort has been made to ensure accuracy, the publisher accepts no responsibility for any inaccuracies in this publication.

Table of Contents Page

To my Darling Wife Sandy, thank you for putting up with me while I was writing this book and for all the other stuff.

To Tayrne and Rohan, thank you for the love and happiness you have brought into my life.

Yes, I was young once.

SYNOPSIS

I'm Bernie, a first-generation Irish immigrant born in England shortly after World War Two. Brogborough, the housing estate where I was born and raised was owned by the Marston Valley Brick Company. It was built to accommodate workers for the local brick factory. Everyone worked at the factory that polluted the estate with the constant day and night clanking of machinery and sulphurous smoke from its chimneys.

The estate was home to many persons displaced by the war. Poles, Yugoslavs, Czechoslovakians, Italians, English, Scots, Welsh, others from a decaying British Empire, and the odd German POW who never went home.

Each year my parents returned with my sister and me for our summer holidays in the fresh sea air of Rosslare Harbour in Ireland. The first recollection of my existence is waking in my grandfather's house to the sound of jackdaws and the smell of sea fish frying for breakfast when I was three years old.

In Ireland, I roamed for miles on the beach, got up to mischief with my Irish friend Terrance, or waited on the pier for my uncle Ben's boat to come in from fishing.

Consequently, I grew up with the condition Irish blood English heart. That means I bow to no man. Well, unless he's six-foot six and carrying a Kalashnikov. Even if he's only five-foot two and carrying a Kalashnikov I'll call him sir and polish his boots.

In Brogborough, my mates and I lived in a world of knights and battles with Red Indians, Martians, Germans, and Japanese. When we heard of a Ministry of Defence dump in a nearby worked-out clay pit, we looted it despite the MoD warning notices.

To my parents' surprise I won the Brooke Bond county art prize and best handwriting award from the Children's Newspaper at primary school. I had another talent. I got paid by parents in the street to make their sons' Air fix models that they received as Christmas and birthday presents.

I joined Beasley's troop operating out of Colonel Beasley's dad's garage. The gang was run by the sinister Colonel, his enforcer Frank and the Colonel's empathetic cousin Ray.

With near-disastrous results, we carried out various tests with ordnance misappropriated from the Army Cadets Summer camp.

A friend and I almost drowned during an amphibious exercise to rob a swan's nest using a home-made raft. Another time, because I was small, I was co-opted on a covert mission. My three seniors concealed themselves in bushes while I gained access to an Army Cadet hut through a small window. I borrowed a .303 Lee Enfield rifle and some ammunition clips as ordered. We went on a shooting spree in the woods and narrowly avoided arrest by the local gamekeeper.

Beasley Troop disbanded when the Colonel left school, and Ray and Frank went off to join the army.

I failed my Eleven Plus, but before going to Fulbrook Secondary Modern, the new headmaster at my primary school triggered in me a fascination with science.

At Fulbrook, I did well in science, maths and art. However, I was undiagnosed dyslexic, and English grammar and spelling were a mystery to me. History was a disaster because my dad insisted that every story had two sides, and what I was learning in school was only one.

Following a playground deal with a rich kid, my middle class friend Peter and I purchased a Spandau heavy machine gun.

In the 1960's, Britain's youth, fashion, and music revolution erupted. The Beatles conquered America, then the world. Kennedy said we were going to the moon, but he was assassinated shortly after. The Vietnam war went into full swing.

During the Big Freeze of 1962-63, I worked weekends on a farm milking cows and delivering milk. One cold winter morning, I experienced the wonder of new life when I helped deliver a calf.

In my last year at Fulbrook, our gay English teacher instilled in me a love of Shakespeare. It wasn't possible to take O Levels at Fulbrook, so I went to Dunstable College of Further education with my mate Buzz for two years.

During the summer break of 1964, I worked as a fare collector hopping on and off a fairground carousel at Woburn Abbey.

In early 1965 aged 16, later than many of my school friends, I lost my virginity. Because Mods got more girls than Rockers, I abandoned my idea of getting a motorbike. I worked weekends and holidays clearing tables at the M1 services to earn money to buy a Vespa Sportique. I became a Mod.

At college, I read a book predicting the invention of the internet and man's destruction of nature. Initially, I thought the book was written in the 1960's, but later, I was amazed to find it was written in 1909. It made me wonder how people could predict the future like that.

I was more interested in chasing girls than studying. Nonetheless, I passed Mathematics, Technical Drawing and Art but failed English and Physics, which was my best subject. I wanted to be a draughtsman, but surprisingly my tech drawing teacher convinced me to become an engineer. However, I couldn't get an interview. I thought it was because I came from Brogborough, I was Catholic Irish, and my father was a labourer. You had to put that stuff in your job application then. Through a chance meeting with a trainee nurse called Sue Brown in the Students' Common Room, I got an interview at her father's Engineering factory in Dunstable. The foreman didn't like the idea of giving a job to someone whose primary qualification was being a friend of the boss's daughter. However, when I answered his 'killer' trig question, I was offered a four-year apprenticeship at Headley's Engineering.

Dunstable college provided another twist of fate. By agreeing to retake O Level Physics, I was allowed to drop technician training and join an experimental course that combined Mechanical and Electrical Engineering.

To broaden our outlook, student engineers had to attend Liberal Study classes, where we read and discussed the books 1984 and Animal Farm.

In late 1966 after some years of complicated relationships, I fell in love with Erika, the girl from the Polish family on the opposite side of the street. This was the start of a three-year love affair.

The same year, I passed my first-year engineering examination. However, I was expelled from the course because I passed physics but didn't attend any classes. I signed on at Mander College Bedford. They were impressed and arranged for me to continue studying both Mechanical and Electrical Engineering.

In early 1967, I bumped into Ray, who was home on leave. I hadn't seen him since he joined the army 5 years earlier. We re-established our friendship, and Ray told me he'd joined the SAS regiment stationed in Hereford. Most civilians, including myself, had never heard of the SAS at that time. But that would change.

Supported by my dad, I had a terrible fight with the Flitwick Rockers, who constantly terrorised the local dance. My dad dealt with three in quick succession. After a tough slog, I was beaten by a formidable opponent. However, my dad and I were local heroes, and the Flitwick boys never bothered me again.

The clutch on my Vespa disintegrated. On my apprentice wages, I couldn't afford to get it fixed. For the next 3 years, I had to thumb it to and from work every day, rain, snow, wind or shine. I was always short of money.

In 1967, Erika and I hitchhiked to Ireland for a holiday, staying with my relatives. In the UK's Hippie Summer of Love, the same year, we hitchhiked to Preston to see Erika's Polish Grandmother. We heard that Brian Epstein, the Beatles' manager, had been found dead from an accidental overdose of barbiturates combined with alcohol during that Bank Holiday weekend.

In 1968, I managed to save enough money for a holiday in Spain. With Erika, our friend Mary and Mary's boyfriend, we travelled overland by coach for a ten-day stay in San Sebastian. This trip started for me a lifelong romantic attachment to Spain. On the last day of our holiday, Melitón Manzanas, head of Franco's secret police in the city, was shot dead by gunmen. This was the first act of terror by the Basque separatist group ETA.

In late 1968, in a Liberal Studies class, I initiated a discussion on why Britain was not a democratic country. I cited the Northern Ireland civil rights movement as a prime example. I got pilloried over this, but no one, not even me, foresaw the coming storm.

That year I saw 2001: A Space Odyssey. The film was prophetic and reinforced my commitment to becoming an engineer.

In 1969 Erika and I, Ray and his Welsh girlfriend Pat, took the train and ferry for a two-week holiday in Rosslare. This was probably the last time a British soldier, especially one from the SAS, could have safely holidayed in the Republic of Ireland before the eruption of the 30 years Troubles. During that holiday, the late President Kennedy's dream was fulfilled when Apollo 11 landed on the moon. On the last day of the holiday Tom McClean, an SAS soldier, landed in Ireland. He was the first man to row single-handed West to East across the Atlantic.

In early 1970 after three years together, Erika and I broke up. That was a very painful period for me.

Following that, I had various girlfriends but nothing serious. I knuckled down and passed my Higher National Certificate in Engineering.

After four years as a poor apprentice, with no commitments and looking for adventure, I signed a two-and-a-half-year contract as a

Junior Engineer Officer with a company operating old tramp steamers around coastal ports of the Far East. Before going to sea, I attended a shipboard firefighting course in Liverpool. By chance, I met Lorraine at a railway station. Lorraine was a girl I was infatuated with at school who would never look at me. We struck up a friendship and started going out together. However, I was secretly in love with a girl I'd only recently met. My feelings were reciprocated, but it was an impossible situation because the girl was engaged to be married.

The day I left to join a ship in Bombay, India, my taxi driver was Dina, another girl I'd loved from afar at school, who totally ignored me.

As my plane took off from Heathrow, heading for the Far East, I wondered what the hell I'd done. But that's another story.

I have indeed been fortunate. All the things I have written about in this book, good and bad, I consider to be gifts. I am the sum of all my experiences.

Prologue

The longest journey starts with the first step

Mallorca

One evening before sunset in early autumn 2018, I was driving on the Felanitx to Cas Concos road. Everywhere was bathed in that golden light so loved by artists in Mallorca.

A kilometre from Felanitx, I turned left onto a rough track not usually used by tourist hire cars. Ahead, the way passed between two buildings. On the left was an old señorial stone farmhouse; on the right was the round tower of a mediaeval windmill. Between these buildings, visible in the distance, rising five hundred metres above the valley floor, was the fourteenth-century monastery of San Salvador.

The farmhouse had seen better days, but the windmill tower was still in good condition even with its six sails and conical straw roof removed. The scene was evocative of old Spain. It conjured up a vision of two figures silhouetted against the twilight sky. Don Quixote mounted on Rocinante, lance vertical, Sancho Panza on a donkey by his side. Dust hung in the still evening air from their mounts' hooves as they plodded wearily along the track. As suddenly as they'd appeared, the ghosts from La Mancha vanished.

As I passed between the buildings, the lane dipped to the right near a vineyard, then curved left past a small plantation of bramble and tall pampas grass. Around this bend came a small boy on a bicycle. Behind the boy, dragging a stick in the dust, ambled a little girl in a straw hat, summer dress and sandals. Following this pair was a young woman pushing a baby buggy. As I drew closer in the fading light, I recognised this group. I stopped the car and wound down the window. Two small heads peered in, and with accented voices echoed. 'Hello, Granddad'. My youngest granddaughter was peeping from the buggy, being pushed by her beautiful Spanish mother. We chatted a while, then I continued on, leaving the four to wander back in their own time.

I turned into an oleander lined drive and parked in front of a red and orange bougainvillea covered house, our home on this beautiful island. Our son, his partner, and three of our grandchildren lived here with us. Our daughter, her husband, and our other two grandsons lived not far near Palma.

In 1985, my wife, me, and our two young children started on this adventure. A two-year experiment from which we could return to the UK if things didn't work out. After thirty-three years, there were now eleven of us, another grandchild on the way, and an extended Mallorcan family of in-laws.

In those early days, we were strangers in a strange land. Trying to find our way then, we never imagined life unfolding like this.

Our family is now irrevocably part of Mallorca, absorbed by this magical place.

It wasn't always like that. I still find it amazing. How did a first-generation Irish immigrant born in England in 1949, a few years after World War II, come to live on a Mediterranean island with all these Spanish grandchildren?

This project started as a series of short stories, so my grandchildren would know something about their roots. When my friend and publisher Phillip first suggested I turn the stories into a book, I initially thought that was a bit grandiose. However, after considering it, I realised I had been part of the Golden Generation with all the opportunities and privileges that went with it.

You might think that being born into a working-class family, brought up in a terraced house rented from the local brick company and living next to a noisy, noxious smelling factory was not the best start in life. Well, you'd be wrong. It wasn't always easy, but it was never dull, and I wouldn't have wanted it any other way.

The 1950's and 60s were probably the best years for a kid like me to grow up in Britain. You may think that is just nostalgia but consider this.

The Second World War was over. National Service was scrapped. You didn't have to go and fight or die in some foreign land unless you wanted to, and boys being boys, some of my friends did. The National Health Service was established based on clinical need, not the ability to pay. If you wanted to see a doctor, you went to the surgery and waited your turn. If you called for a doctor, they came out because they knew it must be urgent. Without the moderating influence of a Health and Safety Executive, this was just as well. Within reason, provided you didn't fall foul of the local constable on his bicycle and the following repercussions from your dad, we kids played where we wanted and did what we liked. Games were

rough and tumble, but Social Services didn't turn up at your home to take your mum and dad away for parental training.
I wasn't super bright, but I got an excellent technical education, for which I didn't have to pay. Unemployment was less than 2%, so generally, there was no problem getting a job.
To be truthful, there was some open racism. Specifically, when visiting my uncle in London, I remember the signs in accommodation for rent saying "No Blacks. No Dogs, No Irish". That was strange to see for a kid coming from cosmopolitan Brogborough.
We did live under the threat of thermonuclear annihilation, but we had Rock and Roll and then the Beatles to take our minds off all that.

Chapter 1

The first step

Irish roots.

My surname has its roots in the 12th century Norman invasion of Ireland, after which King Henry II gave the Butlers stewardship of the country. The Butlers first arrived in England with William the Conqueror during the invasion of 1066. Before that, they were Norman French, which meant they were Vikings. So, you can see I come from a long line of mercenary travellers and troublemakers.

I was born in England, but both my parents were Irish. Morrissey called the condition "Irish Blood, English Heart". I don't have Morrissey's anger, but two versions of history have occasionally proved problematic. My father loved post war England, he thought it was the greatest country on earth, but it never stopped him from commenting on my history homework.

"There's two sides to a story, and that's just one of them".

Consequently, I've had a problem with authority, or at least with The Conventional Wisdom, most of my life.

Rosslare Harbour

As a child and a teenager, I spent my summer holidays with my grandparents in Ireland almost every year. It's not surprising then that Ireland has greatly influenced my life.

I wonder how many people recall their first memory, the first realisation of their existence? I can.

At about three years of age, I woke in a brass framed bed with my older sister Ellen asleep beside me. The chatter of jackdaws from a nearby plantation of trees and the smell of fresh sea fish frying on a paraffin primus stove filled the air. I had a dim recollection of a train and ship journey that lasted into the night, being carried in the arms of someone along a boardwalk with the smell of the sea and the sound of waves crashing below, then ascending steps to the top of a cliff before falling back to sleep.

I woke to see a vaguely familiar-looking man leaning against the wall at the foot of the bed. The man smiled, turned his head to his right and spoke to someone outside the room.

"Winnie, the little Englishman is awake".

The memory of seeing my grandfather, Bernard (Ben) Boyce, for the first time at 1170 Colville Street, Rosslare Harbour, is as clear today as it was then.

My mum's cousin Tommy Boyce, my Welsh auntie Betty and cousins Jimmy, Marggie and Bernard lived in Jameson Street behind my Granddad Boyce's house.

Auntie Emma and Uncle Richie lived across the street at number 1177. They were from my grandmother's side of the family; her maiden name was Constance Siggins. Constance was born in Bombay, India. Her father was a soldier in the Indian Army of the British Raj. Auntie Emma kept a framed photograph of him on her Welsh dresser wearing his black, gold-braided uniform wearing a pillbox hat. I never met my grandmother Constance; she died before I was born.

At that time, Rosslare village ended at the bottom of Colville Street by the plantation where the noisy jackdaws lived; there, at a right angle, it joined Jameson Street that led onto the old Kilrane back road.

My other grandfather, James Butler and his daughter, auntie Mae, came to live just outside Rosslare on the back road to Kilrane in a house called Ozier Lodge. Granddad Butler had been a soldier in the British Army in World War I. He survived the Gallipoli campaign in Turkey only to return blind from Passchendaele. He moved from Rathfadden, a British Legion housing estate in the city of Waterford, later moving to Rosslare in the early 1950's. I don't know why my grandmother Ellen Butler (née Stone), who I only met once, moved back to live in Waterford, where she died in 1957. It's bizarre to think that if granddad Butler had died on the Western Front, I would not be writing this book, and neither myself, my Butler cousins, nor my children and grandchildren would exist today.

My Auntie Mae was an Irish cycling champion. She had a cafe grandly named 'The Butler Arms' and a petrol station on the clifftop where the Dublin road comes up from the harbour. Sometimes I'd help auntie Mae by clearing tables, washing dishes or filling cars with petrol. She'd give me fizzy drinks, ice cream, and chocolate from the cafe's shop in payment for my work.

Once I was big enough to roam the village by myself, I would go down to the harbour and wait for my uncle Ben to come in from a night's fishing. When the crew had offloaded the boxes to go onto the Dublin train, I would help Uncle Ben bring his share of the catch home. We might have plaice, turbot, sole, dabs, sea bass, sometimes great crabs and the occasional big black lobster.

Uncle Ben and I would climb the ninety-nine steps to the top of the cliff and take the four-minute walk to Colville Street. The wire holding the hank of fish through their gills would cut into my hand, but I wouldn't accept any help carrying them. I'd follow my uncle, imagining I was a real fisherman coming home from the sea.

There was a building a little way along from the clifftop, on the left side of the road, opposite Murphy's store and post office. Painted in big, faded letters on its wall was 'Boyce's Tea Rooms,' a remnant from my great-grandfather's time. John Boyce was an Irish civil engineer. He moved from Carrigart, Co Donegal, Ireland, to work for Charles Brand and Son in Glasgow, Scotland, who in 1901 won the contract to reconstruct the pier in Rosslare Harbour. My great grandfather was a travelling inspector for Brand and Son and the block foreman on the pier project. The harbour storm wall was named Boyce's Wall after him.

Following the construction of the harbour, my great-grandfather remained in Ireland. Later he moved to Helvic, Co Waterford, to build the pier there. My grandfather, Bernard (Ben) Boyce, stayed in Rosslare and married my grandmother Constance Siggins.

Back at Colville street, we'd fry the fish and, if we had them, drop the crabs or lobster into boiling water for the family breakfast.

Most times, when my mum took me to see friends and relations in Rosslare, I'd be given a silver sixpence. English or Irish, the coins were interchangeable. However, I liked it best when she took me to see old Mrs Doran. Every time I saw Mrs Doran, she gave me a silver half-crown. Two shillings and sixpence was big money for a child in those days.

I would roam the beach all day, going south to Carnsore Point, seven miles of empty sands where waves crashed on the shore and reverberated against the cliffs. Many battles I had with pirates and buccaneers on that long beach. Or, I'd go north to the rock pools, full of small crabs, shrimp, crustaceans and other strange creatures. Then, I'd walk along the clifftop to Rosslare Strand, where Commodore John Barry, "The Father of the American Navy", grew up with his uncle Nicholas, a fisherman, after his family was evicted from their home in Tacumshane by the British. The 'Strand' is also where Guglielmo Marconi built his repeater station when he transmitted the first radio signal from Britain across the Atlantic to Newfoundland in 1901. Marconi's mother, Annie Jameson, was from the county town of Wexford, about 10 kilometres away. Annie was the granddaughter of John Jameson, the founder of the Jameson Irish Whiskey Company.

Of course, all that meant nothing to me then. I was only interested in going off with my friend Terrance O'Brien, who lived in Goulding street just up from Colville street. Opposite Terrance's house was the three tall, sided ball-alley where we played handball, sort of like squash, but without a racket. We were always up to mischief around the harbour. We'd collect discarded drink mixer bottles on the railway track dropped from the dining cars of the Dublin express and take them to Coady's store to collect the deposit money. That was a profitable little business. Or, when Cadbury shipped sacks of chocolate crumb that looked like brown coal coke to their Dublin factory, we'd spike the hessian sacks on the dock and fill our pockets.

Sometimes we got caught and reprimanded during these criminal activities by the railway company employees.

"Terrance O'Brien and that brigand with ya, feck off home before I tell ya mothers". Then we'd lope off laughing with our ill-gotten gains.

There was a cinema in Rosslare in a small building on St Martin's Road in those days. The seats and the projector were all in the same room. The local boys and girls would gather together, and when the lights went out, there'd be chaos in the front rows. Periodically, the lights would go on, and the lady projectionist would chastise us.

"Settle down at the front, or I'll put you all out. You, Terrance O'Brien and Winnie Boyce's boy from England behave yourselves, or I'll tell your mothers'.

A funny thing in Ireland, it was always your mother you had to be afraid of. The only film I can remember seeing at that cinema was 'Moving Target' with Paul Newman.

After leaving school, I continued visiting Rosslare. Before the Gaelic Tiger economy of the mid-1990's, Terrance had moved away to work in London like many others. Then I spent more time in the Railway Club with Uncle Ben or drinking with my friend Brendan Walsh in the hotel. Brendan was a fisherman and volunteer RNLI lifeboat man; he was the son of RNLI Silver Medal holder Coxswain Richard Walsh. One day Brendan told me that a man from the RNLI

in the UK had come to inform the crew about the new hi-tech lifeboat they were getting. If it capsized, the boat was self-righting.
"What do you think of that," asked the Englishman.
"Well, I think I'd prefer one that didn't turn over in the first place", replied Brendan.
One night, I was drinking in the hotel after hours when suddenly the barman shouted.
"Everyone out. The Guarda are coming".
Pints in hand, everyone made for the door. Not familiar with rapid pub evacuation, I was the last one out. The police car arrived to find fifteen men in a line on the clifftop, hands in pockets or smoking, taking the night air and enjoying the view of the harbour lights. A tall officer walked down the line asking each man by name how his mother was, how the fish were running or suchlike until he got to me." And who are you?" he asked.
"He's Bernard Boyce's grandson", the man beside me answered.
"Can't he speak?".
"He's English", came the reply as if that explained everything.
The Guarda lowered his head and said into my ear.
"Where's the drink?". I said nothing, and the Guarda continued.
"Give us a sup of ya beer, and I'll say nothing about this" he knew how to break a man.
I reached down behind the low wall and brought up a full pint of Smithwick's. The Guarda took it, drank it and handed me the empty glass.
"Regards to ya granddaddy," he said, and then "Grand night lads" and walked back to the car and drove off.

When he'd gone, I asked the barman how he'd known the police were coming.
"The Desk Sergeant telephoned me," he replied.
But Rosslare Harbour wasn't my home. I only tell you about it, so you know something about my roots. What bearing, if any, this has on my tale is for you to decide.

I was one of two children. My older sister Ellen and I were always fighting, but most of that was my fault. Ellen was sensitive, and I took advantage. One incident involved an umbrella. Ellen had just come in from a walk in the rain; she liked doing that. As usual, I lay on the sofa winding her up about something. I stressed her so much that she threw the umbrella at me. Lucky for me, it fell short and went through the side of the sofa, splitting it top to bottom. I compounded the situation by saying, "Temper, temper. What's dad going to say when he sees that?" which caused my sister to burst into tears.
Mum sorted the problem by giving dad some old blarney about the dog taking a fit and running around the room with the umbrella in its mouth and impaling it into the side of the sofa. Like one of those accidental silent farts, the old dog took the fall.
Ellen passed her 11 Plus exam and went to grammar school in Dunstable. After that, she became the secretary for a director of Plysu Plastics in Woburn Sands. Before she left school, she started going out with Peter Hinson, who lived at the bottom end of Ridgway Road. I never gave them any peace when they were canoodling. I'd creep behind the sofa with my fishing rod and

dangle a weight down onto their heads. The only time I ever heard my sister swear was after one of these incursions when she shouted at me. "Fuck off, you little creep and grow up, " which encouraged me even more. However, we did become close when I eventually did "grow up", but we always had a different outlook on life.

My mum had two sisters, Mary and Madge. I never met Madge; she died from tuberculosis when she was young. The consumption, as they called it, was common in those days.

My mum had three brothers. Uncle John was in the merchant navy working deep-sea on oil tankers.

Uncle Billy was also merchant navy working on small coasters around the British Isles and the western coast of Europe. Billy told me all about his adventures, I am surprised he lived as long as he did, but I'll get to that later.

Uncle Ben was the youngest brother, he was a fisherman who'd also been in the merchant navy sailing deep-sea. Ben had his own close calls. Late one night he was drinking in the bar on the pier in Rosslare Harbour. He left and either turned the wrong way to go home or stopped for a pee. Either way, the worse for drink, he fell off the dock by the stubby red lighthouse. Still in his sea boots and working gear, he hung onto the harbour wall all night until someone heard his call for help in the morning. He was pulled out of the sea lucky to be alive. In the end it was too many Capstan Full Strength that got him. He was a big quiet man and I loved him.

Over the years, stories about travel and life at sea fuelled a desire in me to visit faraway places. My dad built a shed in our backyard. It was an old shanty hut made out of bits of planks and sheets of corrugated iron. He'd put in a large glass window made from an old picture frame at the end facing the garden. On rainy days with my jacket over my head, I'd dash from our back door into the shed. I'd fight my way through the junk to the end where the gale lashed rain against the window. There, with white spray streaming off the bow of my ship, battering the window, I was the captain on the bridge of a destroyer ploughing through a raging sea in search of submarines. I had to bend and brace my legs to support myself as the shed pitched and rolled in the mountainous sea.

Mum's brothers were all heavy drinkers but very relaxed about it. Unlike my dad and his younger brother Tommy Butler (not to be confused with my mum's cousin Tommy Boyce, from Rosslare). My dad was an intelligent man with a love of books and Shakespeare. During the war, which neutral Ireland referred to as 'The Emergency', he was in the Irish Army. That's not to be confused with the IRA, which was and still is an illegal organisation in Ireland. He met my mum in Rosslare while he was on coastal defence. After the war, he moved to England for work. He loved England, but he was frustrated and could have got a much better job but for the times he lived in. When he could afford it, he drank too much. He was only five foot eight tall, and although he was never one to start a fight, he was never inclined to walk away from one if it came his way. Like a Kerry Blue dog, all opponents shrunk to fit the frame.

When my dad and his brother Tommy Butler, who lived in London, got together, it was like something out of a John Wayne film. It always started and ended the same, an emotional reunion followed by blood on the floor when they returned from the pub. My dad was no saint, but Uncle Tommy was psycho after a few drinks. It was horrible for my mum and my lovely Auntie Kay, Tommy's wife. My sister Ellen was a nervous wreck during these family reunions. It upset her so much that she refused to say she was Irish. It didn't bother me so much because I lived in a world of my own most of the time, but, no doubt, it left its mark. It was a shame because I never really got to know my cousins - Jimmy, Tommy and Patrick - properly because of the eventual rift in the family.

There wasn't the same animosity between my dad and his older brother, even though Uncle Stephen could easily drink a bottle of whiskey a day. Uncle Stephen had been a professional soldier, a Battery Quartermaster Sergeant in the Artillery Corps of the Irish Army. After he retired from the service, he got a job as a storeman in Croydon, so I often met him. Uncle Stephen knew a lot about ballistics, mathematics and statistics, essential knowledge in the artillery for understanding trajectories, mean point of impact, probable error, and dispersion areas. Until he showed me, I never knew how vital mathematics was for killing people.

Uncle Stephen served as a United Nations peacekeeper with the Irish Army in the Congo and Cyprus. In the Congo, on 8 November

1960, in a place called Niemba, a patrol was ambushed by the Luba militia. It was the first time the Irish Army had been embroiled in battle since the Irish Civil War. 9 Irish soldiers were killed.

In September of the following year, a small contingent of Irish troops was besieged at the mining town of Jadotville by forces loyal to the secessionist state of Katanga. The 150 Irish soldiers resisted attacks by an estimated opposing force of more than 3000 for five days while a relief force of Irish, Indian and Swedish troops attempted to reach them. They were eventually forced to surrender when they ran out of ammunition and supplies. No Irish troops were killed in that engagement, but 26 Irish soldiers lost their lives in the Congo deployment.

Dad had another younger brother, Mossy (Maurice). I only met Mossy once when I was a kid. Remembering him conjures up an image of Buddy Holly, a pair of thick, black-rimmed glasses under dark curly hair. I think Mossy went to Australia, and we never heard from him again. I had four aunties from the Butler side. Nancy (Anne), Mae (Mary), Helen, and Julie (Julia). Julie joined the British Army during the war. She married an Orange man and ended up living in Belfast.

I knew my Auntie Mae best because she lived in Rosslare. I think I had another auntie called Greta who died young, like Madge, from tuberculosis or possibly a heart problem.

That was an introduction to my Gaelic side, the emotional part that acts without too much forethought. The what the hell side of my character that can get me into trouble. Then there's my English side which is more logical and calculating. The how can we sort this to my advantage? That can get me out of trouble.

However, I don't think there is that much difference between the two. The Irish are considered warm because they tend to openly show their emotions. The English are considered cold because they tend to hide their emotions. Either way, as nations, you really wouldn't want to upset either.

Chapter 2
Broken Hill.

If you're ever passing junction 13 on the M1 close to Milton Keynes, the city of trees in Bedfordshire, look north. Less than 300 metres from the motorway, you'll see the Prologis Park of Marston Gate. Marston Gate is a large, modern, industrial estate of logistic warehouses that includes the giant Amazon distribution centre. Obscured by these industrial buildings is the small village of Brogborough. It wasn't always like that.

Before Prologis, there was an enormous brick factory with 25 massive chimneys spewing noxious smoke into the atmosphere 24 hours a day.

In early 1946, shortly after World War II, most of Britain's male working population was still in uniform and scattered across the globe. Due to a labour shortage, the Marston Valley Brick Company recruited workers from Ireland and anywhere else they could find them.

That's when my father, James Christopher Butler, from Waterford in Ireland, arrived in Brogborough looking for work. In June of that year, he married Winifred Katharine Boyce from Rosslare Harbour in Kilrane Church, County Wexford, and returned to England alone. Once he was allocated a house, my mother left her home in Rosslare to join my father in England. It must have been a shock for my mum when she arrived in the brick fields of Bedfordshire.

In 1946, Rosslare was a small village, it had no church, but it did have one hotel and the Railway Social Club for the other spiritual things in life. Atop a grassy cliff overlooking the St George's Channel in the Irish Sea, Rosslare had the highest average sunshine in Ireland.

Brogborough, with just three streets and about one hundred houses, was smaller than Rosslare. But Rosslare was a close-knit community with a common identity. My mum knew everyone, and everyone knew her. In contrast, Brogborough was a diverse mix of humanity from across the globe, unrelated strangers looking for work and a new life after the horrors of World War II. Apart from the Irish, there was a mix of displaced Europeans. Italians, Poles, Yugoslavs, Czechoslovakians, others from the Baltic States, and the odd German POW, like the father of my friends Hans and Steven Pauli and their sister Anna. Mr Pauli married the local farmer's daughter, and, like 30,000 other German POWs, he never went back home after the war. There was also a mix of English, Scottish, Welsh and nationals from a decaying British Empire.

Other than a village full of strangers, the biggest shock for my mum would have been the air. The sulphurous atmosphere from the brickwork's chimneys belching smoke day and night was a far cry from the ozone filled sea air of Rosslare. As a child, I occasionally found my mother softly crying by herself. Over the years, as I came to love Rosslare, and her family and friends, I understood the wrench it must have been for her to leave and come to England.

When my mum arrived in England, her sister, auntie Mary, was already living in the village of Wing, 14 miles away in

Buckinghamshire. Soon after I was born, auntie Mary, her husband Steven Susikow and my cousin Bernadette came to live in an old house two miles away on the road to Marston; later, they moved to 12 Ridgway Road in Brogborough. I'm not sure where Uncle Steven came from, possibly the Baltic States. He didn't talk about the war and said he'd lost contact with his family. Like many displaced persons, he never went home because his country had become part of the Soviet Union.

My sister Ellen was born in Bedford Hospital in September 1947. I was born at 32 Highfield Crescent Brogborough at about three on a freezing winter morning on 27 January 1949. Auntie Mary, who'd come to stay to look after my mum, was the first person to hold me when I came into the world. She and I were very close for the rest of her life.

I was a first-generation Irish immigrant in the UK but being an immigrant in Brogborough wasn't unusual.

By the time I was five, Brogborough had become an integrated community, a multinational place with English as a common language. Residents knew each other and each other's business. Like any close-knit community, there were frictions. But if you were in trouble, there was always a neighbour to turn to.

The name Brogborough comes from the Anglo Saxon, brocc-barrow, meaning The Badgers' Hill. Alternatively, bróc-barrow can mean Broken Hill. A barrow can be a mound, a hill or a fortified hill.

In my imagination, a broken hill fortress conjured up a scene of a great battle. The battle of Broken Hill worked as well for Saxons and Normans as it did for Cowboys and Indians or a Japanese Banzai attack.

There was no evidence of a fortress at Brogborough or a great battle, but Broken Hill sounded exciting, so I stuck to that interpretation and dispensed with the badgers.

Either way, like the Anglo Saxons, we were just a continuation of an old, ongoing migration into Britain.

To us locals, Brogborough was called 'the estate'. We never referred to it as a village. It was built in the early 1930's to house Marston Valley Brick Company workers. It sat on the south-facing hill slope overlooking countryside to the distant Anglo-Saxon church at Husborne Crawley, one and a half miles away. But don't imagine some tranquil pastoral setting. Immediately to the east of the estate, only two minutes' walk, was the brick factory, known to us as the 'brickyard' or just the 'yard'.

The yard had twenty-four tall chimneys, twenty-five when the new Hoffmann kiln was built. Belching sulphurous fumes twenty-four hours a day, the massive factory cooked off bricks made from local Oxford clay. There was an insatiable demand for bricks to rebuild a Britain pounded by the Luftwaffe and for the industrial centres of Europe flattened by carpet bombing and total warfare. Everyone worked in the yard; it was a reassuring constant, always there pulsating as a background to our lives. The heavy cable trucks ran day and night. Clack clacking, they hauled clay from the pits below the north side of Brogborough hill to feed the kilns.

Looking north from the top of Brogborough Hill, the valley was filled with the smoking chimneys of other brick factories as far as the eye could see to the enormous hangars at Cardington, nine miles away, where the ill-fated R101 airship was built.

The estate had three streets. Hill and Highfield Crescent ran east to west, known as the 'top street' and 'bottom street' because of their position on the hillside. Ridgway Road ran north to south, connecting the top and bottom streets. The brick company owned two shops on the west side of the estate by the B557 Bletchley-Bedford road. Next to the shops were a red GPO post box set into the wall and a red telephone box. On the other side of the B557 was the CIU Working Men's' Club, also owned by the brick company.

After the war, with a mass of displaced persons throughout Britain, a condition for my parents getting a house was they would have to take in lodgers. Not forever, but for a few years until housing availability improved.

And so, my mum settled into a new life. Now she had her own home, but soon she would be sharing it with strangers. It would have surprised her to know that her new boarders were setting out on a long journey to Brogborough from a very different island.

1,220 miles west of southwestern Africa and 2,500 miles east of South America, at coordinates 15° 56 S, 5° 42 W, an extinct volcano rises 818 metres out of the open sea, a speck in the vast South Atlantic Ocean.

You may not know this place, especially if history and geography are not your best subjects. Only 10 by 5 miles in size, with a mild tropical marine climate, Napoleon was exiled there after his defeat at the Battle of Waterloo. The island of Saint Helena is one of the remotest places on Earth.

In the late 1940s, two young men from that distant place boarded a ship travelling from Cape Town, South Africa, to England. Union-Castle mail ships occasionally stopped at Saint Helena on a two-hour turnaround before sailing to Ascension Island. Their journey would take two weeks as the ship ploughed north around the coast of West Africa and then across the Bay of Biscay to Southampton. Like any young men, they would have been apprehensive and jubilant about this new adventure.

Imagine their dismay when Kenny and Charlie Wade arrived with their suitcases at 32 Highfield Crescent. With a cloudy sky and damp air holding the acrid smoke from the brick factory chimneys down onto the street, Brogborough was a bleak place in the winter. The houses were cold. On winter mornings, you had to breathe on frosted windows to see out.

Coming from a small coastal community and struggling to adjust to this unfamiliar place herself, my mum understood their feelings. She welcomed the two young men into her home. I was very young when Kenny and Charlie came to stay; it's now a distant memory. However, I grew to know them well. Charlie moved on to live in Leighton Buzzard but visited us regularly. Kenny married Betty

Ring, an Irish girl from Brogborough and moved to the top street. Kenny and Betty often came to see us, especially when my dad rented a black and white television from Simmons Ltd of Bedford for two shillings a week. One of the first in the street, the thing was a chest-high, polished wooden cabinet. The screen was smaller than a dinner plate. During the day, you had to draw the curtains to see the picture, and at night we watched it with the lights off.

Nevertheless, it was standing room only in our house on nights of a big football match.

The biggest problem with that TV was that we had an electric meter under the stairs. You had to prepay for your electricity by putting shillings in the meter. The power cut out if you forgot to top up the meter and used up all the prepaid electricity. Then there was a scramble to find a shilling to get the electricity back on. This could be chaotic at night because not only could you not find a shilling, but you also couldn't find the torch to find the meter under the stairs to put the shilling in.

This event was known as "Mum the shillings gone". Murphy's Law is a constant in life. The shilling usually went just before the critical part of a film or drama or before a goal or penalty in a football match.

Sometimes we were so unprepared we had to go next door to scrounge a shilling to get the power back on.

We eventually lost touch with Charlie. However, I've known Kenny all my life. After I left home, I often met him at Brogborough's CIU Club when I returned to visit my parents.

But that wasn't the end of our relationship with Saint Helena. Sometime in the 60s, another pair of dark-skinned young men with suitcases arrived at our door with a letter for Mrs Butler. Mrs Wade wrote that Kenny and Charlie had spoken highly of my mother and asked my mum if she could watch over her younger sons, who'd followed their brothers' path to England. We rearranged the bedrooms; my sister Ellen got the small front bedroom. Mum and dad moved into the back bedroom, and I shared the largest bedroom in the house with my newly acquired older brothers, Georgie and Herbie Wade.

I have fond memories from that time, not least of the extra pocket money and Christmas presents I got from the brothers. I always found it amusing that the two of them slept with the sheet pulled right over their heads. With the sheet blowing up and down, it was like having two breathing corpses in the room. It made me think there must have been a lot of nasty insects in Saint Helena.

One time, Herbie took an extended holiday from his job in the brickworks and took the Union-Castle ship back to Saint Helena to see his family. He was gone for about two months. When he returned, his suitcase was half full of mangos that had ripened on the journey home. That was the first time I'd ever eaten that exotic fruit so common in supermarkets today. And that's how it was for the next few years until Georgie and Herbie found their own way in the world.

A day in the life.

An average day in Brogborough started at seven in the morning. Mr Bevington, the farmer (Hanns and Steven Pauli's grandfather), delivered freshly bottled milk on a large flat-bed wooden trailer with big pneumatic tyres, pulled by a massive shire horse. Mr Bevington had two shire horses, a black one and a brown one; they were enormously powerful but docile creatures. They plodded and stopped waiting patiently unattended as the farmer delivered milk in pint and quart silver-topped glass bottles to each doorstep. Randomly distributed piles of steaming horse dung rewarded the horticulturally inclined estate residents.

The newspaper delivery came after Mr Bevington. Peggy from the shops usually did this. Peggy was a lovely lady, the daughter of Mr Wolsey, one of the owners of the brick company. Peggy must have risen very early, as she was always made up like Ava Gardner in the mornings. The best was the summer when Mrs Peacock, I think that was her name, took over the paper round. She was a young woman who came on her bicycle from the 'six houses' on the main road. With a skimpy blouse tied in a knot under her bust revealing her navel, in shorts and sandals, with long tanned legs, she was an exotic creature more suited to the Mediterranean than a paper delivery round in Brogborough. A shameful Bridget Bardot, but well appreciated by the men on the estate.

Shortly after eight, the postman arrived in his red Morris or Austin GPO van. He would deliver the Royal Mail, dressed like a military man in a navy-blue uniform trimmed with thin red braid on cuffs and collars, wearing a peaked cap with a brass badge and brass buttons.

About 08:15, the Horseshoe Coach Company buses drove around the streets to take the children to the primary school in Ridgmont and the secondary modern in Aspley Guise. A different company's bus came to the shops for those who'd passed their 11-Plus examination to take them to the grammar school in Dunstable.

Occasionally the call of "Rag Bone, Rag Bone" would be heard. Kids would pester their mums for any old clothes they could trade for cheap plastic toys or a goldfish that the rag-and-bone-man had in his van.

In the summertime, Walls and Mr Whippy ice cream vans, with ping-pong chimes, would compete for clients on the streets of Brogborough. We were also visited by hawkers, door-to-door salesmen and gypsies selling clothes pegs and telling fortunes.

One time, I opened the door to a huge Sikh gentleman with a beard and handlebar moustache with waxed spiral ends. Dressed in a turban and a long silver high collar coat, he had an enormous suitcase full of Indian Object d'art, silk scarves, leather wallets, trinkets, ivory and wood carvings.

On Friday nights, residents congregated outside the shops, waiting for Mr Bitchener's fish and chip van to arrive. With the splattering of boiling lard and steam rising from the vehicle, people stood chatting, getting the local gossip while eating fish and chips wrapped in old newspapers. Sixpence for a bag of chips, one-shilling-and-three pence for a piece of battered cod, and a scoop of batter-bits for free if you asked for them.

There was a dance in the CIU club hall most Saturday nights, which usually ended in a punch-up. After cleaning the blood off the dance hall floor, Sunday night was bingo night.

There wasn't much crime in Brogborough. We didn't have much to steal in those days. You didn't need to break into a house anyway; all you had to do was put your hand through the letterbox in most front doors and pull up a string with the door key. Nevertheless, Constable Vaughn and later Constable Button from the police house in Ridgmont would patrol the streets once a day on a bicycle to ensure all was in order. In those days, the minimum height for a policeman was 5 foot 10 inches (1.78 metres); Mr Button was taller than that, so you didn't give him any lip.

One Sunday in every year was devoted to the brick company's summer outing. A convoy of blue Horseshoe Company buses would arrive at seven in the morning, all governed to a maximum speed of 40 mph, and everyone went to the seaside. Once, like a scene from a film about wartime refugees, the whole village made their way to Ridgmont railway station to catch a train specially laid on for the event.

On these annual excursion days, the estate was abandoned and left like the scene of a mass alien abduction. We'd go to Yarmouth, Clacton-on-Sea or Skegness. I remember one time on our way to Margate, passing through parts of London still with blackened bombed-out shells of buildings left over from the war.

With memories of the fairground, candy floss, toffee apples, and fish and chips, after a day of bracing sea air, paddling in the turbid North Sea or the English Channel, we returned to a sulphurous Brogborough untouched by felons. Quite amazing.

In those days, there were loads of tramps around. But these men weren't criminals or vagrants; they were wanderers. They didn't bother anyone; they kept to themselves. They were probably ex-military men from the war who just couldn't fit back into society

Chapter 3

Paradise Lost

In September 1954, my world extended from my front door to the west, a hundred yards along Highfield Crescent, to the two shops by the main road, and another hundred yards to the east as far as my Auntie Mary's house on Ridgway Road. I hadn't ventured up to the top street at that time.

My world was bigger at the back of our house. We had a long garden separated from our neighbours on either side by a low diamond link wire fence. My dad, like most people in Brogborough, grew vegetables and flowers. His favourite flower was the hollyhock. At the bottom of the garden was a lane that ran the length of the street. On the other side of the lane was an open grass playground with two sets of swings, two seesaws, and a slide. There was also a high vaulting bar on which I could climb, hang by my legs and look at the world upside down. The playground equipment was painted green, the same colour as the houses' doors, windows, and drainpipes. Beyond the playground was a cornfield with a paved pathway through its centre, not surprisingly called the middle path. This path led to a small brick bridge across a narrow brook. From there, the path carried on to the Marston Valley Brick Company factory where my dad worked. The yard was a dangerous place and forbidden territory, but when we were older, we kids went there anyway. That part of my world was dominated by the massive, ever smoking brickyard chimneys and the constant clacking of the clay pit cable trucks riding over their pivoted anti-roll-back levers.

That was the extent of my world, it might have seemed like a small empire, but at the age of five, it was a vast, fascinating place full of mystery. I spent hours lying on my stomach in the grass studying small plants, flowers and hundreds of different types of tiny creatures of all shapes and sizes with spots and stripes of different colours. These little animals had lots of legs and antennae sticking out of their heads. They scurried about, some in huge gangs attacking lonesome wanderers, overpowering them and dragging their bodies into holes in the earth. Great life and death struggles went on every day. My mum said, if I looked hard, I might find some fairies unless they'd all gone to live in Ireland, where there were plenty of the little people. I never found any real fairies as hard as I looked, but it never stopped me from imagining and talking to them. I spent my time chasing after butterflies and bees to see what they got up to, and I found the hiding places and homes of lizards, frogs, toads, field mice, voles and moles.

The Oxford Clay dug from nearby pits was full of fossils. They often had a bronze metallic sheen to them. In my mind, the spiral ammonites were parts of a Roman Legion's standard lost in battle with local ancient Britons. The long-pointed Belemnites were bullets fallen from the sky in the aerial dogfights between the Germans and the British in the war before my birth.

One of my favourite pastimes was lying spread-eagled on my back in the grass amongst the wild sweet peas and insects. Stuck to the earth with my arms outstretched, I wondered why I didn't fall up into the clouds where I saw dragons, knights on horseback, and pirate ships that scurried across the sky. I wondered what clouds were made of and if I could walk on them. I thought, One day, I might go along with the clouds to see where they went, but first, I would have to learn to fly. The birds did it, so it couldn't be that difficult.

I'd get out of bed, have my breakfast, and wander off searching for some new discovery each morning. With a mind uncluttered, everything was possible, enchanting, unexplained and needed to be explored. Communication with my parents usually started with what, when, why, where or how.

I wanted to know about everything. My dad used to smoke Old Holborn tobacco, and I wanted to know what it was like to smoke. He threw a half-smoked roll-up into the empty fire grate and left the room one day. I picked it up and sat in his armchair. Unfortunately, he came back and caught me puffing on the smouldering butt. I thought I was going to get into trouble. Instead, he rolled a big fat new one, lit it and put it between my lips.

"If you want to smoke, don't do it behind my back", he said and made me smoke the whole thing down to a stub. He didn't think I'd do it, but I did. By the end, I was retching, my eyes were stinging, and tears streamed down my cheeks. After that, I threw up and never touched another cigarette until I was eighteen years old.

Sometimes I'd go with my parents down the middle path and over the brick bridge through the brickyard to Ridgmont station to catch the Bedford train. We had to cross the railway tracks to the station house. There was a little hatch in the wall in the waiting room where you bought your tickets. Before you got them, there were 'chings' as the date was stamped on each ticket. Then the man passed them to you through the hatch. My dad said you could pay for your ticket with unused postage stamps if you had them; they were as good as money.

With our tickets, we'd go back across the tracks and up the ramp onto the platform, where passengers waited in an open-fronted shed with a long hard bench on the back wall. I wondered about and annoyed the travellers with questions in this shelter. All except for Mr Burgess, who never tired of my continual interrogation. Mr Burgess seemed to know everything and answered all my questions.

Next to the station house was a fenced-off area full of great levers. Before the train came, the man from the station house dressed in a dark uniform and a peaked cap came out and opened the two great gates across the railway track and swung them over to stop the road traffic. Each gate had a large metal handled key that came free once the gates were locked. The man took the two keys back to the levers, put them into a block and turned them; this allowed him to operate the long levers.

Further along the track, a large red signal plate with a white stripe would swing down from the horizontal to a sloping angle to tell the train driver it was safe to pass. A little later, a monstrous black steam engine, belching smoke and hissing white steam with the driver leaning out of the cab, would arrive hauling a string of coaches. The machine smelled of burning coal, oil and hot metal. Once the guard had checked everyone was on board and all was clear, the doors were slammed shut. Then the guard would wave a green flag from the rear carriage. Then, we'd chug off through the countryside, passing the many brick factories built along the side of the track on the way to Bedford.

I had an idyllic, carefree existence, but it was all coming to an end unbeknown to me. One day my mother sat me down and told me I would soon be going to school. Almost every day for the last year, my sister, Ellen, had gone off early each morning during the week. She didn't come home until well after lunchtime. She told me she spent her day at school, learning to read and write and count with numbers. She said the children were let out for short periods called playtime, but afterwards, they had to go back to school to work.

It didn't sound very nice to me, and I told my mum I didn't want to go, but my mum said I had to go. When the fateful day arrived, a blue Horseshoe Company bus came to take me the two miles up the hill to Ridgmont. When I got back home that evening, my mum asked how school had been. I told her it was alright, but I didn't think I'd bother going back. That led to the first of my life's rude awakenings when my mum forced me to get on the bus the following day. Thus, in September 1954, I started my formal education. I lost my freedom when I was sentenced to serve school time.

For the next five years, I was in the tender care of Miss Boswell and Miss Bolton and the not so tender care of Miss Busbee, the three old spinster schoolmistresses who taught at Ridgmont school.

It's difficult after 65 years to recall a complete picture of my primary education, which is now a series of discrete, fragmented, but enduring memories with a lot of blank spaces. For example, I've travelled the road from Brogborough to Ridgmont many times. It's one of the things that are ingrained in my psyche. I can recall almost every detail of that road as it was then, but I have no recollection of that first journey to school.

However, from the top of Ridgmont hill, on my way home to Brogborough that first evening, I would have seen my first view west across the open countryside almost as far as Northampton 20 miles away. At that point, I would have realised the world was a much larger place than I'd imagined.

Being stuck in school all day was tough. Fortunately, we had morning playtime and free time after lunch to let off steam. Genders were separated at playtimes. Girls had an area at the back of the school closed off by a high wooden gate. The boy's playground was at the front. With no genteel moderating influence, the boy's playground was a battlefield strewn with the bodies of knights, red Indians and Vikings.

Free school milk was delivered by a man each morning at the entrance to the boys' playground. The milk came in crates of one-third of a pint bottles. Some better-off parents paid for their children to have orange juice instead. I was a milk monitor, which meant that another boy and I had to bring the crates in each morning. Sometimes, the milk froze in the winter, and the silver tops would sit an inch above the bottle on a white column of solid milk. On those occasions, we would put the crates next to the coal stove to thaw before we were able to drink it. I hated drinking warm milk.

The school day started with morning assembly, supervised by our three bespectacled spinster schoolmistresses, their brittle grey hair neatly pinned into buns on the back of their heads. Assembly began with the Lord's Prayer and a hymn accompanied by Miss Bolton on the piano. I liked "All things bright and beautiful" and "We plough the fields and scatter". However, my favourite hymn was "To be a Pilgrim" by John Bunyan. It was stirring stuff starting with, "Oh He who would valiant be, let him come hither". Bunyan, a local Elstow man, wrote the hymn and the book "Pilgrim's Progress". A 17th-century Puritan nonconformist and a Protestant, he wanted to purge the Church of England of all Roman Catholic influence. Bunyan believed that the reformation had not gone far enough, and he went around the county preaching as much for which he wasn't authorised. The Justice of the Peace accused him of "perniciously abstaining from coming to church to hear divine service and having held several unlawful meetings". He was imprisoned in the Bedford Gaol and House of Correction for 12 years. As far as my mum was concerned, not going to church on Sunday was a sin, but even she wasn't that severe. Protestant or not, with a total disregard for the law, Bunyan was a man to be admired. He would have been puzzled that his hymn was the favourite of a young Irish Catholic boy.

Mind you; he wouldn't have been as perplexed as my dad when one day, after a BBC Radio school broadcast on folk music, I came home singing the Irish patriotic song, "The Minstrel Boy".

"Who taught you that song?" he asked.

"They taught it to me at school, dad", I replied.

During the war, my father was in the Irish Army. At one time, he was stationed at the Curragh Camp, County Kildare guarding IRA prisoners. He was openly proud of Ireland's fight for independence against the British, the Easter Rising, the Free State and all that stuff. Yet, he was a committed Anglophile believing England to be the greatest country in the world. Typically Bipolar Irish, he wasn't happy about his son going around the streets of Brogborough singing like an insurgent.

However, this pales compared to what the recent German prisoners of war must have thought on hearing the hymn "Glorious Things of Thee Are Spoken". This hymn was sung to the same tune as their national anthem "Deutschland, Deutschland über alles".

Our teachers' temperaments ranged from the gentle headmistress, Miss Boswell, to the generally moderate Miss Bolton, to the very severe Miss Busbee. This was a perfectly natural progression of demeanours as all new children started in Miss Busbee's class. They were suitably psychologically battered into submission by the time they'd moved up the line.

I often wondered why our teachers had never married, well, not so much, Miss Busbee, that seemed obvious. It was only in later life that it occurred to me that they would have been young women during the First World War. With over a million men killed and many more seriously maimed, they'd probably lost or never found love.

After assembly, I'd go to Miss Busbee's classroom in my first year. There we recited our times' tables and the alphabet: two ones are two, two twos are four, two threes are six, and letter A says ah, letter b says buh, letter c says cuh etc., etc. We learnt these things like parrots. I'm not criticising the method. To this day, I can happily get by without a calculator.

I do wish, however, that someone had discovered I was dyslexic. It would have saved me a lot of embarrassment. Raise, Rays, Rase, Raze, Rehs, each sounds the same and their (or is it there?) meaning is clear in context, written or spoken. So why are they spelt differently? And as for that 'I' before 'e' except after 'c' rule, it's just not consistent. At least with arithmetic, you knew where you stood.

We had oak desks with hinged lids with messages cut into them by past inmates at great risk of retribution from Miss Busby. There was a recessed hole for a black ink pot on the far right-hand corner of each desk and a groove for a metal nibbed, wooden dip pen. We carried out the arduous business of scratching out words on ink splattered paper with these implements. Poking the metal nib into the child's back in front of you was a sure way of gaining their attention.

I became very good at writing provided I had something to copy; otherwise, my spelling made my pros unintelligible. In 1958, when I moved up to Miss Bolton's class, I received the Award of Merit from the Children's Newspaper in the National Handwriting Test.

The school presented works for the National Brook Bond painting competition the following year. The subject was 'Teatime'. Miss

Bolton moved from desk to desk, encouraging the children's depictions of teapots, cups and plates of cakes and sandwiches.
When she came to me, she inquired. "Bernard. WHAT IS THAT?".
I'd painted an orange billed blackbird, worm in beak, over three open-mouthed chicks in a nest.
"It's teatime, miss", I replied in all sincerity.
"Oh. Deary me," she exclaimed and moved on to the next child.
When the paintings were judged, I was awarded the First County Prize and went to the Bedfordshire Show with my class and Miss Bolton to collect my certificate. It sometimes pays to see things differently through a child's eyes.
Back to Miss Busby. She kept a large bag of cut squares of material, and when at a loose end - excuse the pun - of things for us to do, she would, under the guise of 'Crafts', distribute these patches to the class. We then had to pick the threads out of the cloth until each pupil created a pile of cotton waste. This exercise was unsurprisingly called 'picking'. It was a cruel sort of weaving in reverse. Some might have found it meditational, but to me, it was mind-numbing, which probably amounts to the same thing. Another tedium was making bloody pom-poms; this involved cutting two cardboard disks, putting them together and winding wool through the hole and back over the top while moving around the disc, over and over until you had a woollen doughnut. When finished, you cut into and around the doughnut's circumference between the two cardboard disks, tied it off, removed the discs and fluffed it up, voilà, a pom-pom. No experience is wasted; in

electrical engineering, I was an expert at hand-winding toroidal transformers in later life.
A more enduring memory of Ridgmont school was the time around Guy Fawkes Night.
As the 5th of November approached, the Ridgmont Post Office started selling fireworks. In the 21st Century, with the ever-present Health and Safety Executive, it is incongruous to think that a gang of five to eleven-year-olds could legally purchase objects filled with gunpowder and the matches to ignite them. Even more unbelievable. The small shop at Alec White's petrol station, opposite the school, was stacked to the ceiling with boxes of explosives from the Standard Fireworks Company. These were on sale to children. Mr White spent his war years in Bomber Command, so to him, a few fireworks were inconsequential compared to the odd 1000-pound bomb.

I resigned myself to a life of forced servitude and settled into the daily routine of learning reading, writing and arithmetic. I have few clear memories of specific things that impacted me or broke the monotony of that desk-bound confinement. History was good; it always involved a lot of bloodshed between the British, Romans, Saxons, Vikings and Normans that had practical application in the playground.
The school was built in 1878, and the original toilets were still in use in the 1950's. A water tower was built to serve Ridgmont in 1913, but the plumbing didn't extend to the school toilets. The boys' lavatory comprised a long trough urinal at right angles to a

long wooden bench. The bench had five bottom sized holes spaced along its length with buckets beneath that were periodically hooked out and emptied by municipal workers. The place resembled an ancient Roman communal latrine with no partitions for privacy. With shiny-hard Izal disinfectant toilet paper, the heavy aroma of Jeyes Fluid and other natural fragrances, it was not a place to linger.

Opposite the school on Eversholt Road, there was a pretty whitewashed semi-detached thatched cottage. The front of each household was a mirror image of the other in perfect symmetry with identical windows and doors. At each end of the building, there was a low entrance door. Between the doors, each home had a small window of square leaded-glass panes above which was a small arched bedroom window cut back into the thatched roof. The thatch came down to just above the level of the tops of the front doors. A single brick chimney with two terracotta chimney pots protruded from the centre of its high, steeply sloping roof. The strip of front garden was only a few feet wide and enclosed by a low picket fence with two thick white posted gateways for each home. It was a wonder how the straw roof had survived so many Guy Fawkes Nights.

Each year, on a suitably warm sunny day, we were released from class with small rigid boards, pencils and paper. Supervised by a teacher, we'd sit on the grass on the opposite side of the road and draw this picturesque cottage. After an hour of enthusiastic sketching, an old lady would come out of the tiny house to inspect our work. She would then award the most promising Canaletto, a shiny silver sixpence.

My dad often returned from jumble sales with boxes of books. I'd found a book with the fundamentals of perspective drawing in one box. I may not have been good at reading, but I understood the pictures in that book and put the principles to the test in my sketch. That year I won the sixpence. It was enough to buy a 1/2-pound bar of Cadbury's Dairy Milk Chocolate. And so, I learned the value of art and books.

On spring days, we went out for nature walks. It's funny, but rainy days don't take up much of my childhood memory. We always took the same route along Eversholt Road into the lane leading to the roofless church in the abandoned Anglo-Saxon settlement of Segenhoe. Standing in the ancient ruins, I imagined myself to be a Saxon noble confronted by mounted Norman knights in chainmail wearing helmets with nose guards. They'd come to announce a change of ownership. In time I'd learn my ancestors, from the House of Ormond, came to England with those Norman invaders, but for the time being, I was content to be a Saxon ready to fight the oppressors.

Someone said that a secret tunnel connected Segenhoe church to an old building in a field near Brogborough called the Roundhouse and that King Charles had escaped the Roundheads during the Civil War through this tunnel. There was no historical record of this escape, and it was unlikely that anyone could have dug a three-mile tunnel with such accuracy. Nevertheless, we searched for a floor slab or gravestone that concealed this elusive passage.

Springtime was enchanting with woods full of bluebells and meadows carpeted with yellow celandines, cowslips and tiny white daisies. Bumblebees and butterflies busily pollinated the wildflowers and hedgerow blossoms. Ponds abounded with newts, frogs, tadpoles, and dragonflies. And the blue sky was full of migrant birds, swallows and martins, returning from wintering in southern Europe and Africa. So many things seen for the first time.

The height of school technology was a Bush valve radio that received educational programs from the BBC Home Service. "Music and Movement" was one program where a woman's insipid voice spoke to us as if we were introverted mice. She encouraged us to prance around looking for imaginary objects, pretending to be bears waking from hibernation or trees blowing in the wind, all accompanied by suitable sound effects. What I enjoyed best were the broadcasts on Greek and Roman mythology: Theseus killing the half-man half-bull Minotaur with the sword of Aegeus in the labyrinth. The adventures of Jason and the Argonauts. Daedalus and Icarus flying on home-made wings into the sun. Horatio's defence of the bridge against the invading Clusiums. All these stories were what school was all about, stuff you could put to practical use. In late 1957 things began to change. Men arrived with long tape measures and peered at red and white banded poles through small telescopes on tripods. They demolished the old toilets and knocked wooden stakes into the ground.

By the start of 1959, we had two brand new bright classrooms with large windows. We had new boys' and girls' wash rooms with sinks with running water, soap and paper towel dispensers and flush toilets with doors.

There was a long wide corridor with pegs to hang our coats. The pegs were in rows of different colours red, blue, yellow, and green. Now we were divided into 'houses' that competed against each other.

Teachers gave each house points based on the performance of its members in things like study, sports, and manners. At the end of each month, they totalled the points. The house with the highest points was then declared 'top house' for that month.

I didn't like this new competition with my friends. However, after being asked to be a school prefect and house captain, I thought it was a great idea.

Soon another change occurred that would have a fundamental impact on my life. The sympathetic headmistress, Miss Boswell, retired and was replaced by a new headmaster, another 'B'.

With an air of 'Not to be messed with', Mr Briggs was a stern-looking man. However, first impressions can be deceptive. Mr Briggs was dedicated to the enlightenment of children. He introduced a revolutionary new subject that changed my life.

I still remember my first science lesson in one of those new bright classrooms with awe. Science meant Time-travel, Dan Dare, Flash Gordon, spaceships and ray-guns, and I made sure I was at the front of the class.

However, the lesson didn't unfold the way I expected. Mr Briggs wrote "The Earth's Atmosphere" on the blackboard. He took an empty one-gallon oil can and poured a cup of water into it. Then, he pumped up and lit a paraffin primus stove and put the can on it. Before long, steam emerged from the can.

He took the can off the primus and screwed its cap on tight, trapping the steam inside. Then he turned off the primus, put the can to one side without referring to it again.

He told us the atmosphere was like an ocean, and we were submerged in it. The atmosphere pressed down on us, like water in a swimming pool, with a pressure of 14 pounds on every square inch of our body.

I kept looking at the can, wondering why it was there. Mr Briggs told us the atmosphere was 20 % Oxygen and 79 % Nitrogen. The other 1% was all the other gases, but mainly Argon. None of this meant anything to me at the time; I just kept wondering why the can was on the table. Eventually, there was a strange creaking sound, and the can began to distort. The class looked toward the sound. Suddenly there was a loud bang, and everyone jumped in fright. The can collapsed in on itself. It fell over on the desk, crushed by some invisible hand. Mr Briggs explained that as the steam cooled, condensed, and turned into water, it created a partial vacuum in the can. As the vacuum increased, 14 pounds per square inch of atmospheric pressure squeezed on the empty container's thin walls and, like a man with an empty cigarette packet, it crushed the can. I wondered why the atmosphere did not crush me, then realised that I was full of air as the can was at the start of Mr Briggs's demonstration.

To some, this might have seemed like a clever party trick. To me, it was a revelation. I learned how one teacher can make the difference. School would never be the same again.

Before I leave Ridgmont, I have to tell you about a family that had a small but not insignificant influence on my life. I say small because these things are incremental. As I learned in Chaos Theory much later, small differences at the start of a process can dramatically affect its final outcome.

Brogborough and Ridgmont were different worlds. Brogborough was a new place of uniform construction built for the specific purpose of housing a group of cosmopolitan brick factory workers. Conversely, Ridgmont was an old Bedfordshire village. Its residents had occupational names like Farmer, Cook, Garratt, Clark and Woodland that went back to before their entry into William the Conqueror's Domesday book of 1086. My sister became friends with Rosemary from the Barnwell family, and I became friends with Rosemary's younger brother Stephen.

Mr Barnwell had a market garden business, and Stephen lived in a big old farmhouse off the High Street, a short walk from the school past the church. I loved cycling up to see Stephen on Saturdays because Mrs Barnwell, a lovely lady, always asked me to stay for lunch. On Saturday, she always did the same thing, smoked haddock cooked in milk, served with a large knob of butter.

Mr Barnwell had a car; on some Sundays, if he wasn't busy, the family would drive down to Brogborough and take Ellen and me out for the day.

Those trips expanded my world. We went to fascinating places like Chipping Norton in the Cotswold Hills, Stow-on-the-Wold and The Model Village in and of Bourton-on-the-Water.

Mr Barnwell was a Luton Town FC fan. One time he asked me if I'd like to go to a match with him and Stephen. I didn't really like football, but I thought it would be rude not to go, so I went.

There were no seats then, just a stepped concrete terrace. Stephen and I were small, so we stood on the top step in an empty corner to see the match. Three bigger Luton boys lower down saw us and came up to give us some grief.

"You're not from around here," they said aggressively.

Unfortunately, embarrassment, anger or just self-consciousness, I blush very easily.

"Look at him," said one of them. "He's gone red like a traffic light."

Stupidly I responded without thinking.

"It's better than being yellow".

He was bigger than me, but he wasn't that bright. He looked straight into my face because he was standing one level down on the terrace.

He went to pull my shirt, but I saw it coming and instinctively pushed him away. The bully fell backwards and bumped heels-over-head down the concrete steps, followed by his concerned mates.

Mr Barnwell, who'd seen this commotion came over.

"You're not in Brogborough now, Bernard". Said Mr Barnwell, having seen only part of the incident. A football hooligan, I wasn't invited to another match at Luton.

Nevertheless, Mr Barnwell didn't give up on me. My next trip with the family was to the Cutty Sark and the Maritime Museum in Greenwich.

Chapter 4

Oh Baby Baby, It's a Wide World

Back in Brogborough, my world was getting bigger.

In addition to the middle path through the cornfield, there was another path to the brickyard. This path ran down the west side of the cornfield from the B557 Bedford-Bletchley road. The path was unpaved, with the cornfield on one side and a hedgerow bordering farmland on the other side.

The two paths formed a V with its apex on the small brick footbridge over the brook. From there, they joined to become a single path. The paths gave access to the brickyard and passage to Ridgmont railway station and the Cambridge-Bletchley line.

In my imaginary world of knights, pirates, and great peril, these tracks with the mystical names of 'the middle path' and 'the side path' were places of conflict and adventures.

Before being felled in the early 1970's because of Dutch Elm disease, there were two large trees halfway down the side path. Not surprisingly, this area was named 'the two trees' and was a meeting place for kids from the estate.

You could walk directly to the two trees, but that was too easy. There was a more exciting way to get there.

There was a river at the back of Highfield Crescent, where the lane met the side path. Well, in truth, it was a drainage ditch.

Enclosing this ditch was an impenetrable canopy of brambles and hawthorn bushes, screened on the path side by groves of stinging nettles and cow parsley.

We used to cut the long hollow stemmed cow parsley with our sheath knives to make peashooters and use the hawthorn buds as ammunition. We were lucky to survive because none of us knew the difference between cow parsley and poisonous hemlock. Only after surviving my childhood did I learn the rule 'spotty and bald is bad' to tell the difference between the stems of the two plants. It was good advice too late.

Back to the ditch, to the adult observer, the path's edge was a long strip of undergrowth. However, we could crawl through a concealed entrance into a dim green tunnel that arched over the ditch. This tunnel led to the two trees. A world illuminated by beams of filtered sunlight dancing with light reflected off swarms of flying insects. It was a secret passage to a fortress. Or a jungle stream in Burma that we waded through in our war against the Japanese. Often, we sat silent, listening for intelligence from the enemy as they passed along the track above. It could take an hour of careful patrolling and a stop to eat the sandwiches our mothers made before we travelled the 100 yards and emerged from the undergrowth at the two trees.

Some said that the two trees were a way into the underworld, but search as I might, I could never find the doorway in their trunks. Their branches grew out over the path. One of the more courageous kids, probably Ray Papworth, had climbed up and tied a rope on an upper branch. We'd climb into the lower limbs, take the rope and swing out over the path and the edge of the cornfield.

One day, my friend Johnny Mac (McNamara) was in the tree and given the all-clear to jump. Through negligence or because he thought it would be fun, the lookout didn't tell Johnny Mac his grandfather, Mr Tilley, an old man with a bushy white moustache and bottle bottom spectacles, was pedalling up the path on his bicycle.

I suppose the lookout imagined Johnny Mac first swooping in front of Mr Tilley and then swinging back behind him as he passed on his bike. That would have been funny, but the timing didn't work.

Johnny Mac sailed in front of his grandfather, who understandably braked. In the resulting collision caused by the return swing of the pendulum, the birdman, bicycle, and cyclist hit the ground in a unified heap.

Understandably, Mr Tilley was not happy with this Robin Hood event and accused his grandson of attempting to kill him for his inheritance. This claim was unjustified, although Mr Tilley did have a lovely old, black Model T Ford at the time.

Another day my mate Les Parker and I were sitting under the two trees talking when we heard a high-pitched whistling sound. We fell silent. A man dressed in white overalls and a flying helmet, sitting in a metal-framed bed, floated over the rooftops and headed south-east across the cornfield at about 30 miles an hour. We watched, amazed until the contraption disappeared into the distance. When I got home, I told my dad what I'd seen.

"Dad, I saw a man in a bed fly across the cornfield".

I thought he'd laugh and tell me I was imagining things again, but he didn't.

"That must have been the Rolls Royce 'Flying Bedstead," he said. "I read about it in the paper. They're trying to make an aeroplane that can take off and land vertically. It must have been up at RAE Bedford for testing or something."

Les and I would sometimes lay flat, each of us on one of the elms' lower branches. Unseen, we could peer through the leaves from our concealed perches and listen to people's conversations as they passed underneath. To make this pass time more fun, we would drop small pebbles on the heads of passers-by, nothing injurious, just little stones big enough to get their attention. We'd lay dead still as they looked into the tree. Peeping down through the leaves, we could see them, but they couldn't see us. It was exciting. They must have thought it was birds or other small animals in the tree, and they would check their head and shoulders for signs of droppings. No one ever realised it was us up in the branches.

However, one day a tall man in an army greatcoat and a Cossack hat that looked like a piece of rolled-up carpet on his head came up the path. As he passed under us, we dropped a pebble on him. The stone hit his hat, then his shoulder, from where he watched it fall to the floor. He bent down and picked it up, rolled it around between his thumb and index finger for a moment, then looked up into the tree. We soon realised our folly. He must have been over six and a half feet, taller than anyone else we'd molested before. He could have pulled us out of the tree if he'd stretched up his arm. We looked down into a rugged face. He had a nasty scar that ran down from his right eye over his cheekbone to the bottom of his jaw. It looked like a sabre slash. His mouth was drawn down and frozen on that side. We lay petrified and silent on our branches. He continued staring until his eyes finally narrowed, and we saw the hint of a sinister smile. He could see us.

We'd been caught for the first time. It was unlikely that we would escape if we tried to get down from the tree. The Cossack continued looking at us for a few seconds, then slowly put his right hand into his greatcoat pocket and withdrew what appeared to be a short fat wooden stick, but we were mistaken. He hinged the knife open, and it emitted a 'CLICK' as its long blade locked. We were filled with fear, but he wasn't finished. He put his left hand into his pocket. When his hand came out, he was holding an apple. He cut the apple in half. What he did next was unexpected. He stretched up a hand holding two pieces of apple. Petrified, we didn't move. He gestured with his raised hand to take the offering. Not wanting to upset him more than we already had, we cautiously reached down and took the pieces of apple. With sorrowful eyes and a rueful lopsided smile, the giant nodded his head, closed the knife against his hip, slipped it back into his pocket, and went on his way. After that, we were more careful about choosing our victims.

I didn't think much about the event at the time. However, in later years, that man often surfaced in my memory. He must have been one of the hundreds of displaced persons from Europe who washed up in or passed through Brogborough and the brickyard after World War II. I often think of that sad, lonely giant and his small act of kindness to two naughty boys. Where was he from, where was his family and did he ever see them again?

Another time at the two trees by myself, an old mongrel dog with a white coat and a big black patch around one eye came up and adopted me. It followed me around until I took it home and pleaded with my dad to let it stay. After that, there was never a time in my childhood when I didn't have a dog, which was invariably called Rex.

Behind the two trees, there was a field we called the 'bullock field' because that's where Mr Frances, a farmer from Husborne Crawley, kept his bullocks.
This field ran from the two trees to where the side path met the middle path at the bridge across the brook.
The field extended along the brook west to the B557 road. Near the corner of this field, close to the bridge, was a sturdy old oak tree. We called this oak 'Merry England'. In our minds, it had a mysterious connection to Robin Hood. The tree being eighty miles from Nottingham was of no consequence to us.

Large dome-headed iron doornails had been driven into the tree's trunk. These nails allowed you to climb into the oak's lower branches. At the top of the climb, the older boys, Ray Papworth, his cousin Roger Beasley and their friend Frank Reader walked like high-wire artists along a stout bough ten feet above the ground. These boys had tied a rope that hung down from one of the higher branches. Aided by someone below flicking it, they would catch the rope and swing out over the field. However, unlike the two trees, where we skimmed a couple of feet off the ground, here you could do serious damage to yourself if you fell from the bough or slipped off the rope. You also had to drop from the rope when the swinging stopped.

Initially, I was happy enough to climb the tree and sit in the cradle of its lower branches. Gradually all the other boys my age had a go on the rope. Eventually, under peer pressure, they shamed me into having a go. I was not good with heights, so I crawled along the bough on my hands and knees. Holding onto a branch with white knuckles, I sat with my legs dangling in space and stared into the void. I was small for my age, and it looked like an awful long drop to the ground. I sat petrified. I couldn't take the rope and couldn't crawl back. If Roger or Frank had decided to resolve my predicament, the outcome would have been swift and brutal. "You're holding us up. Take the rope or jump. Either way, you're getting off this branch".

Fortunately for me, Ray Papworth decided to come up the tree. Ray was no saint; he and his cousin were always getting into trouble, but he was an empathetic rogue.

Ray was fearless, but he knew his boundaries, well, most of the time. One of his most infamous exploits was riding his foot steered plank and pram-wheel trolley down the north face of old Brogborough hill. The hill was on the main road with an incline so steep that lorries had to be in first gear to get up it. The trolley was deficient in four of the five design features necessary to prevent instability-Tyers, Wheel Area, Axles, and Brakes (Engine: not applicable). Consequently, halfway down the hill, the machine went into a speed wobble. Ray lost control, and in the resulting tumble, the bent six-inch nail holding the driver's plank seat to the foot steering plank ripped into him. He was left bleeding to death on the side of the road. Fortunately, the ambulance came in time. After numerous stitches in his knee, he was released from the hospital, lucky not to have lost his lower leg.

Ray was lucky; at that time, there was a large concrete block directly at the bottom of the hill in the V-shaped verge where the road split left to Bedford and right to Lidlington. The block supported a steel frame for the overhead cable buckets that carried clay from the pits to the brickyard before the truck line was put in. He'd probably have been killed if he'd hit that block and wouldn't have appeared again in this story.

Back on the tree, I was going nowhere. Ray walked along the branch, sat down and called for the rope. He showed me the knot above which I had to grip the rope, so my hands didn't slip. He told me I'd be closer to the ground when I stopped swinging so I could safely drop off. Explained like that, it seemed simple enough. I took the rope and slipped off the branch. There was an initial jerk as I dropped and took up the slack, then for a few seconds, I was flying like a bird. It was exhilarating. I dropped off and got back into the queue for another go. After that, there was no stopping me, well, not until the rope broke with some unfortunate swinging on it. Preventative maintenance wasn't a consideration in those days.

Skydiving wasn't the only game we played on Merry England.

I had to sit in that tree by myself for an hour once while the bullocks took shelter under it from the rain. The animals favoured the east side of the tree for these gatherings. Consequently, that side had a slimy black pond of bullock urine and churned up cowpats. Due to the prevailing wind, the tree leaned slightly toward the slime pond.

The oak was wide. It took about five boys with outstretched arms to encircle it. This led to the invention of another game, the object of which was to use your fingers to grip the grooves in the oak's bark, then, with your feet on the slight bulge at the bottom of the tree, work your way around its trunk, starting on the slime pond side.

One day, egged on by my mates, I took up the challenge. I was about eight at the time. Starting at the slime pond's edge, I carefully inched my way around the trunk. When I was at the pond's centre, I felt the bark between my right-hand fingernails start to give. I froze, hoping things would stabilise, but they didn't. The bark came away in my hand. I should have assumed a sitting position and surrendered to my fate. Instead, I tried to hang on with my left hand. My body twisted with my right arm swinging out and my left hand fixed to the tree. I fell horizontal into the black slime. None of my friends rushed in to help me. I got myself up and sploshed out of the ooze. The right side of my body, head to foot, was covered in the glutinous foul black liquid. It was in my hair, running out of my ear and nose. I was spitting it out of my mouth. All down one side, my clothes were stuck to my body with black glue.

My friends escorted me up the middle path to my garden gate at a distance, then made themselves scarce. My mum wouldn't let me in the house until I'd stripped naked in the yard. I had to take a cold bath because it was springtime, and the coal fire wasn't alight to heat the back-boiler. Curiously, I never came down with some nasty disease. In all probability, the immersion strengthened my immune system.

The middle path and the ancient oak tree 'Merry England' are long gone and confined to history. In their place, the ground is covered by industrial buildings and warehouses.

About every fourth or fifth house in Brogborough had a communal air-raid shelter at the bottom of the garden. These weren't the small, family-sized Anderson shelters prefabricated from corrugated iron and covered with earth and sandbags. The Brogborough shelters were made of brick about 18 feet long, ten feet wide, and just high enough inside to stand up. They were buried with just their flat reinforced concrete roof and a few rows of bricks showing above ground. Single bricks were omitted at intervals around the above-ground perimeter wall to let in air. A concrete stairway led down to a small opening that gave access to the structure.

The shelters were off-limits or playgrounds and camps for the local kids depending on whose garden they were in. Our Italian neighbour on our east side had three daughters, Rosetta, Luigia and Michelina. He also had a bomb shelter where he grew mushrooms, or more precisely, fungo. He used to ask my dad for our dandelion leaves for his salad. He also used olive oil on his bread instead of butter, which was strange because we had a little bottle of that oil at home for putting in our ears if we had an earache.

My friend, Kenny Yates, who lived next door to my auntie Mary on Ridgway road, had a bomb shelter in his garden. One Saturday morning, I decided to go up to Kenny's house to see what was going on.

Before I continue, I have to tell you that I lived in a world that was part reality and part fantasy during this part of my development. Sometimes it wasn't easy to distinguish one from the other.

I could be a buccaneer, a space pilot, a Saxon warrior, or a soldier fighting the Germans or Japanese. I might even use my superpowers to help Flash Gordon against Ming the Merciless.

However, after seeing 'She Wore a Yellow Ribbon' on our black and white telly a few times, I quite fancied myself a lieutenant in the US 7th Cavalry.

This morning, I went onto the street, called my sergeant over and told him to assemble the troops. We then galloped up the road with me ahead of the column.

When I got to Kenny's, he and Johnny Mac were prancing around with dustbin lids and battering each other with sticks. Also, from Ridgway Road, Peter Hinson wandered in and out of the bomb shelter with a wartime baby's gas mask respirator on his head, with a big Perspex visor and a bellows hanging off it. He looked like something out of the H.G. Wells film 'Things to Come'.

It was so bizarre; I turned my troop of 7th Cavalry around and left for home. As we trotted off down the street, Richard Cashin, the older brother of my friends Thomas and Ambrose, came galloping towards us, slapping the side of his buttocks. He had a broom handle horizontal under his arm and a Shredded Wheat box pulled down over his head with eye holes cut in it so he could see where he was going. As we galloped past each other, I turned to my sergeant and said, 'Look, sergeant. The idiot thinks he's a knight'.

We were always playing war games in Brogborough. It's not surprising as the estate had its share of soldiers, airmen and sailors who'd been gradually demobilised and returned home. Many men still wore 'demob' suits, a double-breasted dark grey pinstripe jacket with baggy trousers. They'd exchanged one uniform for another, which we mistook for the fashion.

There was a rumour of a military dump in the worked-out clay pit at the bottom of Brogborough hill. So, at the age of eight, my mates and I set out on an expedition and found the dump. There was a padlocked five bar gate behind the cable bucket tower, where the Bedford road branched off to Lidlington. Behind the gate were the steep earth banks to the bottom of the clay pit. There was a Ministry of Defence (MOD) 'No Entry' warning notice, which was of no consequence to us. The MOD tipper trucks must have backed up and emptied the stuff straight over the edge. The sides and floor of the pit were littered with surplus World War II military materials. Heavy webbing shoulder straps with ammunition pouches, canvas-covered water bottles, bayonet scabbards, and thick webbing belts. There were gas masks and chemical warfare treatment kits. I found a copy of "The Infantryman's Training Manual". With pictures and information like "Never look over vegetation, look through it", and "Never look directly out of a window, stand back in the shadows", I found this book very handy for covert operations.

I also found a British Army Brodie helmet. It was complete with a chinstrap and foam shock absorber on a metal cross, fixed with a dome-nut outside the helmet. When my dad found out where it came from, he took it off me, disinfected it with Dettol and returned it to me with a new coat of green paint. He was right pissed off when I sold it to a kid from the top street for sixpence.

My mum stopped my expeditions to the dump by telling me the pit was full of snakes. That put me off rummaging around rubbish tips for a long while.

We never found any weapons, which was a shame, but that didn't matter much. There was no shortage of arms in Brogborough. Most kids had a bayonet or knife of one sort or another. I had two bayonets, an 18-inch World War I type and a short modern one just long enough to penetrate a Russian in full winter clothing. Roger Beasley had a Fairbairn Sykes commando fighting knife. Most kids had a 177-air pistol or rifle of different types. The more affluent had powerful BSA 22 Meteors. There was some real hardware too. Rodney Bombfield's dad had a Lewis machine gun in the wardrobe that had been overlooked for recall by the home guard. My friend Steven Barnwell from Ridgmont had a .32 revolver from the Boer War in a lovely wooden presentation box. I even swapped some medals for a Very pistol flare gun.

I couldn't afford an air gun with my pocket money, and my dad refused to buy me one. However, I got my introduction to air-powered weapons one day when Mr Fagg cleared out his under-stairs cupboard and found an old Diana 177 rifle. Mr Fagg lived on the other side of the street. His daughter Betty was my sister's best friend, so instead of throwing the gun out, he cleaned it up and brought it to our house with a tin of lead pellets. I waited anxiously as my dad examined the rifle, feeling sure he would say I was too young for the weapon. We took the gun out into the back garden, and dad tried it out. To my surprise, he told me I could have it. I thanked Betty's dad, overjoyed with my new toy. My dad stood by while I tried out the gun, and I realised why he'd let me keep it. The spring and piston were worn out. When I fired it, the pellet fell in a curve and hit the ground about fifteen feet in front of me. My vision of being a great white hunter on the African veld evaporated.

Nevertheless, I still got the safety lesson from my dad. He'd been in the Irish Army and knew how stupid people could be with guns.

"Whatever you think, THIS IS NOT A TOY. Never leave it lying around loaded. When you've finished using it, make sure the barrels cleared and the cylinder is not charged"

"If I ever catch you pointing this gun at anyone, loaded or unloaded, I'll smash it. Do you understand?" I nodded.

"And! Remember this. IT'S ALWAYS THE UNLOADED GUN THAT KILLS"

That was a confusing statement, but I understood what he meant after a few careless accidents playing around with my mates.

After a while, I found that I could hit targets thirty feet away if I held the barrel at 45 degrees. Aiming was difficult with the barrel at that angle because you couldn't use the sights. Nonetheless, after a lot of practice, I became a good shot.

One Saturday, I looked out of my bedroom window, just beyond the flat-roofed bathroom that jutted out from the back of the house, a row of about ten daffodils caught my attention. I decided to try out my new shooting technique from this elevated position. After a few practice shots, I hit the stem of one flower, which wavered for a second, then fell flat on the ground. The next shot took off the head of another daffodil. As I was loading for another shot, I heard a shout.

"BERNARD! STOP THAT". Unknown to me, my dad was digging in the garden behind the bathroom.

After that, I was more careful about target practice and made sure my dad was at work or at CIU Club when I did it.

On our west side, Mrs Freeman, our next-door neighbour, had a big tabby tomcat called Garibaldi. A strange name for a cat, she doted on the animal. She was a nice lady, but she always got on at me for making too much noise. Whether it was for hammering nails into wood planks to make a trolley or fighting off Cherokees who'd invaded the garden. She especially got upset when our dog Rex went berserk, barking at her cat that deliberately provoked him from the safety on the other side of the garden fence. When my dad was over at the club one Saturday, I spied Mrs Freeman from my bedroom window that overlooked her yard. She was sitting on her back-door step talking to Garibaldi, who was rubbing up against the fence, driving my dog to distraction. When the cat strolled off and disappeared into the long grass of Mrs Freeman's unkept garden, I couldn't help myself. This time I was careful. As per the instructions in "The Infantryman's Training Manual", I stood back from the window in the shade of my bedroom. I couldn't see Garibaldi, but I could see the movement in the grass. It was a long shot, but I made my best estimate for the fall of the pellet. I squeezed the trigger; there was a delay as the pellet took a high arc and fell to earth.

There was a loud hissing-spitting screech, and Garibaldi leapt vertically three feet into the air. He fell back to earth and hit the ground running, streaking into the house past Mrs Freeman on the step. She jumped up and followed the cat in to find the cause of its distress.

I surprised myself; I never expected to hit the cat. There was little likelihood that the pellet had enough force to hurt it, but I felt guilty about the incident. Mrs Freeman had no idea what had happened. Even so, I never took another pot-shot at Garibaldi again.

Another incident that could have gotten me into serious trouble with my dad involved my mum's piano.

In the 1950's, there were lots of upright pianos around. They were the equivalent of today's home entertainment system. Many people had them in their homes for parties and sing songs with family and friends. However, as television became the main form of home entertainment, the piano's popularity declined. If you wanted a piano, you didn't have to buy one. People gave them away or just dumped them on the side of the road. Some people made a ritual of smashing up pianos with sledgehammers. These scenes of piano vandalism were often filmed and then shown on TV news and current affairs programmes. It was ironic that the destruction of perfectly good pianos was a source of entertainment on television.

My mum heard about the abandonment of one such unwanted piano on the estate.

The streets of Brogborough were tarmacked. Even so, it took a great effort by my dad and a couple of friends to roll the piano on its small castors down from the top street to our house. The whole palaver drew the attention of a band of kids who had to be fended off from attacking the keyboard at the occasional rest break. Getting the thing into our house proved almost impossible. However, by standing it vertically on its side, they got it into the small entrance lobby, then using the instrument's natural L shape, they managed to manoeuvre it into our living room.

The piano was given pride of place against the wall that backed onto our neighbour's living room. Mrs Freeman had another cause to complain when my sister and I fought over who would play the instrument. None of us except my mum could play the piano properly.

The piano was a beautiful piece of furniture made from dark polished chestnut veneered wood. Above the keyboard was an intricate fretwork backed inside by red material.

One day, I came from my bedroom with my air rifle, intending to do some target practice in the garden. There was no one else in the house. As I was about to go outside, two things caught my eye: the piano's fretwork and a box of Swan Vesta matches on the dining room table. A child's brain is an incredibly inventive thing. I've always been amazed at how you can look at two unrelated objects and combine them to create an entirely different function in one moment of inspiration.

I levered down the rifle barrel to charge the air cylinder, then I took a Swan Vest and pushed it, redhead first, into the chamber. It fitted almost perfectly. I stood on the other side of the room, and with my new knowledge of ballistic trajectories, I took careful aim at the piano. There was a satisfying 'twang' as the projectile went through the fretwork and hit one of the taut wire strings inside. I checked the piano. There was little evidence of the match's passage through the material behind the fretwork.

I went back to the Swan Vestas. I was having great fun peppering the fretwork and playing a manic tune on the instrument. That is until the smoke started rising from beneath the piano's lid. I'd overlooked the fact that Swan Vestas were 'strike-anywhere' matches. One of the matches had ignited on hitting a string. Years of cobwebs, dust and the odd piece of paper were smouldering in the bottom of the piano. I rushed to the kitchen, filled a saucepan and flushed the inside of the piano with water. When I was sure the fire was out, I made myself scarce. After a safe time, I returned to the house. My mum was back from the shops.

"Do you know anything about this water under the piano?" she asked

"Oh, sorry, mum. The dog was locked in the house when I got up. He couldn't hold it". Rex took the fall again.

"Poor thing, look at it. He must have been desperate", she said. She got a bucket of water mixed with Dettol and mopped up the great pool on the lino. That was another activity I didn't pursue again.

I found that I could get a little more range from the weapon by putting a drop of diesel fuel for model aircraft engines into its air cylinder. This modification had the pleasing effect of producing a puff of smoke when the pressure rise in the cylinder ignited the fuel.

This led to the worst thing I ever did with that gun, an action that put me in the greatest jeopardy. I used the gun to play a variation of 'Knockdown Ginger,' a game that involved knocking on someone's front door, then running away before they opened it.

The devil finds work for idle hands to do. One dark winter night, I looked through my front bedroom window. The dimly lit street was empty; nothing was going on. I could see the flickering light of a TV where the curtain wasn't closed properly in a house one up from ours on the other side of the street. Mr Bjelatic, who lived in that house, was a big Yugoslav and the father of my friend Dorothea. I guess he was a Tito partisan in the war because he hated Germans. The strange thing was Mrs Bjelatic was a German; it was another of those puzzling relationships in post-war Britain. I don't know how or why these things came into my head, but with due consideration to 'The Infantry Man's Handbook', I turned off the bedroom light and picked up my gun.

I primed the rifle's cylinder, opened my bedroom window and after a few ranging shots, I heard the faint 'tick' as the pellet hit the window. I pulled my window shut, ducked back into the room and peered through a crack in the curtain. A moment later, the front door opened, and Mr Bjelatic came onto his front step. He looked up and down the street, but seeing nothing, he went in and closed the door. That was fun, so I waited for him to settle in front of the TV before taking another shot.

This time it wasn't so funny. Mr Bjelatic came out and walked straight across the street. Now I was scared; my heart started thumping in my chest, and I wished I'd read 'The Infantry Man's Handbook' more thoroughly. I expected him to walk down our path and bang on the front door. To my relief, he walked up and down the street, looking over the garden walls for the culprit.

I sat on the floor with my back against the wall for a long time before I dared peep behind the curtain to see if the street was clear. After that, I decided that antagonising ex-Yugoslav partisans was probably not a good idea.

There were loads of decommissioned mortar bombs, Mills bombs and other types of artillery ordnance in Brogborough; all souvenirs smuggled back from the war. When we got our hands on this contraband, we'd swapped it for bubble-gum cards and stamps or other military stuff we'd collected. For us kids, Brogborough was Dodge City set down in rural England. It's a wonder there weren't more casualties or trips to the Magistrates' Court.

There were a lot of steel helmets, British and American. Kids would patrol the streets with these great metal pots on their heads, obscuring their vision, precariously supported on their spindly necks.

One morning I went to Johnny Mac's house all tooled up for action. He'd dug a slit trench in his back garden, a common occupation; I'd also dug one in my garden. The trench was big enough for both of us. We climbed in and settled down with jam sandwiches and a water-filled Corona bottle and waited for an attack by fanatical Japanese Imperial troops. Our position was about four yards from the garden's rear wire link fence, our first line of defence. Beyond the fence was a lane that separated the bottom street gardens from those of the top street. This route ran from the back of the shops on the main road to Ridgway Road. It wasn't long before Paddy Clifford, who lived at the far end of the lane, came strolling past on his way back from the shops. Paddy, like me, was first-generation Irish. Not being Japanese Imperial Guard, we held our fire and let him pass. This was a significant military blunder. Within ten minutes, Paddy returned with his older brother John. The Japanese threat receded and what happened next was like an extension of the Irish Civil War. The Clifford boys had come armed with a tin of duck egg blue gloss exterior house paint, a bundle of sticks and a box of Swan Vesta matches. There was an abundance of duck egg blue paint in those days. Some entrepreneurs must have bought up a load of green, blue and white surplus military camouflage paint from the war and mixed it together.

We didn't read the Clifford boys' intentions until it was too late. We sat haplessly in our trench, watching John poke a stick into the can, twist it a few times and pull it out coated with thick paint. Paddy struck a Swan Vesta and put it to the stick. It burst into flame. With the action of a circus whip master, John flicked a lump of the flaming goo. We ducked down as the projectile hit the lip of the trench and showered us with blazing molten paint. The bombardment went on relentlessly, with us popping up after each attack to see if we could escape, only to be subjected to another salvo. For ten minutes, we suffered this abuse, with splatters of hot burning paint raining down onto our hair and clothes. The Clifford boys thought it hilarious seeing us cowering in our trench. Unfortunately for them, they had made a fatal miscalculation. Poking a still burning stick into a pot of hot, volatile, viscous liquid turned out to be a bad idea. As the paint went down and its temperature rose, the can filled with vapour. Suddenly, as we cringed in our trench, there was a 'PUFF', a scream, and the firestorm stopped. We popped our heads above the parapet. The last insertion of a lighted stick into the can had caused the vapour to explode. Like a scene from the 'To the Shores of Iwo Jima', John was hopping about covered in burning, hot blue liquid.

"Get some water," they shouted.

"Bugger off," we replied, and the Clifford boys retreated along the lane to their home, routed by their own hand. Johnny Mac and I made a tactical withdrawal from the trench to the safety of his house. Rethinking our strategy, we decided that sitting in a slit trench close to the lane with the Clifford boys around was a tactical error.

My auntie Mary was a fun person, but she did have a serious side. She was a UK Civil Defence Corps volunteer. In the 1950's and 60s, we were living under the threat of nuclear war with Russia, the

Soviet Union, to be more precise. We were told we'd get a three-minute warning before being incinerated by 40 megaton thermonuclear warheads. It wasn't easy to understand how the Civil Defence people would survive when everyone else was toast. Still, Auntie Mary took it all very seriously.

We were advised to put mattresses up against windows and doors during the three-minute warning and fill a bath with water. That was probably a government ploy to keep us busy and stop us from panicking about what was to follow.

My mates and I were more concerned about how we were going to lose our virginity during our last moments on earth. Three minutes would be long enough, but first, you had to find a girl who'd agree to it. There weren't many girls you could approach with a contingency plan. If you did find one willing, you'd probably have to queue up with the rest of your mates.

I wondered how I would know about the coming apocalypse if I were up a tree or what good it would do if I did know. We went around cluelessly, singing "Ashes to Ashes. Dust to Dust. If the bomb doesn't get us, then the fallout must".

But not everything in Brogborough was war and mayhem. Auntie Mary lived just 100 yards up the street from our house at 12 Ridgway Road. Her house backed onto the truck lines that brought the clay from the pits to the brickworks. Auntie Mary had three daughters. Bernadette was a couple of years older than me, Anna and Veronica younger; they came along after auntie Mary moved to Brogborough. Later in life auntie Mary had a son, my cousin, David.

On Sunday afternoons in the late 1950's early 60s, I'd often go to 12 Ridgway Road to watch TV with my cousins. Auntie Mary liked 'I love Lucy' and 'The Liberace Show'. Liberace was a very exotically dressed American pianist. Women loved him, but to most men, he was a 'poof', we didn't know what that meant, and the term gay wasn't in use at that time. My cousins and I would lay on the carpet with our chins supported on our fists, watching this flamboyant character performing his stuff. He always finished the show with the same song, "I'll be seeing you". Whenever I hear that song, especially the lines: "I'll find you in the morning sun. And when the night is new. I'll be looking at the moon. But I'll be seeing you", it makes me sentimental, and I think of my auntie Mary.

We were lying on the carpet watching the ITV channel one Sunday when my cousin Bernadette said.

"Have you seen the new OXO advert? It's in colour; it's red like the box".

"Don't be silly." I replied, "It's a black and white telly".

"No, it's true. You'll see".

During a commercial break, the OXO meat stock advert came on.

I watched in disbelief as the screen started flickering and parts of the advert turned to colour.

"See!" said one of my cousins. "It's red".

"No, it's not. It's purple", I replied because that was the colour I saw for the word OXO.

And that's the truth. OXO had a coloured advert on a black and white television. Later in life, when I knew a bit about physics, I realised how they did it. Making the picture flicker at a lower factor of the frequency of red light caused the optical illusion of colour. However, I still have no idea why I saw it as purple. It was an interesting advert for the time, but it was soon dropped, probably because it brought on epilepsy in half the population who saw it.

My cousin Bernadette was one of my best friends. However, she did have a leaning toward the supernatural. We often sat in front of the fire, talking about spirits and ghosts. Stories of the Banshee, the wailing female spirit, herald of the death of a family member in Irish folklore, particularly filled me with terror.

Some nights, when my imagination got the better of me, Bernadette had to escort me home along the dark street.

All things must pass. Between March 1958 and October 1959, the countryside between Brogborough and the old Saxon church at Husborne Crawley changed forever. Enormous earthmovers and bulldozers cut a great swath from east to west through the green fields beyond the brickworks and Ridgmont station. Like some massive military operation, the forces of John Laing began the construction of the southern section of the M1 motorway from Junction 5 at Watford to Junction 18 at Rugby. Work continued day and night for 19 months.

During that time, our house would be full of Irish navies on Sunday afternoons who'd come to Brogborough club for a drink on their day off. Typical of his habit of collecting waifs and strays, they were invited home for lunch at closing time. I don't know how my mum managed.

With a house filled with the chatter of accents from Donegal, Cork, Kerry and Galway, it was like being in a west coast pub; I couldn't understand a word. They'd return to their digs in Leighton Buzzard by seven in the evening, and the house would fall silent.
At the same time as the M1 construction, my dad's sister, auntie Ellen, from Birkenhead, came to stay with my two cousins, Jimmy and Liam Greenslade, for the summer school holidays.
We spent our time at the motorway construction site watching the building of the slip roads to the concrete bridge that is now Junction 13. Or we'd go up Brogborough hill to the kale field and crawl beneath the tall green plants pretending it was a jungle. Occasionally we'd stop, cut a kale stalk with our sheaf knives, strip off the skin and eat it, imagining it was sugar cane. From the kale field, we'd go up the lane to the cottages between the woods to see my friends Michael and David Shaw, whose father worked at Manor Farm. That's where overcoming my fear of heights, I climbed the enormous pine tree. From that lofty tower, in sunshine under a clear blue sky, I could see for miles and miles and miles. Mrs Shaw was so afraid I'd fall that she coaxed me down with a mug of hot chocolate made with creamy gold top Jersey milk. The best hot chocolate I'd ever tasted.

1959 ended, and we moved into 1960, my last year at Ridgmont Primary. I failed my 11 Plus examination, so I'd be off to Fulbrook, the Secondary modern in Aspley Guise, where life would change again after my summer holidays.

Chapter 5

The summer of 1960

The cousins, Roger Beasley and Ray Papworth, were about two years older than me. They were very different characters. Ray had empathy, which Roger was sorely lacking. Later in life, Roger morphed into a human being, but he was something of a psycho as a kid. They did have one thing in common, though; there was sure to be a high level of mischief when they got together.

At the age of eleven, I was conscripted into Beasley Troop as a boy soldier. Today it would be called a gang, but Colonel Beasley had high ideals to prepare his men through discipline, instruction and training. This required attending formal sessions for military drill, ambush, weapons, ordnance and other training he deemed appropriate. Training sessions were held at a secret military camp at the bottom of his garden, masquerading as his dad's garage. There was a small office attached to the garage. Colonel Beasley's dad used to run a car repair business from home, but he'd given that up. Now Colonel Beasley used the abandoned facility for clandestine activities and to pass on the skills he'd acquired from the local Army Cadet Force in Aspley Guise.

One Saturday morning in the summer of 1960, I couldn't think of anything to do. The Lone Ranger was on the TV in three hours, but that was a lifetime away. To pass the time, I thought I might report to Colonel Beasley's training camp to see what was going on. An informal visit to show my enthusiasm.

I walked up Highfield Crescent and turned North. The camp was in the second back garden of Hill Crescent, in the lane off Ridgway Road. Opposite the training camp was a row of about ten garages that took up some of the bottom street's back gardens. These garages were rented by people who owned a car or wanted storage space. The lane was wider here to allow vehicles to park outside garages without blocking the lane. In those days, few people had cars, so the area was often empty. We used it for football, cricket, trick-cycling and other activities that annoyed the residents, like using it as a parade ground and an explosives testing facility.

I made my way up the path and poked my head through the half-open office door. Colonel Beasley was sitting with his feet on the desk browsing a Dandy comic. He held the comic with difficulty as his left arm was in a sling, having broken it a week earlier after a high-speed bicycle accident.

"Ah! Private Butler. Wait outside while I deal with these reports".

I left him to his comic and wandered up the garden path to the back of the house, where there was a large rhubarb patch. I've always had a sweet tooth, but I also liked sour fruit like crab apples, green plums, and gooseberries. I pulled up a stick of rhubarb and discarded the leaves because I'd been told they were poisonous. I wasn't inclined to test that theory, not on myself anyway. Peeling back the skin like a banana, I started chewing on the crisp bitter centre.

Colonel Beasley stuck his head out of the office and shouted at me.

"PRIVATE BUTLER. WHAT DO YOU THINK YOU'RE DOING EATING MY MUM'S RHUBARB? GET INTO MY OFFICE, NOW".

I threw down the offending stick and scurried into the office. Colonel Beasley was already behind his desk preparing a charge sheet.

"Shut the door," he snarled. "Right, I'm putting you on a charge".

"What for?"

"For eating my mum's rhubarb. What would happen if all the troops took it on themselves to pull up my mum's rhubarb? She wouldn't be able to make any crumble, and I'm very partial to my mum's crumble. You will have to spend time on jankers."

"What does that mean?"

"It means you'll have to clean up the garage, and don't think you can run off because you'll be locked in until you've done it to my satisfaction".

"Well, I won't. I have to go home".

He picked up a Fairbairn-Sykes, brass handled, stiletto commando fighting knife. With the ball on the top of the handle between his good hand's thumb and index finger, he pirouetted the knife by its point on the desk.

"So, insubordination and stealing rhubarb, you'll be here till the sun goes down".

"Well, I won't because I'm going home to watch The Lone Ranger".

I turned to leave the office.

"STOP" he shouted, but I didn't.

There was a thud. I saw the commando knife embedded in the far side of the door at about eye level. He didn't throw it at me, but it was too close for comfort. I was gone.

Outside, I heard the chair screech and fall to the floor as Colonel Beasley came out in hot pursuit. I looked down the pathway to the gate into the back lane. I wouldn't make it. He was too fast for my little legs.

There was a workbench by the side of the garage. Like a wild animal looking for high ground, I jumped up onto the bench, then jumped again. Just in time, I pulled myself up onto the sloping roof with a hand frantically grabbing for my ankle. I made my way to the top and sat on the apex of the roof, looking back. My sense of security didn't last long. Injured or not, Colonel Beasley was hanging horizontal to the edge of the roof by one leg and the hand of his broken arm. He was trying desperately with his good hand to pull himself up. It would have been funny if my position hadn't been so dire, but it looked like he might make it. There was a three-foot length of wood that someone must have thrown up onto the roof to his left. Overcoming my terror, I made my way back down the slope. He read my intention and tried desperately to grab for the wood, but it was out of his reach. I picked it up. He stopped struggling and stared at me. I hesitated, feeling regret that I had ever thought of doing such a thing. Then came a venomous hiss, "Don't you dare".

Benevolence deserted me. I brought the wood down hard onto the hand of his broken arm. He screamed but held on.

Bang, bang, bang, it took three more strikes before he let go and fell with a double thud, first onto the bench and then onto the path. I might have killed him, but I didn't wait to find out. I raced back up the roof and down the other side to the corner overhanging the lane. Leaping forward, I hit the ground running. I could have gone to seek sanctuary in my auntie Mary's house at 12 Ridgway Road, but that would have meant running back past the gate. Instead, I shot down the lane in the direction of the shops.

In my frantic imagination, I saw Colonel Beasley closing fast behind me, his good hand outstretched like an open claw, ready to take me by the neck. I ran on in terror, not daring to look back. Halfway along the lane, like a rabbit trying to avoid the stoop of a raptor, I skewed to the left. Fumbling with the latch of a gate, I burst into a back garden. My brain was working fast. I can't remember making a conscious decision. However, it was an exquisitely logical choice. The garden was owned by Mr Irvine, the father of my friend Mary. He was a lovely man who wouldn’t rebuke me when he saw I was in peril, and Colonel Beasley would think twice before trespassing into his garden. Mr Irvine's house was one of the few terraced homes that were separated by a gap that allowed you to pass from the back to the front of the property without going through the house. I shouted a greeting as I streaked past a surprised Mr Irvine. I was almost home free, but my decision had a fatal flaw.

Teddy, Mr Irvine's dog, may have been a mild-mannered creature, but he was a dog, and the sight of a desperate animal in flight on his territory was too much for him. He was after me like a shot. A side gate was now the only obstacle blocking my escape, but I wouldn't have time to open it before Teddy got his teeth into me. Fear is the key! I did a cross-country running, head-first, gate vault and landed on my back, winded, on the other side with Teddy leaping at the gate but unable to get to me. Teddy needed to lose a little weight.

I picked myself up and looked left and right. With no sign of the Colonel and with Teddy guarding my back, I sauntered across the street to 32 Highfield Crescent, home and safety. I still had two hours before the start of the Lone Ranger, but I could wait. I'd had enough excitement for one day.

After the episode with the commando knife, I avoided going to Beasley Troop for a while. Fortunately, it was time for the family's summer holiday.

My family never had much disposable income. We never had a car. My father never applied for a driving license in all his life, but we always went on holiday. Every year, we went to Rosslare Harbour, stayed with granddad Boyce and spent time with granddad Butler, auntie Mae and our Irish relatives.

However, July 1960 was the first time we didn't go to Ireland. One of my dad's friends from the brickworks had a small holiday chalet in Jaywick Sands near Clacton-on-Sea. He let us have it cheap for two weeks at the end of July. Nipper Gunter, a friend of dad's, drove us to Jaywick and brought us home for petrol money.

Jaywick was all a bit temporary looking. The chalets were like the prefabricated buildings the government put up to solve the housing shortage after the war. There was a small general store close by that sold groceries and souvenirs. One thing that sticks in my memory because I'd never seen them before was milk in white pyramid-shaped cartons with blue lettering.

Our chalet was at the southern end of the village. There was a sea wall with a pedestrian walkway on top, with steps, at intervals, which went down to a beige-coloured beach and the sea. The beach ran along the coast all the way to Clacton. Leaving Jaywick along the beach, you passed Butlins's holiday camp. We couldn't afford Butlins's. I didn't want to go there anyway. With its barbed wire-topped fence, it looked like a prison camp. During the war, it nearly was one, but instead, it was assigned to the Pioneer Corps, who used it as a training camp and almost destroyed the place.

Halfway between Jaywick and Clacton, there was a big round Martello tower. A relic built as a defence against invasion during the Napoleonic wars. There were a lot of these towers along the coast. Each time I passed it, I imagined what it would have been like inside under a cannonade from attacking French warships. However, that obviously never happened as the tower was in very good condition.

If I thought I would get off church service during this holiday, I was wrong. On our first walk into Clacton, we passed a community hall with a sign outside giving the times of Catholic services. I was forced to go with my parents once during the week and the following Sunday as well.

Most days in Jaywick, we walked north along the sea wall to my dad's favourite spot, where there was a pub and an amusement arcade. We'd go onto the beach and sit in the sun if the weather was nice. Sometimes we'd go swimming, but the murky North Sea was bitterly cold even in summer, so swimming wasn't my activity of choice.

While my mum and dad went for a drink in the pub, I'd play the penny slot machines in the arcade. I spent most of my time and pocket money training as an aerial gunner. The Air Combat machine had an oval handgrip that moved up and down and left and right. There was a thumb button at the top of the grip for firing a machine gun. You stood in front of the box and peered into a padded binocular type eyepiece. After dropping your money in the slot, old black and white films from fighter gun cameras started rolling. I'd manoeuvre a white dot on the screen with the handgrip and fire at anything that came into view. I couldn't distinguish friend from foe, so I blasted anything that crossed my sight. There was a sound of machine-gun fire when you pressed the button and a red flash if you hit the target. There seemed to be no relationship between a button press and the stream of bullets you saw on the running film, but it was fun and a great way to pass the time.

The really fond memory I have of that holiday are the songs. For me, it was an awakening to pop music. There was always music in the arcade and the family room in the pub. It came from transistor radios or jukeboxes. Up until that time, I hadn't paid much attention to pop music. I listened to Uncle Mac's, Children's Favourites on Saturday mornings. They played songs like The Laughing Policeman, The Runaway Train, The Ugly Duckling, There's a Hole in my Bucket!-Dear Liza, The Bubble Car Song, Magic Moments, Champion The Wonder Horse, The Deadwood Stage, and The Ballad of Davy Crockett. They were nothing like the music I heard on that holiday in Jaywick. - Cathy's Clown by the Everly Brothers - Apache by the Shadows - and Tell Laura I Love

Her by Ricky Valance (not to be confused with the American singer Ritchie Valens). This is the music I remember from that time.
However, the song I still find the most evocative is Only the Lonely by Roy Orbison. Play that, and I'm immediately back in Jaywick as a kid.
Then there was a dark-haired girl my age called Edythe. I met her in the arcade, and we became friends. We spent our time together sitting on the sea wall, dangling our legs over the sand, talking about all sorts of stuff. Or we'd buy ice cream and stroll along the beach, saying not much at all. The day she went home, we kissed with closed, puckered lips because that's how we thought you did it. I'd never done that with a girl before. I'd never wanted to, but with Edythe, it was different.
And so, my most enduring memories of that Jaywick Sands holiday are four pop records and an Anglo-Saxon princess from Colchester. An appropriate opening to the 1960's.
That summer holiday was nice, but Jaywick was not like Rosslare. In Jaywick and Clacton, the beaches were crowded. In Rosslare, I could walk for miles along the sand without seeing anyone. Even by myself, I was never lonely. There was too much to investigate with the prospect of finding strange sea creatures or some treasure washed up on the shore. In Rosslare, the water was so clear you could look over the side of the pier's viaduct and see fish swimming deep below the surface. In Jaywick, you couldn't see your feet when you were paddling.
I missed how everyone in Rosslare seemed to know me. I missed the banter of the Irish kids. They made fun of my English accent,

but they always looked out for me. I hoped my dad didn't intend to make a habit of these holidays in England.

Ordnance safety training

We returned to Brogborough a few weeks before I was due to start at Fulbrook Secondary Modern School in Aspley Guise. By then, weeks had passed since the Fairbairn-Sykes Commando knife incident. Colonel Beasley's arm had healed up, the plaster cast had been removed, and he, Ray and Frank had been to the Army Cadets' summer training camp. Now they were back from their adventures, I thought the Colonel might have forgotten about my attempted manslaughter on his dad's garage roof. I figured I could probably slip safely back into the fold.

One day, I hid by the side of the lockups that overlooked the garage. I didn't want to go blundering in to face the Colonel alone. There was some activity going on, the side door was slightly open, and I saw Stanley Novak wander down the garden path and go in. That was my cue. I summed up my courage, strolled across the open ground, and casually entered the garage.

Colonel Beasley was standing between the workbench and three boys sitting on a long wooden bench.

"Private Butler, where have you been?" he didn't wait for an answer. "If you're not careful, you'll be on a charge. Now get sat down, so I can get on with this training session".

I took my place at the end of the settle. The Colonel held up a brass cylinder.

"This is a three oh three blank cartridge. It does not have a bullet head in it, but DO NOT let the name blank fool you. This is a dangerous thing".

He handed it to the first person on the settle who looked at it, weighed it in his hand, and passed it on. When it came to me, I inspected it closely. The cylinder was slightly tapered at one end and closed off with a star-shaped crimp where the bullet head should have been. There was a raised rim with a circular recess in its centre at the other end that contained a small domed copper cap. This cap was the primer, where the gun's firing pin hit to ignite the propellant charge inside the cylinder. I passed the cartridge back to the Colonel.

"We are going to do a little test just to see how dangerous this thing is".

He put the blank horizontal into the workbench vice with the primer facing out and tightened the vice. Then he picked up a hammer and a four-inch nail in a pair of pliers. He put the point of the nail against the cartridge's primer and struck it with a hammer. Nothing happened.

Shifting like a golfer preparing for a putt, he put the point of the nail against the primer and struck it again. Nothing happened. Someone yawned and put the back of their hand to their mouth in mock boredom.

"Stop that, or you'll all be on a charge for insubordination." said the Colonel. "This must be a dud. I'll give it one more try".

We sat in the dim light, patiently waiting as he carefully re-positioned the point of the nail against the primer. When he struck it this time with the hammer, there was a blinding flash and an almighty BANG.

Four heads and torsos recoiled with such force from the shock that the settle tilted over. All four of us, legs in the air, along with the settle, fell backwards onto the concrete floor. Something hit the back wall of the garage with a clang. It ricocheted around the room, pinging off anything it hit and finally fell to the ground with a tinkle. We lay with our ears ringing from the concussion and our eyes temporarily blinded by the flash from the explosion. The air was filled with smoke and the stench of burnt cordite.

After a while, we recovered our senses and got to our feet. Blinking from the flash, we tried to accustom ourselves to the dim light. Colonel Beasley was standing stunned by the workbench.

Whatever he'd expected was obviously not what had just happened. The vice was empty, a lump had been knocked out of the garage's back wall, and the blank cartridge was nowhere to be seen.

With four subordinates peering at him through the fog, he soon recovered his composure.

"What are you lot gorping at. A fine bloody shower you'd be if we came under fire. Now find it".

We hunted around and eventually found the cartridge in a dark corner. It was split open with a long-serrated gash running from end to end.

You'd have thought we'd have learned something sensible from that experiment, but the only thing it taught us was not to let off explosives in a confined space.

The following week I saw the Colonel, Ray and Frank by the swings in the playground beyond my garden gate and wandered down to see what they were doing. Frank was sitting on the ground with a box of real .22 bullets. He was pulling out the lead heads using two pairs of pliers and emptying the flakes of explosive propellant into an empty matchbox. Frank held up one of the small empty brass cylinders between his thumb and index finger. He put it on the solid base of the swings, and then he hit it with a hammer. It went off with a CRACK. After that, he rolled up his sleeve to show me a nasty looking graze that ran from his wrist to just below his elbow, where a bullet head or cartridge case had run up his arm.

"That's what happens if you leave the head in," he said and continued dismantling and emptying the bullets.

Colonel Beasley was disassembling a № 36 Mills hand grenade. It was a real grenade with all its mechanical parts, but it was painted white and drilled with holes, indicating it was a practice device and harmless! However, with Colonel Beasley, you could never be sure. He removed the safety pin and lever, unscrewed the base plug with his fingers, put a screwdriver into a hole inside the bomb, and unscrewed the striker-detonator tubes joined together on a threaded metal disk.

"Look, we've made a little modification" he pointed to a hole drilled in the top part of the detonator tube. "Hand grenades are single-use. This one is reusable".

While I was trying to figure out the concept of a reusable hand grenade, he handed the parts to Ray and Frank, who poured some propellant into an empty brass .22 case. They placed a length of fuse cord into the open end of the case and pushed the case and cord into the detonator tube. Then, they put the spring and striker into the other tube and refitted them into the grenade. With a screwdriver, Frank pushed the striker up the tube against the pressure of the spring. When the grooved end of the striker came out of the top hole in the grenade, he fitted the safety lever and retained it with the ringed split pin. He put the loose end of the fuse cord into one end of a metal olive and an empty .22 case into the other end. Finally, he put the metal olive, with the percussion cap of the .22, facing up the striker tube and screwed in the base plug to hold the parts in place.

Frank stood up and pulled the safety pin out of the grenade. Uncurling his fingers from the safety lever, he carefully removed it, so it didn't fly off. The striker went down with a crack. Immediately he tossed the grenade a few yards into the grass. After a few seconds, there was a muffled bang and puffs of smoke were ejected through the holes drilled in the grenade.

"Well, that works," said the Colonel. "Now, let's give it a proper test".

They disassembled and then reassembled the grenade with a new fuse and detonator. Frank unscrewed the filling plug at the top of the grenade's casing and poured in the propellant flakes from a matchbox before refitting the plug.

"This grenade has a five-second delayed fuse." said Frank, "When I release the lever, I'll count to three and throw it".

He pulled the pin, brought his arm back in the classic cricket bowling position and released the safety lever, which flew off into the grass.

"One, Two, Th....". Before he finished counting there was an almighty BANG.

"Fuck, Fuck" shouted Frank, dancing around holding a blackened hand chard from the flashes that came through the vent holes in the grenade. Fortunately, he still had all his fingers.

The loosely fitted base plug had blown out, relieving the pressure inside the grenade.

That was, unfortunately, not my final armaments training exercise with Beasley Troop.

You may be wondering where all this military hardware came from. Well, when the senior members of Beasley Troop went for summer cadet training, it was considered a test of resourcefulness to see how much property they could misappropriate from the Ministry of Defence. It's incredible how some of us Brogborough boys ever survived our childhood.

While I was involved in all this mayhem, other forces were in play, attempting to forestall my move to the dark side.

Before starting this part of the story, I'll tell you that I'm an Atheist. I have tried to believe, but I have failed. I know it may be comforting to have a god and the hope of an afterlife that you can put your faith in, but I can't. I wonder what I'd do with my time for the next five billion years if one day I found myself in heaven.

However, even if the vast universe cares nothing for me, I still give thanks for the short time I have here with my family and friends.

It seems that it's only human nature to create a deity to explain the great mystery of life. I have no problem with people of faith, providing they don't try to force their various gods onto me.

Having said that, despite the reputation of the Catholic church regarding paedophilia, their treatment of children, abortion, contraception and other things. I can honestly say that my life has been better for once knowing a Catholic priest.

Coming from an Irish Catholic family, my mum ensured we all went to Mass on Sunday.

Our priest, Father Edmund Golston, took up his position as pastor of the parish in Woburn Sands in February 1939, ten years before I was born. At that time, services were held in an old 1914-18 army hut on the corner of Wood Street and Theydon Avenue. The hut had been donated by a parish in the diocese of St Albans after they bought a disused nonconformist chapel. Before that, services were held in the Club Room of the Fir Tree pub at the bottom of Aspley Hill. The proprietor Brigadier Beresford was by chance a Catholic. I remember going to the army hut with my parents and sister Ellen. It was closed in July 1956 when St Mary's, the new church, was opened on the top of Aspley Hill. Half the money for the new church was donated by Miss Christine Chichester from Port law, County Waterford, Ireland, after her death in May 1951. That in itself was coincidental as my father came from Waterford. To my knowledge, Father Golston never met Miss Chichester. He communicated with her by letter for some years, and she decided his desire to build a church was a cause worthy of her support.

Father Golston looked like a rural French curate with black-rimmed spectacles, a black cassock, and a black beret with a stalk sticking out of the top. Rain or shine, he'd ride around his parish on a large-wheeled black bicycle to care for his flock. Eventually, in the early sixties, the congregation secretly collected enough money to buy him a new Ford Anglia car and a course of driving lessons. Before this, he would peddle the three miles from Woburn Sands to Brogborough. There he gave the Catholic immigrant children instruction in the basic principles of Christianity, the Catechism.

We had the Catechism classes in a different family home each Saturday on a rotational basis. Father Golston said he enjoyed coming to our house. Standing by the open fire, looking out through the front window, he could see the reflection of the flames superimposed on the lilac bush in our front garden. He said it was the only house he visited where he could gaze upon the burning bush like Moses.

Fr Golston's ideas on religious education were a little unorthodox. He wanted us to understand the values rather than learn words like parrots. One day, I remember, he asked me what religion I was. This seemed a strange question to a boy from an Irish family.

"I'm a Catholic father", I replied confidently. He asked me the question again and got the same answer. After the third identical response, praying for guidance, he put the tips of his fingers together on his lips and closed his eyes. When he opened them, he shook his head slightly and said.

"No, Bernard. First, you are a Christian". This was a revolutionary concept for a young Catholic boy in late 1950's early 60s England.
On another occasion, he presented me with a problem about morals.
"Bernard, imagine there is a tribe who live in a really harsh desert. These people have to travel constantly foraging to find food and water to survive. If they don't, then they will all die. When members of the tribe become too sick or old to keep up with the tribe, they're left to die in the desert. What do you think about that?"
"They should look after the sick and old people, Father. It's terrible to abandon them like that", I replied.
He repeated the exact same facts and posed the same question once more. My response was the same. This time he never gave me the answer. He just let me think about it. Years later, I realised that he was trying to get me to understand that I shouldn't judge people by my own standards and try to see things from their perspective.
The priest taught me that you should always follow your own conscience despite the' conventional wisdom'. He used the example of the Duke of Norfolk and Sir Thomas More. Norfolk showed More a list of the noblemen who'd signed a document agreeing that Henry VIII's marriage to Anne Boleyn was legitimate. Norfolk asked More to do the same and "come along with them for fellowship". More's reply was:

"And when we die, and you are sent to heaven for doing your conscience, and I am sent to hell for not doing mine, will you come with me for fellowship?".

I understood what he said, but I don't believe I would follow my conscience if it meant, like More, having my head cut off.

Paddy Clifford (of the flaming paint attack) was another good Catholic Irish boy who lived in Highfield Crescent. He was one of the ten Irish kids on the estate who passed their 11 Plus examination. He was also an altar boy at St Mary's church. An altar boy helps the priest during the church service or mass, as referred to in the Catholic church. By definition, an altar boy should be morally pure and virtuous. It says a lot about Father Golston's Christian charity that Paddy was chosen.

Paddy pestered me continually to join him as a helper on Sundays, but there was no way I would put on a knee-length dress and parade myself in front of all and sundry. Finally, Paddy wore me down, and I agreed to serve.

As soon as the bus arrived at St Mary's, we'd jump off and run to the vestry, the small room by the side of the altar, where the priest prepared for the service.

Father Golston would generally be already dressed, sitting in a chair having a last drag on an untipped Players Medium Navy Cut. Paddy and I would quickly pull on our white smocks and, at the appointed time, follow the priest and two of the older acolytes out to the alter. One of the procession would pull the cord on the small bell by the door as we left the vestry to announce the start of the service. For the first few weeks, I just followed Paddy's lead. I hated it, but my mum loved it. She was proud of me, I was obligated, and it was a sure way to get me up for church.

After a few weeks, Paddy said it was time I did something useful and put me in charge of the small handheld altar bell.

This bell was chimed once during the service as an indication that the bread and wine were about to be consecrated by the priest before Holy Communion. This was too much of a responsibility, and I didn’t want to do it. Paddy assured me it was no problem. He said he would nudge me at the appropriate time, so I reluctantly agreed.

I kept the bell close on my right side during the service. I felt sick with anxiety, consumed by the thought of having to ring it. As we approached the time for Communion, I felt a nudge in my ribs. I grabbed the handle of the bell and rang it. When I looked up, Father Golston was peering down at me over his black-rimmed spectacles. I’d rung the bell too soon. I should have waited until he'd stretched out his hands over the bread and wine while he said the epiclesis. If the Holy Spirit had struck me down then, I would have been grateful. I looked at Paddy. He knelt in pious reverence, his head bowed, eyes closed, and hands clasped in prayer to his lips. However, I could see his shoulders shuddering slightly as he tried to suppress a snigger.

I don’t know if Paddy was laughing because he'd pre-warned me, and I’d rung the bell too soon or if he'd deliberately given me the nod early. As a Christian, I guess you have to give him the benefit of the doubt.

Fortunately, others were willing to take up the burden. To my mother's dismay, I was able to quietly relinquish my duties as an altar boy and stray from my path to priesthood.

Chapter 6

School Years Before the Revolution

1960 was my last year at Ridgmont Primary School, and I failed my 11-plus examination. I moved to Fulbrook School in Weathercock Lane, Aspley Guise in September. On the boundary of Aspley Guise, the small town of Woburn Sands was a short walk across the road from the school. Unlike the village of Ridgmont, Woburn Sands High Street was lined with shops for clothing, groceries, sweets, newspapers and magazines, stationery and books. It had a baker, a butcher and a fishmonger. It had a hardware store that sold Air fix and balsa wood models. It also had a chemist where kids could buy chemicals like Sulphur, potassium nitrate and granulated charcoal from big glass jars behind the counter, no questions asked. There was a bank, a doctor's surgery and two dentists. The town had at least six pubs. Two of which were hotels, one by the railway station and one at the other end of the town where the Bedford-Bletchley road crossed the High Street. In the middle of that crossroads, there was a tall, four-sided, white stone clock tower with a Celtic cross on its top. The clock tower was a memorial to the 43 men from Woburn Sands who lost their lives in the First and Second World Wars.

This was 'Middle England', very refined, a posh metropolis compared to the brickwork's estate of Brogborough.

Before starting at Fulbrook, I had to go by train to Woburn Sands with my mum to get my new school uniform. There must have been a government allowance because I don't know how we could afford everything on the list without one. Shirts, socks, a tie, black shoes, and a blazer with an aspen leaf badge. You could choose to have long or short grey flannel trousers. My mum chose short trousers for her 'little boy'. Clueless, I went along with it because I'd always worn short trousers to school.

My first day at school was an embarrassment. There were only two other kids in the whole place wearing short trousers. When I got home that evening, I told my parents I wasn't going back unless I got long trousers. My mum was sympathetic, but my dad had none of it, and I got the 'do you think money grows on trees' lecture. I had to go a whole year before I got long pants.

Fulbrook was a big, three-story building that opened 1958, to replace the old school near to the Woburn Sands clock tower. It was a Secondary Modern School providing basic education to the age of 15 years only, with no provision for pupils to go onto university.

The school had a car park, bicycle sheds, and a large mixed-gender playground that doubled as a netball court. Behind the school, there was a large sports field with a football/rugby and cricket pitch, an oval 440-yard running track and sand pits for long, high and triple jumps.

The headmaster, Mr Nailer, was a big man with a commanding presence. He was strict but fair with a passion for music.

Until 1960, the morning attendance register had been very English at Fulbrook. In the 1960's, when Brogborough's post-war immigrants started attending, it became a more cosmopolitan affair. Along with Brown, Baker, Smith, and Jones the register call now included the more exotic Sokolowski, Cusack, Novak, Matysik, Bjelatic, Pauli and Susikow. With a name like Butler, I was pretty ordinary.

Each year's intake of scholars was divided into three classes, A, B and C based on the students' reports from primary school. Surprisingly, I was in 1A, the class for children with supposedly higher intellectual ability.

I don't remember much about my first year at Fulbrook. There was too much to take in. What I do remember clearly, though, was an introduction to sports. For me, it wasn't a pleasant experience. With three grey-haired spinsters at Ridgmont Primary, I can't remember doing many sports or physical exercise other than the BBC Radio's 'Music and Movement' programs with the insipid voice of a lady commentator. I was, however, used to playground rough and tumble and unruly football matches on waste ground.

Physical Education

What a shock I had when I was confronted by Fulbrook's PE teacher. Everyone called him Spud Taylor. Why Spud? I have no clue.

He had the empathy of an army instructor trained by Attila the Hun. He'd 'slipper' anyone for the most minor offence. Slipper being a euphemism for him waking the victim across the arse with a twelve and a half-inch, heavy, rubber-soled tennis shoe. Not the casual footwear used for wandering around the house. These beatings were usually administered six times in the changing rooms in front of the class. He'd be up in front of a magistrate today, but it was an accepted form of summary punishment then. Fortunately, Taylor's wroth never came down on my arse.

My first cross country run was a trauma. Taylor led us out into Burrows Close up Mill Way and then across the golf course. We came out at the top of Weathercock Lane and crossed the road heading for Aspley woods. A few yards into the woods, I'd had it. I doubled over and threw up. Despite Mr Taylor's gentle' coaxing, I wasn't going anywhere. It had nothing to do with defiance, I was physically incapable, and we'd only run a mile. It may have had something to do with me having pneumonia a few years earlier; I like to think so. I had to take the walk of shame back to school and wait in the changing room. What an embarrassment.

When the horde returned, we had to strip off and take a communal shower. We stood around the walls inspecting each other's dicks until the sadistic bastard turned on the ice water. After five minutes, we came out with teeth chattering.

At eleven, almost twelve, some boys had already gone through puberty. There were a few who already had pubic hair and dangling appendages. One boy had a dick that hung down to his knee. If it grew any more, he'd trip over it. It made me wonder if maybe he passed out when he got an erection from blood loss to the brain. He also had a complete set of rotten front teeth, which was some consolation to the rest of us.

On the Ropes!

The only good thing about Physical Education was I had my first orgasm when I had to climb the stairway to heaven on the thick static ropes that hung from the gymnasium ceiling. Fortunately, I was pre-puberty, so it wasn't a messy affair. I wasn't sure what had happened, but it was really pleasant. After that, I didn't mind rope climbing, even though Mrs Taylor, Spud's wife with big tits and an equally nasty personality, screamed at me for climbing too slow. The funny thing was, the more she screamed at me, the more I enjoyed the experience! I could just imagine what role slippering took in their ritual foreplay.

Judo

During our last year at Fulbrook, Spud Taylor decided the fourth-year boys would learn judo. I suspect it was just a way to legally beat us up. The first thing we had to do was learn to fall correctly. This entailed throwing yourself forward or backwards to the ground. The technique was to relax and strike down with one or both arms with palms open to break the fall before your body hit the ground. This, we were told, would absorb the force of the fall and save damage to your more delicate organs. That all worked fine on the training mats, but I wondered how it would work out

on a concrete floor, stony ground or a bar brawl where the floor was covered in broken glass.
I can only remember one throw by name: O-Goshi, a hip throw. With this throw, you had to pull your opponent's arm up and forward. When they were off-balance, you turned into them and used your back and hip as a fulcrum to throw them.
Another throw, I can't remember the name of, was a foot sweep. I remember this one well because Spud chose me to demonstrate it. We were all sitting on the floor at his feet, students in front of the master.
"You," he said, pointing to me. "Get up here".
I thought, 'The sadistic bastard, he's going to hurt me', but I was too scared of being slippered to disobey him, so I got up.
He took me by the lapels and told me to do the same with him. He was bigger than me, so I had to stretch up. He went through the throw slowly. He moved me to the left and then back to the right. As I was putting my foot down, he put his instep on the outside of my ankle in the direction we were moving and swept it towards my other leg. I lost my balance, and he let me fall to the floor. This was all in slow motion, so no harm was done.
Then he said we would do it for real. This time he pulled me really hard left and right. His actions were so violent I was scared of what he would do to me. Survival instinct kicked in, and before thinking about it, I did exactly what he had just demonstrated. As his left foot was coming down, I swept it towards his other leg. He let go of me and hit the mat with an almighty bang. He wasn't expecting the wimp to do that. In truth, nor was I. I don't know who was more

surprised. It took him a second or two to regain his composure, and then he sprang to his feet.
'Oh, God. I'm dead,' I thought.
But, as if it had all been part of the demonstration, he said, "Very good" and told me to sit down.
I was a hero for the day. I was expecting a severe reprisal for that incident, but strangely it never came.

The Escape of Smudger Smith

Spud Taylor didn't always supervise us for sports. Sometimes, Mr Gough, our Welsh woodwork teacher, took the class. We all thought Mr Gough and Mrs Welch, our maths teacher, were having an affair. They always seemed to be together in their free time, in the staff room, or on playground duty. Who wouldn't have wanted to have an affair with Mrs Welch? Most of the boys in my class fancied her.
Mr Gough was more sympathetic than Spud. However, he lost his temper on one occasion while we were in the gym. I don't know what caused the altercation. I just remember Mr Gough shouting, "Come here, Smith," and Smith replying, "Fuck off, Gough".
After that, Smith ran for it with Mr Gough in pursuit.
Smith went up the wall bars like a Barbary macaque ape with Mr Gough shouting from below for him to come down. This request was again followed by "Fuck off, Gough".
A stand-off continued for some time until Mr Gough decided to climb the wall bars. When he was halfway up, Smith, hanging by

his arms, moved hand over hand along an 'I' beam supporting the ceiling high above the gym's floor.
Mr Gough froze with fear on the wall bars, and we stood below open-mouthed, watching Smith dangling seven metres above the gymnasium floor. The teacher cautiously retreated back down to the ground.
"OK, Smith, I won't come up after you. Just get back onto the bars, and we can talk".
Smith made his way back to safety. No matter how much Mr Gough pleaded with him, Smith wouldn't come down.
Soon, Smith, tired of this battle of wills. Above the wall bars was a row of top-hung awning windows used to ventilate the gym. Smith opened a window, squeezed through it and ran across the flat roof outside. Then, he shinned down a drainpipe and ran off. Mr Gough, visibly relieved, disappeared to inform the headmaster of Smith's jailbreak.
I don't know the complexities of the negotiations, but Smith was back at school the following week as if nothing had happened.

Girls

Apart from Edythe in Jaywick, I didn't think much about girls until I was twelve. They were just a nuisance; they got in the way in battles with Roman legions, Danes and Mediaeval knights. In Ridgmont, we only interacted with girls in the classroom. Or in the canteen across the road in the village hall. Boys had a separate playground and enjoyed rough and tumble playtimes.

In Fulbrook, we shared the playground with the girls. In class, we tended to segregate, boys didn't sit next to girls, but we all shared the same space at break times. At least in the junior years, the genders tended to stay in their own groups. However, there was a marked change as we became teenagers. During that time, my feelings for girls started to change. I became particularly attracted to a girl in my class called Lorraine Hopkinson. It was a strange feeling, not sexual, I just became madly infatuated with her, and I fell in love with a girl for the first time. She didn't want anything to do with me, which caused me terrible heartache.

Nevertheless, I persisted in doing stupid things to gain her love. Her dad owned the Halt Garage just across the M1 bridge from Brogborough on the road to Aspley Guise. I'd often ride back and forth past the garage on the chance I might see her, but she was rarely there. On one occasion, while I was engaged in this stupidity, she walked out of her dad's office just as I was passing. I stopped, and she actually came to talk to me. I tried to act nonchalant, as if this was just an accidental meeting. However, she'd probably seen me riding up and down most of the morning. I gave her some story about where I was going and then rode off before I fainted. Wherever I told her I was going, I couldn't go back past the garage again and had to take another long way home.

That painful period lasted for the first few years at Fulbrook until my affections shifted to another girl, Dina Humphries. Her family owned the bakery and Sibley's taxis at the bottom of the hill into Aspley Guise coming from Brogborough. Again, this girl showed no interest in me, and my cycling trips became more extended in another forlorn quest. She was in a class a year lower than me with my friends Erika Matysik and Mary Irvine from Brogborough. I found out their class schedule and would strategically position myself in corridors where I knew they'd pass at break times just to get myself noticed. I even joined the school's Country Dancing Group. Dressed in an embroidered smock and straw hat, I'd attend the extracurricular dance classes because Dina and her friend Cheryl were in the group. It was more like non-contact stick swiping than intimate hot-blooded South American Tango, but it was as close as I could get. To the great amusement of my mates, I ridiculed myself by country dancing at the Woburn Sands' summer fete. But what care I in my pursuit of love.

Because Dina and Cheryl were in it, I joined the Canoe Club. The club was run by Spud Taylor, which shows how desperate I was. We used a lake on the Hockliffe road on the other side of Woburn, so I had a long bicycle ride to get there.

These activities improved my physical condition and weight problem, so they had some benefits.

One Christmas, I bought Dina a charm bracelet from Woolworth in Bedford. It was made with dangling farthing coins sprayed with gold paint. Farthings stopped being legal tender in 1961. I wrapped the bracelet in a silk (well, more likely, rayon) scarf and Christmas paper. However, I was too embarrassed to give it to her, so I asked Erika, who was friends with her, to do it for me on the last day before the school holidays. She didn't even thank me for it, but no matter, I was just some hopeless imbecile.

Later, my mum told me she thought the bracelet and scarf were for her when she saw them in my room. She'd been very disappointed when they didn't materialise on Christmas day.
These crushes were painful adolescent affairs that, fortunately for me, eventually ran their course.

Film Stars

Around the same time, I had a more impossible crush on the British film star Janet Munro, who I'd seen in the Walt Disney film 'Swiss Family Robinson'. I was so infatuated that I wrote her a letter in my best handwriting. I didn't know her address, so I sent it to: Janet Munro. c/o Walt Disney. Thanks to the good old GPO the letter got to its recipient. To my surprise, a month later, I received a handwritten reply and a portrait photograph signed ' To Bernard. As Aye, Janet Munro'. I believe 'As Aye' is a Scottish term meaning 'As Always' or 'Yours Always'.
After that, I thought I might go to drama school, become a famous actor and win her affection. However, Janet broke my heart when, in 1963, she married the actor Ian Hendry, so then I thought I might join the Royal Air Force and become a fighter pilot. Janet Munro died in 1972 from a heart attack. She was only 38 years old. Her letter and photo went missing from my mum and dad's house around the same time while I was away travelling.
I also had a crush on Julie Christie, who I first saw in the 1961 seven-part BBC TV series 'A for Andromeda'. Encouraged by my previous success, I wrote another letter. Julie Christie replied with

a photograph with a handwritten note on the back. The picture she sent me was of her in a slinky nightdress, which I thought was a little inappropriate. However, evidence of being on first name terms with film stars gave me a certain kudos in the playground for a while.

Other Lessons

Studying at Fulbrook secondary was a lot tougher than at Ridgmont primary.

History was no longer about great battles and heroes of the Greeks, Romans, Saxons and Normans. History meant learning dates and consequences. My dad made things difficult. To him history was about points of view; there was always an alternative perspective. He taught me to try and stand in other people's shoes before opening my mouth. That caused a complication because things were no longer black and white; they were different shades of grey.

My dad loved books. If he went to a jumble sale, he'd always return with a large cardboard box of books. History, travel, geography, politics, science, and Shakespeare, he loved Shakespeare. There was never a shortage of something to read in our house. The books weren't for show; he spent hours reading. He was well known for winning debates with colleagues in the brickyard. Once, a co-worker got so frustrated with him during a discussion he said as if he were cheating. "You only know that because you read it in a book".

The Irish have a 700-year memory when it comes to the British, but my dad was no Irish rebel. He loved England, he thought it was the best country in the world. I found that confusing considering the long, complicated relationship between the two countries. For my dad, history was about the past, not to be forgotten but not to be picked at like a festering wound. History wasn't today.

I found it hard to understand the British view of Irish history. Many adults and consequently their children seemed to think that the Black and Tans were Irish terrorists when they were British forces with a reputation for extreme brutality.

Some books on the Irish War of Independence were banned in the UK. I saw confiscations by British customs in Fishguard when we came back from Ireland. One book on the list was Guerrilla Days in Ireland by Tom Barry, which my dad smuggled through to add to his collection. This was censorship, but the Irish were as bad in their own way.

One of my relatives worked for Irish customs. When I was on holiday in Rosslare, I'd sometimes hang around with him while he was on duty in the harbour. A prize piece of literary contraband coming into Ireland at the time was Playboy magazine. These were confiscated on the spot, but they weren't sent to the incinerator by young Irish customs officers.

My dad taught me to be sceptical, read as much as I could and consider conflicting opinions. That was a good approach and probably why I got terrible marks for history.

Geography was another subject that lost its charm at Fulbrook. It was no longer about exotic places and people as portrayed by the

BBC, but about maps, Geo-political relationships and Gross National Product.
Tom Maybe, came from a well-off family who lived in a big house in Aspley Guise. His father was high up in the nascent British computer industry. Tom's summer holidays consisted of road trips to the South of France and cruises around the Mediterranean. One year Tom brought in a box of slides from one of these Mediterranean jaunts. The geography teacher, a very large woman whose name escapes me, set up the projector. Tom talked us through the slides until the last one, which was of a big black goat with stubby horns and a tufty beard standing in short grass. Tom said nothing. The geography teacher came in and waxed lyrical about this final picture.
"Ah yes. A typical beautiful scene from the Mediterranean", she said with nostalgic romance.
"No, Miss. That's my back garden," replied Maybe.
We all sniggered behind our hands. That was no accident.

English Lit and Shakespeare

As always, English was hard work for me. English grammar, what little we were taught, was beyond me, and spelling was a total mystery. I could write the same word ten times in an essay, and it would be spelt differently every time. My writing would come to a halt when I had no idea how to spell a word. I went into a mental block once because I couldn't figure out how to spell the word 'who'. I was filled with fear when asked to read something to the class. Stumbling over each word was an embarrassment. And yet I could read to myself with no problem. I remember the excitement of reading 'Treasure Island' under the blankets with a flash lamp when I was supposed to be in bed asleep.

I enjoyed English Literature, except for when I had to read passages aloud to the class. One book we read was 'Prester John' by John Buchan. The only thing I can remember about it now is there was a place in the story called Blaauwildebeestefontein. This translates as "the spring of the blue wildebeest". Everything else in 'Prester John' except that name and its meaning is a blank to me. Maybe when I have the time, I'll read the book again.

English and English Literature were taught by Mr Mellor, a man with light hair and bright eyes. He had lips like Mick Jagger and occasionally sprayed you with spittle when he spoke. We thought he was queer (the word for homosexual before gay) because he lived with his 'man servant' in Mount Pleasant, Aspley Guise. If they were gays, they were discrete about it. The relationship would have been illegal because homosexuality wasn't decriminalised in the UK until 1967. Mr Mellor was mild-mannered, dedicated, and a patient teacher who rarely lost his temper. I thank him for giving me an appreciation of Shakespeare during my last year at Fulbrook when he decided we would learn 'The Merchant of Venice'. To enlighten us, he arranged for the class to see the play performed in a London theatre.

My dad was taught Shakespeare at school in Ireland, and he loved it. Whenever a Shakespeare play was on television, I found it so dull I had to find something else to do. I never got past the first five minutes.

I told Mr Mellor this, and as the trip was voluntary, I said I wasn't going. That was not the end of the matter. In the weeks leading up to the trip, Mr Mellor pestered me continually to change my mind. He wore me down in the end, and I reluctantly agreed to ask my parents if I could go. I was sure my dad would say we couldn't afford it, but to my great disappointment, he thought it was an excellent idea, so I resigned myself to my fate. At least it would be time out from school.

On the day, we filed into the first rows of a dimly lit theatre a few feet from a low stage on Shaftesbury Avenue in London's West End. From the start, when the stage lights came on, I was blown away. It was beyond anything I'd expected. The loud, heavily made-up performers with perfect diction and colourful clothes looked right into the audience. They spoke directly to me. I wasn't just watching a play; I was part of it. I came out of that theatre in a trance. I had never seen anything like it.

If anyone tells me they don't like Shakespeare, the first thing I ask is, "Have you ever seen one of his plays in a theatre?".

Invariably they haven't, so I try to convince them to go and see one. Especially now, I tell them to go to the new Globe Theatre on the South Bank in London. Those who do go come away with the same experience I had all those years ago. For that, I am eternally grateful to Mr Mellor.

Music

Music lessons with the headmaster Mr Taylor were great. The magic of Peer Gynt, The New World Symphony, Peter and the Wolf, Carmen, and Fingal's Cave. The sheer majesty of Gustav Holst's The Planets. All of these recordings were a joy to hear. However, musical notation was and still is a mystery to me. One of my biggest regrets in life is that I never learned to play a musical instrument.

Maths and Science

In my first year at Fulbrook, I found a love for mathematics and Science that stayed with me. Mathematics was a pleasure, not least, because it was taught by the lovely Mrs Welch.

On the other hand, Science was taught by 'Salty' Sellers, an ex 'Desert Rat' from the North African campaign. Salty was a small thin man with weasley eyes and a pencil moustache. His favourite pastime was to creep up on an unsuspecting boy chatting to his mate and pull a few hairs out of the back of their neck.

One of his experiments involved boiling water in a conical lab jar plugged with a stopper with a copper tube that came out at a right angle to demonstrate superheated steam.

First, he'd get the water boiling. Then he'd put the flame from a Bunsen burner under the copper tube. When he did this, the steam coming from the copper tube disappeared.

"This is dry steam. It's very dangerous," he told us. Then he'd take a Wills Woodbine and put it between his lips. To demonstrate the danger, he'd carefully bend forward until the cigarette's tip was next to the end of the copper tube. The end of the cigarette would glow red. Puffing on the Woodbine, he'd straighten up, hand the class over to the lab assistant and go outside and finish his smoke. Another experiment involved heating a needle to red heat and then selecting someone, a boy, to come to the bench. The boy was told to open his hand palm up. Salty, would then drop the needle into the boy's hand, who would immediately drop it but with no damage to his skin. Salty then heated up a half-inch washer to red heat. He'd assure the class that a red-hot needle and a red-hot washer had exactly the same temperature and asked for a volunteer to repeat the experiment. Naturally, no one was stupid enough to oblige. It was a clear demonstration that the temperature and the amount of heat in an object were two different things. Mr Sellars' teaching methods may have been unconventional, but they worked for me. When I was at Fulbrook, I came top of the class in Science every year.

Art

I always enjoyed drawing and painting, and I was good at it. At Fulbrook, our art teacher was Mrs Watson; today, you might label her a hippie. That expression didn't come in until later in the 60s. However, Mrs Watson was no revolutionary. She wasn't going to mould us into Vincent Van Goghs. One year she decided there would be a competition to see who could paint the best Easter picture. The paintings were to be displayed, and the school would vote for the winner. Under Mrs Watson's direction, most of the work was of rabbits, little yellow chicks, and chocolate painted eggs.

My picture was Jesus in a loincloth nailed to the cross. His head was bleeding from a crown of thorns. He had blood running out of a gash in his side administered by a Roman legionnaire standing beneath the cross with a blood tipped spear. The painting was inspired by a Dali I'd seen in Bedford library, but full frontal and very colourful. It was bloody and brutal, not to Mrs Watson's liking, and not her idea of Easter.

Nonetheless, to Mrs Watson's displeasure, I won the most votes. The barbaric painting probably appealed to the boys and the less sensitive girls, of which there were many at Fulbrook.

Mrs Watson was not happy with me, which wasn't unusual. One year she got me into a lot of trouble with my dad. In my annual report, she gave me a low grade and wrote 'Argumentative. Thinks he knows best'. This seemed to strike a chord with my dad, and I got a right bollocking. I never understood how he thought I was free to argue the toss in history and politics but not in art.

I talked Mrs Watson into allowing me to do an abstract wood carving, which could only be done in the woodwork room. I think she was glad to see the back of me, and I strung out the creation of that masterpiece for weeks.

I remember the arrival of a brand-new potter's wheel, which Mrs Watson forbade anyone to touch. For the time I was at Fulbrook, that wheel stood unused at the entrance of the art room. So infamous was the mechanism that Tom Maybe, never short of words, made up a little jingle about it.

"We must not touch the potter's wheel.
We cannot touch the potter's wheel.
We can't have a piss cos we ain't got a pot.
But we cannot touch the potter's wheel".

We'd sing it reverently and surreptitiously touch the sacred artefact when we entered or departed the art room.

I find myself softly singing that song even now when I think of that character Tom Maybe who sadly has now passed.

Religion

I can't say that being an Irish Catholic was a particular problem for me at school. Most of my friends were Church of England, at least in name, but they weren't all dragged off to church on Sundays like I was. Until we were old enough to make up our own minds about religion, my mum was adamant that my sister, and I went to church on Sunday. That included my dad, even if he'd overdone it in the working men's club the night before. It even included her brother, uncle Billy when he came to stay with us for a year or so. Billy was recovering from tuberculosis, not helped by neglect due to an over-fondness for the strong drink and Capstan full strength cigarettes. I'll come to Uncle Billy later.

Religion may have been an issue when I left school and looked for a job. In the 1960's and 70's, job applications included a question on your father's nationality and religion. Even until 1980, you were still asked about your religion in the job applications. I always put Christian because our priest Father Golston had always told me that's what I was. I'm not sure if religion was dropped from job application forms in the 80's because I didn't do much job hunting after 1982.

In 1962 morning school assembly was an Anglican religious service that involved hymns and the Lord's Prayer. Some misguided but probably well-meaning progressive had the bright idea that Catholics should be allowed to choose whether or not to attend the assembly. To me, self-imposed segregation seems a dumb thing to do now. However, being an adolescent at the time, it gave me a sort of identity, and I chose to stand outside the assembly hall with a couple of others. I was thereby saved from the slightly differently worded Anglican version of 'The Lord's Prayer' and radicalisation by hymns such as 'All things Bright and Beautiful.

That was not the dumbest thing I did at school, but it comes close.

Library

In 1962 I volunteered to be a library monitor. My lunchtime activities included inscribing the spines of books with appropriate Dewey Decimal Classification numbers and plotting them and returned books back in the proper place. Browsing around and peering between books on shelves allowed me to study the more erudite females who frequented the library. Now, increasingly girls of any kind occupied my mind.

School-yard black market in machine guns

Not all of my friends at school were from Brogborough. By the end of my first year, I'd become good friends with a boy called Peter Worthington.

It was an unlikely friendship. Peter was from a very English middle-class family who lived in a detached house on the Bow Brickhill Road on the outskirts of Woburn Sands. I was from an Irish immigrant family living in a Marston Valley Brick Company's terraced house on the workers' estate in Brogborough. He was a super athlete; I was a wimp in that department.

However, we had common interests like Roman and post-Roman Anglo Saxon Britain, Vikings, history in general and science.

For Christmas 1961, mum and dad bought Ellen and me a BSA Star Rider bicycle from Brightmans in Bedford. This was unusual because stuff like that was typically purchased second hand cleaned up and repainted by dad. I don't know where the money came from in this case; possibly mum paid them off monthly. Anyway, we weren't complaining. Ellen's lady's bike was blue and mine, with a crossbar, was red. The film El Cid came out in December, starring Charlton Heston and Sophia Loren. I went to see it at the Granada in Bedford and was so taken with the story that I painted the word 'Babieca' on the chain guard of my bike. It was the name of El Cid's warhorse; it meant simple-minded or fool in Spanish, which I didn't know then. Legend had it that the horse was a gift to El Cid, then the boy known as Rodrigo Díaz by his godfather. Rodrigo was allowed to choose a horse from a herd. The boy chose a lumbering colt, which grew into El Cid's faithful steed.

Peter and I both saw the film. Peter read the book. I didn't need to; Peter always filled me in on the detailed information in books he read that never got into the films. He read a lot of historical novels.
I began reading books by Henry Treece, who died in June 1966, he was only 54, but he wrote over 70 historical children's books. I remember reading the Legion of the Eagles, The Eagles have flown, and The Green Man.
Some Saturdays, I'd ride to Peter's house on Babieca. We'd take our swords and shields to Danes borough, the old iron age Viking hill fort in Aspley Woods just across from his house. The fort was long gone; all that was left were the remains of the three defensive ditches that encircled the hill at different levels. Evidence of these ditches was overgrown with tall trees and difficult to find. You had to have a good imagination to visualise the old structure, but we did. Many battles were fought on that hill, leaving the place awash with the blood of Scandinavian Norsemen. After resting and eating the sandwiches made for us by Mrs Worthington, we would wander home in the evening. Sometimes Peter would come to Brogborough. We'd explore the worked-out clay pits or spend time rummaging in the municipal dump at the bottom of Brogborough hill.
Mrs Worthington was a lovely lady. She had grey hair and looked much older than my mum. She must have had Peter quite late in life because Peter had a forty-year-old brother who'd served in the Far East, Burma, I think, during the war. Peter's father looked much older than his mum. I met Mr Worthington but never got to know him. He couldn't speak because he had throat cancer. He had

a hole in his Adam's apple about the size of a penny covered with a lint pad that had to be changed, especially after severe coughing fits. He died shortly after I came to know Peter.

Peter's auntie was ahead of her time. She wouldn't have a television in her house because she said the people on it could listen to her and watch what she was doing. We thought this was hilarious and that she was crazy. Not so crazy now, though, with smart TVs, Alexa, and remote access to microphones and cameras on smart devices.

The Worthington's had friends on one of the local American air bases. Even at the age of 12, Peter was a fervent anti-communist. He told me about the domino effect and that America was starting to get involved in a war in East Asia in a country called Vietnam. There was nothing on the news about it, and I'd never heard of Vietnam, but we all soon would.

Peter and I were both interested in science. When we weren't reading Mad magazine, we spent many hours with our heads in Knowledge magazines looking for something to build. We decided on liquid propellant rockets. Peter's interest was chemistry, and we set about making the fuel and creating a venturi nozzle for a combustion chamber. This involved wrapping a wax former with copper wire, putting the assembly into a bowl of copper sulphate solution and connecting it to a car battery. This coated the whole thing by copper deposition electrolysis. After weeks of innovative evolution, we took our device to a nearby field for launching. The idea was to pressurise the fuel tank and then ignite the engine from a distance by detonating an open pan of gunpowder beneath the venturi with a battery-operated primer using the filament from a flash lamp bulb. Our ballistic missile development and hard work ended in a ball of flame, so we switched to solid fuels, with only marginally more success.

Our most outlandish interest was collecting old military hardware. Between us, we had an assortment of bayonets and swords. We had a 2 and a 3-inch diameter mortar shell, a Bakelite hand grenade, different anti-tank and small arms bullets, a Very pistol and an 18-pounder artillery shell, which we presumed to be decommissioned.

When our form teacher asked the class to give a talk on our various interests, Peter and I brought our collection in. We assured the teacher all the ordnance was decommissioned, although none of it had come with a certificate saying such. To her dismay, we explained the purpose of the blood grooves in swords and bayonets and the purpose of Shrapnel shells. We described explosives mechanisms, fusing, and detonation in shells that we learned from Peter's Encyclopaedia Britannica. All this was in contrast to the needlework, stamp collecting, fishing, music, and other genteel interests presented by the rest of the class.

The Spandau machine gun.

At school, we acquired a reputation as collectors. One day in the playground, we were approached by a boy called Paul Jay, who said he had a machine gun he wanted to sell for ten shillings. That was a lot of money in those days. I didn't have that sort of money, but Pete recently had his birthday and was flush with cash. We arranged to go to Paul's house on a Saturday to check out the hardware.

Paul's place was on Aspley Heath, a super posh area. It was a substantial detached house with a double garage in a secluded setting in the woods. Paul's dad was definitely not a labourer in a brick-works factory.

The gun was well kept with oiled metal and a polished wooden stock. It was similar to a British Sten but German over-engineered. Paul said it was a 9mm Steyr Solothurn MP34 submachine gun. We asked if he had any ammunition for it, but he didn't, probably just as well. However, he did have some 32-calibre automatic pistol ammunition. You couldn't feed it from the magazine, but if you wrapped some insulating tape around the cartridges and put them into the chamber one at a time, you could 'probably' fire it single shot. Peter said he didn't want it. That may have been a middle-class bargaining technique; I noticed they did that sort of thing.

Paul said he had something else we might be interested in and took us into the garage. He pulled back a tarpaulin to reveal a Spandau MG 08 heavy machine gun. Not the WWII Spandau that looked like a length of metal pipe, but the larger water-cooled, tripod-mounted version that was similar to the British Vickers. There was no ammunition for it, but it was so impressive that we bought it anyway, even without the tripod mount. We carried it home, wrapped in a hessian sack, me at the front with the barrel under my arm and Pete behind at the trigger end. We struggled back from the Heath down Church Road past the Old Oak pub, the clock tower in the square by the Swan Hotel and then down the street back to Bow Brickhill Road. I don't know what Mrs Worthington made of it all as we entered the house exhausted with the weapon, but the tolerant woman she was, she asked us what we would like for lunch.

You may wonder why much of what I write about as a kid growing up in post-war England is a world of Cowboys and Indians and battles with Germans and Japanese.

We had shields and helmets, bayonets, knives and swords. We had toy guns, air guns, bows and metal-tipped arrows, and catapults with ball bearings. Our battles, ambushes and raids were not video games; they were really rough and tumble with hand-to-hand combat. Cuts, bruises, black eyes and ripped clothing were common. Did anyone get killed? They didn't, there was no malicious intent, but we were fortunate. In the 21st century, we'd be considered feral, a Social Services' nightmare. But attitudes were different then. It was accepted that's what kids did for fun.

In 1960, World War II had only been over fifteen years. It was current history. Most young men in their early thirties had experienced war. Our lives were full of stories, medals, cap badges, uniform flashes, army paraphernalia, and military contraband smuggled home from foreign parts. We also had the local dump where we scavenged discarded MoD army surplus.

We had comics like Commando and War Picture Library. With titles like Unleash Hell, No Surrender, Kill or be Killed, and Cold Steel, we weren't short of heroes, enemies, spies and traitors. Things weren't very PC then. We were soldiers, cowboys and knights, armed and ready to wreak havoc on our foes.

The Firearms Act of 1937 didn't help. It raised the minimum age for buying a firearm or air gun from 14 to 17. However, Section 19 paragraph (2) said:

"No person under the age of fourteen years shall accept as a gift or borrow any firearm or ammunition to which Part I of this Act applies, and no person shall give or lend any such firearm or ammunition to any other person whom he knows or has reasonable ground for believing to be under the age of fourteen years".

So there you have it. If you were over the age of fourteen, you could legally carry a firearm and ammunition provided you borrowed it, or it was given to you by someone over seventeen.

In retrospect, it's debatable if a 7.65mm Spandau machine gun with a rate of fire of 500 rounds a minute was covered by Part 1 of the Firearms Act of 1937.

The Firearms Act of 1968 brought in stricter regulations for the ownership and safe storage of guns and ammunition. Applicants had to have a good reason to obtain a Firearms Certificate. However, anyone could apply for a Certificate to own a shotgun.

The Act was accompanied by an amnesty where guns and other weapons could be handed to the police without conditions. I don't know if Peter handed in the Spandau MG 08 because I'd lost contact with him by then.

Buzz

In early 1961 a new student joined our class 2A. Philip Burrell. I can't remember how it came about, but he acquired the nickname Buzz. He missed our first year at Fulbrook because he lived in Cranfield, where his parents ran the shop and post office. Cranfield was in the catchment area for Stewartby.

His parents moved to a semi-detached house directly opposite the school on the other side of Weathercock lane, so he just had to stroll across the road in the mornings. Buzz and I became lifelong friends, we did a lot of stupid things together, but the one that could have gotten us into the most trouble happened at school.

In the summer, I often biked from Brogborough to Fulbrook so I could stay after school and spend time with my friends. The distance was a little over three miles, and the journey took less than half an hour.

One evening I stayed a while at Buzz's house. Buzz's mum was older than my mum, or she looked it. Mrs Burrell smoked, and so did my mum; many people did in those days. But Mrs Burrell smoked a lot; she had a persistent cough and didn't seem to be in the best of health. She was a lovely lady and always made me welcome. Mr Burrell was also a nice person. He told a lot of jokes, but they were outside the range of Buzz and my sense of humour. However, you couldn't help but laugh when he told one because they were so bad. The only one of Mr Burrell's jokes I can remember went like this.

Man 1. 'Were you wounded during the war?'

Man 2. 'Yes, I was squatting with my pants down having a crap, and some German shot me in the backside'.

Man 1. 'Rectum?'

Man 2. 'No, straight up the arse.'

Mr Burrell thought that was hilarious.

We went to Buzz's bedroom this particular evening, where he kept three guns.

He had a Four-Ten shotgun with a folding stock that you could hide in the inside pocket of a poacher's jacket. A .300 bolt action with a rifled barrel that took bullets or small shotgun cartridges. He could only get shot cartridges for that gun. He also had a .22 BSA Meteor air rifle.

Buzz's bedroom faced the school, and we saw that the second-floor window of the classroom opposite his house had been left open. On its stand, framed in the open window, was Mr Bowles' inflatable world globe.

The reaction was simultaneous. One of us opened the bedroom window. The other went for the Meteor.

The classroom was 70 metres away, beyond the sight range of the Meteor. It took a few ranging shots, but once we got an aiming point on the wall above the globe, we could hit it almost every time.

In my imagination, I see the globe slowly deflating from our abuse and Mr Bowles' reaction the following morning when he encountered the flat earth. That's just wishful thinking because the Meteor couldn't penetrate the plastic at that range. That was fortunate for Buzz and me. With air-gun pellets scattered on the

classroom floor and a punctured globe, it wouldn't have taken Sherlock Holmes to figure out where the shots had come from. At best, the situation would have been resolved in-house at school. At worst, we would have ended up in front of a magistrate.
All I can say is, it was a period of temporary insanity with no malicious intent (as such). With no thought of the consequences, we just couldn't resist the challenge.

Aston Martin

One Saturday morning in October 1961, Ray Papworth, Johnny Mac, and I went for a bike ride. We turned off right before the M1 Motorway. It was a glorious day, and when we arrived at the village of Salford, we continued on along the country road. We came into the small town of Newport Pagnell on Tickford Street, where Aston Martin had its factory. When the cars came off the production line in those days, they were road-tested by white-coated drivers. After that, they were parked on the street, waiting to be picked up by customers or dealers. We arrived outside the factory where a couple of Lagonda Rapides and two or three DB4s sparkled in the sunlight on the public street. With nothing between us and the cars, we peered in wonder through the windows at these fabulous machines' pristine leather upholstered interiors.

In 1964, the cars built in that small Buckinghamshire town became world-famous when the new DB5 model made its film debut in the third Bond movie Goldfinger.
We rode over Tickford Bridge and headed out of town towards Northampton, but it was autumn. The nights were drawing in, so we turned our bikes around and headed for home.
Aston Martins are no longer built in Newport Pagnell. In 2007, manufacturing was moved to a former RAF V Bomber airbase in Gaydon. The original factory is gone, but there is a modern service facility for heritage service, spares and restoration.

There is also a sales department where cars are parked on an unfenced forecourt. Day or night, seven days a week, you can still roam among bespoke supercars worth hundreds of thousands of pounds.

Chapter 7

More about the 1960's

The Barber of Aspley Guise.

Vic Thomson was the closest barber to Brogborough. He had a little shop off the square in Aspley Guise.

When my dad said it was time for a haircut, my mum would give me a couple of shillings, and I would take the train from Ridgmont and walk up to the square from Aspley Guise station. Or I would ride my bike to Aspley Guise and buy sweets with the train fare. Generally, you had to wait for a haircut, especially on Friday evening or Saturday morning when demand was high.

During my wait, I used the time to expand my mind by reading the Reader's Digest. However, I was fascinated with the girly mags lying around for the older clientele. With titles like Modern Man, Playboy and Titbits, I was too embarrassed to pick one up to 'read'. However, I couldn't help taking a peep at what the older men were studying.

When the men were paying, Vic would ask them casually,

"A little something for the weekend, sir".

If they gave Vic the nod, he would give them one or two small packets of Durex or Ona.

I eventually found out about this little ritual when a friend enlightened me in the playground, and that was the start of my sex education.

Before the Beatles came along in late 1962 and the whole Merseybeat pop revolution took off, and before I discovered that girls were not just an annoyance, hair care was not my prime concern. Getting a haircut was simple; there were only two hairstyles to consider. One style was the Teddy Boy haircut, used mainly by older boys of working age.

The Teds' hairstyle was greased, longish on top, with a quiff sticking out at the front that hung slightly over the forehead. The sides were combed all the way round to the back of the head. This crease or 'duck's arse' ran from a square cut Boston at the nape of the neck up the centre line of the back of the head.

For schoolboys, things were more straightforward. Our cut of choice was a short-back-and-sides. The barber tucked the sheet around your neck, trimmed the top short, and combed it to each side with a left parting. He then ran a mechanical hand-operated clipper up the sides and back the head to about an inch above the ears. Vic would blow off the loose bits of hair with a talc puffer, pull out the sheet and you were done. Or, for a little extra, he would massage a dab of Brylcreem into what was left of your hair. For the next few days, you'd be obsessed with stroking the bristles up on the back of your head, something akin to poking your tongue into the hole left by a recently lost tooth or filling.

That's not to say there wasn't the odd rebel without a cause who came to school with a quiff and a duck's arse, but that was asking for trouble.

Swimming Pools:

Continuing with hair styling. Brylcreem was very popular when I was a kid, especially at swimming pools. I can't remember a swimming pool I went to that didn't have a Brylcreem dispenser. After swimming, a line would form at the dispenser when we were dried off and dressed. The machine would discharge a great glob of white emulsion resembling shiny whipped cream for one large bronze, 1.2 inches (3.1 cm) diameter penny. It was far too much product for a young boy's head, especially if you'd recently had a short back and sides. You could share it with your mates or spend ten minutes trying to massage it into your scalp. After that, you could impress the girls with your clean-smelling slicked-down hair. All that changed in the mid-sixties with the Beatles and their 'mop-tops'. When the long-haired rebellion came along, Brylcreem went out of fashion.

There were four swimming pools within cycling distance of Brogborough in the sixties Husborne Crawley. Woburn, Eversholt and Stewartby. The closest was halfway down Mill Road in open countryside outside Husborne Crawley. This was an average public village pool, about 8 by 20 metres in size. The pool was a little over a mile from Brogborough, so sometimes we walked to it. One lovely late August afternoon, I walked back from a swim with Michael Shaw and his younger brother David from the farm at the top of Brogborough hill. Returning home after our swim, we passed Hobbs' Orchard. Seeing the ripe apples hanging from the trees was too much temptation, so we nipped over the fence and scrumped (euphemism for stealing) some fruit from the trees. We ate a few, put some more in our pockets, and continued on our way. As we passed the large brick house just before Ridgmont Station, out came old Mrs Hobbs. She must have been spying on us through the large bay window of the house.

"You've been stealing apples," she said.

"No, we haven't".

"Yes, you have", she retorted, pointing to our bulging pockets. "Hand them over."

She told us to wait outside the house while she went to get paper and a pencil.

We didn't know what to do, so we stood there like idiots. I knew plenty of boys who'd have been off like whippets.

We waited ten minutes before she came out again. She wrote our names and addresses on the back of an old magazine.

I've no idea why we didn't run off as soon as she went into the house or why we didn't give her false names and addresses.

She dismissed us, saying, "This isn't the last you've heard of this. Expect a visit from the police".

We never heard any more about it. She probably expected us to high tail it as soon as she went inside. She'd not expected to have three witless criminals standing outside her house all day. After that, I always went on my bike to Husborne Crawley pool. I peddled, head down, as fast as possible, on my way home, past Mrs Hobbs' house.

On another lovely summer's day, I went to Husborne Crawley pool with my dad's brother. I guess I was about eight at the time. Uncle Tommy was down from London with my auntie Kay to spend their summer holiday with us. Tommy was riding the bike, and I sat on the handlebars using the towels as a cushion, but it was still uncomfortable. As we turned into Mill Road, we were confronted by a man on his bicycle coming in the other direction.

The man put his hand up for us to stop. He got off his bicycle and pushed it across the road towards us.

'Oh Shit!'. It was constable Vaughn.

He was off duty and out for a spin on his bike or on a covert operation. Constable Vaughn took the law very seriously; I tried to avoid him whenever possible. We were caught two on a bike, with me perched precariously on the handlebars.

Ever the policeman, in this situation, constable Vaughn saw himself as a vigilant plain-clothed CID Inspector on the prowl for desperate criminals like us. To uncle Tommy, a young Irishman in his mid-twenties up from the big city, the policeman was just some young bloke on a bicycle.

The confrontation had the potential for a very bad outcome.

"You know you're breaking the law carrying a child on the handlebars of a bicycle on the public highway," said constable Vaughn.

"What's it got to do with you?" replied Uncle Tommy curtly.

"I'm a police officer".

"How do I know that? You're not in uniform".

I suppose Mr Vaughn could have flashed his warrant card, but he didn't. I hadn't known Uncle Tommy long, but if he were as fiery as my dad in such a situation, the resolution could be swift and final. I had a vision of Mr Vaughn lying unconscious on the road. Fortunately, it would have meant dropping the bike with me on it, so it didn't happen. Nevertheless, I quickly confirmed that the man was telling the truth.

What followed was a heated dispute that ended in a compromise. After issuing a verbal warning, Constable Vaughn went on his way. We dismounted from the bicycle and walked the few hundred yards to the swimming pool.

With the possibility of constable Vaughn in uniform concealed in the bushes after our swim, there was no way I was getting back on that bicycle. To uncle Tommy's annoyance, we walked home pushing it.

We told my dad what had happened, but not my mum. Otherwise, we'd have been in more trouble.

While I'm on the subject of policemen. There used to be a municipal rubbish tip at the bottom of Brogborough hill on the road to Lidlington opposite the MOD dumpsite. This tip was a small worked-out clay pit used by Bedfordshire County Council and anyone else with rubbish to dispose of.

It was like a free hardware shop and a favourite haunt for us kids. Old bicycles could be cannibalised into working machines. Sometimes there were even complete bikes. Broken down prams could be converted into trolleys.

Old radios and televisions were full of treasures like electronic vacuum tubes, coils of copper wire, and especially highly prized magnets from speakers.

Many machines used mercury-filled glass tilt switches and rectifiers in those days. With no supervision at the dump, it was common to find these discarded devices. The glass could be broken, and the silver liquid recovered. Mercury was fun to play with and a very swappable commodity amongst kids.

One time I found a roll of high-quality white paper a metre long by 50cm in diameter. It was probably from a printing company, and it weighed a ton, but I managed to get it home, carrying it up Brogborough hill on my shoulder. I didn't have to buy drawing paper for years. Once I found a large book on English cottages. Each page had a coloured painting of a cottage set in a beautiful garden or countryside.

On another occasion, one of my friends, Stephen Williamson, found a set of the Encyclopaedia Britannica still in its packing box. You could find all sorts of stuff on that tip. It was amazing what people threw away, lovely ornaments, vases and framed paintings. National Geographic and Readers Digests were plentiful, but the prize for adolescents' foragers was when we came across what passed as porno mags in the 60s. Pretty mild by modern standards, just tits and bums with not a hint of pubic hair. The closest thing to full-frontal nudity was found in discarded naturalists' Health & Efficiency magazines. Still, these were subject to the censor's razor. The magazine seemed to be more popular than it should have been in respectable British society. Along with comics, these magazines were another tradeable item. The problem was getting them into the house without your mother finding them.

The dump was a dangerous place, not just because of the rats attracted by rotting refuses. The pit was gradually being filled in with rubbish. Now it's just a field covered in topsoil and grass. Then, the rubbish lorries dumped their loads in great piles that were bulldozed into the pit. The boundary between the tip and the pit was a rubbish wall sloping down from uncertain ground to infested water.

Consequently, the place was cordoned off from the road with a fence and no trespassing signs. However, it was bordered only by a scrappy hedge if you came in from across the fields.

One Saturday morning, I was rummaging in the tip when along came constable Thompson on bicycle patrol from Lidlington. I got a right bollocking and was told to get off the property, or he'd book me. I didn't argue and made myself scarce for a while.

At the time, I thought he was an arrogant prick. Little did I know then that I would meet that same policeman in an encounter that would change my life forever ten years later.

Continuing with swimming pools. In Aspley Guise, behind the shops, in the V formed where Church Street and the Bedford Road meet at the square, there is the grand old manor house. This is Aspley House, with its drive and gated entrance on Bedford Road. In the 1960's, the property was owned by the Sturdee family. At that time, there was a large swimming pool in the house's grounds.

One day in the week during the summer school holidays, the family allowed the children from the surrounding area to come and swim in the pool. They were a tolerant lot to let hordes of unruly kids descend on their beautiful grounds and splash about in their private pool. These days, the Health and Safety Executive would require: a Risk Assessment, a sanitary water certificate, Pool Safe Operating Procedures (PSOPs), Emergency Action Plan (EAP), Safety information signs, Poolside supervision, and Rescue Equipment such as poles, throw bags, buoyancy aids.

Today, this act of kindness would result in the Sturdee family being hauled up in front of a judge. Nevertheless, we never had any serious mishaps with a pool full of screaming kids, jumping in and out and ducking each other.

I have enduring memories of afternoons lying on the grass, drying out in the summer sunshine in the beautiful grounds around that old house. Childhood memories are strange; I can't remember any rainy days at Aspley House.

That old property was in stark contrast to the terraced houses and back gardens in Brogborough. But we never had any egalitarian socialist ideas about the people who owned the enormous house or why they had so much money. We were just grateful they were kind enough to share it with us.

Conkers, another victim of the Health and Safety Executive.

Towards the end of summer, returning home from Sturdees' pool on our bikes, we'd stop at the horse chestnut tree before Husborne Crawley to see how the horse chestnuts were doing. Soon we'd be back at school, and it would be time to play conkers.

Taking turns to strike an opponent's horse chestnut threaded on a piece of string is another activity far too dangerous for children to play at school today. At least not without the requisite Personal Protective Equipment (PPE) and supervision. Today, flying shrapnel from exploding conkers and the fear of anaphylactic shock to combatants with nut allergies pose too high a risk to allow the game to be played in the school-yard. Curious because we would dare each other to eat a whole conker. No one got a quarter way through the bitter nut before spitting it out. The nuts looked beautiful when broken out of their spiky green shell but biting through the shiny brown skin to get to the kernel was usually enough to admit defeat. Just as well, because a belly full of an aesculin filled nut, if not fatal, would have certainly ended with a bad stomachache and excellent intestinal cleansing. We didn't try this challenge very often because your teeth would be on edge from the acid in the nut for the rest of the day. No one I knew ever suffered from anaphylactic shock, not that we had any idea what that was in those days.

The greatest danger I found playing the game was from boys, who didn't like to lose. They tended to strike the hand of their opponent instead of their conker, intimidation, to make less aggressive boys concede defeat and abandon the game.

More of Beasley Troop Amphibious operations.

Staying with the theme of water sports, the following incident would give any self-respecting Health and Safety Executive person seriously disrupted sleep.

The old clay pit at the bottom of Brogborough Hill where the MOD used to dump their army surplus stuff is today a 220-acre lake used by windsurfers.

In the 1960's, that lake didn't exist. It was an abandoned clay pit known as 'The Knot-Hole', more than 20 metres deep. With precipitous sides, its floor was a series of long, parallel, rain-filled channels separated by low islands of soil deposited by a machine to expose the Oxford Clay below. For good reason, the pit was fenced off with notices saying, PRIVATE PROPERTY KEEP OUT. TRESPASSERS WILL BE PROSECUTED. There had been several drownings in the man-made crater. However, these warnings did not deter Beasley Troop, who used the area for Covert Operations, Survival, Escape and Evasion training.

In the school summer holidays of 1961, Colonel Beasley led a team into the pit to carry out a dangerous amphibious operation. Intelligence had informed the Colonel that a rival force had built a raft in a large water channel close to an island with a pair of nesting swans. The team included the Colonel, Stan Novak, Johnny McNamara, me, and young Melvin Burr on his first active

operation. Melvin's mother was not happy with him mixing with the more feral elements of Brogborough's juvenile community. We managed to turn him to the dark side on this day as his parents had, uncharacteristically, gone out and left him home alone.
We entered the pit through a hole in the fence concealed by a low bush. Momentarily we stood on the edge gazing in awe at Conan Doyle's 'Lost World' before descending the gradient into that mysterious landscape.
It was difficult to spot us from the road when we were at the bottom, where we could operate freely, untroubled by adults.
Removed from civilisation, it was a peaceful, natural, primaeval world disturbed only by the calls of lapwing, moorhen, curlew, peewits, ducks and gulls. An enduring memory of trips into the pit is lying on my back on the warm earth. Squinting into a bright cloudless blue sky, searching for the dark dot of a skylark singing high overhead. There were bulrushes, frogs, frogspawn, tadpoles and grass snakes. We'd hunt for the eggs of ground-nesting birds. We'd jump with fright from tripping over a hare or rabbit that dashed off unexpectedly from underfoot. The sheer variety of animals, plants and wildflowers was overwhelming.
We jumped the narrower water gaps that separated some of the islands. We carried a square plywood board on a long string with a spike tied to the string's free end for the broader gaps. We'd put the spike into the earth, throw the board into the centre of the gap, run down the bank, leap onto the board like a steppingstone, and push off hard onto the next island. Provided you were quick and hit the board's centre, the upward pressure of the water took the

impact allowing you to clear the gap. Occasionally, landing off centre, the board would skid, causing the jumper to fall, arms raised into the water. The last person across pulled out the spike and jumped with the string so we could retrieve the board for the next wide channel.

We eventually found the raft tied to a post in a lake with the swan's island. It wasn't a big raft at about two and a half metres long by one metres wide. The raft was made from an angle iron frame covered with wooden planks to form the deck. Onto its centre, nailed to the deck, a bent metal sheet made an open-ended, inverted V-shaped cabin about one-and-a-quarter metres high. The whole thing was kept afloat with round ten-gallon oil cans stuffed beneath the angle iron frame. It was not the most elegant of vessels. It sat very low in the water and was only sensibly capable of taking a crew of three. Johnny Mac decided to go for a swim. Stanley sat on the bank and lit up a Sobranie Black Russian.

Colonel Beasley took up a position aft. Melvin disappeared into the cabin to shelter from the sun. I was ordered forward on the raft with a stick to fend off any aggression from the swans. We untied the line and pushed off. Colonel Beasley slowly manoeuvred the craft across the water towards the island using a plank as an oar. The raft wallowed in the water under its own weight and that of the crew. The swans became agitated at our approach. The cob took to the water with his wings outstretched, aggressively hissing and flapping its way towards us. Attempting to scare off the angry bird, the Colonel began bobbing up and down, bending and straightening his knees, causing the raft to see-saw along its length. So violent became the motion that I had to hold onto the cabin for support. At one rise of the bow, an oil can shot out from under the raft. It sailed in a lazy arc, hitting the water in front of the swan. The splash from the projectile hitting the water caused the swan to retreat back to its island. The Colonel, seeing my discomfort, continued rocking the raft. The subsequent rise of the bow was higher than the last, and two more cans shot out. As the bow rose up even higher for the third time, cans shot out one after the other and didn't stop. Colonel Beasley floated off and swam for the land. I was left floundering as the raft, standing at an angle like the Titanic, slipped beneath the turbid green water. For a moment, I was left stunned and floating among the cans. It had all happened so fast. Then I was struck with a terrible realisation.

'WHERE WAS MELVIN?'

He'd gone down with the raft. He couldn't swim. I spun around, but he was nowhere to be seen. The water was too murky to see below the surface, and I didn't even know how deep it was. Anxiety turned to fear. If his mother found out I had a hand in this, she'd kill me; my mother would kill me. Treading water and contemplating how I would explain all this at the inquest, I slipped into a stupor, not knowing what to do.

In this state of dejection, I began to pray, 'Oh, dear God, please don't let Melvin drown'.

Suddenly, I started to rise up out of the water: 'I didn't mean, take me instead, God'.

Melvin's head popped up like a cork between my legs. The next thing I knew, his arms were wrapped around my neck in a drowning man's grip. Now we would both die. In a moment of clarity, I remembered a life-saving technique I had seen on TV. I closed my fist and smashed it into his face. It didn't work. I did it again with more force. He let go, bringing his hands up to his bleeding nose. I grabbed a nearby oil can and thrust it at him. Melvin grabbed the can and floated on his back with his arms and legs wrapped around it. I swam away from him, trying to think what to do next. That's when I heard the thud of running feet and a splash. Johnny Mac swam past me doing a fast crawl, took Melvin by the back of his collar, and swam back to shore, dragging Melvin with him with a one-handed breaststroke. A little shaken but none the worse for his experience, we dried Melvin off and managed to get him home with his mother, none-the-wiser.

I don't know if Mrs Burr ever found out about that incident. I certainly wasn't going to ask her. Still, a while later, the family moved to the six houses a little way outside of Brogborough, away from the immediate influence of Beasley Troop.

Borrowing the Short Lee Enfield rifle.

Buying the Spandau MG 08 heavy machine gun and the shooting of Mr Bowles inflated world globe was not the only gun-related incident during my secondary school years. There was another that potentially had more serious consequences.

One summer's morning in 1961, I was walking down the street in Brogborough. Coming the other way were Colonel Beasley, his cousin Ray and Frank. They were about fourteen or fifteen then, a lot older than me. Two years difference in age doesn't seem much, but when you're twelve, it is. I was astonished when they said they were undertaking a clandestine operation and would I like to come along.

Wow! Being asked by the big boys to go on a special mission.

Without a thought, I said, "Yes, where are we going?".

Colonel Beasley put his finger to his lips and winked. "Top secret. Don't tell anyone. Get your bike." he replied.

I felt guilty about telling my mum I was off up the top street to play with some friends, but it was justified because I was on a secret mission. The least she knew, the safer she'd be if I was caught, and she was interrogated by the Gestapo police.

We rendezvoused with our bikes on the B557 main road. Then we headed off in the direction of Bletchley across the bridge over the newly opened M1 Motorway.

My bike was a lot smaller than theirs. Even with my little legs peddling like mad, they kept having to stop and wait for me. We got to the Bell pub in Aspley Guise and peeled off into Woburn Lane about thirty minutes later. I can't remember exactly where, but they suddenly dropped their bikes on the verge and disappeared ahead of me. When I got to the spot, a finger beckoned from the bushes. We lay concealed, peering through the hedge. Across the field was an Army Cadet hut, a long black creosoted shed with a bitumen covered pitched roof.

Colonel Beasley started issuing instructions.

"You see that small window?" silence. "Are you listening to me, Private Butler?".

I didn't realise he was talking to me. "Yes, Sir".

He gave me instructions for what I had to do, finishing with:

"Frank's the tallest, he'll go with you and help you get through the window".

Frank and I ran in a crouch across the open field and dived into the bushes by the hut. The window was in two parts, a fixed pane at the bottom with a small window hinged along its top edge above it. The small window had a swinging handle with holes along its length. The holes were there to fit into a centre stud. This allowed the window to be propped open for ventilation or kept shut.

The window would normally have been securely shut. However, after Cadet training the previous night, my accomplices had left the handle free to facilitate this operation. Frank lifted me on his shoulders, and I pushed the window up. While wriggling through the restriction, stretching down my hands to support myself on the sill, and bringing in my legs, it occurred to me that the morning's meeting was not accidental. The thought passed as I fell to the floor; I was now focused on completing my task. I found the massive steel gun safe in the room to my right. I pulled on the brass handle and, with an effort, swung the heavy door open. A thin brass shim that had stopped the locking bolts from dropping into place fell to the floor. Propped up inside the safe was a Short Magazine Lee Enfield rifle. On the floor were several five-round clips of .303 blank cartridges. I took the gun and ammunition and put the shim back in position when I shut the door. Back on the windowsill, I passed the ammunition and heavy rifle down to Frank. Like an arched caterpillar, with the help of Frank, I made the difficult head-first exit through the window. We ran back with the prize and dived into the tree line. After a quick inspection of the goods, Colonel Beasley slung the rifle on his shoulder. We made a tactical withdrawal on our bikes along Woburn Lane in the direction of Aspley Wood.

Once in the wood, we concealed our bikes in the bracken, made our way along a track further into the wood, and then cut off onto a lesser-used trail. Once we were far from any houses, Colonel Beasley loaded a five-round clip into the rifle's magazine. Within a few minutes, with loud blasts, my three seniors had emptied the magazine. The place was filled with the sound of flapping wings and unseen creatures scurrying for safety in the undergrowth. I did as I was told and collected up the spent cartridges. In the confines of the trees, the air was heavy with the smell of burnt cordite. Shoot and scoot tactics were adopted. The three of them ran off and turned onto another track. I scampered after them, my pockets jingling with empty brass cylinders. The last thing I wanted was to be lost and alone in this forest. To my relief, once they were a safe distance from the previous shooting position, they stopped. While Colonel Beasley was fumbling in his pocket for a new clip to reload the rifle, a man stepped out from the trees some way ahead.

"Oh shit!" someone said.

The gamekeeper, with a broken shotgun on his arm, approached us.

The conversation that followed sounds absurd now, but it was another era. The 1937 UK Firearms Act had raised the age of buying a firearm from 14 to 17 and was still in force until the new Firearms Act of 1968. Fortunately, Roger and Frank were fifteen-year-olds but big for their age.

"Someone is shooting around here. Do you know anything about it?".

With quizzical looks and waggling heads, someone said.

"No! But we did hear some shooting from over there".

"What's that then," said the gamekeeper pointing at the rifle.

"Oh, this. This is a Lea Enfield. Look here," said Colonel Beasley, holding the gun out for inspection.

"D P O", the gamekeeper read the letters stamped into the rifle's metal.

"Yes, that means it's for Drill Purpose Only. This gun's been disabled. It's only good for arms drill and marching practice.

"Oh, I see. Well, I'd better go and find out who's doing all this shooting," The gamekeeper went off to the last shooting position, where they'd indicated the shots had come from.

In truth, DPO did stand for Drill Purpose Only, which meant that the army's armourer wouldn't issue the weapon to a soldier and expect him to hit a target using it. That's why it was passed down to the Cadets.

Once the gamekeeper was out of sight, we set off at a pace in the opposite direction.

Eventually, after more volleys, we got to where the Woburn Road separates Aspley Wood from Aspley Heath. By this time, I was moaning because I hadn't had a shot with the rifle.

"Look, these blanks can do serious damage or even kill. This is a real rifle. It's not for kids to play with", growled Colonel Beasley.

I whined on, "It's not fair. I got it from the Cadet hut".

"Alright, I'll show you just how dangerous these blanks are", he retorted.

He looked around. There was a cardboard box that must have blown off the back of a lorry in the undergrowth. He tore the side out of the box and handed me a large square piece of cardboard.

"Now stand over there. Hold it by its top and bottom and away from you as far as you can".

He picked up the rifle, pulled back the bolt, pushed it forward and loaded a new cartridge. Standing six feet from me, he raised the gun and aimed at the card between my hands.

"Don't look at me. Turn your head away". As I did, there was an almighty BANG, my ears rang, my hands stung from the blast, and I dropped the cardboard.

He came over, picked up the card and showed it to me. The ragged hole in the centre looked like a golf ball had gone through it.

"See how bloody dangerous these things are. Let that be a lesson to you, never mess around with blanks".

After more whining, they finally let me take a shot, but someone had to support the barrel because the gun was too heavy for me to hold level. It didn't kick much, but it was a thrill to shoot it.

When all the cartridges were used, we cleaned the weapon with the cleaning kit in its stock.

By late afternoon we were back at the Cadet hut. I returned the Lee Enfield and empty clips to the gun safe. This time I didn't use the shim and allowed the safe's door bolts to drop into place, leaving the scene undisturbed except for the missing blanks. We didn't really do anything wrong. We just borrowed the rifle and returned it in good order. You might say we stole the blanks. However, in our eyes, we were preparing for covert operations to save England in the event of a Russian invasion. Apparently, this was a distinct possibility at the time.

I often wonder what would have happened if I'd been caught in that cadet hut with my mates long gone. How would it have turned out when the Special Branch arrived at our house to question my Irish father.

"Can you explain why your twelve-year-old son was caught in possession of a rifle on government property, sir?"

Then taking him away with his illicit copy of Guerrilla Days in Ireland!

Railway Saboteurs.

Ray Papworth was nearly three years older than me; nevertheless, we became good friends. Ray was quieter and more considerate than his cousin Roger. In modern terminology, you might say Roger was 'empathy-challenged'; however, he did eventually morph into a reasonable human being.

When Ray, Roger and Frank Reader got together, you never knew what trouble they'd get into.

One Saturday in 1961, the police, in the form of a uniformed constable and a plain-clothed CID Inspector, came on a door-to-door enquiry around Brogborough. The railway hut between Ridgmont and Lidlington stations had been broken into, and some items had been stolen. My dad called me to the door and asked me. "Do you know anything about this?".

The police interrogated me on the doorstep for a while. Fortunately, I knew nothing about it. That was just as well because lying was not one of my strong points. The inspector would have seen through me in seconds. As it was, I felt guilty just being questioned. There was no shortage of suspects, but fortunately, I'd not been singled out as a culprit. They moved on to the next door but didn't get much out of the Italian girls Rosetta, Lucia and Micolina.

At that point, I had no clue what had been taken, but it must have been a serious crime for the police to spend the time questioning every household.

Some months later, while I was waiting to go to school, the bus came down from Ridgway Road, where it had picked the kids up from the top street. As the bus proceeded slowly down our street, Stan Novak ran along its side and dropped something under its back wheel. Nothing happened, so he picked the object up, caught up with the bus and dropped whatever it was under the bus's wheel again. When the bus got to us, Stan was red-faced from running. He popped what looked like a wristwatch, a silvery grey disk the diameter of a penny with metal strap-like tags on either side, into the top pocket of his shirt. Stan was the last one to get onto the bus, and when he did, the driver demanded that he show him what he'd been throwing under the bus's wheels.

It turned out that the wristwatch Stan put into the pocket next to his heart was actually a railway warning detonator.

These types of detonators are used to give emergency warnings to trains.

If three of the devices are fixed at intervals on the track by the two soft metal tags, they explode with three loud bangs when they are crushed between the rail track and the iron wheel of a passing train. This signals the driver to stop.

The Colonel, Ray Papworth and Frank Reader had been the villains who had taken the detonators from the hut. Like saboteurs, they'd placed four devices side by side on the track, so they'd all go off together when the train ran over them. That wouldn't have derailed the train, but it would have certainly derailed the train driver. Years later, Ray told me Frank had instigated that particular mission.

Stanley found out about this and relieved a detonator from Colonel Beasley's dad's garage. Stanley was trying to get one to explode under the bus. Fortunately for him, the detonators, usually crushed between a steel rail and a locomotive, weren't sensitive enough to go off under a coach's rubber tyre.

When the CID returned to investigate, Frank, the oldest of the three Musketeers, had left home to join the British Army's Tank Regiment. Whatever Stanley told the bus driver, the culprits were never apprehended.

In 1962, A friend gave me a small travelling chess set in a plastic box with pieces that fit into small peg holes on the board. I had no idea how to play the game. Ray, who was still at Kingsbury Grammar School, taught me one evening while we were sitting on the front doorstep of my house. I learnt all the moves and bought a book on the game, but I was never good at it. I could never think of more than one move at a time.

Ray's dad had a pile of bricks delivered by the gate of his back garden for something he wanted to build. As his dad hadn't started on the project, Ray dug a hole about twelve feet from the back fence of the garden where the side path came up from the brickyard. Around the hole, Ray built a three-foot-high wall of four bricks thick. The construction had a corrugated iron roof held down with more bricks. There was a small entrance into the hole on the side facing away from the garden fence and a couple of spy holes the size of a brick in the wall facing the path. From the safety of this fortified bunker, we'd sit and wait for unsuspecting workers coming up from the brickyard. When we saw one through the spyholes, we would shout abuse at them and then snigger in our den as they looked around for the culprits. After a while, they would go on their way. However, one time a young man came past who was more persistent. When he realised where the abuse was coming from, he leaned over the fence and took some bricks from Mr Papworth's pile. He then began hurling the bricks at the bunker. Some rattled off the tin roof; others hit the front-facing wall, denting it into the hole's edge. After a few minutes of this constant barrage, some bricks began falling off the inside wall of the bunker. It seemed like the whole structure might collapse on us. If we tried to get out, there was a distinct possibility we'd be hit by a flying brick, so we remained in our hole amidst falling dust and debris.

Eventually, the man got tired of this game, and with the parting words, "That'll teach you, you little bastards", he relented and went on his way.

1962 brought a lot of changes. Frank had already left Brogborough and joined the Tank Regiment. Now just plain Roger, Colonel Beasley had left school and worked as an apprentice mechanic in the brickyard, and Beasley Troop was disbanded.

In April, Ray, now fifteen and a half years old, joined the British Army and went off to the Army Apprentices School in Harrogate. I wouldn't see him again for another five years.

But these weren't the only changes. There were things going on that would change our lives forever.

In July 1962, the communication satellite Telstar 1 was launched. Public television and telephone signals were transmitted around the world for the first time from space. In September, the British group the Tornados' instrumental record Telstar went to number one on the UK charts. In December, it went to number one on Billboard Hot 100, making the Tornados the first British group to have a number one hit in both the UK and the USA. Little did we know, we were heading into a science and music-driven cultural revolution.

On Saturday, about a month after Telstar hit number one in the UK while walking to the shops, I bumped into Johnny Mac coming the other way with a transistor radio.

"Listen to this," he said, holding out the radio. A new group called the Beatles were singing 'Love Me Do'.
Nothing would ever be the same again.

Music

In the early 1960's, I listened to Radio Luxembourg in bed under the sheets with a transistor radio when I was supposed to be asleep. Radio Luxembourg, which transmitted from the European Grand Duchy of the same name, broadcast game shows and religious programmes from Billy Graham. However, I was only interested in the music. It was the only source of pop music available on the radio then.
Luxembourg was a commercial radio station financed by advertising. I can still remember three advertisements transmitted by the station.
One was for Horace Batchelor's "Famous Infra-Draw Method" for winning the football pools. The 'pools' were the only way to win big money at the time. Horace had a very distinctive way of making sure you got the correct spelling for the address to send him money. "Horace Batchelor, Department One, Keynsham, spelt K-E-Y-N-S-H-A-M, Keynsham, Bristol". I don't know how successful his method was because I was too young to do the pools.

A second ad was more interesting to me as an adolescent. It was for Clearasil zit gel for teenagers. Of course, they didn't call it zit gel. The ad worked for me, and I bought the product. I can't recall if it was effective, but it did have a lovely smell.

The third ad I remember was for Pro Plus caffeine tablets. The jingle went.

"If you've got a date with a girl and you're feeling down, down, down.

Get up and go with Pro Plus. Paint the town, town, town, town, town".

Pro Plus was the closest thing we had to hard drugs in those days. It was basically concentrated caffeine. You could buy it over the counter from the chemist. It had the effect of drinking sixteen cups of coffee without the inconvenience of multiple trips to the toilet afterwards.

Continuing with Billy Graham and his Radio Luxembourg ads. It must have been during his mid-1960's Crusade in Britain that my friend Mary Irvine travelled to Earls Court, London, to hear the words of the American Evangelist. She returned the embodiment of Mary Magdalene, the 13th Apostle and took it upon herself to guide all of us, sinners, to the path of righteousness. Mary cajoled a large group of us into gathering one Sunday afternoon on the grass area by the main road end of Highfield Crescent. There we awaited the coming of one of Reverend Graham's travelling acolytes. We all sat at his feet when the preacher arrived and received the word. Some signed up for further guidance after the sermon. I was happy enough with father Golston's interpretation of Christianity, so I didn't bother. I don't know what the evangelist's conversion rate was. All I can say is it didn't take long for Mary to stray from the path. However, she did become a lifelong Christian in the end, but not the way you might think. I'll come to that later.

When it came to holidays, some of the middle-class kids at Fulbrook School, other failures in the egalitarian 11 plus system, went to France, Spain or Italy. Some went on the British India company's educational cruise ships, the Uganda or Nevasa, on exotic trips around the Mediterranean.

Of course, we didn't have that sort of money, so I never went on one of those sea trips. Still, I wasn't psychologically scarred and didn't need therapy for being a disadvantaged child. I did alright. I was obsessed with aeroplanes; my mum paid 1/6p a month for my' Flying Review' magazine and 6p a week for 'Look and Learn.' The middle-class kids had 'Knowledge' magazine at 2/6 a week. Nevertheless, I won Fulbrook school's High Sheriff Cup for General Knowledge. This proves you can take kids to the fountain of knowledge, but you can't make them drink it.

I was always short of cash. If I wanted something, I had to save my meagre pocket money for it. One time I wanted a long plastic Tennessee rifle from Brightmans' shop in Bedford. It took me fifteen weeks, saving 6p a week to accumulate the 7/6p to buy it. On Saturdays, when I went to Bedford with my parents, the stress was terrible in case it had been sold. It was a happy day when I finally walked out of the shop with that rifle. And what joy when my Uncle Tommy and Auntie Kay came back from Bedford one day with a Davy Crockett suit and a coonskin hat. To think I used to walk around Brogborough dressed like that, imagining I was the famous frontiersman who was killed at the Alamo.

One way of earning extra money was potato picking. Mr Hunter, a farmer from Bletchley, came every year to pick up women to go potato picking. They worked in pairs, my mum and her friend Mrs Hinson worked together, and in the summer holidays, we kids went along in the back of the open Land Rover. Initially, we didn't work; we just roamed the fields and woods and splashed around in lakes and ponds that we came across, generally making a nuisance of ourselves with the locals. Orchards were of prime interest. I remember one time a group of us got caught. When the man asked us for our names and addresses and found out we came from Brogborough, it seemed to explain everything. Still, nothing came of it, and we just got a ticking off. When we got to about twelve, Mr Hunter, a very nice man, thought we were responsible enough to work for pay. We did piecework, getting paid by the sack, which we had to tie up with a personalised coloured string. It was great getting a wage at the end of the week. Today it would be considered child exploitation, I suppose. However, they were happy days, with warm tea from thermos and lunchtime picnics. The problem was, the work was seasonal, and I needed a regular income.

In 1962 I was thirteen. I was friends with Rodney Bonfield. He was a few years older than me and lived up the top street. Rodney was a trainee farmer studying one day a week at Silsoe Agricultural College. He worked on Bevington's farm, a short walk from Brogborough. To give the head herdsman a break, Rodney asked if I would be interested in a job helping to get the cows in, milking, bottling up, and delivering milk to the houses in Brogborough. It also involved taking full churns to a farm at Ridgmont. I'd work four hours a day on the weekends and be finished by 09:00 am.

It was over one hundred years since the Slavery Abolition Act. The eight hours' wages were 15 shillings old money, 75p new decimal, but I took the job anyway. There was a problem, though: young farmers have a reputation for partying. Rodney always slept through the alarm clock on the weekends. Consequently, I had the additional responsibility of getting him out of bed.

At 04:30 on crisp winter mornings, I'd make my way to his house in clouds of frozen breath. Under a black star-filled sky, it was so quiet I could hear the freight train coming down the track from Bedford. At Rodney's, I'd go to the back of the house, climb the drainpipe onto the flat balcony, and bang on his bedroom window. Sometimes it would take minutes before he opened the window bleary-eyed so I could climb in from the freezing cold. Taking his record player and a bundle of LPs (Long-Playing Records) with us, we'd quietly sneak downstairs so as not to wake his parents. We'd raid his mum's drink cabinet and sit in the kitchen with a tumbler each of Cinzano Bianco. Our spirits raised; we took the record player and LPs and made our way to the farm.

At the milking shed, we'd set up the record player. We had Eddie Cochran, Billy Fury, and Elvis, but we'd put on Buddy Holly before getting the cows in. They liked Buddy, he relaxed them, and a relaxed cow gives better milk.

While Rodney cleaned the cows' udders and got the milking equipment on, I got the bottles ready for filling. Once the milk started coming, I'd take the buckets into the bottling room, climb the ladder and fill the header tank. The liquid then ran down over what looked like a corrugated washboard cooler before bottling. Each bottle had to be filled and capped by hand. Capping involved putting a foil top into the rubber insert of the hand-held capping tool and pressing it onto the bottle. I had a quota of pints and quart bottles to fill; the excess went into the churns for Ridgmont, where it was used to make cheese. It was impossible to bottle up with gloves on. It was a wonder I didn't get frostbite in the unheated shed in winter, handling nearly frozen bottles. With numb fingers, sometimes, a bottle would slip on the stainless-steel table, and I'd get soaked in milk. When this happened in the heat of summer, I'd get home stinking of spoilt milk.

It was a pleasant time, the two of us working in synchronisation. The cows' heads locked into the stalls, happily chewing on straw. Their tails flicking back and forth to the beat of That'll be the day, Summertime Blues, Halfway to Paradise and 'Jailhouse Rock; a scene of pastoral tranquillity.

Once the cows were milked and returned to the fields, we'd load up the churns and crated bottles and hitch the trailer to the big farm tractor. With Rodney driving and me jammed between him and the wheel arch, we'd go off to Brogborough to deliver the milk and pick up the empties. We had to collect payment for the week's deliveries to each house on Saturdays. We either knocked on the door or picked up the money that had been left out on the step overnight by those who wanted a lay-in. After dropping off the

churns at Ridgmont, we'd go back to the farm, wash and sterilise the empties for use the next day and go home for breakfast.
The concept of a bottle bank hadn't been invented then. In those days, milk, beer and pop bottles were all returned to the supplier for washing and refilling. Discarded bottles were like treasure to kids. They would collect them and return them to shops and pubs for the deposit money.

The money was crap, but working on a farm was a good experience, it was a learning curve. One morning we arrived around five to find the headsman had been called in because a cow was in trouble calving. He had his arm right in her up to his shoulder, trying to turn the calf. Then with the headsman holding the cow, Rodney and I had to haul on a rope tied to the calf to get it out. There was a lot of heaving and bellowing from the cow until a new long-legged life form came stumbling into the world, steaming in the cold winter air.

The Big Freeze.

The winter of 1962 to 63 turned out to be one of the coldest winters on record in the United Kingdom.
On the Saturday 29 and 30 of December 1962, England's Southwest and Wales were hit by a blizzard from gale-force wind-driven snow. Some places had snow drifts over 20 feet high (more than six metres). Power lines came down, roads and railways were

blocked, and villages and towns were cut off from the outside world.

It was Sunday 30 of December when the blizzard came our way. I was working on the milk farm when it arrived. Like any other winter's weekend morning, my day started early with me on the freezing balcony banging on Rodney's bedroom window, trying to wake him.

When we arrived at the farm, it started to snow as we got the cows in for milking. I began collecting the milk and pouring the warm steaming liquid into the tank at the top of the refrigerated cooling unit. It was colder than usual in the bottling shed. Slivers of frozen milk began dropping off the corrugated cooling plate. My fingers were so cold they turned as white as the milk I was bottling. I had to keep stopping to blow on my hands and flick to get the blood back into my fingers. The snow was falling so heavily that it was difficult to see the old lean-to covering some old farm equipment across the yard. The roof of the lean-to was covered in an ever-increasing thick white blanket of snow.

I was working as fast as possible, but the cold was slowing me down. Suddenly, I heard a loud crack followed by an almighty crash. When I looked through the window. I saw the lean-to had collapsed onto the equipment.

The snow kept falling; by the time we'd loaded the crates onto the trailer, it was more than a foot thick on the ground. Rodney fired up the tractor. We headed out of the farm with me huddling between Rodney and the wheel arch. There was no traffic on the road, but even with the massive tread on the tractor's tyres, we had to take care in the treacherous conditions. Trudging through ankle-deep snow with a metal pannier full of milk bottles was a miserable and perilous task, especially on the sloping pathways to and from the houses. My socks were soaked from the snow that had fallen into my shoes and melted. My feet and hands were frozen.

When we finished our delivery in Brogborough, we headed down the B557 past the farm turning off left towards Ridgmont to deliver two churns to the farm close to the bottom of Ridgmont hill. We passed the entrance of the desolate brickworks and crossed the Bletchley to Bedford railway line. The snow-covered tracks showed no indication that the trains were running. The single tyre track of an earlier intrepid traveller was almost indiscernible in the snow. Driven by an ice-cold wind, the snow had drifted three or four feet deep in some places on the road. Rodney kept up a constant speed and ploughed through. After each thud, a wave of snow crashed over the tractor, covering me with cold white powder. The wind cut into us like an icy knife, covering us with more snow. We reached the base of the Ridgmont hill, but as the tractor took the slope, its progress began to falter. Soon the wheels were spinning. It was apparent we weren't going to make it. Rodney carefully reversed back down the slope and skilfully manoeuvred the tractor and trailer to face the opposite direction. We unloaded the churns on the side of the road, then trudged up the hill to tell the farmer he would have to figure out his own way to recover them. Fortunately, with the churns being gradually coated in snow, there was little chance of the milk going off.

We fought our way back through the ever-increasing drifts. We finished off our work at the farm and then, with great difficulty, made our way home on foot.

Back at Brogborough, a ten-foot-high drift had blown across the main road just beyond Hill Crescent, leaving the Bedford-Bletchley road completely blocked.

On Monday morning, when we opened the front door, we were confronted with a translucent wall of compacted white snow that had drifted above the height of the door. Even if the buses could get through, which they couldn't, we were trapped in the house, so there was no possibility of going to school. Our only escape was for my dad to dig his way out. When we did get out, we built snowmen and slides everywhere. Unfortunately, it was only a few days before the roads were cleared and salted, and we were back at school.

The air temperature remained so low that the snow cover lasted for more than two months.

At Fulbrook school, we brought water from the changing room wash basins in bottles to make a long slide. The slide ran almost the entire length of the playground. Skating down this sheet of ice was a dangerous sport. The slide terminated up against the solid brick wall at the back of the bike sheds.

In the anarchy of the playground with no stewards or track inspectors, boys would run uncontrolled onto the slide. With little spacing between them, a line of valiant skaters' arms outstretched, flapping like wings to keep their balance, would streak down the run. Like railway trucks heading for a cliff face, you had to jump off before slamming into the bike shed wall or get crushed by the following horde. The mere act of exiting the slide invariably ended in a tumble, grazes, bruises and minor injuries. The teachers let this mayhem continue until a fat boy with large prominent front teeth hit a piece of the slide where the ice was worn through to the asphalt. The result was an object lesson in Newton's Laws of Motion.

Law 1. A body will continue its state of uniform motion in a straight line unless acted upon by an external force.

The external force was the friction braking of the asphalt on the soles of the boy's shoes.

Law 2. The rate of change of motion is proportional to and in the direction of the applied force.

The rate of change of motion due to his feet being stopped by contact with the asphalt was immediate. Unfortunately, the top half of his body tried to follow Law 1 and continued to move forward. This resulted in a rotational torque that caused his head to rotate down towards the floor.

Law 3. To every action, there is an equal and opposite reaction.

Too slow to react, the boy's face hit the floor like a hammer. There was an interchange of momentum between the falling boy and planet Earth, and Planet Earth wasn't going anywhere. The boy's head bounced like a ball. Two front teeth, roots and all flew in an arc out of his mouth onto the playground. The teeth were enormous, complete with their roots they looked like tusks from some undiscovered miniature elephant. Some thoughtful child found the teeth and put them into the victim's hand. Blood streaming from his nose and mouth, the boy was taken away for medical attention.

After that, the slide was salted, and further slide making was banned.

Through January and February, the snow persisted on the ground. We threw bread and seeds onto the snow, but it was survival of the fittest, and thousands of birds died of starvation.

It wasn't worth hunting pigeons. They were just feathers and bone. The poor things wander up to you without fear just to be put out of their misery. It was pitiful.

Even for us kids, the novelty of the winter landscape wore off after two months. The temperature continued just above freezing during the day and back to freezing at night. The snow turned from powdery flakes you could play with into a shell of white ice, and we longed for sunshine and green grass again.

One Saturday morning in early March 1963, I peered through my bedroom window that was unusually frozen over. The sun was shining, and water dripped in glistening drops from the icicles on the roof gutter. I jumped out of bed, fully dressed because it was the only way to stay warm at night in our unheated homes. In excitement, I shouted to my sister that the snow was melting.

Soon the spring flowers and blossoms would fill the fields, and hedgerows and life would return to normal. I was like a bear coming out of hibernation.

Army Cadets.

In 1963, Morris Maroney, another first-generation Irish immigrant, lived outside Lidlington close to the automatic railway crossing on the Marston back road. Morris kept badgering me to join him in the Lidlington Army Cadets. I'd done my military training with Beasley Troop, which was by then disbanded, so I declined. Morris continued to pester me every time we met, so in the end, to keep him quiet, I joined.

I was issued a short jacket battle dress with leg gaiters for the trousers, a tie and an itchy hairy shirt. I had a thick khaki 1937 issue webbing belt with a brass buckle and brass adjustment loops at each end. The brass fittings had to be kept polished, and woe betides anyone who got Braso on the webbing. My boots were made of dimpled black leather. I spent hours with a hot spoon smoothing and polishing the toe caps until you could see your face in them. I also had a black beret with a brass Army Cadet Force cap badge. The badge had to be kept polished unless you were on night training, then it had to be blacked up. Again, woe betides anyone who left Braso or black in the crevices of the badge.

Because they were so comfortable, I liked the fatigues best. Fatigues were a light grey/olive green boiler suit with button-down breast and thigh pockets, something like a flying suit.

When we assembled at the cadet hut on Friday evenings, the first thing was inspection. I always made sure I was well turned out, but some of the others got a right earbashing.

We had two older sergeant instructors, about 17 or 18, who took things very seriously. After inspection and some parade ground drill, we got to the real army stuff.

Fieldcraft: involved learning infantry skills such as patrolling, laying an ambush, camouflage clothing and face makeup, reconnaissance, and hand signals for stealth.

Navigation: included using a compass with Ordnance Survey maps, six-figure grid references, distances between points, understanding contour lines and map signs, magnetic bearings and the three different types of north.

I still remember the term "in the door and up the stairs" for fixing coordinates by tracing horizontal latitude before vertical longitude.

Skill at Arms: included stripping, cleaning and using a Lee-Enfield .303 rifle and .22 target practice.

Close to Lidlington, there used to be a gun range where cadets could fire off .303 blank rounds. This place was the source of an incident that became part of Lidlington Cadet Force folklore on how not to clean a rifle. After one blank firing session, the cadets were told to clean their rifles. With a Lee-Enfield, this involves holding the rifle vertically with the muzzle resting on your boot to avoid getting mud in the barrel. You then remove the bolt from the rear of the gun and drop a pull-through with a cleaning cloth attached to a string into the breech.

An instructor checking things were being done correctly saw that cadet S, also a first-generation Irish immigrant, still had his rifle cocked.

"S - - - - - -, your rifle is still cocked," shouted the instructor. Upon which, cadet S pulled the trigger. Unfortunately, the rifle still had a blank in the chamber.
BANG! The wadding from the blank went through the cadet's foot and out through the bottom of his boot.
My dad always said, "It's the unloaded gun that kills, " and as Colonel Beasley remarked in Aspley Wood, "These blanks are bloody dangerous".

Lidlington Cadets was an educational experience. It was something like Beasley Troop but without the beatings and jail time. I stayed in for about eighteen months but stopped going when I left school and went to college. I lost contact with Morris after he joined the British Army.

Rosslare Holiday 1963

Early Saturday morning, 27 July 1963, there was a lot of excitement in the house. We were off to Ireland again for our summer holidays. After breakfast, my sister Ellen, mum and I followed my dad carrying two suitcases down the middle path between the two cornfields, through the brickyard to Ridgmont Railway Station. My dad bought the tickets at the little hatch, and we sat and waited on the platform. The big black locomotive came hissing into the station in a cloud of smoke and steam. The guard in the rear coach waved a green flag and blew his whistle. The train chugged out of the station under the M1 motorway and passed the old MOD fuel dump on the Husborne Crawley road crossing. Our railroad adventure by steam engine began. Half an hour later, we arrived at Bletchley after a trip through English summer countryside, stopping at Aspley Guise, Woburn Sands, Bow Brickhill and Fenny Stratford. There we changed trains for London's Victoria station.

From Victoria, we usually took the Underground Circle Line to Paddington. On this occasion, we took a London black taxicab. We travelled through Belgravia, passed Buckingham Palace, and then between Hyde Park and Mayfair to Marble Arch. We saw so many elegant buildings and statues. London was such a fascinating place. The weather was sunny and scorching, and the air was gritty. The place was opulent and noisy, with the constant chatter of pneumatic drills from the reconstruction going on everywhere. We saw a column of mounted cavalry with swords and polished breastplates. The riders had plumed helmets with chin straps just below their mouths. Riding with ramrod straight backs, the soldiers glistened in the afternoon sunshine.

There was no shortage of foreigners in Brogborough. We were almost all immigrants, but in London, there were people dressed in traditional clothing from their own countries. Arabs looked like they'd just come off the set from the recently released film Lawrence of Arabia. They wore long white robes and Bedouin headdresses, striding in front of veiled women and groups of children. There were black African men dressed in coloured flowing wide-sleeved Agbada robes sporting round rimless patterned hats and women wearing vibrant costumes and massive matching turban-like headgear.

The taxi dropped us at Paddington among a host of other travellers arriving and leaving. The station was bustling and filled with the chatter of strange dialects and foreign languages. Farewells and reunions. As we followed my dad onto our platform, the chatter became more and more Irish. Some accents were so strong I couldn't understand what was being said.

The train's carriages were the kind that had separate polished wood compartments that seated travellers in two long, upholstered seats facing each other. A long corridor that ran the length of the carriage gave access to each compartment via a sliding door. Some of the carriages were 'NO SMOKING'. My dad avoided these and chose one that already had the strong scent of pipe and cigarette tobacco.

While my dad loaded the cases into the overhead string net shelves, I took a seat by the window facing forward. I thought our carriage was moving backwards; only when the train next to us disappeared from view did, I realise we were still in the station and the other train had moved out. That was an observation I would have to think about.

After an interminable wait, there was a slamming of doors and a shrill whistle. My head jerked backwards, and we began to move out of the station on our way to Fishguard.

Soon we were out of the city grime and rattling through green countryside, flashing through small towns and villages in brilliant sunlight, leaving a cloud of smoke and steam in our wake.

These journeys to Rosslare instilled in me a love of rail travel.

The poem "From a Railway Carriage" by R L Stevenson sums up the experience, especially if it's recited to the rhythm of the fast-pounding pistons of a steam railway locomotive.

"Faster than fairies, faster than witches,
Bridges and houses, hedges and ditches.
And charging along like troops in a battle
All through the meadows, the horses and cattle.
All of the sights of the hill and the plain
Fly as thick as driving rain.
And ever again, in the wink of an eye,
Painted stations whistle by.
Here is a child who clambers and scrambles,
All by himself and gathering brambles.
Here is a tramp who stands and gazes.
And here is the green for stringing the daisies
Here is a cart run away in the road
Lumping along with man and load.
And here is a mill, and there is a river.
Each a glimpse and gone forever."

All the carriages had a toilet at one end of the corridor. I liked visiting this little room. When you flushed the toilet, a flap swung down, and you could watch the track whizzing past beneath the train.

One time I went for a pee and found a signet ring had been left on the side of the hand basin. It must have belonged to another child

because it fit my finger. I took it back to our carriage and showed it to the affluent looking Englishman on the seat opposite. He inspected it, looking especially carefully at the inside of the ring. After a moment of contemplation, he brought his bottom lip over his top lip and nodded knowingly. He handed the ring back to me.
"That's Spanish gold," he said.
"Wow. Should I find the owner?"
"Oh no," he replied. "It's the plunder of some pirate. He won't want to be found. Best you keep it and say nothing."
I was happy with that and put it back on my finger. I wore the ring for the rest of my holiday and told all my Irish relatives I got it from a pirate on the Spanish Main. Of course, it was only an old piece of brass, but it had a secret history of blood and adventure to me.

We went through the rail tunnel under the river Seven into Wales and got our first glimpse of the sea as we passed down the Bristol Channel's west side to Cardiff. We had a long stop at Swansea station and may even have had to change trains if I remember correctly.
From Swansea, with the occasional sight of the setting sun glinting off the sea, we travelled inland.
It was dark when we pulled into Fishguard station. There, lit up against the dock, floating serene, was the TSS St David waiting to take us on the next leg of our journey across the St George's Channel in the Irish Sea.

Cars were being loaded into the hold by a crane as we made our way onto the ship. At the top of the gangplank, a seaman checked our tickets and recorded our numbers, clicking a hand counter that looked like a stopwatch. There was a low hum and vibration of unseen equipment running below decks. People were milling around, stowing their luggage and finding a place to settle. Children were running around, and the space was filled with excited chatter.

Before long, the propellers rumbled into life, and the ship inched its way out of the harbour. Passing under the beam of the Strumble Head Lighthouse, we made our way into the night. Unknown to me then, we sailed by the area close to Fishguard, where on the night of 13 June 1941, the SS St Patrick, en route from Rosslare to Fishguard, was bombed by the Luftwaffe. The ship broke in half and sank in five minutes with the loss of thirty lives.

The coastal lights of Wales disappeared, and we headed into the night towards Ireland. The St George's channel can be a stormy place. On that night, it was relatively calm.

Nevertheless, the gentle rolling of the ship caused a number of the less hardy to be seasick and throw up. This always infected other passengers who followed suit. Soon that obnoxious smell had me retching. I've never been seasick, but I've often been sick at sea because of others.

A gathering of Irish travellers, strangers or not, anywhere on the planet invariably results in music and singing. This erupted from the bar, adding to the misery of some of the more nauseous passengers.

We made our way onto the port side deck in the dim light of dawn. First, the Tuskar Rock Lighthouse came into view. Like many from Rosslare, my uncle, Billy Boyce, did time on Tuskar Rock. A lonely job but something of a period of solitary rehab in Uncle Billy's case.

Shortly after sighting Tuskar, the grey colour perspective of the coastal strip came into view. Even since I was a child, the first sight of Ireland always filled me with excitement.

Soon, we could see the harbour wall. 'Boyce's Wall', was built under the supervision of my great grandfather John Boyce at the beginning of the 20th century. At the end of the wall stood the red-painted harbour lighthouse, where my uncle Ben fell off the pier in his overcoat and sea boots one night when he left the harbour bar and turned the wrong way to go home. He hung onto the wall all night until workers found him in the morning and hauled him up to safety. He was lucky to have survived.

As the ship came alongside, my mum pointed out my grandfather waiting on the dock for us.

We disembarked. Granddad Boyce was leaning against a stanchion, smoking an untipped cigarette.

Characteristically he held the cigarette between the thumb and middle finger. His right-hand index finger was just a stump. He lost his finger as a boy, cut off by a lever while he and his friends played in the cab of a steam engine on the railway siding near the pier.

Everyone on the pier knew granddad. He'd walked straight through the customs shed to where the ship berthed. He'd been a crane driver before he retired. While working on the pier one day, the crane he was operating malfunctioned and tipped over into the sea with him in it. He was lucky to get out alive. He said that he saw an image of the Virgin Mary beaconing him while under the water. He swam to her, and that's how he got out of the crane's cab.

With a connection to the Mother of God or not, we still had to go through the customs ritual and put our case on the long table. After inspection, the customs officer marked the cases with chalk, and we left the shed. Other than Playboy magazines, I'm not sure what was contraband in those days. Certainly, cigarettes, cigarette lighters, beer and spirits were cheaper in Ireland then.

We made our way to the viaduct while passengers boarded the train, and cars were being loaded onto open flatbed rail trucks to take them ashore. The viaduct was a black steel box section that supported two railway tracks. It bridged the gap from the concrete pier across the sea and beach to dry land, where the train line went off to Wexford and on to Dublin.

Hanging off the left side steel wall of the viaduct was a pedestrian walkway. The walkway was about two metres wide and made from thick wooden planks. The planks had gaps between them where you could see down to the waves crashing against the mussel and seaweed covered viaduct support pillars below. There was a steel handrail to stop you from falling into the sea, but it was still an unnerving experience for novices and small children. That walk is an enduring memory of arriving in Rosslare.

From the viaduct, with granddad Boyce carrying one of the cases, we made our way up an inclined bridge over the train lines to the road, then up the 99 steps to the top of the cliff by the Pier Hotel and took the short walk to Colville Street.

When we arrived at grandfather's house, uncle Ben was in from the night's fishing. Uncle Ben was a big man with dark hair and a ruddy complexion from working long hours on deck at sea. He was a quiet, gentle giant who liked to drink Smithwick's or Guinness in the Railway Social Club with his friends. He chain-smoked Sweet Afton, Majors, Players Navy Cut, or other non-tipped strong cigarettes. Uncle Ben was quite relaxed with his drinking, unlike the Butler brothers of my dad's family, where a quiet drink invariably ended in a fight.

If you said anything controversial, all you got from Uncle Ben was a nod, a knowing smile followed by silence. Whatever his opinion, he kept it to himself to not upset the tranquillity. Of course, I only learned this side of his character when I was old enough to accompany him to the Railway Club.

Soon the house was filled with the smell of fresh-caught fish cooking on the paraffin primus. We all sat down to breakfast of fried plaice and turbot, soda bread and strong Irish tea.

Granddad's house at 1170 Colville street was a small mid-terraced bungalow that belonged to the railway company. It had a narrow strip of front garden with a beautiful smelling, pink honeysuckle growing up the right side of the front door. There were three bedrooms, one with its entrance directly across from the front door in the small entrance hall with a door to the living room. The living room had doors at each end of the far wall to each of the other two bedrooms. The room was furnished with a round table, hard-backed wooden chairs, and a small writing desk. In pride of place against the back wall was a black wooden organ with stops above the keyboard and pump peddles below. A peat' turf' fired stove stood against the wall between the two-bedroom doors. The stove had an oven on one side, used for baking soda bread, and a flat surface on top that supported a large stew pot. The shiny brown peat briquettes were stacked neatly by its side.

On the left side of the back wall of the living room was a doorway to a long narrow kitchen that ran the width of the living room. The kitchen had a long work surface for preparing food and a large paraffin primus stove supporting a big frying pan. The kitchen had a tall, shelved pantry with a wire mesh door, and on its back wall below the window, it had a sink and draining board with cupboards beneath.

There were three steps down to a large concrete-floored backyard surrounded by a seven-foot-high wall from the kitchen's back door. On the left of the steps was a low open shed that contained a tin bath and other bits and pieces. In the far-right corner of the yard was a latch door to an outside WC that had a flushed toilet connected to the village sewage system. Another latched door in the centre of the far wall of the yard opened onto the lane that connected Goulding street to Jameson Street. Behind this door was an ornamental cast-iron water hydrant that supplied water from the mouth of a lion for the households.

To the right, across the back lane, where Colville Street turned the corner into Jameson Street, was the backyard of my mum's uncle

Tommy, his Welsh wife, auntie Betty and my second cousins Margie, Jimmy, and Rene Bernard.

Uncle Tommy was a slim, quiet man with a soft Irish accent. Auntie Betty was Welsh, stout, full bosomed with a flushed complexion. She was effusive and always greeted me with great emotion when I went to see her. There was never a dull moment around auntie Betty; it was always a joy to be around her.

My cousin Margie was 15, the same age as my sister Ellen. They were very similar in appearance and size. They both had fair hair, and you could easily mistake one for the other from a distance.

That summer, my cousin Margie worked in Murphy's general store and post office on the corner where Colville Street crossed St Martin's Road and continued on to the Pier Hotel on the clifftop. There weren't many telephones in Rosslare, but there was a green Irish Telephone box outside Murphy's shop. The box was similar to a British phone box, but it was green, not red. Instead of a crown, it had the word Telefón, in Gallic letters, embossed above its door. The box was connected to a manual plug-in exchange board in a room behind the counter of Murphy's store.

When I was on my way to the beach one day, I stopped at Murphy's shop to buy some sweets. The shop was empty except for Margie and a lady customer in conversation at the counter. I knew better than to interrupt the trading of local intelligence. I used my time to choose a purchase.

A German lady, a tourist, came into the shop. She waited about ten seconds, then impatiently interrupted Margie's conversation. With that unfortunate use of the English language that seems to turn a

Teutonic request into an order, she demanded to make a long-distance call to Germany.

Margie asked the tourist to write down the number on a pad.

"The telephonist isn't available at the moment. When she is, she'll make the connection for you. She won't be long, but to make sure you don't lose your place, you should wait in the phone box outside. I'll let you know when she's ready to make the connection. Do you have enough change for the call?".

"Of course I have", replied the German lady dismissively. Showing her disdain at the inefficiency, she left the shop with no choice but to wait in the phone box lest a local got ahead of her on a rambling call.

When Margie finished her conversation with the customer, she served me. After inquiring about my grandfather and parents, Margie went outside. She told the German lady in the phone box to get ready for the long-distance call. Margie came back into the shop, morphed into the telephone operator and disappeared into the back room. I stayed for a while to listen to Margie, communicating with the caller in her posh telephone voice. The German lady was shovelling silver coins into the coin slot from a pile beside the telephone cradle when I left the shop.

Walking to the clifftop, it was clear to me that there was a more relaxed attitude to time, life and authority in Rosslare. For centuries, the English had tried to come to terms with that part of the Irish psyche. The Germans didn't stand a chance.

I used to sit on the flat concrete roof of the old gun emplacement buried in the cliff that overlooked the harbour, looking out to sea or watching the activity on the pier. I'd wait for Uncle Ben to come in from a night's fishing in the mornings. I'd scan the ocean with granddad's old brass binoculars until I saw the boat chugging in, trailed by a flock of seagulls. Sometimes, other large ships passed back and forth further out to sea. I'd wonder what they were carrying and to what exotic places they might be going.

At fourteen, I was on my tenth summer holiday in Rosslare. But this year, there was something very different about Ireland.
Between June 26 and 29, 1963, John Fitzgerald Kennedy, President of the United States of America, visited Ireland.
He visited the cottage at Dunganstown, near New Ross, County Wexford, where his ancestors had lived before emigrating to America. The President also visited the town of Wexford, where he laid a wreath at the John Barry Memorial on Crescent Quay.
Commodore John Barry was known as "The Father of the American Navy". He grew up with his uncle Nicholas, a fisherman in Rosslare Strand County Wexford after his family was evicted from their home in Tacumshane by the British.
Consequently, when we arrived on holiday in August, the country was still in a celebratory mood from Kennedy's visit. One day we took the train from Rosslare to Wexford town. Pubs, hotels and shops were full of pictures of the President and his visit to the city. Wexford had a lot of souvenir shops. Along with shamrock and leprechaun, cigarette lighters and figurines, these shops were full of religious statues, crucifixes and framed pictures of the Virgin Mary, Christ with a Bleeding Heart. Now, alongside figures and

pictures of St Patrick were those of Kennedy, who had achieved virtual sainthood.

This outpouring of emotion and pride was understandable. The 35th President of the United States of America was the first Irish American Catholic and, at the age of 43, the youngest person to be elected to that office. More significantly to us, his ancestors came from Wexford.

Too soon, our holiday in Ireland was over. As we sailed for Fishguard on the ferry, I watched with sadness as Rosslare Harbour and the coastline of Erin's Isle disappear below the horizon.

On Sunday, August 11, when we arrived back at Paddington Station, my dad bought a newspaper. The paper was full of The Great Train Robbery that occurred while we were away on holiday. On August 8, at three in the morning, a gang stopped a train travelling from Glasgow to London, near Mentmore in Buckinghamshire. The train was carrying used banknotes to be incinerated in London.

The investigation was led by Detective Chief Superintendent Tommy Butler, a man with the same name as my dad's brother but with no connection to our family. By mid-September, the robbery was unravelling, with the police arresting some of the perpetrators. It was believed that 15 men were involved in the robbery. However, only 11 were convicted, and most of the money stolen was never recovered.

The crime was such big news because the gang stole bank notes worth 2.6 Million Pounds (equivalent to £55 million in 2019). In 1963 this was an unbelievable amount of money.

The most memorable thing about 1963 was Kennedy. You didn't have to be Irish or Catholic to admire Kennedy. Being young was enough. We had JFK; the youngest person elected as the president of the United States. It seemed that things were changing and changing fast.

Kennedy had already made his "We do these things not because they are easy, but because they are hard" speech at Rice University. We were going to the moon, and Kennedy said it would be done before the end of the 1960's. Now, Dan Dare, Flash Gordon, and Buck Rogers were more than just fictional comic book characters. They were the future, and the future was now.

Kennedy may have stirred up things in politics, but there was another youth revolution on the boil in the UK. The Beatles were on the verge of changing the music scene forever. They arrived on the music scene in 1962 with Love Me Do. That record didn't do so well, reaching only № 17 in the UK charts. However, by the end of January 1963, Please, Please Me went to number 2. This was followed by three № 1s: From Me To You, She Loves You, and I Want To Hold Your Hand.

By the autumn, the country was in the grip of the new phenomena of Beatlemania, an outpouring of hysteria and screaming that followed the group wherever they went. Everyone loved the Beatles, children, teenagers, mums and dads, grannies and even the odd grumpy grandpa. I was no exception; I was hooked from that first time I bumped into Johnny Mac in the street one Saturday playing Please, Please Me on a transistor radio. After that, Saturday mornings with Uncle Mac on a Saturday morning would never be enough.

Little did we realise, a dark cloud loomed on the horizon. In November, the storm broke.

THE ASSASSINATION

Friday, November 22, was fish and chip night. Mr Bitchener's fish and chip van parked outside the shops in Brogborough in the evening, and for a couple of hours, the place became a meeting point.

My parents were watching something on the BBC that didn't interest me, so, shortly before 7pm, I volunteered to go to the chip van to get our supper. Before I got to the shops, coming in the other direction, I met Margaret, one of seven Coleman's sisters from the Irish Catholic family in Highfield Crescent. Margaret and I were the same age, but she didn't go to my school. Like all of her sisters, she'd passed the 11 Plus and attended Kingsbury Grammar School in Dunstable with my sister.

In the dim light, I could see she was agitated. As soon as she saw me, she burst out with.

"They've shot Kennedy".

It was like being hit in the head with a brick. I replied without thinking.
"You're joking". That inane response people use when they've been told some monumental news that they can't grasp.
Understandably this made her angry.
"DO YOU THINK I'D JOKE ABOUT A THING LIKE THAT?"
she snapped back. Exasperated by my stupid reply, she left me standing alone on the street.
I was stunned, but the memory is still seared indelibly in my brain.
The assassination and state funeral dominated the news in the following days. At the time, the political implications of Kennedy's death didn't mean much to me. I was distraught. The whole world seemed a sadder place. The results of that day ended, not just for me but for many other young people, a great hope for the future.
During all that confusion, remorse and sorrow, the day after the assassination, Saturday, November 23, the BBC aired the first-ever episode of Dr Who. I still remember the old man with long white hair, a couple of children, a police telephone box bigger inside than on the outside, and the time travel. That's all I can remember. I have no recollection of the storyline of that first episode.
We moved toward Christmas and the New Year in a greyer world from which the year had started, and I wondered if we would still be going to the moon.

The Kennedy assassination was the first world event that really affected me. Following it, Lee Harvey Oswald was arrested and accused of the assassination.

On November 24, in Dallas, Texas, just two days after the assassination, Jack Ruby shot and killed Oswald while being transferred from Police Headquarters to the city jail. My dad said it was all very suspicious. The final events of 1963 had a tremendous impact. The world was different from the one I'd constructed in my own head. The good guys like the Lone Ranger didn't always win.

Chapter 8

The year that changed everything.

At the beginning of 1964, there was a sea change in popular music. A tsunami of British artists began the conquest of the world.

A collision of attitudes, technologies and events made 1964 the most fantastic year for popular music and consequently the most amazing year for U.K. youth.

On Wednesday 1 January, at 6:35 in the evening, the BBC's Top of the Pops descended on the British public for the first time. It erupted with The Rolling Stones doing their version of The Beatles' song, "I Wanna Be Your Man". The rest of the show included Dusty Springfield with "I Only Want to Be with You", The Dave Clark Five with "Glad All Over", The Hollies with "Stay", and The Swinging Blue Jeans with "Hippy Hippy Shake". The show ended with The Beatles doing "I Want to Hold Your Hand", that week's number one. One month later, on 1 February, from nowhere, with the same song, The Beatles shot to № 1 in the U.S. singles charts.

On 7 February, the group landed at New York's JFK International Airport. Two days later, on 9 February, they appeared on The Ed Sullivan Show. The country was hit by a shock wave of Beatlemania. The British invasion and conquest of America had begun, and it just didn't stop. On 1 April, The Beatles went to № 1 in the U.K. charts with Can't Buy Me Love.

By 4 April, they held the top 5 positions on the Billboard Top 40 singles chart in America. The songs in order were: "Can't Buy Me

Love", "Twist and Shout", "She Loves You", "I Want to Hold Your Hand", and "Please, Please Me". An achievement not equalled to this day (4 April 2021).

On 11 April, The Beatles had 14 records on the American Billboard Hot 100. The highest number of records in that chart simultaneously since Elvis Presley's 9 in December 1956.

Over the next months and years, The Beatles were followed into America by The Rolling Stones, The Zombies, The Kinks, The Dave Clark Five, Herman's Hermits, The Hollies, The Animals, The Searchers, The Yardbirds, The Who, and Gerry and the Pacemakers. The Invasion by the groups was supported by solo singers such as Dusty Springfield, Cilla Black, Petula Clark, Tom Jones, and Donovan.

The dominance of British over American music in 1964 was undeniable, not just in America but also at home. In the U.K. TOP 20, of the 22 № 1s that year, only three were by U.S. artists. Two were by Roy Orbison with - Oh, Pretty Woman and It's Over. The other was Baby Love by The Supremes. Of the remaining 19 № 1s, one was by the Irish harmony trio, The Bachelors. The remaining 18 were by British artists, the top being The Beatles, who had 3 № 1s with I Feel Fine holding the № 1 position for five weeks.

On 28 March 1964 – The wax likenesses of The Beatles were displayed in Madame Tussauds Wax Museum in London. They were the first pop stars ever to be displayed at the museum.

THE PIRATES

But there was more to come. On the same day that the Beatles were immortalised in wax, the "pirate" radio station Radio Caroline began broadcasting from a ship anchored just outside UK territorial waters near Felixstowe.

Caroline transmitted 20 Thousand Watts of pop music power from six in the morning until six in the evening, when it shut down for two hours to avoid competition with Radio Luxembourg. The station returned to the airwaves at eight and continued transmitting until past midnight.

Radio Caroline was followed on 12 May by Radio Atlanta transmitting from the motor ship Mi Amigo anchored off Frinton-on-Sea. However, its audience and advertising revenue didn't meet expectations. Radio Atlanta merged operations with Radio Caroline to become Caroline South in July.

On 27 May, Radio Sutch began broadcasting from an abandoned WWII Anti-Aircraft fort at Shivering Sands in the Thames Estuary. The station was launched by Screaming Lord Sutch, later the leader of the 'Official Monster Raving Loony Party' and a persistent parliamentary candidate. A true Child-of-the-Sixties.

The quartet of pirate stations was completed on 23 December when Wonderful Radio London started transmitting from an old US Navy minesweeper also anchored off Frinton-on-Sea.

THE 'TRANNY'

The final facet making 1964 the year of music was the availability of cheap, portable transistor radios. The 'tranny' was everywhere. Britain was filled with pop music. Music pervaded every part of society on buses and trains, in parks, on the streets, and in places of work. Few people used the small earphone that came with their radio. This caused grumpy old men to complain bitterly at the decline in courtesy and moral standards. We did not care, and the music played on.

By law, a License was required to own a transistor radio, but nobody bought one at a cost equivalent to more than £20 at today's prices. Kids just could not afford it. Tracking a bicycle mounted radio or none license holder among hundreds lazing on crowded beaches or riverbanks or picnicking and wandering through parks was impossible for the BBC detector vans. By early 1971 the radio-only license was dropped.

The exception to all this musical free expression was at school. At our place of education, transistor radios were banned under threat of confiscation. Some of the school bus drivers tuned in to the music stations, so we generally got a morning dose of pop to get us through the day and an evening dose to brighten our mood on our way home.

However, the school did make one concession. On Friday nights, the assembly hall and toilets were opened up as a youth club where we could play music and dance. The more mature got up to more unsavoury activities behind the bike sheds. I was just coming off my Air fix model stage of development, but my time would come.

MODS & ROCKERS

Along with the music revolution, The Beatles, Pirates and the transistor radio, another phenomenon hit Britain. In 1964, Mods and Rockers battled it out on Clacton and Brighton beaches.

Mods were a youth culture obsessed with fashion and music. They wore suits and smart clothes and rode on Italian, Vespa and Lambretta scooters. Mod music in the mid-60s was primarily: rhythm and blues, Motown, Soul, and Bluebeat (ska). The main attribute of any self-respecting mod was well-groomed hair and a clean, smart appearance, often wearing Hush-Puppy shoes.

Rockers were the nemesis of Mods. The centre of their culture was the motorbike. They often wore protective black leather jackets, jeans or leather trousers, and motorcycle boots. Although many had bikes of 1000cc and rode at 100 mph, they seldom wore helmets. They styled themselves on Marlon Brando's movie character in The Wild One. They generally had greasy teddy boy haircuts and their music was Rock and Roll by Elvis, Eddie Cochran, Gene Vincent, Marty Wild and Billy Fury.

Rockers looked on Mods as a load of effeminate poofs. Mods considered Rockers unwashed yobs and called them greasers. Both groups, at times, acted like hooligans.

Now, with a tendency for a mop of uncut hair, an attachment to Billy Fury and Eddie Cochran, and an intention to buy a motorbike when I left school, I supported the Rockers, for a while!

However, music wasn't the only thing that defined 1964.

A black heavyweight boxer came onto the scene. Known as the Louisville Lip after the city he came from in Kentucky, he was young, mouthy and arrogant. He continually belittled other fighters and bragged about how great he was. You wanted to see him floored in the ring just to shut him up. But when he beat Sonny Liston in six rounds, in Miami Beach, Florida, on 25 February 1964, everything changed. At 22, Cassius Clay became the youngest boxer to take the title from a reigning heavyweight champion.

In his own words, "The Greatest and the Prettiest", on 6 March, Clay became a Muslim and changed his name to Muhammad Ali. Love him or hate him, Muhammad Ali became one of the most eminent sports, political and cultural personalities of the 20th century, and I learned to love him.

Following the Great Train Robbery during our holiday in Ireland the previous year, on 6 April 1964, twelve of the men involved in stealing the £2,600,000 used banknotes from the Glasgow to London express were sentenced by the Assize Court in Buckingham. The sentences totalled 307 years, with seven men getting 30 years each. Two of the robbers escaped after being imprisoned. Charlie Wilson was recaptured in 1968. After a 28-year cat and mouse game with UK authorities, the other escapee, Ronnie Biggs, voluntarily returned to the UK. He was arrested and continued to serve his sentence. Four of the robbers were never caught.

1964 saw us closer to President Kennedy's dream. On 28 July, the spacecraft Ranger 7 was launched. Three days later, it reached the moon. Before its planned impact into the moon's surface, Ranger 7 was able to take 4,316 high-definition pictures, 1000 times better than anything that could be viewed from earth at that time. However, with their Luna 3 craft, the Russians had already photographed the far side of the moon as early as 1959. This was one of the reasons Kennedy lit a rocket under the US space program.

FILMS

In 1964 I saw three great films on St Peter's Street, Bedford in the Granada cinema. They were all A-rated, so we didn't have to be accompanied by an adult.

Zulu and 633 Squadron were exciting stuff for any age group but particularly for 15-year-old boys. After those two films, we fought and flew our way back to St John's station to get the train home to Brogborough.

The other film was Goldfinger. It was the first Bond film I ever saw. The film had a naked, gold-painted Shirley Eaton and Honor Blackman as Pussy Galore. Blackman wore catsuits and open front blouses that produced an open-mouthed, silent excitement in pubescent boys. The conversation after that film was more about tits and bums than the heroics of James Bond.

I really liked going to the Granada, It had a cinema smell all of its own, and it was plush. It had a grand staircase that went up to the circle seats.

In front of the curtains that covered the screen was a stage for live acts. In 1963 The Beatles performed there on their nationwide tour, but I never saw that. However, while I was at school, I did go to a pop extravaganza there. It included Billy Fury, Marty Wild, Joe Brown, the Shadows, Cliff Richards, and I think Roy Orbison.

Below the stage was a pit that held a Wurlitzer organ. The organ and organist would rise up and provide a musical distraction before the films started and during the intermission. A lady with a torch and a tray came around selling ice creams and Kia-Ora orange juice during the intermission.

Cinemas in those days were filled with cigarette smoke because then cigarettes were 'healthy'. All the adverts before the picture started told you so. It amazed me how a flickering cone of light from the projection room could penetrate the cloud to produce an image on a screen. It's a wonder we weren't encouraged by ads to drink cool, pink methylated spirits on the rocks as the latest in-drink.

The Granada had an elegant restaurant on the second floor overlooking a little park area across St Peter's Street. The restaurant was too expensive for us kids. However, close to the ground floor entrance, there was a Wimpy Bar where you could get hamburgers and chips to eat there or take away. There were four other cinemas in Bedford then:

The Empire was at 27 Midland Road. It was close to the bus station, so you didn't have to walk far to get a bus home at the weekend. The buses only ran to Brogborough on Saturday and Sunday.
The Plaza Cinema, which could seat 1000, was the closest in style and size to the Granada and was in a lovely position on the embankment of the Ouse.
The Picturedrome was on the river's south bank on the east side of Bedford bridge. It was the oldest cinema in Bedford, and it was showing its age. It was prone to flooding when the river was high. Locally it was known as the Flea Pit. I only remember seeing two films in the Picturedrome, Old Yeller and Davy Crockett - King of the Wild Frontier. They were both by Disney. After seeing Davy Crockett, I saved my pocket money and bought the plastic Tennessee long rifle from Brightmans in St Johns. I carried that rifle around and lived in my coonskin hat and Davy Crockett suit that my uncle Tommy and auntie Kay bought me until I grew out of it. The Picturedrome was demolished in 1964 to make way for the Moat House Hotel.
However, with seating for 1700, the Granada was the biggest and best cinema in Bedford.

Uncle Billy

An event that significantly disrupted the tranquillity of the Butler household in 1964 was the arrival of the old sea-dog, mum's brother, uncle Billy.

All my mum's brothers were seamen.
Uncle John worked deep sea on tankers. If I remember correctly, he was a helmsman with Shell Oil. His home was in Drogheda, just north of Dublin. He worked long periods at sea, and I never met him until I'd left school when he and my auntie Vera came for a holiday with us in Brogborough. Dad had to raise the glass lampshade in the living room because Uncle John was tall and kept banging his head on it.
Uncle Ben was also a big man. He was a fisherman working out of Rosslare, so I knew him well. Uncle Ben had also worked long trips deep sea. One time the girl next door took a shine to Uncle Ben. They walked out for a while, but nothing came of it. She wanted Ben to give up the drink and settle down. Uncle Ben was too much of a free spirit for that. They never fell out over it, but Uncle Ben remained a bachelor.
Until 1964, I'd never met Billy, mum's other brother. Billy worked as a 'fireman', a stoker on a coal-burning coaster. These were small shallow draft ships trading around the British Isles and the European coastline. Doing four-hour watches below decks and shovelling coal into a steam boiler in temperatures of 50ºC was a hot, hard, and dirty job. The work had a detrimental effect on a stoker's health, mental and physical. Billy was no exception. With a preference for spending shore time in the nearest bar, smoking Capstan Full Strength cigarettes, and not eating correctly, he eventually succumbed to Tuberculosis.
The Seamen's Hospital Society (now the Seafarers Hospital Society) was a maritime charity, especially for people like Billy.

They took care of him, and his health improved, but there was no way he could go back to sea.

My mother decided to take him in. She found him a job at the brickworks in the smudge dump. This was a place where fine granulated coal was stored for use in firing bricks. There were no boilers involved, unlike stoking, and it was outside work, but with 25 factory chimneys spewing smoke all day long, you wouldn't say it was working in the fresh air. There was no sea breeze, but the sulphurous smell from the chimneys and the aroma of coal dust meant Billy wouldn't suffer a cultural shock.

One day a taxi arrived at 32 Highfield Crescent. Out stepped a small man about five foot eight inches tall. He was dressed in a clean white shirt, a new dark suit. His hair was neatly oiled and combed, and his black shoes were polished. He'd obviously tried, or had been helped, to make himself look presentable. He was so thin his clothes hung limp on his bones as if they'd been purchased with the expectation, he'd grow into them. Having the same long nose, you could see the family resemblance to my mother.

My mum introduced Ellen and me to our uncle Bill, and once more, I was sharing my bedroom with a stranger.

Once Billy settled in, he quickly reverted to his old ways. He seldom drank during the working week, but he spent most of his weekends at Brogborough CIU Club. Generally, he only drank beer, mostly pint bottles of Whitbread Forest Brown Ale or draught Guinness. He rarely drank spirits in the Club, but if someone put one in front of him, he wouldn't refuse it. If mum had spirits in the house, she'd keep them out of Billy's reach.

I liked my uncle Billy. He was a character, harmless in as much as he didn't go around starting trouble, although he could be irritating at times. Unlike Georgie and Herbie, who had slept like the dead with the sheet over their heads, when Billy was drunk, which was every weekend, he had the annoying habit of conversing with himself and old shipmates in the night when I was trying to sleep. He was like the old sea-dog, Billy Bones, in Treasure Island. My uncle Billy wasn't menacing like that character, but he was loud. Unlike Dr Livesey, the local magistrate in the story, I couldn't shut Billy up with the threat "you shall hang at the next assizes", so I had to endure his rants until he fell asleep. However, that wasn't always the end of it. Often, he'd reignite a conversation with a shout to some unknown person in the night.

The favourite song of the ruffians in Treasure Island was "Fifteen men on the dead man's chest — Yo-ho-ho, and a bottle of rum!"

Uncle Billy had his own nocturnal serenade. It started, "The life of a fireman is anything but grand. He goes down in the stokehole with a shovel in his hand".

My mum would have to intervene some nights, especially when Billy was trying to negotiate the steep stair to the bedroom. Billy always called my mum 'ma' because she helped bring him up after their mother, Constance, died young. The conversations usually went something like this.

Mum: "Billy, do you know what time it is?"

Billy: "No, ma. What time is it?"

Mum: "It's past eleven o'clock".

There'd be a delay while Billy processed the information, followed by.

Billy: "And can ya tell me ma. Is that day, or is that night?"

Or if he was feeling smart.

Mum: "Billy, what are you doing down there?"

Billy: "I'm trying to get a crate of Guinness up the stairs, ma".

Mum: "For goodness' sake, leave it down there and get to bed".

Billy: "I can't, ma. I've already drunk it".

One Sunday morning, I woke after an unusually quiet night and saw that Billy's bed was empty. When I got downstairs, there was no sign of him. I thought he may have passed out or even died on his way home drunk from the Club, but we would have already heard about it if that had happened.

We only had one bathroom and toilet, which was downstairs. When I looked in there, I found Billy asleep in the bath. He'd gone for a pee, and while he was trying to zip himself up, he fell backwards into the tub. He was so drunk that he couldn't get out. After a struggle, he gave up and fell asleep where he was. Fortunately, the bath had been empty. It would have been ironic if the old salt had drowned in a bath instead of at sea.

Billy had an unfortunate knee reflex. One Saturday in the Club, he was drinking with a group at a table. Someone returning from the loo fell into the seat next to Billy. To steady himself, he grabbed Billy's leg. Billy's knee jerked up hard under the table. A heated discussion followed about who was going to pay for five pints of beer and the broken glasses.

Like most old sea dogs, Billy had a lot of yarns.

An ex British Army colonel lived in Rosslare years ago. One day there was a booze-up in the hotel on the clifftop. The colonel started bragging about what a good shot he was with his .22 rifle. He said he could shoot a miniature bottle of Powers Irish whiskey off a man's head at 10 yards. This claim caused a dispute, bets were taken, and the colonel went off to get his rifle. When he returned, the crowd left the hotel bar and found a suitable wall. The colonel had a lot to drink, so there wasn't a rush to stand against the wall, so Billy volunteered. He stood against the wall with a miniature whiskey bottle balanced on his head.

The colonel passed off the ten yards and turned to face the target, pulled back the bolt, loaded a .22 cartridge into the rifle and squinted down the barrel. There was a CRACK and the bottle shattered over Billy's head. The colonel collected the money. With the drinks on him, everyone returned to the bar. It made me wonder what Bill thought he would do with his winnings if the colonel had missed the bottle with a low shot.

Another time there was a wake in Rosslare. After a drinking session, with the prospect of a few bottles of Guinness, Billy visited the deceased's house to show his respects. The wife was seated behind her dead husband, laid out on a trestle table. Having been given a bottle, Billy went to toast the departed. Unfortunately, after expressing his condolences, he tripped over one of the trestles. The table collapsed, depositing the late departed into his wife's lap.

Again in Rosslare. Billy was offered 2/6p to shave a corpse to make it presentable at the wake. He'd not shaved a corpse before, but it seemed simple enough, so he took the job.

The deceased was laid out on a table in the corner of a room. The near side of the face was easy enough to shave. However, with the table against the wall, the far side of the face was difficult to get to. Leaning over, Billy put his hand on the body's chest. As his hand pressed down, the corpse's head raised up, and it groaned as the air was expelled from its lungs.
Billy dropped the shaving equipment and ran out of the house shouting. "He's still bloody alive".

Then there were the old sea stories.
One time, Billy's ship was tied up in Bremerhaven. When Billy stepped off the boat to go ashore for a drink, it was at the same level as the dock. After a few hours and too many German dunkel beers, Billy made his way back to port. Not realising it had dropped a few metres with the tide, he stepped back onto the ship and fell like a stone onto the steel deck below. He could have easily been killed. Drunk's luck, he walked away without serious damage.

Billy was once in a pub, I think it was in Cardiff, Wales. The landlady took particular pride in the bar counter, which she kept polished like glass. Her other obsession was an old ginger tom that had free run of the place. Billy was in the pub for a quiet drink when the old cat wandered down the counter. Purring happily, the old tom brushed itself against Billy, then proceeded to piss over the hand which was holding his pint. That habit was probably the reason the bar was always being polished.

The cat could do no wrong, so there was no point complaining to the landlady. Billy took a drag on his Capstan Full Strength and gently touched the cigarette's tip to the cat's testicles bulging out under its raised tail. There was a terrible screech as the animal tried to escape, but the counter-top was so polished its claws couldn't get a grip. The cat ran on the spot until its nails dug in. It shot off, skidding and sliding until it fell off the bar and disappeared.

The commotion brought the landlady rushing up from the cellar, but the cat was nowhere to be seen. Other than some scratches on the counter, there was no evidence of the crime. Billy denied seeing anything and drank up and left, leaving the woman to find the unfortunate creature.

Then there was Belfast. The ship used to visit that port often. One of the crew, a local Belfast man, knew a place not far from the docks, a private house, where you could buy cheap booze and maybe a drink after hours. On one trip, after the pubs had shut, some of the lads from the ship visited this house. After a few drinks, one of the men, a new crew member who'd never visited Belfast before, asked where the toilet was. His shipmates eagerly directed him to the back door to the outside WC. However, they didn't tell him that the house owner kept a full-grown pet lion in the backyard. A few moments after he left, they went to the back door to see the result of the joke. They were in time to see the old toothless lion stand on its hind legs and put its paws on the man's shoulder just before he fainted.

I thought this may have been a tall story. However, later I found out there was a man in Belfast named Alexander Robinson. Known as "Buck Alec", he was a boxer, street fighter, loyalist paramilitary, and an Ulster Special Constabulary reservist. He was also famous for owning, at one time, as many as three pet lions.

Apart from his stories, Billy had a few prize sayings. If you asked if he wanted a drink, even if he'd already had too much, his response was "You only pass this way once" or "You're a long time dead", which you took for a 'yes'.

If you asked him about someone's behaviour or character, he'd answer with a wink and "A shut mouth catches no flies".

My mum wasn't overly religious, but her faith was strong, and she was a good Catholic. If you were family and lived under her roof, you were obliged to go to Mass on Sundays, at least until you were old enough to make up your own mind. The 'until you were old enough' rule didn't apply to my dad or uncle Billy, especially Uncle Billy. For them, age wasn't a consideration when it came to devotion; they had to go to Mass.

There were enough, mainly Irish, Catholics on Brogborough estate to hire a minibus to take them to St Mary's church in Woburn Sands on Sundays. We'd get up early, get dressed and ready for inspection by mum and then take the minibus for the 10 o'clock service.

An incident occurred at church one Sunday morning after Billy had a particularly heavy night on the booze. My mum was very easy-going, but she could be extremely stubborn when it came to church. She was determined Billy was going to church to atone for his sins. This morning, he wasn't just hungover, he was still drunk. Like it or not, he was going for absolution. It turned into a battle of wills, but Billy was no match for my mum when she was on a mission. This confrontation held up the departure of the minibus.

Father Golston was a very popular priest; his church services were always well attended. The church was packed with only a few seats free in the back rows when we arrived late. We shuffled in quietly and filled up the back pews. When mum came in, leading Billy by the collar, there was only one place left for her to sit with the family. However, there was a straight-backed chair behind the pews, so she dragged Billy to it and tried to sit him upright. Billy kept swaying in the seat, so mum pulled it and Billy a few feet to the large font of holy water by the door. She left Billy asleep propped up against the stone pedestal with his head resting on one arm on the font.

All was well for a while, and the service proceeded undisturbed. Then Billy started a conversation between himself and some unseen shipmates. We lowered our heads and cringed with embarrassment. Heads turned to the back of the church, but the congregation was too polite to act. Father Golston continued undeterred with the service. This situation continued with lulls and occasional outbursts from the back of the church until it was time for the sermon.

The church fell quiet as the priest mounted the pulpit. Father Golston began to deliver his holy words of wisdom over the PA system. This triggered a verbal response from the back of the church. Still drunk and asleep, Billy struck up a conversation with imaginary friends in the pub. Now, Farther Golston was a very Christian and tolerant man. He understood we were all sinners and all redeemable in the eyes of Jesus. There was no way he would have Billy evicted from his church. However, determined to get his sermon across, he raised his voice. Unfortunately, he couldn't help himself and made a comment on the misuse of alcohol. At the sudden emphasis of the word DRINK, Billy sat up straight and exclaimed in a loud voice.

"IT'S MY ROUND, JIM?". Jim being my dad, with whom he'd spent the previous night drinking.

Following that, Billy settled down against the font and fell back to sleep.

As with most priests, it was Father Golston's habit to go to the back of the church to say a few words to his congregation as they left. My mum dispatched me to get Billy out of the church before that happened.

The final straw came for mum on another Sunday morning. She came downstairs to find Billy sleeping on the floor with an empty bottle of gin he found in the sideboard. He might have gotten away with drinking her gin, but when she saw the ash remains of a Capstan Full Strength that Billy had lit up, dropped and left to burn out on the carpet, it was just too much for her. She went ballistic. It wasn't the fact that he'd burned the carpet. It was what might have happened if the carpet had caught fire with her children asleep in bed. And that's how Billy got evicted from 32 Highfield Crescent.

Billy was moved out to the workers' hostel on the Lidlington-Marston road. In typical Billy fashion, unapologetic and equally unresentful, he recited one of his famous sayings on his day of departure. "Well Ma. As one door closes, another door opens".

Over the next few years, I often bumped into Billy in the Marston CIU Club, where I'd go to chase girls and consume pints of real beer shandy that they allowed youngsters to drink there.

Then one day, we received the news that Billy was discovered dead in his room in the hostel. He was found kneeling on the floor with his head on the bed. I doubt very much that he was praying.

Chapter 9

College years 1964 to 66

1964

Farm to Fairground

In the summer of 1964, before I left Fulbrook school, I stopped working weekends at the milk farm. That job had been hard work, the hours were terrible, and the pay was poor. Getting up early on dark winter mornings and bottling up in freezing conditions was horrible. The summers weren't much better because I continually smelled of sour milk as the weather warmed up. Nevertheless, the job had its moments. Rodney had a shotgun, and we often went hunting for rabbits in the fields around the farm. Sometimes, I'd take four fat rabbits' home. My dad would skin and clean them, something I still don't have the stomach to do. We'd have roast rabbit or rabbit stew. During the week, I'd often hang out with Rodney at his house. He was an only child. Apart from his bedroom at the back of the house, the smaller bedroom at the front was his personal den, where he kept a record player and a large collection of LPs (Long Playing records.). We'd spend our time listening to Elvis, Buddy Holly, Eddie Cochran, Billy Fury, and other famous rock stars. Rodney had Goon Show LPs with Spike Milligan, Harry Secombe, Peter Sellers and Michael Bentine. We thought the Goons were hilarious, their insane humour may have waned over the years, but it certainly influenced the Monty Python crowd and even the Beatles, especially John Lennon.

Rodney also had an extensive collection of what passed as porn magazines in those days. Parade, Escort and Men Only before Paul Raymond took it over. He also had some mags like American Modern Man and Playboy. They were all very mild by modern standards, just tits and bums, not a sniff of a vagina or pubic hair. But there were the occasional educational articles where you could practice reading instead of looking at the pictures. These articles included such obscure subjects as premature ejaculation, the G spot, venereal disease and the strange phenomenon of a woman's rudimentary penis. One article may have used the word clitoris, but it must have slipped my memory. I didn't realise the importance of that information until much later in my development.

And so, still friends with Rodney, I gave up the unsociable hours working at the milk farm and got a job at Woburn Abbey on Mr Beardow's fairground with Erika, Mary, Vicky and some of the other kids from Brogborough.

During school time in the spring and summer months, we worked weekends only, and during the summer months, when the school closed, we worked every day if we wanted.

We would ride our bikes from Brogborough to the Abbey.

On the other side of the road at the White Horse pub in Husborne Crawley was the Great Wall of Woburn. This was a red brick wall fourteen feet high and four bricks thick at its base that ran for nine miles encircling Woburn Abbey's parkland. We'd ride up Turnpike

Road from the White Horse to a great iron gated entrance to Abbey grounds. Once past the gatehouse and across the cattle grid that stopped the free-roaming deer escaping from the park, we'd ride through beautiful, wooded lanes to the Abbey.

This was before the Duke of Bedford, who owned the Abbey estate, opened the Woburn Safari Park, so we rode through the woods without the fear of being confronted by an escaped African Lion or Bengal Tiger.

The journey of about four and a half miles took a little over half an hour. We rode along, chatting carefree in the summer sunshine. It was a pleasant time.

The first job I was given by Mr Beardow was looking after the model railway. This was a large miniature landscaped model with multiple electric train lines, including stations, bridges and tunnels. It was impressive and situated in its own shed. My job was to open up and get all the trains running at speeds that didn't cause them to career off the tracks and then collect the money from visitors. Sometimes during slack periods, I'd experiment with the rheostat speed control to see how fast I could make the trains take the bends. This often resulted in some horrific disasters, which invariably occurred just before a sudden rush of clients. Then, I had to multitask as a ticket collector and a railroad repairman. It didn't take me long to settle for the quiet life and leave the speed control alone despite being pressed at times by more demanding clients looking for an adrenaline rush.

Just as I thought I would die of boredom in the model railway shed, I was moved to the carousel, another piece of equipment with speed control. The carousel's regulator comprised a massive mercury arc valve rectifier driving a powerful DC motor. Speed was controlled using a big crank handled switch that rotated over a semicircle of brass contact studs.

Looking after the model railway was probably a test. A sort of personality assessment to see if I had psychopathic tendencies before entrusting me with the care of human clients on the carousel. I'd done my experimentation in the simulator, learned the lesson about the use of excessive speed and resisted the temptation of creating further havoc.

There was no way I was going to wind up the speed of the carousel for the manic pleasure of hearing the screams of clients as they and their children were flung off by centrifugal force. I would never push the speed lever into the red zone to see how fast it could rotate. Well, not while I had clients on the machine.

The disc floor of the carousel was five or six metres in diameter. About two and a half metres above the floor was a circular, gaudily painted canopy supported from the circumference of the base by twirled gold-painted rods. The carousel's centre had a vertical core that contained the drive mechanism and motor. The bottom of the round-about contained two rows of mainly horses but a few other animals like an ostrich or zebra.

A twirled post went up from the floor through each animal to the canopy. In front of the animal's saddle, this post acted as a handhold for the rider. A mechanism caused the animals to move up and down as if they were galloping when the carousel was in motion. At the same time, the machine played fairground music on an organ operated by perforated cards stapled together to form a continual loop.

Before starting the carousel, my first job in the morning was to fire up the mercury arc rectifier that controlled it. This was long before the invention of solid-state semiconductor rectifiers that could handle the high current required to drive the DC motor. The mercury arc rectifier, contained in its own cupboard separated from the round-about, was like something from Frankenstein's laboratory. Opening the cupboard door revealed what appeared to be an enormous thick glass-walled light bulb about four feet high. Instead of hanging from the ceiling, the bulb was plugged into the cupboard's floor. Four glass tubes connected to thick electric cables projected out of the bulb horizontally close to its base. At the bottom of the bulb was a shimmering pool of silver liquid mercury.

First thing in the morning, the device was deceptively innocuous, but it was a sleeping dragon. Once switched on, there was a "bzzzzzz" as a fiery arc flashed into the silver pool. The glass jar filled with mercury gas and began to glow an eerie luminous blue as the beast came to life, ready to power the machine.

Working outside on the carousel was a great job. I suppose there were rainy days, but I can only remember working in sunshine. It didn't take long before I became adept at hopping on and off the machine. Yes, I became that cocky bastard chatting up the pretty girls while collecting the money.

Mr Beardow periodically came to collect the takings. Sometimes he'd take over to give me a break. During those breaks, I'd go to the

Abbey's cafeteria and sit with a large creamy coffee or a dimpled bottle of lemon Hubbly-Bubbly and a sugary Berliner jam doughnut. I felt like Micky Dolenz in the TV series Circus Boy watching the ordinary people enjoying their day out.
And thanks to the transistor radio, there was music and song everywhere you went.

"You're My World"	Cilla Black
"Here I Go Again"	The Hollies
"My Guy"	Mary Wells
"Shout"	Lulu and The Luvvers
"The House of the Rising Sun"	The Animals
"Nobody I Know"	Peter and Gordon
"It's All Over Now"	The Rolling Stones
"A Hard Day's Night"	The Beatles
"I Just Don't Know What to Do with Myself"	Dusty Springfield
"Do Wah Diddy Diddy"	Manfred Mann
"Tobacco Road"	The Nashville Teens
"I Get Around"	The Beach Boys
"It's Only Make Believe"	Billy Fury
"Have I the Right?"	The Honeycombs
"From a Window"	Billy J. Kramer and the Dakotas

Just to name a few.

That idyllic summer of 1964 on the fairground drifted into September, and it was time to continue my education.

A bus came to the shops in the morning to pick up the Brogborough kids for Kingsbury Grammar school. I was registered to take the same bus to Dunstable College. Some of my friends from Fulbrook would already be on the bus that came through Woburn Sands. My sister Ellen had left Kingsbury by then and got a job as a secretary at Plysu Plastics in Woburn Sands. My friend Ray Papworth had enough of grammar school and, being adventurous, had joined the British Army. Several other kids from the estate who'd passed the 11 plus took the Kingsbury bus. One was my friend Norman Stewart whose dad was the Orangeman from Northern Ireland. Norman was a funny guy and brightened every morning. After Brogborough, the bus picked up in Woburn and Leighton Buzzard. It dropped us college kids off at the Quadrant in Dunstable before going to Kingsbury. With stops for pickups, the journey time was about 50 minutes.

Every morning we passed Dunstable School, a boarding school where the Hollywood actor Garry Cooper, star of the 1952 film High Noon with Grace Kelly, was educated. We also passed the Carousel Cafe, which became a popular hangout with a jukebox frequented by teenage girls.

It's funny how a song can put you back in time. Whenever I hear Rag Doll by the Four Seasons, it reminds me of the Carousel because that song was playing on the bus radio the first time, we passed the cafe. Just for the record, the B side of Rag Doll was Silence is Golden, which, three years later, went to Number 1 in the UK charts for The Tremeloes.

Going home was a drag because the Kingsbury bus left before we finished college. We had to take the public bus from Dunstable through Leighton Buzzard to Heath and Reach and wait for a bus to Woburn Sands. At Woburn Sands, I could wait for a train to Ridgmont station and walk home through the brickyard. However, it was quicker to carry on to Husborne Crawley and walk the 2km home if the weather was good. Either way, it was a drudge. Sometimes, to break the boredom, as the bus slowed on the A5 to take the Stanbridge turn to Leighton Buzzard, we'd do a pole dance on the open rear platform of the double-decker. We'd swing out over the grass verge and then back onto the platform, which really upset the conductor and driver. Sometimes, Buzz and I would jump off the moving bus at the Stanbridge turn and walk to the Hockliffe junction. From there, we'd thumb it home. This was a risky strategy because it was a 7.5 mile, two and a half-hour walk to Woburn Sands, where Buzz lived, or a 9 mile, two- and three-quarter hour walk for me to Brogborough. Mind you, there were worse things than strolling on a sunny evening along an English country road talking shit with a mate. We were irresponsible and carefree, and I don't remember ever having to walk very far before someone was kind enough to stop and give us a lift.

If I were lucky, we'd get a lift with someone going to Bedford, and then I'd be home in 15 minutes. They'd drop Buzz off in Woburn, where he'd thumb it to Woburn Sands. Then they'd drop me off at

Brogborough before going on to Bedford. There were far fewer cars in those days, but people were much more sympathetic.
Aston Martin had their factory in Newport Pagnell then. They used to test the cars on the public road when they came off the production line. On one occasion, we were picked up by a white-coated test driver in a brand new silver-grey DB5. After a high-speed run along Mill Road, Husborne Crawley, I got dropped off at the crossroads near M1 junction 13, less than a 10-minute walk to home. The driver then dropped Buzz off in Woburn Sands on his way back to Newport Pagnell. A driver would probably get fired for doing that now.

Going to Dunstable should have been a transition from school to adulthood. College was like school but with fewer boundaries. You were supposed to be self-disciplined and work studiously because you wanted to, not because you were forced to. Unfortunately, we were only 15 years old and still acted like school kids. I should have known better. My mum had to get a job so I could continue my education. I feel ashamed now that I didn't take it more seriously. I wasn't the only one, but that's no excuse. That's adolescent boys for you, too much freedom too soon.
Most of the lecturers were experienced and kept us under control with their sheer personalities. However, there were a couple that must have dreaded entering the classroom.
The Irish geography teacher, Mr Monaghan, would get so wound up he'd call on the almighty for assistance.
"FURR GAD'S SAKES. WILL YAS AL SETTLE DOWN AND SHOT UP".

You couldn't have blamed him if he'd said, "For fuck sake, shut up", but he never did.

The one that got the worst deal was the physics teacher who replaced Mr Harper halfway through the first year. It would be unfair to name him, so I'll just call him Mr S. He couldn't control the class, which gave him a tough time. His classes were absolute bedlam. He must have been a Buddhist who "Ummmed" himself into a higher plane of enlightenment before the lesson. He was the only teacher I'd known who could carry on writing on the blackboard with a paper dart stuck in the back of his head and others bouncing around him. That sort of group idiocy would come back on me later.

Laughing gas.

At the end of one physics class, Buzz and I filled a large polythene bag full of gas from a Bunsen burner tap on the lab bench and ran out of the classroom with Mr S in hot pursuit, shouting.
"COME BACK WITH THAT GAS".
We stopped at the end of the corridor and turned to face him. I held the bag between my legs. Buzz flicked his cigarette lighter and held it down by my knees. I closed my legs on the plastic sack while releasing the neck of the bag. Buzz jumped sideways as a napalm-like flame rolled down the length of the corridor, driving Mr S back into the classroom. Oblivious of the consequences of the

bag splitting between my legs, we escaped down the stairs in hysterics. Yes, we were that stupid.

One time, Tom Maybe, our compatriot from Fulbrook school, was lucky not to have been expelled from college.

He was asked why he put his hand up Ilene McGuire's skirt while she was sitting in the headphone booth next to him during a language lesson. He told the French teacher he was so overcome by the passion of the language that he couldn't help himself. Fortunately, Ilene, a beautiful girl, understood Tom's dilemma and didn't press charges.

The stupidest thing we got up to was instigated by a student in our year called Malcolm Robinson. I think Robbo was from Leighton Buzzard. Malcolm was a lanky guy, nothing out of the ordinary to look at. The visual impression he gave was of being very conventional and straight-laced.

One day, we were all gathered around the coffee machine on the mezzanine floor above the college entrance. To stop people from falling off this floor into the reception area below, there was a safety barrier with a flat teak rail around the top, similar to a ship's rail. There was a drop of about five metres from the rail to the reception floor.

While we were all talking, Malcolm sidled over to the fence. With his back to the fence, he put his open hands on either side of him, pushed himself up, and sat on the rail with the void behind him.

"You want to be careful doing that," someone said.

It looked as though Malcolm was getting off the rail when suddenly his legs came up, and the top part of his body began rotating backwards. His arms shot out from his sides and started flapping in an attempt to regain his balance. At the same time, he uttered a cry of distress. Seeing him falling backwards over the rail, some girls started screaming.

Malcolm's legs were thrashing, and his arms continued flapping. We didn't know what to do because it could precipitate his fall if we all rushed forward. After a few moments of terror, Malcolm's torso came upright, and he dropped back onto the mezzanine floor, laughing. It was all a joke.

After Robbo's fearless demonstration, boys being brainless boys, we all had to have a go. I tried it once, but once was enough.

A quick calculation from a physics lesson showed that a body that fell from five metres would hit the floor at 36km per hour. If it didn't kill you, it would certainly ruin your day.

Robbo taught me that first impressions can be deceptive in more ways than one.

In October, there was going to be a general election. The windows of nearly every house in Brogborough were plastered with posters showing the political affiliation of the household. The posters were predominantly red for the Labour Party, blue for the Conservative Party (the Tories) with the occasional yellow for the Liberals.

In some instances, a house might have a red and blue poster in the window indicating a family political conflict. My dad had already converted young Jimmy, the son of the Northern Ireland 'Orange

Man' Patsy Stewart, from conservatism to socialism five years earlier.

In 1959 my sister Elena and Jimmy's younger brother Norman had both passed their 11 Plus examination. They were due to attend Kingsbury School Dunstable. The two families shared a Sibley's' taxi to Woburn Sands, where we caught the United Counties double-decker bus to Dunstable. Jimmy was already at the school and came along to the September preterm open day for new students.

While the rest of us sat chatting on the top deck of the bus, Jimmy and my dad sat together in serious political debate. To the consternation of his father, this debate converted Jimmy into an ardent socialist. Later, Jimmy joined the Labour party and even stood as a candidate.

I remember walking through Dunstable with Norman, clueless to the heresy I was committing, singing the slogan on one of the enormous political posters to a made-up tune.

"Life is better with Conservative, so don't let Labour ruin it".

On 15 October, the Labour Party won the general election. Winston Churchill, a Member of Parliament for 63 of the last 65 years, retired.

After 13 years of Conservative rule, Britain was ready for a change. There were several reasons for the Tories' defeat. The new Conservative party leader, the aristocratic Sir Alec Douglas-Home, seemed out of touch with the lives of most of the British public. Home was unable to compete in the rough and tumble of political debate with the charismatic Harold Wilson, leader of the Labour Party.

But there was another reason. It's said that "Behind every great man there is a great woman, and behind the fall of a great man there is usually another woman".

In this case, there were two very young women, Christine Keeler and her friend Mandy Rice-Davies.

A few years before the election, John Profumo, the Conservative government's Secretary of State for War, began an extramarital affair with the 19-year-old Keeler. He may have got away with this indiscretion, except at the same time, the young Christine was involved with Captain Yevgeny Ivanov, a Soviet naval attaché. At the height of the 'Cold War' between the Soviet Union and the West, this suggested a possible serious national security risk. It might have been a brief affair, but its repercussions were enough to eventually bring down the Conservatives.

My dad, a lifelong socialist, was ecstatic about the election result. I was more fascinated with how these young women were attracted to old men when I couldn't find a girlfriend. I still had a lot to learn about the world.

By the close of 1964, I was less interested in model aeroplanes and more interested in girls. It wasn't the unrequited love from afar I'd experienced with Lorraine and Dina. This wasn't love at all. It was a more basic instinct. It involved strange movements in my lower regions, especially at night when I could think of nothing else. It was a messy business, and it was probably a mortal sin coming from a Catholic family. I was damned and on my way to hell, but I didn't care. There was no way I was going to ask for absolution from Father Golston when my mum sent me off on Saturdays to the confessional in Woburn Sands. My friend Buzz had already begun a sexual relationship with a girl from school. I guess I was a late developer.

Dances were a good way of meeting girls. The Students' Union hired the Civic Hall in Dunstable for the end of term Christmas dance. They booked a relatively unknown group from London that had a good review in the Melody Maker but wasn't too expensive. Unfortunately, I couldn't go to the dance because there was no reliable way of getting home from Dunstable late at night.

There was no sign of the group when the event started, and the dance had to open with an impromptu disco. The band's van had broken down on the M1, and they didn't arrive until shortly before the hall was due to close. There was no way they were getting paid for the gig. However, to their credit, they set up and played a few songs before the night's end.

The group was called the Who.

There was another hunting ground. Every weekend there was a dance at the CIU Club in Marston, sometimes two if they had one on a Sunday.

If you couldn't get a lift, there was a Saturday evening bus from the shops in Brogborough that stopped outside the club.

You could also catch the train on Saturdays from Ridgmont to Millbrook Station, a ten-minute walk to the club. Going home after the dance wasn't too much of a problem. There was no public transport, but if you couldn't scrounge a lift, it was a little over an hour's walk back to Brogborough.

An advantage with Marston Club was that although we were underage, they served us pints of real beer shandy. You could even get a pint of beer if someone older bought it. Either way, standing with a pint of shandy, indistinguishable from beer, was intended to impress the girls with your maturity. However, even after a few pints of shandy, I was still awkward around girls.

This was the time before Discotheques when there was live music at dances. Marston Club hired some good bands, but I only remember two of those groups now. One was the Fireflies from Rushden. They were the best band I ever heard at Marston. I always made sure to go to the club when the Fireflies performed there. I don't know why they never turned professional. They recorded a farewell disk at Derek Tompkins' Shield Studios in Kettering before breaking up in 1967. And that, unfortunately, was the end of the Fireflies.

The other band was the local Marston group, the Concords. They weren't as good as the Fireflies, but they played some brilliant R&B stuff like 'Long distance information, give me Memphis, Tennessee' (Chuck Berry); 'You Better Move On' (an Arthur Alexander's song covered by the Rolling Stone); and 'Tell Me -You're Coming Back-' (The Rolling Stones).

Inevitably a fight erupted on the dance floor during the evening. These conflicts, usually over a girl or just due to high testosterone levels and too many shandies, were resolved by Mr Ellis. He would pacify the combatants and then take them outside for a fatherly chat and a severe beating.

My dad's younger brother, uncle Tommy, my auntie Kay, and my young cousin James were driving from London to spend Christmas with us on Christmas Eve. We were going to have a full house. Me and my friend Stanley Novak, who was a year younger than me from the top street, were going to the Christmas Eve dance in Marston club. Mrs Novak offered to drive us there and pick us up after the dance. Mrs Novak was a lovely lady, Stanley was her only son, and she doted on him. Every day she'd send him to school with a bar of Cadbury's milk chocolate. He smoked and was never short of cigarettes as a kid, but not Woodbines or anything like that. Stanley smoked Sobranie Black Russian, black cigarettes with gold foil tips. Sometimes he even smoked the more exotic Sobranie Cocktails. They also had the gold tips and came in pairs of five different pastel colours in an elegant ten pack box.

Stanley had an older sister whose name was Carol Cook. I thought Carol was beautiful, and I often wished I were older so I could ask her out without her laughing at me.

There were a lot of complicated relationships in Brogborough, with children having different surnames in the same family. I guess it must have been something to do with the war.

I can't remember much about that dance that night, whether it was the illicit vodka and limes we'd been drinking or the event that followed, I can't say.

When Mrs Novak picked us up, she told me my mum had come to see her and asked if I could stay at her house for the night.

Apparently, my mum had been behind with the washing. She hadn't got enough bed lining for everyone staying over for Christmas. That was not the real reason mum wanted me to stay at Stanley's, but I'd had enough Smirnoff and was happy to sleep at Stanley's.

Christmas morning, we got up late. Mrs Novak cooked us an English breakfast, and I got home to my house at about 11:30.

The house seemed the same as usual, but there was no sign of my sister Ellen, uncle Tommy, auntie Kay or my cousin James, which was strange for a Christmas morning. When I saw my dad's state, the realisation of what had happened dawned on me. His face was puffy and bruised like he'd been in the ring with Sonny Liston. But worse than that was his mouth. The left side of his bottom lip had been sliced open down to his chin. It looked like someone had opened it up with a scalpel. When he spoke, it was grotesque. The lip flapped about, and his words came out distorted, like after having an injection for a filling before the numbness wore off.

When they returned from Brogborough club on Christmas Eve, Tommy accused dad of ignoring him and spending too much time talking to his friend Mr Clifford. The argument turned into a fight. This wasn't unusual. It happened almost every time the two brothers met, especially when they went out drinking. There was always tension when they got together. I have no idea of the history that caused that problem. It always started well but inevitably turned into a fistfight.

This time it was more than a fistfight. Tommy had pushed a broken glass into my dad's face. My dad had managed to get Tommy out of the house. He then took the 18-inch First World War bayonet from my military collection, stood in the doorway and told Tommy if he came back in the house, he'd run him through with the bayonet. He might just have done it too. It must have been terrible for everyone in the house. My sister was so scared by that event that she would never admit to being Irish for the rest of her life.

Tommy, who must have still been drunk, had to drive my auntie Kay and cousin James back to London.

After such a great year, that was our Christmas of 1964. It was the worst Christmas ever. We never saw Tommy for a long time after that.

The incident didn't seem to upset me much. But the brain is a complex thing. Sometimes we bury stuff in it, only for it to rise up again later.

On a brighter note, The Beatles' song 'I Feel Fine', starting with that great guitar feedback, was number one on the Christmas chart.

Something I didn't know then. Arthur C. Clarke had just finished the first draft of "Journey Beyond the Stars", later adapted by Stanley Kubrick and released as the film 2001: A Space Odyssey. A film that was going to have a significant influence on my life.

As we moved into 1965, I was still a virgin.

1965

After the disruption and trauma of Christmas caused by my dad and his brother, the New Year started surprisingly well.

On Saturday night in the first week of January, I was at the Marston Club dance when a pretty girl walked past. She had short brown hair and wore a tight bottle green sweater, tight white jeans and white tennis shoes.

I was still awkward where girls were concerned, but on this occasion. I followed her into the lounge at the side of the dance hall. She sat with a group of girls who didn't seem to be attached to any boys. When they moved to the hall, I followed and summoned the courage to ask the girl to dance. To my surprise, she agreed, and we spent the rest of the evening together.

When the dance ended, I passed up the offer of a lift back to Brogborough and walked the girl home. We stopped by the gate into the grounds of the Church in Marston. That's where I really kissed a girl for the first time. I'd had some experience under the mistletoe at Christmas, and as you do, I'd practised on the back of my hand. But none of that compared to kissing warm lips on a cold winter's night with my arms around a real girl. I walked her to her house and asked if I could see her again. She agreed to meet me on Wednesday evening.

By then it was midnight, and I had a long walk home. I can't explain the feeling, but it was magical strolling home alone on that freezing winter's night under a star-filled sky.

That was the start of my first sexual relationship with a girl. I'm not writing a kiss and tell story here, that wouldn't be very gallant, so I'll refer to my girlfriend as Laura.

There weren't many places a courting couple could go and be alone in Marston. However, St Mary's church was close by. That's not the St Mary's Catholic church miles away in Woburn Sands. This was a Protestant church of the same name in Marston. I don't mean we did our courting inside the church, even in a Protestant church, that would have been sacrilegious. The building had two entrance doors on opposite sides, one facing north and the other south. The entrances were of the same design, a covered stone porch with an open Gothic arch leading to a sturdy wooden door. On either side of the porch, there was a stone bench to sit about three people. These benches proved very convenient for us two young lovers. The north entrance faced the church gate that led to the main road. This was the main entrance where the congregation came in and departed from services. The porch on the south side led to the graveyard, beyond which was countryside and a footpath that led to Jubilee Cottages and Marston CIU Club. The porch on the south side was lit only by moonlight, and the door there was permanently locked. It was pretty bizarre on the nights when the choir was practising. The hymn singers were oblivious of what was happening on the other side of the door.

It was the closest I'd ever been to heaven, and heaven was warm and wet.

You may think this a creepy place to carry on a romance. However, we never had a supernatural visitation by any of the cemetery's occupants. Or, if we did, we were too preoccupied to notice.

As far as my mum was concerned, if she ever found out, I would have by then broken every rule in the book. Without absolution, I was definitely on the road to hell. But, again, these transgressions would not be shared with Father Golston in Saturday confessional. He'd have to do with the more acceptable alternative of "improper thoughts about girls". A sin by any other name. This was close enough to the truth because those thoughts occupied almost all of my time.

This passionate affair lasted about six months. It taught me that as most boys were obsessed with making babies, some girls were equally obsessed with conceiving them. I was terrified we'd have an accident, intended or not, and I'd end up having to take the other entrance into the church.

When the split came, it was a painful time for both of us. More so for her, because she seemed to love me so intensely, it was frightening. I didn't really understand that strength of emotion at the time.

A little over a year later, Laura got pregnant and then married. It relieved my guilt for breaking our relationship, and I was glad it wasn't me taking on the responsibility. I think she got what she wanted. I hope so because it was something I could never have given her at the time, and she deserved better than me.

I can only speak for myself, but first love and the strange intimacy with a female that goes with it is a memory that has stayed with me all my life.

After the intense relationship and emotional parting with Laura, I adopted a casual approach to girls. Don't get me wrong, I was still hormone-driven; I just didn't want to be that committed, at least not for a while. I'd learned a lot from Laura, certainly from a physical perspective. However, girls were still a mystery to me, and they were all so different.
As Racy put it in their song, "Some girls will, some girls won't. Some girls need a lot of loving, and some girls don't".
My problem was trying to figure out which were which. If you were too amorous, you could get dumped because "you only wanted them for one thing". If you weren't amorous enough, you could get dumped because you were "too nice". It was all very confusing. Every encounter was an adventure, and for sure, chasing girls was never dull.

The Machine Stops.

I don't remember much from the academic side of college, but I do recall for English Literature, we had to read a short science fiction story of about 12,000 words called The Machine Stops.
The story is set in the future, where humans no longer live on the surface of the Earth because it's too polluted.

Each person lives in isolation in a standard room with a life support system below ground. All their physical and emotional needs are taken care of by an omnipresent machine. Their connection to the rest of the world is made via a video console. Using the console, they can order what they want, which is brought to their room by a tubular delivery system. Through the console, they can have conferences and talk to anyone worldwide. Their only activity is sharing ideas and what passes for information with others. There is no need for books because the Machine can access and deliver all human knowledge.

Air travel above ground is permitted, but it's unnecessary and rarely used.

The central characters in the book are Vashti and her son Kuno. They live in rooms on opposite sides of the planet but communicate with each other frequently.

There is more to the story, but towards the end, the life-support system needed to visit the surface of the Earth is shut down. Then a new religion called Technopoly arises, and people begin to worship the Machine. People who don't worship the Machine, now a deity, are threatened with Homelessness. The Machine's self-repair mechanism starts to fail, but people are not concerned because they believe it is omnipotent.

Initially, humans accept the failings as they are now wholly subservient to the Machine. The knowledge of how to repair the Machine has been lost, so things continue to decline.

Finally, the Machine fails completely, bringing down civilisation with it. Before they die, Kuno and Vashti realise that humanity's connection to the natural world is what really matters. It then becomes the responsibility of the homeless exiled to the surface to rebuild the human race and prevent the mistakes of technology from being repeated.

The book's theme may seem familiar now, but you have to remember this was 1965. Few people had a telephone. If you wanted to get in touch with someone urgently, you went to the Post Office and sent a telegram hand-delivered by a postman. We didn't have pocket calculators. Our physics and maths problems had to be worked out with pencil and paper or with a mechanical slide rule. This was before the internet and before the almighty Google search engine, Social Media, Amazon and online shopping. It was before the concept of climate change. At the time, the story was pure science fiction.

Sixty-five years later, during the lockdown and travel restrictions caused by the COVID 19 virus pandemic, I decided to revisit the book and called it up on my computer. I was amazed at how accurately it had predicted the future. I'd always assumed that the book had been written in the 1960's when I'd read it. However, I was astonished when I discovered that the author, E. M. Forster first published the book in 1909. One hundred and eleven years earlier. And so, I found myself living in the future. It appears that life is a time machine.

Long days and late nights at the M1 Granada service station

Because of the slog of travelling to and from college every day, I decided to get my own transport. I set my heart on a 250cc Royal Enfield Continental motorbike.

To finance this venture, I got a weekend job at the Granada Service Station near Junction 12, the Toddington turn on the M1 motorway.

The money was good, and because they were always short-staffed, you could do double 16 hour shifts to make extra money. They also had a staff minibus service, so there was no problem getting to and from work. However, 16 hours was a long day, especially if you had to get up the next day for another shift.

The work was mind-numbing. Cutting up tomatoes, cucumbers and eggs and washing and spin-drying lettuce to make salads and sandwiches. The worst job was clearing tables, especially on Saturday nights when coach loads of drunk football fans descended on the cafe for the toilet and something to eat. Depending on whether they'd won or lost, they were either jubilant, rowdy and looking for trouble or belligerent, rowdy and looking for trouble. They treated the staff like shit with their load and malicious insults. On Saturday nights, I learned the lesson of not upsetting restaurant staff, especially if you're ordering food that's coming from behind the swing doors of the kitchen.

After they left, we had the job of clearing the plates and cleaning up the tables, seats and floors after their excesses. I found it amazing how supposedly ordinary people combined with a group identity could be so stupid.

Fortunately, we didn't have to wash the dirty dishes. We just had to scrape them off and load them into the carriers for the industrial dishwashing machine. There was always a machine minder on duty to take care of stoppages and detergent levels and ensure the equipment was working correctly. One of the minders was a West Indian lady from Luton. I don't know if it was her real name, but everyone called her Big Bertha. She was a nice lady, but every so often, she'd call for silence in the clatter and chatter around the dishwasher.

She'd listen intently with one ear pressed against the stainless-steel housing of the machine. With one arm outstretched behind her, she'd flap her hand to quiet any noise from the staff.

The first time I saw this, I thought she was listening for imminent equipment failure.

"What's she doing?" I whispered to one of the old-timers.

"She's listening for a message from the machine."

"What sort of message?" I asked.

"A psychic message." came the reply with great reverence. "The machine communicates with her".

I looked at him, but my smile faded. He was serious.

After a while, Bertha would raise her hand to indicate the message had been received, and the clatter of carriers on the loading shoot would continue.

"What does the machine tell her?" I inquired.

"Oh. Bertha doesn't reveal that information to us," replied the disciple with great solemnity.

The object of the job at the motorway cafe was to get enough money to buy a motorbike. However, during the late weekend shifts, I noticed something, a revelation that changed my mind.

The Rockers, the large groups of macho, leather-clad motorbike boys, usually had just one or two females with them.

In contrast, the Mods on scooters dressed in smart suits, Hush Puppies, Ben Sherman shirts, and fancy haircuts were each accompanied by a well turned out, stylish young lady.

I made a strategic reassessment and decided I'd buy a scooter.

Mr Charles

I needed money for petrol and clothes to develop my new mod persona, so I continued working at the M1 services during weekends, bank holidays and college breaks.

One day a supervisor came up to me while I was clearing tables in the northbound cafe and told me I'd been transferred to the Grill Restaurant in the southbound service area. I was to report to the head chef.

I crossed the footbridge and presented myself.

"And what's your name?" asked the head chef.

"Bernie", I replied.

"No. What is your full name," he asked again.

"Bernard James Butler", I replied.

"OK. You are going to be my new commis, assistant chef. I will call you Bernard, and you, Bernard, you will call me Mr Charles."

Mr Charles was a big, thick-set black man. With a nose flattened on his face like a boxer, I had no problem complying with his instruction.

"I understand, Mr Charles", I replied politely.

The grill was a very different place from the service cafe. The tables had place mats and were set with glistening cutlery, serviettes and condiments.

The waiters wore crisp, clean white shirts and black trousers. I was issued with blue chequered patterned trousers and a white double-breasted jacket with a one folded lapel. I felt pretty smart; it was certainly better than being a table clearer in the cafe.

The kitchen was spotless and well organised. It was hectic when the restaurant was full, but Mr Charles ran a tight ship and always kept things under control.

I enjoyed working in the grill. Mr Charles was at all times the boss, but he was kind and respectful. Because I was a novice, he always took the time to show me something new that he wanted me to do, but he didn't expect to show me twice. He never shouted or used foul language to motivate; just telling you was enough. I did everything he told me to do and followed his instructions to the letter, and we got on fine. For the first time at the Granada services, I enjoyed going to work.

The only time I saw Mr Charles lose his cool was once when a waiter came in with specific instructions from a client on how he should cook a medium steak.

When the waiter left, Mr Charles said calmly.

"Bernard, would you please go to the cold room and bring me a prime steak. Choose it carefully. Plump, cherry red, no gristle, no edge fat but with a slight trace of marbling".

When I returned, Mr Charles inspected the steak carefully and congratulated me.

"That is an excellent choice, Bernard. You will make a good chef one day".

What he did next surprised me.

"The cheek," he said. "Telling me, Mr Charles, how to cook a steak".

He hurled the steak across the kitchen with such force that it stuck to the white tiled wall. He walked over, peeled it off the wall, and flung it back across the kitchen. This time it slid down the wall to the floor.

He picked it up between his thumb and index finger and handed it to me with an outstretched arm.

"Bernard. Please make sure this is well washed, cleaned and dried. Then bring it to me. When you've done that, wash the walls. I apologise for that little outburst".

When Mr Charles had finished, we put the steak on a plate with deep-fried new potatoes and slightly al dente broccoli florets.

"Bernard." he said quietly, "Take this to the window. Call that waiter and tell him to serve it immediately, or he will have me to deal with".

The waiter did what he was told, and I returned to my work.

Twenty minutes later, the waiter came back into the kitchen.

"Well?" enquired Mr Charles.

"The client said to give his compliments to the chef. It was the best steak he ever had".
Mr Charles just nodded and went about his business.
That incident taught me to be extremely careful about how you treat the staff in a restaurant.

My mum's sweet tooth.

During this time, my mum had settled into her job as the tea lady in the brickworks. She loved working there, it got her out of the house, and she met lots of different people to talk to, and she loved to talk.
My mum had a very sweet tooth; in her mid-forties, she already had a full set of false teeth, as did my dad. In those days, false teeth seemed fashionable. A large percentage of the adult population of Brogborough had them. Every so often, one of the populous men and women, who previously had a set of their own teeth and a reasonable smile, suddenly transformed into toothless wonders. This was a sure sign they had made a trip to see Mr Costigan at his dental surgery up Church Road in Woburn Sands. The practice was conveniently near the Royal Oak pub. However, as many patients found out, it was not recommended to have a pint before surgery to calm the nerves where gas extraction was concerned. It was a strange phenomenon. Rather than having teeth drilled and filled with the help of a cocaine injection, they would have the gas and have all their teeth, the good, the bad and the ugly, removed in one go. I had a back tooth extracted when the travelling dental van

came to the school one time. Feeling sick after gas to find a gaping bleeding hole in your gum was not a pleasant experience. To wake up with no teeth at all must have been horrific.

Following surgery, the patient, often a young or middle-aged person, would take on the appearance of an old pensioner, their lips forming a concave depression into a toothless mouth. They'd stay like that for a month or so until their gums healed and shrunk. Once this stage was reached, they returned to Mr Costigan to give the dental technician an impression of their gums to manufacture a new set of teeth. When the new dentures were fitted, the person was transformed with a film star smile from a mouth full of white crockery on pink plastic gums.

Now, back to my mum's sweet tooth. She was very fond of Cadbury's milk chocolate and always had some to nibble on the tea round. She often complained about an Italian worker who knew she always had chocolate and continually pestered her for it. He would not leave her alone until she gave him some. One Saturday, she was so fed up with this constant badgering that she took the train into Bedford. At Boots the Chemist, she bought a large bar of Ex-Lax laxative chocolate. The following Monday, when the Italian pestered her, she feigned exasperation, saying, "Here, take the lot and leave me alone". She gave him the whole laxative bar.

He didn't turn up for work the next day, and that was the last time he ever tried to bum chocolate off my mum.

Transformation

When my mum found out I'd changed my mind about getting a motorbike, she offered to pay half if I went ahead and bought a scooter. She thought that scooters were a safer form of transport, and I said nothing to change her opinion.

As soon as I had enough money, I went to Graymac Motors in Luton and, for one hundred and forty-five pounds, I bought a Vespa 150 Sportique. The machine was second hand but in excellent condition. It was silver-grey with chromed front mudguard, side panels and spare tyre rack that doubled as a passenger backrest. They took my money, stuck L plates on the machine, gave me a handbook, showed me the accelerator, clutch and brake. Then they pushed the scooter out of the showroom onto the road and left me to it. It was a miracle how, without any previous experience, I got out of Luton onto the country roads without causing a serious traffic accident. Nevertheless, I got myself and my scooter home in one piece.

To the consternation of my motorbike enthusiast mates, I got a new haircut and shamelessly converted from a Rocker to a Mod.

As a Mod, I had to get some smarter clothes, but now I didn't have much disposable income. My friend Roger Aranela, from Lidlington, had a Lambretta 150 with chrome panels. I liked going to Roger's house. He had a pretty sister called Sue, and you often got a glass of his dad's Strega Italian liqueur or a shot of crème de menthe. One Saturday evening, the two of us drank a whole bottle of crème de menthe and I was as sick as a dog the whole of the next day. The two of us spent time trolling the shelves of Millet's Army Surplus store in the high street in Bedford. There you could buy greatcoats and stylish officers' jackets. From Millet's, I bought my first pair of Levi 501's. Jeans are expensive now, but they were cheap working gear in those days. You had to buy them larger than you wanted, then put them in the bath and shrink them to the correct size. Some people bought the right size and then sat in the bath wearing them so they would shrink to a tight fit around the legs and bottom. These 'drainpipes jeans' were worn by Rockers with winkle picker shoes or motorbike boots. They were definitely not for Mods; we wore baggies.

Before they became hard to get, I managed to buy an original US Army olive green M-51 fishtail parka from Millets. Parkas were popular with mods because they were water-resistant and protected your smart clothes underneath. Sitting on the fishtail stopped the wind blowing up your back when riding a scooter. You could use the hood to protect the ears and keep your hair in place in cold, wet weather, a crucial consideration for a Mod. However, like wearing a crash helmet, riding around town with the hood up was unthinkable. That was so uncool.

The other thing about a parka was its charisma. It had a military appearance and made you look bulkier than you really were. Just for effect, I had a Union Jack the width of the sleeve sewed onto the lower right arm of my parka.

Frayed shirt collars were definitely uncool. Roger and I bought officers collarless shirts with button-on stiff paper collars and cuffs. These had the advantage of prolonging the lifespan of a shirt.

It also allowed you to purchase different shaped collars that made it look like you owned more than one good shirt.
Another economic clothing solution was to buy a cheap light grey or white school blazer and a tube of clothing dye. I dyed a blazer red, and no one knew the difference.
One thing I didn't skimp on because there was no alternative was a pair of light brown suede lace-up Hush Puppies. These were an essential addition to the Mod uniform and especially good for dancing.
And so, without too much expense, with my chromed-up Vespa 150 and reasonable smart clothes, I morphed easily into an acceptable Mod.

The GPO Telephone Box.

We had a red GPO (General Post Office) telephone box in Brogborough. It was just before the garage/stockroom of Peggy Wolsey's shop, the first shop you came to as you walked up from Highfield Crescent. A red GPO post box was next to it, set into the high wall around the shop's garden. To those who today don't understand the concept of the red box in the wall, it's what we used before the coming of email and messaging. There were two methods of functionality. With the first, you wrote a message on a piece of card and popped it in the box. This was a cheap, unsecured transmission that anyone could read. With the second method, you wrote on a piece of paper and put it into a sealed envelope. This was more expensive but a private, secure form of transmission.

That is unless you lived in that nasty Soviet Union where they steamed open and read everyone's mail. Either way, you had to buy a stamp from the Post Office and stick it on the message before posting it in the box.

A man in a black military-style uniform turned up once a day in Brogborough to collect the messages and deliver replies to the relevant houses. It was an asynchronous form of communication with a minimum of four days between sending and receiving.

The phone box and the box in the wall were the only methods most of the estate's inhabitants had to communicate with the outside world.

If you met a girl at a dance somewhere, you might give her the telephone number of the box and arrange a time for her to call you. If she phoned at the appointed time, it was a sure sign she was interested. It did have its drawbacks, though. You could never be sure the box would be unoccupied when you arrived to receive the call. If the other caller stayed in the box too long, your girl might get fed up with the engaged tone at her end and just give up calling. Of course, the lines of communication could be reversed. A girl might have asked you to phone her in a box to test your interest. Either way, an occupied box could spell the end of a budding romance.

It wasn't so common in Brogborough, but sometimes a queue would form outside a box. Then things could get heated with people banging on the window because they thought the current occupant of the box was taking too long and hogging the phone.

Before you made a call, you needed to have the right coins, and enough of them for however long the call might last. By design, there was a little shelf to stack the piles of coins you might need. There were no credit cards then. It was not unusual to see a caller grab a passer-by and frantically try to obtain change to make a call or continue a call that had taken longer than expected.

If you had your coins to hand, you'd push them into the slot, dial the number and press button A when you made the connection. Shortly before the money ran out, there'd be a beeping sound warning that you needed to put in more to continue the call or be cut off. If the conversation wasn't going your way, this was a good time to pull the 'I've run out of change' ploy.

Supposing you didn't make a connection or finished a call earlier than expected. In that case, you could press button B to retrieve any unused coins.

It was common for kids when passing a phone box to pop in and press button B on the off chance that the previous occupant had forgotten to do so. This was a good way of supplementing your pocket money.

The GPO telephone box in Brogborough was more than just a link to the outside world. It was also a meeting point for the kids of the estate. A place where you could get out of the house and meet your friends on cold, wet winter nights. It was surprising how many kids fit into a standard K6 box. The Guinness Book of Records put it at fourteen, but five was about a comfortable maximum for us.

Around the late-1960's, the GPO introduced a 'Dial a Disc Service. The service started after six in the evening and ran until six in the morning. This was great for us kids as it was outside school time.
This caused havoc as the phone box became a mini youth club, to the dismay of irate adults who wanted to use the phone. If we pooled our loose change, we could monopolise the box for hours. For a few copper coins, you could dial 160 and listen to records from the top ten. You very rarely got the beginning of the tune as It depended on where the tape was playing when you got connected. The sound quality was rubbish, and you would have to keep passing the phone's handset around to others or all try to listen at the same time around the telephone speaker. Still, it was a great way to hear the latest hits.
For a while, there were a few 'hacks' you could use to listen to the music for free. The system allowed you to listen for the first ten seconds before pressing button A to make the connection. If you pressed button B just before the ten seconds were up, you were cut off, but you got your money back. If you had the patience, you could do this repeatedly until you'd heard a very disjointed version of the whole record. Not very satisfactory.
When the service first started, you could press button B just before the music finished, get your money back, and then use the coins to listen again. This only lasted for a short while until the GPO cottoned on and adjusted their equipment.
Then there was another quirk with the STD system. You could make an open connection if you rapidly tapped out the 'Dial a Disk' numbers 1-6-0 on the telephone's handset cradle with a slight gap

between them. This was a very hit and miss method that only worked occasionally; it was almost impossible to get the timing right.
During this hack, a telephone operator often cut in to inform you that the police had been alerted to this illegal activity and were on their way.
However, it was doubtful that Mr Button would cycle two miles from the Ridgmont station to find an empty telephone box recently evacuated by a gang of misfits.

August Bank Holiday 1965. Clacton on our scooters.

On Friday, 27 of August 1965, at midnight, I finished a 16-hour double shift at the Toddington Granada M1 services. It was my third double shift that week. I was knackered, but I'd done the shifts because I needed the money. On Saturday, we were off on our scooters to Clacton-on-Sea for the August Summer Bank Holiday. I told the personnel department that I couldn't work the weekend as I had to go away with my parents. I said my dad didn't trust me to stay home alone during the bank holiday. It was a lie but a very plausible one.
My house was the most convenient assembly point, so five of us met up there late Saturday morning.
My dad went apeshit when he found out I was off on a jaunt to the coast instead of going to work. He'd have blown a gasket if he'd found out that I'd used him as the excuse to bunk off. Once again, my mum had to calm things down.

A little after one in the afternoon, this uniquely British subculture riding Italian scooters set off on a 95-mile journey to the coast. It was cloudy and cool, not good excursion weather, but it didn't rain. We headed to Ampthill, then on to Bishop's Stortford and Braintree.

According to the press, during the Easter weekend of the previous year, 'hordes of rampaging mods and rockers descended on Clacton hell-bent on fighting and hooliganism. The press probably exaggerated the conflict, although there would inevitably have been a few punch-ups.

This particular group of 'hooligans' stopped in a lay-by before we got to Colchester to eat the sandwiches our mothers had made us for the journey.

By 1965 battles between mods and rockers declined as mods moved into pop art, music and psychedelia, The Small Faces, The Kinks, The Who, The Yardbirds, and The Spencer Davis Group.

We were definitely not on our way to the coast for conflict. Nevertheless, whatever the reality, there was a significant police presence to greet us when we arrived in Clacton, and they were belligerent.

Even with the fixing screws tight, my scooter's headlight rattled. I'd put vertical and horizontal strips of blue insulating tape across the light's glass and housing to stop this. This fixed the rattle, and the resulting blue cross gave my machine an extra bit of character.

A young, helmeted constable threw himself in front of my scooter, causing me to make an emergency stop.

"Remove that blue tape. That colour is reserved for police lights only," the constable shouted.
I was smart enough not to argue and indignantly removed the offending colour. I wondered how two strips of insulating tape made my scooter look like a police vehicle.
That set the tone for the next few hours. We were harassed by the police, not allowed to park up and continually moved on. This went on until sunset giving us the distinct feeling that our patronage wasn't wanted in Clacton. In the dark, we tried to group our scooters in a recently harvested cornfield and set up camp. The police arrived with torches and turfed us out. They lined us up and searched us for weapons and drugs on the road.
An offensive weapon under British law was defined as "any article made or adapted for use to cause injury to the person or intended by the person having it with him for such use". That's a broad description and could include a wheel spanner from any scooter tool kit. Fortunately, it had been a long day for the cops. They probably wanted to get home rather than pull us in on some trumped-up charge with the inevitable paperwork. None of us did drugs, so we were OK on that score, or so we thought.
The police made us turn out our pockets and found nothing until they came to the last person. A nice fellow but a sickly youth with health problems. They found an unmarked, plastic screw-capped tube containing about twenty yellow pills when he turned his pockets out.
"What are these?" demanded the policeman suspiciously.
"They're my hay fever tablets", replied the youth with a sniffle.

"Hay fever!" said the cop scornfully. "Where did you get them? The container isn't marked".

"From my mum. She's got a big jar of them at home".

Fortuitously, at that point, the romp through the cornfield took over. The boy sneezed into the face of the policeman. With disgust, the policeman handed back the boy's medicine and told us all to be on our way.

We eventually found a piece of cop free, open ground where Clacton's Butlins Holiday Camp met Jaywick Sands. There we set up camp for the night.

The next day I stayed behind at Jaywick to look after the tents while the rest of the gang went into Clacton to reconnoitre the police activity. To keep me entertained, they left me a transistor radio. The pirate ship Radio Caroline was transmitting less than 20 miles away, and the reception was brilliant.

Some great songs were being played, but the four that put me right back in that place and time are.

You've Got Your Troubles - The Fortunes.

Mr Tambourine Man - The Byrd's.

We, Gotta, Get Out of This Place - The Animals; and

Woolly Bully - Sam The Sham & The Pharaohs.

There were other songs, but those four are the ones that remind me most of that weekend by the sea.

Late that morning, a pretty girl in a white tank-top and denim miniskirt walking by the sea wall, attracted by the music, came and sat with me. We sat in the sun and talked about singers, bands, fashion, scooters and other Mod things. We got on so well that I

thought I'd try my luck, and I casually asked her if she'd like to continue our discussions in one of the small tents.
To my surprise, she thought that was a good idea, so we withdrew to the privacy of the canvas. She was a wonderful kisser. I was just getting her panties off when there was the rumble of scooters returning to the camp. The engines went quiet, and then my mates, who'd been to a pub, started jeering and jumping on the tent. The poor girl was right put out. She made herself respectable, got out of the tent and stormed off. I never saw her again, and I didn't even know her name.
"You bastards", I shouted, but they just curled up in fits of laughter. And that's about all I can remember about that little sojourn to the Essex coast in the summer of 1965.

All too soon, it was winter again.

There was a youth club in the assembly hall at Fulbrook school every Friday night. One Friday in the middle of November I started going out with a girl at the youth club called Margaret. Margaret lived in Ridgmont. I'd known her most of my life because we both went to Ridgmont Primary school when we were kids. You miss a lot when you are familiar with someone, and I'd missed a lot about Margaret. At 16, she'd grown into a very attractive young woman. She'd been going out with a boy named Nigel
Nigel had been in the same year as me at Fulbrook school. The previous Friday, I noticed Margaret and Nigel were both at the club

but no longer together. Margaret was by herself, so I sat with her and struck up a conversation. I came on my scooter, but I only had a provisional driving license. By law, I wasn't allowed to carry a pillion passenger unless they had a full license, and Margaret didn't have one. When she had to go home, I walked to the bus stop to get the late bus back to Ridgmont. While we were kissing, waiting for the bus, a car pulled up next to us. The vehicle was driven by a guy called Keith Austin, another ex-pupil from Fulbrook school. Leaning out of the passenger window was Nigel.

They were both hostile, and I thought, "This is not going to go well for me".

Fear is the key. A sudden injection of adrenaline into your system can sometimes be misinterpreted. I stood in silence, staring into the car. The driver leaned across, looked at me, and whispered something into Nigel's ear. To my surprise, they stayed in the car, said something derogatory and drove off laughing.

Margaret went upstairs and sat on the empty back seat when the bus came. I waved goodbye and returned to Fulbrook to get my scooter. I caught up with the bus going down West Hill in Aspley Guise and followed it the three miles to Ridgmont.

After a short canoodle on her front step, we arranged to meet the following evening. I had homework during the week, so I could only see Margaret again on Wednesday evening, but things were going well, and we arranged to meet again on Friday at the youth club.

On Friday, before I left for the youth club, I put the lining back in my parka for the winter and found my wool-lined mittens. I took my crash helmet with me. I always did this to stop my mum from worrying, but I rarely used the helmet and strapped it to the back rack that held the spare wheel. However, it was a cold dark winter night, so when I got to the main road at the edge of the estate, I put the helmet on to keep my head warm and my hair in place. I'd stop and take the helmet off before I drove from Weathercock Lane into the youth club. Looking cool was important.

As I crossed the Ridgmont Salford crossroads and started up the incline to go over the M1 Motorway bridge, I saw a vehicle's lights pull off the slip road of the northbound carriageway. The vehicle crossed the road and stopped on the bridge facing my direction. Another vehicle had stopped on the slip road, indicating it was waiting to cross the road in my direction. As I got closer, I could just make out the vehicle on the bridge to my right was a dark-coloured Bedford van. It was too dark to identify the one waiting to come off the slip road.

I dipped my headlights, for the van that was facing me. Then! To my utter horror, as I was about to pass the van, I saw a taut steel cable about eighteen inches off the ground in the beam of my headlight. Travelling at 60 miles an hour, I hit the cable almost as soon as I saw it.

The metal tow rope snapped with the impact and skidded off like an elastic band. Instead of being thrown over the top, the scooter rotated anticlockwise. The end of the handlebar hit me in the ribs, and I was thrown off the machine. My head hit the road, and I slid along the tarmac on my hands and knees with the scooter on my back. I passed a lorry stopped on the motorway slip road and came to rest about 40 yards down the road.

I threw the scooter off my back and stood up. I felt no pain, just a burning rage as I walked back to the van.

The soles of my hush puppies flapped where they had been torn away from the bottom of the shoes. The knees of my Levi 501's were worn through, and the skin beneath was missing. Thanks to my Levis, I still had my kneecaps. The right lower arm of my parka was ripped away, and the palms of my mittens were burned where I'd outstretched my hands to stop my face from scraping the tarmac. I took off my helmet and felt a dent at the front where the right side had hit the road.

When I got to the van, I hit the driver's side door hard with my helmet. I slid the door open with such force that it made a loud bang as it hit the stop. The driver and passenger looked surprised as if they hadn't realised what had happened. I screamed at them.

"YOU BASTARDS. WHAT THE FUCK DO YOU THINK YOU'RE DOING?".

After that, I passed out on the road.

I was sitting in the van's passenger seat, with my scooter loaded in the back when I came too. The driver was questioning me, trying to find out where I lived.

They took me home and dropped my now severely bent scooter outside my house. My mum went to the phone box and called the doctor. When the doctor arrived (they came out in those days), it was about 9 at night. Other than grazes and bruises he found no serious damage. I had no broken bones and I didn't need stitches.

We should have reported the accident to the police because I was well damaged, but we didn't. There were no 'Ambulance Chasers' to get involved, so we exchanged insurance details, and the two tow truck men left.

The van had been towing a large Pickfords' removal lorry that wasn't firing on all cylinders. They managed to get the vehicle off the motorway, but the lorry stalled on the slip road when the van crossed over the bridge. The taught steel tow rope was well over 30 feet long because it stretched from the slip road across two lanes to the other side of the bridge. That's when I came along.

The following day I felt like I'd been run over by a steam roller, and I couldn't get out of bed for a week.

It was fortunate it had been such a cold night that I used my crash helmet, or things may have turned out a lot different. I was lucky not to be dead, a cabbage or a cripple.

Margaret had gone to the youth club that Friday night, but she must have thought I'd abandoned her, and so I lost my girlfriend because I couldn't contact her to let her know what had happened.

What made it worse was my best mate Buzz stepped in. Opportunistic scoundrel. A classic case of, I trust you with my life, but not with my wife.

When Buzz and I met up again, he was no longer going with Margaret. He told me he didn't know I was going with her. A likely story.

I asked him how he'd got on with her. He said she was very nice but had not let him touch her. I told him I'd had sex with her, which

was a blatant lie, but that's what boys do, to make themselves feel better.
Though we only lived a few miles apart, I never saw Margaret again. I never had the opportunity to apologise and explain why I didn't meet her that night. I don't suppose I would have had the nerve to apologise for the lie I'd told Buzz. I was probably off chasing other girls.
I think the word you're probably looking for is - shallow.

When I was able to walk again, I phoned Graymac Motors in Luton, who told me to get the scooter into them. They gave me the name of a lawyer, Mr Marriott in Luton, who would handle the insurance claim. Once I felt up to it, I straightened out the front wheel of the Vespa and very cautiously drove the machine to Luton.
As Christmas approached, I no longer had a scooter. I didn't have a girlfriend either, but that wasn't so bad as it meant I didn't have an extra present to buy. I was lucky to be alive and not to be a vegetable, so I didn't have anything to moan about.
One consolation, the Christmas charts in 1965 were great. The Beatles were number one again with the two-sided hit Day Tripper, and We Can Work It Out. The Who were in the top ten with My Generation, along with Len Barry with 1-2-3, and The Four Seasons with Let's Hang On. Those were my favourites. However, our parents were still represented by the likes of Ken Dodd, who had two records in the top ten, The River and Tears. You can't knock him for that, but that stuff wasn't for my mates or me.

Christmas 1965

I was on holiday from full-time study for my O Levels at Dunstable College on Christmas Eve.

My sister's boyfriend Gary told me to meet him at Brogborough CIU Club at lunchtime. A group from the Brickyard's forklift repair shop, where Gary worked, were going to the club for a Christmas drink. I told him I didn't have any money, and he said I shouldn't worry about that; I wouldn't need any. Gary was with his co-workers Tim Garrett and Roger Beasley (Colonel Beasley from when we were kids). They were drinking rounds of Captain Morgan's dark rum mixed with blackcurrant cordial. They took great pleasure in making me keep up with them; I didn't mind because they were buying.

By 2 o'clock, when the others had to go back to work, I'd drunk fifteen shots of Captain Morgan's with blackcurrant. To say I was pissed was an understatement. I managed to get home by feeling my way along the low wall that ran the length of the street. When I got to my house, I was in a state of collapse. The wall between our path and our neighbour's path was only a couple of feet high. If I'd bent down to use it for support, I would have fallen over it into the neighbour's front garden. While I was swaying on the edge of the step, wondering how I would negotiate the five or so yards down the incline to my front door, I felt a steadying hand on my arm.

Squinting to focus, I looked around and saw Erika supporting me. She must have seen my predicament from her house on the other side of the street. Erika guided me down the path, retrieved the

front door key hanging on a string behind the door's letterbox flap and helped me into the house. Mum and dad were still at work. By herself, she managed to get me laid out on the sofa.
She looked like a heavenly angel hovering over me.
"Do you want me to make you some coffee?"
"No", I replied, "I want a Christmas kish".
She leant forward and, before I passed out, I felt her warm lips on mine
When I woke up, the room was spinning. I was alone, and my head was splitting with the worst hangover I'd ever had in my life. I got up, stumbled to the toilet and was violently sick. I was still feeling ill the following day. Christmas Day was a subdued affair for me that year.
Nothing developed from that incident. I suspect Erika had a boyfriend. She may well have been going out with my friend Pinch at the time.

In January 1966, I was going to be 17 years old. I was studying, but as a self-absorbed, immature adolescent hedonist, my main focus in life was the pursuit of girls. I don't carry tremendous guilt about that, but I do sometimes regret not being more sensitive. Mind you, girls that age can be pretty awful too. More importantly, I could have been more conscientious, considering my mum had taken a full-time job to fund my education.
I reckon it wasn't my fault. It was Mother Nature's way of ensuring that the human race survives. She fills boys with hormones so that they go on a mindless quest to promulgate the species. Then, like a

variation of the female spiders' mating ritual, She sends them off to some testosterone-charged war designed to control the population.

The difference for my generation was that on the last day of December 1960, conscription for military service was formally ended in the UK. After that, it was a personal choice if you wanted to get yourself killed in some foreign land fighting for Queen and Country. Of course, boys being boys, there was no shortage of volunteers. My friends Ray, Frank and Maurice and my cousin Jimmy Greenslade had already signed up for a bit of adventure...

As it had done for millennia, dance played an important role in the mating ritual. Locally, there were Brogborough, and Marston CIU Clubs and many village halls had regular dances. Because of lack of supervision, these venues usually ended in a punch up.

Further afield, there were the Corn Exchange and Conservative Club in Bedford and the Civic Hall and the famous California Ballroom in Dunstable. The Civic had a dance on Monday nights. That dance cost three shillings and sixpence (3/6p) plus sixpence to put your coat in the cloakroom. After spending four shillings, I was usually broke for the week. Still, if a girl stayed with you when she knew you had no money, at least you knew she was serious.

There were a few youth clubs and the Blue Angel in Lidlington High Street just up the hill from the Green Man pub. Having taken over the abandoned Wesleyan Chapel, the Blue Angel acted as an unofficial weekend youth club. Teenagers frequented it and played loud pop music on a Sunday night when there was nothing else to do. The villagers considered this a satanic place because it was dimly lit except for a crude rotating Hypno-disc illuminated by a blue spotlight close to the entrance. They probably thought the disc would turn us all into zombie sex slaves. I suspect the place was run by someone with a grudge against the village council just to annoy them.

Other popular hangouts that played pop music were Maratelli's cafe in Bedford, the Milk Bar and the Carousel in Dunstable.

Before we went for a night out, we'd get dressed up and splash on the Old Spice. Later, Brut became very popular. I found Brut too overpowering and preferred the more subtle 12 Bore. This came in a red cylinder with a rimmed brass screw cap that looked like an oversized shotgun cartridge.

As 1965 came to an end, I didn't have a girlfriend. That situation would change on New Year's Eve, but that was not necessarily for the better.

I was about to find out what it was like to be subject to a 'Mafia Hit' and how girls can complicate a young boy's life.

Here's some background information on this little tale.

I've changed the names of some characters in this story to protect their privacy and for my own self-preservation.

With about 14,000 residents per 100,000, Bedford has the largest collection of Italian families in the UK. The link to Bedford is so strong, that the town has its own Italian Consulate.

During WWII, thousands of Prisoners of War (PoWs) were held in the UK. There was a camp near Brogborough. The Germans were kept in very secure facilities and subject to de-Nazification.

By contrast, the perceived threat from the Italian PoWs was such that they were allowed to roam in relative freedom.
Consequently, the Italians who returned to their families in Italy had a reasonably good impression of the UK. I can't comment on British food's impact on them, but the Empire was at war at the time and subject to severe rationing.
However, that is not the sole reason for the high number of Italians in Bedford. Marston Valley Brick Company didn't have enough labour to handle the post-war demand for bricks. In the late 1940's, the company recruited 7,500 workers from villages in southern Italy. Like my father, who came from Ireland to work in the brick-fields, many Italian workers brought their families over to settle in Bedfordshire.
In the mid-1960's, I knew a lad my own age from Bedford called Marco Lombardo. We weren't exactly friends, but we were on first-name terms. He was from a Sicilian family and quite tall, about five foot eleven. He had fair hair, which I thought was unusual for an Italian. His ancestors may have been part of Sicily's Norman conquest, as the Butlers were from the Norman invasion of Ireland. They got around those Vikings. At a stretch, you might say we were family.
Marco became a well-known businessman around town in later life, maybe not always for the right reasons. To my knowledge, he had a shoe shop and a barbershop, food outlets, arcade game machines, and a property development company. When my friend Norman Stewart was at university, he got a holiday job on Marco's ice cream vans. Norman said the first order of business in the

mornings was to go out and slash the tyres of the opposition. Norman was a funny guy, so I suspect that was a joke, but I couldn't say for sure. Regardless, I always found Marco to be a very nice guy.

On 31 Dec 1965, I went to a dance at Ampthill, Parkside Hall. Curiously, a pretty mod girl named Jillian Brook, who I'd never met before, decided I was going to spend New Year's Eve with her. We ended up on the mattress in the back of my mate Ken's Bedford van. There was a lot of French kissing, but to her credit, I never got further than getting my hand up her jumper. Typical teenage boys, I got a lot of ribbing from my mates about the love bite on my neck, and I did nothing to dispel their fantasies.

I met Jillian the following Friday at the same place. Our relationship blossomed slightly up against the wall at the back of the dance hall during the band's break. After the dance, I walked Jillian home. We arranged to meet two days later at the Sunday night dance at the Conservative Club in Bedford.

Because I'd told Ken and my mates not to wait for me, I had to thumb a lift home. It was a cold January night, but there was a full moon, and I felt good having been with Gillian. Nevertheless, I had a 6-mile walk ahead of me.

A car passed me about a mile out of Ampthill and stopped about fifty yards down the road. Believing someone had taken pity on me, I ran up to the car. When I reached it, the passenger side window wound down, and I was confronted with the face of Nigel, Margaret's old boyfriend. In the driving seat was the gloating face of Keith Austin. My first thought was they were going to beat me up. But they just wanted to see me run and my disappointment when I reached the car. The bastards drove off laughing, leaving me panting white clouds of breath into the cold air.

On the bright side, I wasn't lying unconscious on the road, and I now felt considerably warmer.

A little while later, another car passed me and stopped about 100 yards down the road. While I considered who else might want a laugh at my expense, the car began reversing towards me. I walked cautiously forward, ready to jump onto the grass if the occupants had some evil intent. It turned out to be Kay Cashin and her boyfriend. Kay was from another Irish family in Brogborough, so I got a lift all the way home.

I stayed in on Saturday. As usual, with only nine shillings, my finances were stretched. I was due to meet Jillian the next day in Bedford, and I wanted to keep some money over for the Monday night dance at the Civic Hall in Dunstable. I had an on-off relationship with a girl called Dot, who lived near the AC Delco works close to the A5 Watling Street north out of Dunstable. Dot looked like Cher from 'Sonny and Cher'. She was fun to be with, and I hadn't seen her for a while.

I didn't go to church on Sunday morning, nor did my dad after his Saturday night session in CIU Club. Nevertheless, he had a real go at me for my mortal sin. I thought it best not to tell him I was already on the road to hell because of my occasional use of condoms.

On Sunday evening, I hitched a lift into Bedford. I met Jillian at Martarelli's cafe, a popular hangout for the mod fraternity on Midland Road. I used to go there a lot. However, as I'd badly bent my Vespa Sportique and myself on the M1 bridge before Christmas, I hadn't been to Matarelli's for some time. Jillian was at Matarelli's with some friends; she said she had to go into town, and she'd meet me at the Con Club. Later. While I was walking through Bedford bus station on my way to the dance, I was approached by two youths. One was Marco Lombardo, the other I'd never seen before. Marco looked surprised and awkward when he recognised me. Before exchanging any pleasantries, the other fellow asked if I was going out with Jillian Brook.

"What's it to you if I am?" I replied. And that was the end of that conversation.

I woke up on the pavement with a fat lip, with my assailant and Marco walking away.

A Bedford boy I knew helped me to my feet and told me the guy who'd hit me was Jack Peters, an amateur boxer. Strangely, I didn't find that fact surprising. He also said Jack was a very nice chap, something I didn't feel qualified to comment on.

At that point, anyone sensible would have gone home. However, it seems that being Irish, I might have been born with an irrational gene. I tidied myself up and headed for the dance.

At the Con Club, I bumped into Marco. Marco's response was like the cliched line from a mafia hitman in a movie.

"Bernie, it was nothing personal. I didn't know it was going to be you."

Nevertheless, we parted on good terms. We all make mistakes.

I met Jillian in the dance hall and told her what had happened. She told me the guy who hit me was her ex-boyfriend. The ex-boyfriend

Jack was also in the dance hall. Dented pride is a powerful motivator; I kept staring at him. Jillian asked me not to start anything. In retrospect, antagonising someone on their own turf was a stupid thing to do.

In the end, he came over, and to my surprise, he apologised.

"Sorry," he said. "If she likes you better than me, I can't do much about it".

He offered me his hand. Stupidly, I took it, which could have turned out badly if he'd been a southpaw and hadn't finished with me. However, it was a genuine gesture.

Jillian was sitting alone in a corner, so I went over and sat with her. When I approached the subject of her ex, she said she couldn't decide who she liked best. That was too complicated for me, so I raised my hands in surrender and left her by herself. When the dance finished, Jack took her home.

Girls were difficult to understand. That wasn't the end of things between Jillian and me, and life would get a bit complicated for a while.

I didn't go to college on Monday. My tooth had cut into my bottom lip, and the right side of my face was swollen. I told my mum I had a stomach problem and stayed in bed until she and dad had gone to work.

John Button, the policeman's son from Ridgmont, had promised to pick me up on his scooter and take me with him to Dunstable, but he never turned up. That was probably no bad thing as his scooter was constantly breaking down, and I might have had a 13-mile

walk home. It also saved another confrontation with my dad about being too ill to go to college but well enough to go out to a dance.
A pretty little girl I was attracted to came to college on day release on Mondays. Often at break times in the common room or restaurant, we'd make eye contact, not strange, as I always looked out for her. It's funny how you look at a girl, she looks at you, and something happens, a sort of chemical reaction.
I began bumping into her during the week when I was with friends at lunchtime in the Carousel Cafe. At first, I thought it was a coincidence, but I wasn't so sure after a while.
Her name was Sylvia, and she worked at AC Delco on the same street where Dot lived.
One Monday in January, I was with my mates at Civic Hall dance in Dunstable. Dot was there, but she wasn't happy with me, probably because I hadn't made an effort to see her for a while. Quite unexpectedly, I bumped into Sylvia. We had a dance, and suddenly I had a new girlfriend.
For a few weeks, Sylvia and I had a serious relationship. We met up at college every Monday. Most other days during the week, she'd catch the bus up from Delco's during her lunch break, and I'd meet her at the stop outside Dunstable Grammar school. We'd sit in the park if it were sunny, but the weather was terrible on most days, so we went to the Carousel cafe and listened to the jukebox. Sylvia generally bought the coffees because she had a job, and I was always broke during the week.
During this time, Mr Marriott, my solicitor, wrote to me. He asked me to settle for £40 damages for my clothing and loss of wages at

the Granada M1 service station where I'd worked at the time of my accident. However, the claim for damage to my scooter was still pending, so I still didn't have any transport. As Dunstable was a long way from Brogborough, I never got to see Sylvia at night unless I managed to get a lift with friends to the Civic Centre dance. Then, I had to put Sylvia on the 10 O'clock bus home. I didn't want to become prey for Sylvia's dad, who I had never met, so I made sure she caught the bus. Consequently, apart from snogging and some furtive petting in the park, we didn't have an intimate relationship, but it was a pleasant time.

28 January 1966, one day after my 17th birthday. It was a Friday; I hadn't intended to go out that night. However, I bumped into my friend Kenny Yates. He said he was taking the Brogborough girls Erika, Mary, and Vicky to Leighton Buzzard and did I want to come along for the ride. When we got back to Brogborough, we met Johnny Mac and Pinch in the club, and we all went with Kenny to the dance at Ampthill. At the dance, someone said Jillian Brook was looking for me. After the last fiasco, I wasn't too interested in seeing her. However, Jillian found me. She apologised for what had happened and said she was no longer going with Jack, so I went out with her. When the dance ended, Jillian asked if I would go babysitting with her the following evening. A meeting like this alone with Jillian could only end up one way, but I had Sylvia to think about. After some very careful consideration, I said, "Yes".
The following evening I walked the two miles to Ridgmont. While waiting for the bus, a friend from Brogborough, Stephen Hall, and

his girlfriend stopped and gave me a lift to Ampthill. It seemed all my old school friends had cars while I was generally broke and bumming rides or catching public transport. Still, I had no time for self-pity; tonight I had a hot date with Jillian.

I found the large, well kept, detached house on Flitwick Road on the way out of Ampthill. The owner was obviously not short of money. There was no car in the drive, so I knocked on the door. Jillian let me in and introduced me to the owner's amiable Scotty dog. After our introduction, the dog went off and returned with a pair of slippers for me. I thanked it and patted its head. The little animal dropped the slippers on the carpet and retired happily to its basket. Jillian went upstairs to check on the baby. I settled on the large brown leather Chesterfield sofa. I wondered if I would ever be able to afford a house like this with its plush carpets, drapes and central heating. It didn't seem likely. It was a far cry from 32 Highfield Crescent, freezing in the winter, with linoleum floors, one downstairs bathroom and toilet, and a coal fire with a back boiler for hot water. It was all quite depressing.

My mood lifted when Jillian returned and joined me on the sofa.

I must admit I felt a little uncomfortable carrying on with a girl in a stranger's house under the scrutiny of a Scotty dog and a baby sleeping peacefully upstairs. I couldn't stop thinking that the house owners might return and catch us at any moment. Nevertheless, I overcame my moral reservations and got on with it. That's what adolescents do.

Like Cinderella, I had to leave the house before midnight when the owners were due to return. Fortunately, the bouncer from Ampthill

Parkside Hall, and his girlfriend, recognised me walking along the road and gave me a lift home.

Friday, 4 February, I met Jillian at Ampthill dance. Jack Peters came in, and Jillian went back with him. She was leading us both by the nose, but at least we weren't fighting over it. I really liked Jillian, but I took Jack's approach. If she liked him better than me, I couldn't do anything about it. I wasn't complaining; I'd done alright out of the intrigue. However, it was time to stop being a pawn in Jillian's game.

Erika was at the dance and had seen what had happened. She came over and asked if it bothered me. I told her it didn't, but I felt a bit of a fool, only because my friends didn't know the whole story of this love triangle.

I had no hard feelings. That's life; it was time to move on. Sometimes fond memories come at a cost; even so, it's nice to have them.

Saturday 5 February started peaceful enough. I cooked some dehydrated Vesta beef curry for my lunch. After that, I went to Bedford on my scooter, which had been finally repaired after the accident.

I met up with some Bedford boys at Matarelli's cafe and went with them to Clanfield Lawrence to buy stuff for their scooters. After that, I went to Millets Army and Navy surplus store. With my insurance money, I purchased a grey reefer jacket, a coat made of heavy wool with broad lapels, a double-breasted front with four large buttons in two rows, and vertical pockets. Originally reefers were worn by sailors, and you could get them cheap from Millets. I also bought a new pair of Levi's. I never threw out the old pair, even though the knees were shredded from my scooter accident. My friend Roger Aranela and I had a new fashion statement. We both wore worn-out jeans everywhere, except for special occasions, even though they were totally faded and falling apart. My mum said we looked like a couple of old tramps. She threatened to burn mine, but she never did. Roger and I thought we looked really cool.

In the evening, at about 8:30, I went to the dance at Brogborough. Kenny, Pinch, Unca and Johnny Mac, Erika, Mary, and some other Brogborough girls were there.

Later, a Lambretta turned up driven by a guy named Dingle, with Marco Lombardo on the back. I'd not seen either of them in Brogborough before, so I went over to say hello.

Johnny Mac and his girlfriend Margaret, also from Brogborough, fell out some weeks earlier but were now back together. When they were split up, Dingle made a play for Margaret. Now, Johnny Mac was one of the nicest people you could meet, he seldom lost his temper, but things went ballistic if he did. Someone told him about Dingle's indiscretion. It took a while for the pressure to build, but then the volcano erupted. Mac came through the dancers like a bowling ball through skittles, followed by Kenny, Pinch and Unca. To Dingle, it looked like the Four Horsemen of the Apocalypse were about to obliterate him. He didn't realise that three of the four assailants were trying to prevent the carnage and save Mac from a court appearance on charges of manslaughter. The three restrainers managed to get their hands on Mac just in time, leaving him like a Rottweiler on a short chain going for Dingle's throat. Mac's blood was up, and there was no guarantee he could be held back for long. In the resulting confusion, I bundled Marco and Dingle into the small changing room by the side of the stage and bolted the door.

When the scuffle outside subsided, I quietly reminded Marco he was fortunate I wasn't vindictive.

"Remember that day at Bedford bus station? Well, you really owe me one for this, Marco".

After a short while, there was a bang on the door. I thought Dingle was going to pass out.

"You can get them out of there now. They've dragged him home and locked him in the bathroom".

I escorted the two celebrities from the changing room through the crowd to the car park like a pair of rock stars.

Dingle tried to fire up the Lambretta, but he was so shaken he flooded it. He and Marco then tried to bump start it.

In the meantime, Mac escaped through the tiny bathroom window. Pursued by his mates, he came thundering back like a charging rhinoceros. He was so focused on getting into the dance that he ran straight past Dingle and Marco, still running up and down in front of the hall, trying to start the Lambretta. Fortunately, the machine burst into life. They jumped on it and disappeared into the night over Brogborough hill, last seen heading for Bedford.

All I can say is that life is a series of recurring events. You just never know which side of the fence you'll be on when they happen. And Marco Lombardo still owes me one.

By mid-February, my relationship with Sylvia had run its course. We weren't getting on very well. She certainly wasn't happy with me because I never tried to go and see her in the evenings even though my scooter was back on the road. Occasionally, I'd arrange to see her at the Civic Hall Monday dance. Even then, I'd spend a lot of time with my mates or dancing with other girls. There was a mod girl with short-cropped hair who wore a long mustard suede coat that I was particularly attracted to.

The last straw was when Sylvia's friend confronted me and told me she knew I'd been going out with a girl from Ampthill. I don't know how she knew, but she did, and if she knew that, she would have already told Sylvia. The world was a smaller place than I'd realised.

And so Sylvia and I split up. I knew a boy called Roy from Delco's was making advances, so she probably went out with him. I don't blame her; I was a bit of an arse. I was attracted to many girls, but I never gave them the commitment they were looking for. Just the previous year, I had a wonderful girlfriend called Gil Richards. She was beautiful, soft and kind. I still feel guilty about the way I treated her and how I ignominiously dumped her for no good reason.

I often wonder if it was because I came from Brogborough, and she lived in a beautiful house at Ivinghoe Beacon just outside Dunstable. Maybe I didn't want to get too close because I'd have to bring them home to meet my mum and dad, and she'd think I was a fraud. I guess that's another characteristic of adolescence.

It was a complicated time because while this stuff was happening with Sylvia and Jillian, a girl from the college called Linda wrote me a letter to tell me how much she liked me and how she thought I was a great dancer.

And then there was Stephanie, a buxom girl with large breasts and excessive sexual appetite. She was not a beauty, but adolescent boys are easily swayed, especially when their mates aren't around to take the piss. I know it's shallow, but nature has stacked the cards against us. The truth is boys are hard-wired to spread the gene pool with little consideration of risk or recipient.

One day Stephanie decided to keep me company during an art class. She immediately started telling me how she'd lost her virginity. She continued with an in-depth description of her lovers and told me that she had once experienced a 13-inch cock. This made me wonder if she carried a tape measure around with her and if you had to have your erection measured and recorded before the act. If she thought being catalogued and compared on her scorecard would turn me on, she was mistaken. As Clint put it, "A man's got to know his limitations!" and I'd never been that competitive.

Because I'd told her I liked the song, Stephanie gave me a present of the Small Faces single, I've Got Mine. She kept asking me for my address. I kept trying to put her off, but she forced it out of me in the end. I hoped I lived too far out of Dunstable for an impromptu visit. Stephanie's appearance on my doorstep demanding a bonk wouldn't go down too well with my Irish Catholic mother after her lectures about sex before marriage. My sister was as bad. I guess her boyfriend Gary wasn't getting any.

I also kept bumping into an old girlfriend in Bedford called Maz, who came from Cardington. She kept hinting that we should get back together. Maz was a tall blond who often wore a long red leather coat that she looked stunning in. I was tempted, but life was complicated enough at the time. What with the girl from Dunstable in the mustard-coloured suede coat, who I was unashamedly chasing, I thought I might be developing a leather fetish.

Sex and drugs, rock, and roll

One Saturday in mid-February, I went to a dance at Stewartby Village Hall, close to the brick factory. I got chatting with a girl from Wootton called Melanie. After a couple of dances, we went out and sat in a car that belonged to a friend of hers. We started kissing, but the car was outside the entrance to the dance hall with too many people passing, so we went for a walk. We crossed the road to the brick company's swimming pool. The pool was closed, but the secluded entrance doorway made a suitable spot to continue what had begun in the car. Before long, she had her panties off, and I was fiddling with a condom. Unfortunately, we'd just started our nocturnal activity when we were caught in the beam of a night watchman's flashlight.

"Oi. Clear off," he growled. "You can't do that ere".

Caught with our pants down, he was discrete enough to divert his torch long enough for us to make ourselves respectable and vacate the premises.

When we got back to the Village Hall, the bus to Wootton was about to leave, so we had to say goodbye.

The following Wednesday, when I got home from college, Terry, the son of Peggy from the shops, gave me a note from Melanie.

I don't know how he knew her. I doubt very much if he'd had a sexual relationship with her or anyone else for that matter. The poor boy was studying theology.

In the letter, she asked me to go to the public telephone box at 6:30 that evening. Fortunately, no one was using the box when the call came. She wanted me to go to see her in Wootton. I said I didn't want to get serious. That was somewhat superficial, considering she'd been willing to let me shag her.

Not surprisingly, she was upset. She sounded like she was in tears, so I told her I would see her at the next Stewartby dance. Whenever that might be.

18 Feb Friday

At the Ampthill dance Friday that same week, a beautiful girl from Marston called Kristine told me Melanie would come to see me at the Brogborough Club dance the following night. I told Kristine I probably wasn't going. But, after some consideration, I thought - maybe I just might.

The following evening Melanie did come to the dance with some friends. The dance wasn't very good, and I didn't go with Melanie; instead, fourteen of us from Brogborough piled into Ken's van and went to the bowling alley in Bedford. I can't believe now how badly I treated that girl.

On the Monday after college John, the policeman's son from Ridgmont, picked me up on his new Lambretta Pacemaker, and we went to the Civic Hall, Dunstable. After paying the entrance and cloakroom fees, I was again financially challenged.

The girl in the mustard coat was with a dark-haired friend at the dance. Sometimes, when I really liked a girl, I didn't know, I found it daunting to ask her for a dance. That was probably a fear of rejection or a dented ego. That night, I finally dared to ask her for a slow dance. Surprisingly, she was very talkative, and her name was Sylvia. Another Sylvia.

After the dance, John and I took a ride to the Chinese chip shop on West Street. While we were queuing for our chips, the two girls came in.

"Fancy meeting you here," commented the one with the dark hair. Because of my infatuation with Sylvia, I hadn't taken much notice of her. She was gorgeous and very friendly. She kept smiling at me, and I was really attracted to her. I was a moth to the flame; was there any hope for me?

They were really lovely to us and also very affectionate with each other. We didn't know what to make of them and wondered if they were a couple of pinks. They might even have been bisexual or just having fun at our expense. I knew women were supposed to be mysterious, but sometimes I found them totally incomprehensible. Nevertheless, it was game on for another day.

The following day in the students' common room, I was popping a red multivitamin pill in a vain attempt to boost my IQ. I really had to catch up on my neglected studies. A girl called Sid came over to talk to me. Sid's real name was Uraina. I have no idea why we called her Sid. Like many at college, she was a first-generation immigrant, her parents came from Ukraine. She was British born like me, but with a more refined accent.

Sid was an exceptionally beautiful blond girl. She asked me what I was taking, and for some inexplicable reason, I told her they were sex pills. I thought she'd realise it was a joke, but curiously she asked if she could try one, so I gave her one. A little while later, I met her in the corridor. She told me the tablet was working because she felt a little bit 'funny'. I wasn't sure what she meant by 'funny', and I didn't have time to find out because I was late for my maths class. After that, I found it very difficult to concentrate on maths because I kept thinking about Sid. Why had she looked straight into my eyes when she said she felt a bit 'funny'. I couldn't help wondering if I'd missed an opportunity.

When I bumped into Sid again, she was back to normal, and the moment had passed.

At lunchtime, I had to go to the chemist with a prescription for my mum. I came back to college with twelve large purple pills in a white paper bag. I didn't know what the tablets were, but I told everyone they were big purple hearts, which were then used illegally as recreational drugs.

I forgot about the flippant remarks I'd made about drugs until a few days later when I bumped into Ags in the milk bar.

Ags was studying at the college, and we crossed paths occasionally. He was much taller than me. He looked very similar to Mick Jagger and had long hair below his shoulders. A few months earlier, he'd had a run-in with the college principal, who gave him the choice of a haircut or expulsion. Ags declined both options. The battle of wills that followed caused such a stir that the BBC got involved. They sent a team to interview Ags. The news and camera crew caught up with him in the park when Ags and I were walking back from town. That evening, I had a few minutes of fame when I appeared briefly on the evening news walking with Ags. The publicity for the college was so bad that the principal had to back down.

Back to the drugs! In the milk bar, Ags asked me if it was true that I was pushing drugs at the college. He was deadly serious. I told him that I'd given Sid a vitamin C pill and made up a story about my mum's purple prescription tablets just for a laugh.

Joke or not, if people were talking about it, I could get into serious trouble. After the embarrassment with Ags, the principal would be happy to expel someone to reassert his authority. If he thought I was pushing barbiturates and providing aphrodisiacs to young girls, that someone could easily be me.

If that happened, I'd have a lot of explaining to do at home. My dad would not be happy that I'd become a drug lord to supplement my

meagre finances. And to compound things, I'd implicated my poor innocent mother as my primary supply source.
Fortunately, nothing came of it, and I dropped any jokes about drugs from my repertoire.

Saturday 26 February, at about 8:30 in the evening, Erika and Mary came to my house to see what I was doing that evening. I said I was going to Marston club because the Fireflies were playing there.
I went to Marston on my scooter, and the girls got a lift later in Ken's mini. The dance hall was almost empty, which was sad because the Fireflies were brilliant as ever. After the dance, we went to the Blue Angel, where I spent most of the time fooling around with Erika and Mary.
The following morning my mum dragged me off to Mass, but I'd rather have stayed in bed. I only went because it kept my mum happy and stopped me from getting grief from my dad even though he was still in bed suffering from too much Watney's Red Barrel from the night before. My dad's mantra was always, "Don't do as I do. Do as I say".
There were some incentives to go to church, though. All the young girls attended in their Sunday best. If you were lucky and some girls took the seat in front of you, you could gaze at their backs and smell their perfume and freshly shampooed hair. You could study their bottoms pressing against their skirts when you were kneeling at the pew with your head lowered in prayer. My thoughts often wander from the path of righteousness. It was unadulterated, erotic voyeurism. Something I wouldn't share in the confessional.

In the evening I went to the Blue Angel. Erika, Mary and Vicky were there. There wasn't much going on. The music was too loud to have a conversation, so Erika and I walked down to the Green Man pub. We were both underage to drink, but the landlord didn't ask any questions. I bought a beer and a whiskey and lime for Erika, which I couldn't really afford, and we spent the next hour talking.

Back at the Blue Angel, the girls got a lift back to Brogborough with, Ugy and Gina, two boys from Flitwick. I followed on my Vespa. When they dropped the girls off at the shops, I took Erika to her house on the back of my scooter. Without a full license, that was illegal, but it was unlikely the cops would have been around Brogborough at that time on a Sunday night. If the cops had caught me, I'd have been done for drinking underage and carrying an unqualified passenger. My dad would have gone apeshit. Still, as Uncle Billy used to say. "You might as well be hung for a sheep as a lamb.

Later in the week, I walked to the shops with Erika and Vicky. Erika bought us each an apple. Vicky asked me quietly if I would take Erika to the pictures the following week. I said I couldn't because I was always short of cash or completely broke.

Curiously the following day, I received 20 pounds additional compensation for my accident in a registered letter from my solicitor. I was left with 16 pounds after paying off my family debts. I should have taken Erika to the pictures, but in truth, I was still hopelessly obsessed with Sylvia Mustard Coat.

On Saturday, although Bedford was much nearer, I went to Dunstable shopping for new clothes with my windfall. I bought a maroon blazer at Foster Brothers for 3 pounds 7 shillings.
While I stopped at the traffic light crossing on West Street and London Road, not entirely by coincidence, I saw Sylvia. She smiled at me, and I coolly responded with a nonchalant raised hand. Bloody hell, I did fancy her.
After lunch on Sunday, Erika gave me a haircut. She wasn't a hairdresser, but she did a good job. She cut my hair every few weeks and wouldn't take any money because I was invariably destitute.
That evening, eight of us went with Mac and Ken in their minis to the Green Man pub at Little Brickhill.
There wasn't much room for ten people in two minis. On the way home, Erika sat on my lap and asked if I didn't mind if she went to sleep.
That was fine by me, and we cuddled up. I was tempted to kiss her, but we were good friends, and I didn't want to spoil that. Also, I had this other preoccupation in Dunstable, which complicated the situation.

On Monday morning I told my mum I had a headache from too much studying, and I wasn't going to college. Basically, I was being lazy. Shortly after 1 o'clock my mum brought me lunch in bed.
By the evening, my headache had miraculously gone. John, Bill and I went on our scooters to the Civic Hall Monday dance. Before we left, I got the "too sick to go to college, but" lecture from my dad.

At the Civic, Sylvia Mustard Coat was sitting talking with a boy I didn't recognise. I didn't know if she was going with him or not. But to hell with it, I went and asked her to dance. She wasn't with the guy. She'd come to the dance by herself. After three dances I asked her if I could walk her home. I couldn't take her on the scooter because I was still a learner driver. After a long kissing session outside her house we made a date to meet at the California Ballroom on Friday night.

The dentist from hell

The following day I had an appointment with my Irish dentist because I needed two fillings. While he was injecting my top right molar the nurse came in and called him to the phone. After a few minutes he returned and drilled out and filled my top tooth.

After that, to my horror because he hadn't injected it, he started to drill out my bottom right molar. I tried to tell him, but he had the drill in my mouth. The drill hit the nerve, my hands clenched on the handles, and I tried to push myself out of the chair.

He was strong, and wrestled me back into the seat, kept his left arm pressed against my throat to fix me in position, and kept on drilling. For ten horrendous minutes I struggled to get out of the chair with him holding me down telling me not to be so stupid. Having me in a throat lock with a high-speed drill whizzing around in my mouth like a buzz-saw, he got the upper hand. By the time he'd plugged my tooth with amalgam, my shirt was stuck to the back of the chair with sweat.

I didn't know what the phone call was about, but he was certainly in a foul mood when he finally released me from the chair after the worst dental experience of my life. For all I know he may have been a relation of Mr Monaghan who'd phoned to tell him to give me the full treatment for the disruption I caused during his geography classes. Or he might have been a student of Ravens Bruck concentration camps Walter Sonntag. Either way I'd be finding a new dentist. To his credit, that filling lasted for fifty years before it fell out.

Back at college we were given a talk by Mr Swales, the employment officer.

It was getting close to the time we had to join the real world.

In the evening Erika and Mary came round to my house for a coffee. We had a good laugh but sadly most of the time I was thinking about Sylvia Mustard Coat.

On Friday, I met Sylvia in the California. I can't remember who was headlining there, but we had a good evening. She didn't look it, but she was two years older than me. She lived a short distance across the main road from the Cali, so I walked her home instead of taking her on the Vespa. With L plates front and back, I'd be sure to be stopped by the police, who were always at the junction after the dance.

After a kissing session on her doorstep, we made a date to meet at the Civic Hall Monday dance.

Sylvia Mustard Coat stood me up at the Civic Hall. Maybe she thought I was too immature; she may have been right. Or perhaps it was because I couldn't take her somewhere nice and romantic as I never had much money. Possibly I was just not her type. Either way, being attracted to girls was one thing. Understanding them was a totally different matter.

On Friday night at Fulbrook Youth club, someone said a lorry carrying oranges had overturned on the M1 near Brogborough. Bill, our friend Peter Humphries, no relation to Dina, and I went off on our scooters to investigate.

The accident was close to the railway station where the Ridgmont Road passed under the M1 bridge. This was the same place where one night, a few years later, a policeman stopped his panda car to check a vehicle at the entrance to a field. The suspect car was empty. The policeman entered the field with a flash-light and found a man scratching out a shallow grave to hide the body of a dead girl. The man, who I think was from Leighton Buzzard, had picked the girl up at the M1 Newport Pagnell services. Whatever transpired, he killed her and then tried to get rid of the body. But for the vigilance of a policeman going off duty, he may well have gotten away with it. As far as I know, that was the worst crime to occur around Brogborough. In comparison, riding two on a bike, scrumping Mrs Hobbs' apples or stealing railway detonators paled into insignificance.

Back to the oranges, we had to climb the bank and walk along the M1 for a short distance. The lorry was on its side on the hard shoulder. There were thousands of oranges scattered from boxes all down the bank. I got a box full, put it on my scooter's running board, and took it home.

Back at the youth club, Erika, Mary, and Vicky wanted to go to the old Hulcote church because it was supposed to be haunted. Ken offered to take them in his mini, so I followed on my scooter.

There wasn't much of a moon, and it was pretty dark when we parked on the country road just before Salford village. We walked through a sombre avenue of tall trees to the church, guided by Ken's torch. The tension was electric amongst the girls. Erika clung to me as we crossed the graveyard. The heavy nail-studded wooden door creaked open as Ken, and I leaned against it. Inside it was pitch black, so I borrowed Ken's torch and entered the church. I found a door and made my way up steps that led to the belfry. The stairway was filled with hanging, dusty cobwebs. When I got to the top, I couldn't help myself, and I heaved on the wheel of the headstock of one of the bells. When I let the wheel go, the mechanism swung back, and there was an almighty 'CLANG' as the ball on the clapper struck the inside of the bell. It was a stupid thing to do, the noise was deafening, but I still heard the scream from Mary, always the first to over-react, from below.

By the time I got back outside, the others had scattered. As Alistair MacLean put it, Fear is the key. Even in the darkness, the girls had found their way back to the car.

Enough excitement for one night, we departed before the cops arrived.

After college the following day, Buzz and I rode to the M1 to see if there were any oranges left. All the fruit had been squashed, and the whole area doused in diesel and set on fire. Swilling diesel fuel over the ground in preference to letting squashed oranges rot! It was a different world then.

Job Hunting

Back home, I began filling in the job application forms I'd received from Allan's, Skefco and AC Delco. Erika and Vicky came to the house and asked me to go down to the motorway to get some oranges. I told them they'd all been squashed and burned. It was a two-mile walk there and back, so I was amazed when they insisted, I go with them after what I'd told them. I should have carried on filling out my job application, but it was a lovely evening. How could I refuse the offer of a stroll with two pretty girls? Ken and my sister's friend Betty joined us despite my scepticism about our scavenging venture. Of course, it was a waste of time, and I really should have completed my job applications. In my defence, I was a seventeen-year-old boy. What would you expect me to do?

Then it was Friday again, dance night. At Fulbrook youth club, someone said the Who were playing at St Albans, so we decided to go there on our scooters. However, our friend Paul Rogers from Brogborough said he'd take us all in his car, so we piled in. The Who weren't playing at St Albans. It was the Birds. Not the American Byrd's of "Mr Tambourine Man" and "Turn! Turn! Turn!" fame. It was the English Birds with Ronnie Wood in the line-up, who went on to join the Faces and then the Rolling Stones. It cost six shillings to get in, but the place was packed, and you couldn't dance, so we left St Albans and went to Ampthill, where the Bow Street Runners were playing. Their drummer Mick Fleetwood had recently left the group. Nonetheless, it was a good night. They were a great R&B band that unfortunately disappeared into oblivion later that year.

By the time I got home, I was lamenting that I'd spent thirteen shillings and sixpence with little to show for it.

On Wednesday 23 March, at 10 o'clock in the evening, Buzz's mum died. Buzz was really upset, but he came to college anyway. I suppose it was better than staying at home.

Poor Mrs Burrell was a lovely lady, but she had never been in good health for the short time I'd known her. She had returned home from the hospital at the end of February. She had lung cancer. In those days, the only treatment was surgery, which was rarely successful. Mrs Burrell smoked a lot, and so did my mum and dad. Even Buzz and many kids at school smoked. When I was about five, my dad caught me puffing on one of his discarded roll-up butts. He rolled a big fat cigarette and made me smoke the whole thing. After that, I vomited violently and never touched a cigarette again.

In those days, smoking was considered a relaxing, stress-relieving, pleasant pass time. The medical fraternity was only just getting an inkling of the damage smoking did and not only to the lungs. Those findings were generally suppressed and countered by advertising and contradictory medical reports from the tobacco companies.

Apart from Peter Worthington's dad, who was really old and had throat cancer, Mrs Burrell was the first of my friends' parents whose death was smoking-related.
It was a sobering realisation that we were all destined for the graveyard.

On 25 March, Bill passed his scooter test. It was a surprise because he never told anyone he was taking it. That meant Bill, and Buzz and Malcolm Robinson who'd passed in the previous weeks, all had full licenses. Now, they could take anyone, especially girls, as passengers on the back of their scooters.
I was the odd one out, I failed my first attempt when I almost put the examiner in hospital during a surprise emergency stop. He leapt out from behind a parked car like a Japanese ninja. My only consolation was seeing him leap for his life back onto the pavement as I skidded towards him on the wet road. Still I had an appointment for a second attempt on 11 May, but that seemed a long way away.

That evening I went to the Friday dance at Parkside Hall Ampthill. The Mojos were playing. This was just before the group's first break up when Lewis Collins, later famous as 'Bodie' in the late 1970's TV series The Professionals, was the bass guitarist.
Melanie was there, and I finally went out with her. We made a date to meet in Wootton on the coming Sunday.

When I got up Saturday morning, Vicky and Erika were in the house. They'd come to see how my sister Ellen was because she was suffering from tonsillitis.

Ellen gave me six shillings to go into Bedford to pay five shillings at Stones for some clothes she'd bought.

Sunday morning, I went to church to atone for any sins I might perpetrate later in the day.

At 8:15 in the evening, I met Melanie at the bus stop, where she was returning from her weekend job in Bedford. Just up the road from the bus stop was a building site. The place wasn't fenced off, and there was no sign of any security, so we went in. The house under construction had walls and a roof but no doors or windows. Inside it was pretty dark, but there was enough dispersed light from a streetlamp to make our way in the gloom. We started kissing, standing up against a wall. It wasn't the most romantic of places, but we didn't have much choice.

Soon I was fumbling around in the dark to find the only condom I had with me. Everything was going well until disaster struck once again in our brief relationship.

Even in the height of passion, it was impossible not to have known what had happened. Melanie probably would not have realised, but there would be no concealing the disaster by the end.

For me, it was the difference between paddling the shoreline of the cold North Sea in wellington boots compared to strolling the water's edge of a tropical island, waves gently lapping my feet and my toes sinking into warm golden sand.

A young man's basic instinct is to think, what the hell and press on regardless. I must admit it did cross my mind. However, the constant lecturing of my Irish Catholic mother on the consequences of premarital sex sprang up like an unwanted weed in a beautiful flower garden. That, reinforced by articles I'd read in Rodney's porno mags on venereal disease and premature ejaculation, did it.

"Oh, shit," I groaned. "The rubber's split", and with chivalrous consideration, I withdrew. Fortunately, after the previous fiasco with the night watchman, Melanie took pity on me.

After tidying ourselves up, I walked her home. However, it seemed like fated Romeo and Juliet, our love affair was doomed, and we never arranged to meet again.

I often wonder about the reaction of the workers the following day on finding a discarded foil sachet, a torn sheath and a stained floor. I hope it didn't offend their sensibilities.

All I can say about that little episode is that I'd done the right thing, but no way was I going to confide in my mother and thank her for her guidance.

That's enough for now about chasing girls, dances, mods and scooters.

My mum had gone out and got a job to see me through college, and during the two years I was there, I should have been diligently pursuing my studies. However, that was the exact time of my adolescent development when responsible behaviour and raging hormones were in constant conflict. A time when parents didn't understand, your old man knew nothing, and the world owed you a living.

It didn't help that we were in the midst of the 1960's revolution of - sex, and drugs, and rock and roll.

Girls were a disposable commodity for puerile boys, as were boys to some girls. Dance halls were hunting grounds, and dancing was, and still is, the mating ritual. Strutting and prancing, fashion was the key.

Scooters and cheap petrol represented freedom. We were knights on chromed up steads immortal and indestructible. Or so we thought.

The spring of 1966 was crunch time. I had to pass my exams and get a job. I could probably flannel my mum, but my dad was a different matter. If the brickworks were good enough for him, it would do for me.

It was a rude awakening to find that time gone is not reclaimable. I had a few months to knuckle down and do some serious work.

We had to sit mocks to prepare for the actual exams. The pass mark for mocks was 50%. This was higher than the GCE requirement of 40% for a low pass. The college reimbursed one pound from the exam fee for each mock subject you passed. The reimbursement was made in cash which was a great incentive. You could surreptitiously pocket the money without your parents knowing.

The exams for real started in mid-May and ended in June. The clock was running.

I was taking Mathematics, Physics, Technical Drawing, Art, English, and Geography. I don't know why I signed up for geography, and I wasn't concerned about taking that exam either.

English was going to be a problem. Mr Harmer was a great teacher, but the English language was a mystery to me. I struggled with the grammar. I understood the basics like nouns, adjectives, verbs, and adverbs. However, subject, predicate, independent, and subordinate clauses; Subjective, objective, possessive, personal, reflexive, interrogative, demonstrative, indefinite pronouns, and all the subspecies of adjectives, verbs, and adverbs. Ask me about any of that, and I was lost.

At the time these mysteries were explained to me, I understood. However, ten minutes later I didn't have a clue.

Spelling was a disaster. I could stop while writing an essay just trying to figure out if I should write whether weather or wether to describe a climatic event. I even froze once because I couldn't remember how to spell the word 'who'. Dyslexia is something I've struggled with all my life.

Mathematics was different. It was logical with unbending rules. Some of the concepts might be difficult to grasp at first, but they were constants. You knew where you stood with mathematics.

I was sure I'd pass art. I'd always been good at sketching and painting. Mr Lawrence was a great art teacher. He'd been a reconstruction dentist during the war, putting people's jawlines back together after battle trauma. He'd been so fascinated by the human face's structure that he studied and became an art teacher after the war. Mr Lawrence was good fun in class, but he wasn't a man you'd want to piss off. He didn't suffer fools gladly.

Technical Drawing, I was a proficient draughtsman and didn't foresee any problems passing that exam.

The one that I was worried about was Physics. I'd been really good at Science at Fulbrook and had received the school prize, even beating my friend Peter Worthington, who I considered a whizz in the subject. The first year at college, we had a teacher called Mr Harper. He was fantastic, and I got excellent marks. However, Mr Harper had moved on, which was a terrible loss. His replacement could not control the class, and physics degenerated into a practical demonstration of Chaos Theory.

My study regime went something like this. If I had a free study period first thing in the morning, I wouldn't bother taking the Kingsbury school bus from the shops at ten past eight. I'd stay in bed until about nine, walk the one km to junction 13 of the M1 and hitch a lift south to junction 11. I'd catch the bus from the stop opposite Luton and Dunstable Hospital and generally be on time for my first class of the day.

If I had a free study period in the afternoon, I'd walk to Costin's coach station in West Street, catch the coach before it went to pick up the Kingsbury school kids, and be home before five.

Despite the urgency of the situation, I'd fit my homework and revision in between riding around on my scooter and going to dances and youth clubs.

In the midst of all this, on Wednesday, 11 May, just before the GCE examination period, I took my scooter driving test for the second

time in Bletchley. This time I passed. It was a good omen. However, you should never trust your life to superstition!
By the first week of June, the exams were over. We had to wait until August before we received the results.

My time at College was coming to an end. If I passed my O-Levels, A-Levels were out of the question. My parents couldn't support me for another year. I could imagine how that discussion would go down with my dad.
I wanted to be a draughtsman. I'd seen them in films working on projects for aeroplanes, ships, and spacecraft. Each morning, I saw myself leaving for work, smart in a suit and tie. The neighbours would be very impressed. I told my tech-drawing teacher and was amazed when he disagreed with me.
"No. Be an engineer. Engineers have the ideas, do the calculations, and work things out. They give their sketches to a draughtsman to make the drawings. No doubt you'd be a good draughtsman, but engineers innovate. They know what can be made and how to make it".
Uncharacteristically, I took his advice and decided to become an engineer.
Before the exams were over, I'd sent job applications to Allan's, Skefco, AC Delco, Vauxhall, Thermo-Plastics, Bagshaw's, Hunting Aircraft and more with little success.
Getting a job should have been easy in 1966. UK unemployment was less than 2%, and there were many local towns with

engineering firms looking for apprentices. The problem was no one seemed to want me.

The result of each application ended the same way.

"Dear Mr Butler. Thank you for your interest, but unfortunately, on this occasion, we cannot offer you a position with this company".

I wondered if the problem was because I was Irish Catholic or because I came from Brogborough and my dad was a labourer. The UK's first Race Relations Act of 1965 had been in force for a little over six months. The Act banned racial discrimination in public places but not discrimination in employment and the workplace.

I still remember as a child walking down Ladbrook Road in London with my dad and uncle, Tommy. There were signs in house windows with rooms for rent saying, 'No Blacks, No Dogs, No Irish.

I can't remember any racial problems in Brogborough. We were a mongrel bunch from across the world.

The British residents were mostly domestic migrants, Northerners, Welsh, Scottish, Northern Ireland and the colonies. Everyone just wanted to earn a living and live their life. That's not to say there weren't animosities, but that was human nature, Generally in Brogborough everyone got on.

My dad was OK being referred to as 'a Mick' or 'a Paddy' amongst his mates. It was a term of endearment. However, the derogatory use of those names didn't go down well with him. He was only about five foot eight, but you didn't want to upset him because he had no concept of size if you did. He was like a Kerry Blue where all dogs, Jack Russell to Dobermann, morphed to fit the same frame. He wasn't daft, if he did spark off, it was always swift and unexpected. If an aggressor was standing too close and towering over him, the knee went into the groin, followed by a head butt as they buckled. If they were standing off, it was a kick to the groin followed by a right hook to the jaw as they slumped forward. It was normally over fast, but if it turned into a scrap that was OK too.

The brickyard had hundreds of workers. A lot of them used the CIU Workingmen's Club at the weekend. Some were ex-soldiers. They may have harboured grudges about foreigners or were just still fighting their own demons. Either way, after a few drinks, the aggression came out, but it didn't occur often.

One Saturday night in the CIU club an ex-Scotts Guard made the mistake of disrespectfully calling my dad a 'thick Irish git' which ended up rather badly for him. The following day at work in the brickyard the ex-Guardsman accused my dad of taking advantage of him because he'd been drunk. My dad looked up at him and offered to meet him in the field next to the factory at lunchtime for another go, but the man declined the offer.

Being a white boy with a Bedfordshire accent I'd never experienced any discrimination, although I'd heard the term 'Bloody Irish' banded about often enough. However, in those days, you had to put your religion and your father's nationality in a job application, so I guess that information must have been important for someone.

The adult world was a difficult place. I'd had a big row again with my dad because I wouldn't take a job, he'd lined up for me in the brickyard. We were working-class, and he told me I was aiming too high above my station. Maybe I was aiming too high, but I was determined I would not work in the brickworks. Things were uncomfortable in the house over the issue. As usual, my mum had to calm things down. She understood because her great grandfather had been a civil engineer who was instrumental in the building of Rosslare Harbour.

I became very depressed.

Some people tell me that they put a lot of effort into achieving success in life. I don't dispute it. However, more people would be successful if it were just a question of talent, hard work, persistence and planning. Of course, it all depends on your definition of success; after all, there's no future in being a successful Kamikaze pilot.

Like many things in my life, I got my first real job through a happy accident. A chance meeting that only happened because I was in a particular place at a specific time. If this overlap had been displaced by a moment, I would be writing a different story or maybe no story at all.

It was a branch in a series of coincidental events more influential in my life than my meagre talent.

I was sitting in the student's common room feeling dejected when in breezed that little ray of sunshine, Sue Brown, looking for someone. Sue was a pretty girl with blondish hair, a beautiful fresh complexion, bright eyes, and an engaging smile that showed a centre gap between her top teeth. She was not tall, probably a little over five feet, and slightly plump. She was dating a bespectacled fellow called Oz. They made an odd couple; Oz was about six foot something, maybe an exaggeration, but next to Sue, he looked it. We all fancied Sue and thought she was far too good for Oz. Sue had a lot of outstanding qualities, not least of which was her sympathetic, friendly character and full bosom. She was training to be a nurse. I wondered what effect she might have on a poor male patient if she materialised from behind the screens, bursting out of her crisp white uniform, armed with a hypodermic.

She was perceptive, though. A good quality for a nurse.

"You look down, Bernie. What's wrong?" she asked.

"I am Sue. I've been looking for a job for two months, with no luck".

"What do you want to do?"

"I want to be an engineer Sue, but no one will give me a chance. It's probably because I live out in the sticks, and they think I'll have trouble getting to work. That seemed a less convoluted excuse.

My dad says he can get me a job in the brickworks, but I don't want that".

"Well, that's a coincidence," she replied. "My father has an engineering firm here in Dunstable. I'll speak to him".

Then, not finding who she was looking for, she was gone. The incident happened so fast that I didn't give it much thought. Lots of people offer help with the best intentions, but in the end, they have to deal with their own problems, get on with their lives and probably just forget.

I bumped into Sue a few days later. This time, it wasn't by accident because I was coming out of a maths class, far from the nursing section.

"Hi Bernie, I spoke to my father".

She handed me a piece of paper. Written on it was Headley's Engineering, Southfields Road. Interview with foreman Roland Wilson, and a date and time.
"Good luck," she said and off she went. I was astonished, I'm sure I thanked her, but to tell the truth, I can't remember.
On the day, I dressed as smart as my wardrobe would allow and presented myself at Headley's Engineering. I introduced myself to the receptionist, who pushed a button on an intercom and informed the foreman of my arrival. She indicated for me to sit. Interviews have always bothered me, probably due to the overproduction of adrenaline. Fortunately, other people often see qualities in me that I don't see myself.
Nevertheless, I sat like a man waiting to be called to the gallows. A few minutes later, the connecting door to the factory opened. The low rumble of machines increased significantly as the foreman, Roe Wilson, entered the office. He was an average-sized man dressed in a white knee-length work coat with several pens and a propelling pencil in his top pocket. I have always had problems estimating peoples' ages, but I guess he was probably in his early thirties with thin grey-blond hair hinting at a progression to premature baldness. His face had a fading tan, and his nose looked a little raw from too much sun, probably from a recent holiday in a more exotic clime than Dunstable. His eyes were narrow, pale in colour, but bright and penetrating.
We left the office and made our way through an area where a few young girls were making flat-pack cardboard boxes. We entered a long workshop that housed a small number of lathes, milling

machines and a row of pillar drills. There were no workers here, but from the double doors at the end of the room, the noise of other machines could be heard running somewhere in the near vicinity. The place had an oily smell, not unpleasant, but something I'd not experienced before. At one end, there was a flight of stairs to a cubicle with a large window that overlooked the workshop. We went up the stairs and into what appeared to be an abandoned office. He sat down and offered me a seat on the opposite side of a desk. I got the impression that the last thing he wanted to do was interview someone whose only apparent qualification was being the friend of the boss's daughter. To his credit, he did not seem concerned about my family background or whether my father was an Irish insurgent bent on overthrowing the British Government.

He went straight to work, asking me questions like, what is Pythagoras's theorem, what was the value of Pi, how do you divide a circle into six equal parts, how do you use log tables to multiply, divide and find square roots (no calculators then). It seemed I had frustrated his every move to get me out of the factory. Now, believe me, every interviewer has the killer question for times like this, it is something dear to them, and your answer will be the difference between success and failure. Roe Wilson had his killer question up his sleeve ready.

"Alright, what's the sine of 30 degrees?" he said like a cobra striking without warning.

"Naught point five." I parried, then the coup de grace "And the cosine is naught point eight six six".

He was beaten, and that's how I started on my journey to becoming an engineer.
Don't ask why I carry such pieces of information in my head. I have no clue.
You just never know when some inconsequential piece of knowledge will come in handy.

My college time came to an end in the summer of 1966. Serendipity, in the form of a chance meeting with Sue Brown, meant I would not be joining the ranks of the unemployed. My mum and dad had to take time off work to come to Headley's Engineering in Dunstable to sign my apprenticeship papers. The indenture paper was like a mediaeval document written on thick tan coloured paper that looked like parchment. The document was scattered with shiny embossed red discs reminiscent of old wax seals. I was now legally bound to Headley's for four years of servitude. My starting pay was £3 – 10 shillings a week, rising incrementally each year to £5 – 15 shillings in my fourth and final year. With that sort of money, I would still need the support of my parents until I finished my training and became a skilled man. My dad may not have been too happy about this. However, he did have the satisfaction of telling his mates that his son was training to become an engineer.
For my 'O' Levels, I passed Art, Pure Mathematics and Technical Drawing. I failed English which I expected. I never took Geography, which I thought at the time was of no use to me.

The worst thing was I failed physics. I'd always been top in Science at school, and I received the school prize for the subject. I loved physics, but I'd wasted too much time messing around in class and not spending enough time studying.

Nevertheless, I had enough 'O' Levels to get onto the Technicians course, which was above the Craft Apprentices. However, I was really disappointed with myself, and I decided that I wouldn't get overconfident again. In the future, I would stop arsing around and take things seriously. I guess I was growing up.

In September, I would enter the real world, working full time in a factory at Headley's Engineering, Southfields Road in Dunstable.

Chapter 10

The life of an apprentice

Welcome to Headley's Engineering.

In September 1966, Thanks to that accidental meeting at college, I started my apprenticeship in precision engineering at Sue Brown's father's factory in Dunstable. I was fortunate to have a job with day release at college once a week. I was also happy I didn't have to go to work in the brickworks in Brogborough, even though it was only a few minutes' walk from my home.

When I finished work at Headley's on my first day, I found a pair of women's frilly pink knickers tied to the back of my scooter. The knickers had a note pinned to them saying - They're still warm.

I assumed this was a welcome from the girls who worked in the factory's section making cardboard boxes. No one owned up to the prank, and I never asked. I did not find out who they belonged to, but I kept the undergarment in the side bubble of my scooter and used it to polish the chrome work. It was a very erotic duster.

Headley's was a typical World War Two factory. There was still an old air-raid shelter in the car park at the back of the building. There was a canteen where you could buy filled bread rolls at morning tea break and a hot meal at lunchtime. I could not afford lunch on my wages, so my mum made me sandwiches to take to work. Later, the mother of one of the other apprentices, Robin Beagarie, insisted that I go for lunch every Friday at her house. At least I got one hot meal in the week. That was great, especially when Mrs. Beagarie cooked fish, chips and peas. Dessert was followed by a cup of tea and one of Mrs. B's Embassy cigarettes. This was after I foolishly started smoking.

Occasionally, I would go to a Chinese restaurant for lunch on my college day. This restaurant was near the corner of West Street and London Road, opposite Woolworth. There you could get a three-course meal for 3s/6p.

Clocking in and out of the factory and having my pay docked if I were a few minutes late was a far cry from the freewheeling life I had had as a student. There was no more skiving off or staying in bed when I felt like it. This was the working world of eight to five with an hour for lunch and a couple of short tea breaks.

One ray of sunshine in this austere world was that I had one day off work each week to go to Technical College. The same Dunstable College of Further Education where I recently squandered my education.

This time I promised myself, hormones permitting, I would take full advantage of the opportunities that came my way.

Filing bloody blocks

Another account of how, unplanned, I blindly stumbled into an opportunity, not of my making.

In September 1966, as a Headley's apprentice, I was required to enrol with the engineering department of Dunstable College of Further Education for day release and evening classes.

At enrolment, I was given two options. Option one was the City and Guilds craft course; Option 2 was the Technician's course. As I already had GCE O Levels in Mathematics and Technical drawing, I was advised my best choice would be the Technician's course. It was more prestigious than the craft course, so I enrolled as a technician.

On the first day, I went to the engineering department and was sent to the main workshop. This place was full of lathes, milling machines, and workbenches. Each bench had a metalworking vice, and an assortment of hand tools fixed to a backboard, with the shape of each tool outlined and marked in red on a white background. The whole place smelled of mystic water-soluble cutting oil. After an introduction to the powerful machines, we were subjected to a safety lecture where the instructor pointedly informed us:

"Remember! The day you cut your finger with one of these tools is the same day you almost lost your hand".

We were told that turning on a lathe with the chuck key still in the chuck just to see how far the key travelled across the workshop was not recommended.

We were instructed NOT to wear ties when working on the machines. It didn't take a lot of imagination to picture a tie wrapped around the spindle of a whirling lathe with the owner's head dragged into the spinning chuck. Gross! Like the climax of a scene from the 'Pit and the Pendulum' except much faster without a tense build-up.

We were told to keep our shirt cuffs buttoned and no finger rings or hanging medallions. These were all potential sources of decapitation, amputation and other forms of mutilation.

Next, we had the horror stories about the misuse of pressurised air lines, the thin braided plastic tubes with trigger nozzles that hung down from the workshop's ceiling. These tubes delivered 80 pounds per square inch of compressed air for cleaning metal shavings, cutting fluids, and dust from the machines and workpieces.

Air lines are found in every engineering factory. It's not uncommon to see apprentices, even experienced skilled workers, misusing them. They would fool around and spray each other with the compressed air or blow the air on themselves to clean up before going off shift.

It all looked pretty harmless, but all this was also NOT recommended. We were told that compressed air in the mouth could rupture the lungs; directed into the navel, it could inflate and rupture the intestines even through clothing. As little as 12 pounds of pressure could blow an eye out of its socket or disintegrate an eardrum. If directed onto the skin, it could cause bubble embolisms in the bloodstream, resulting in coma, paralysis, heart failure, and death. It could strip a body part of its flesh, leaving naked, bloody bone. In fact, it was used for precisely that purpose in meat processing factories. The list went on. Playfully spraying air up someone's anus just didn't bear thinking about. These innocuous tubes took on the appearance of green mambas hanging down, waiting to ambush unsuspecting passing prey. The workshop was a primordial jungle full of countless unseen terrors.

However, the most serious workshop jeopardy, the one with fatal results, was kept until last. Anyone caught fabricating metal discs the size of a sixpenny piece to fit the student union's common room coffee machine would be instantly expelled from college.

Suitably instilled with a terror of our new environment, we were each assigned a workbench. We were given a rough-cut lump of iron and a drawing of a rectangular block with the dimensions: seventy-five by fifty by twenty-five millimetres. Using only a file, a metal set square, a scribing tool, a micrometer and the vice, we had to make a block to the dimensions shown on the drawing. The block had to have perfect right-angled sides with zero point two of a millimetre dimensional tolerance.

I started this task enthusiastically, but after fifteen minutes of trying to produce just one flat, straight-edged, right-angled corner, my enthusiasm waned. With time slipping away, iron filings mounting on the workbench like sands in an hourglass and the muscles in my arms beginning to ache, I wondered why I'd ever considered becoming an engineer. The other techs were happily engaged in whittling away their blocks while I was thinking about how I would make it through the next hour until the lesson ended. Was this a test of endurance? More likely, the instructor wanted to know what he was letting himself in for with this new batch of Isambard Kingdom Brunel hopefuls. Either way, I wasn't happy with my new career path.

While I was descending into a Slew of Despond, an officious looking man in a grey suit carrying a clipboard entered the workshop. The man spoke to the instructor standing close to the door on the other side of the room. I couldn't hear what was being said over the rasping of files on metal, but I stopped my endeavours to observe this welcome distraction. The suit drew the instructor's attention to something on the clipboard. The instructor, frowning slightly, read pensively, scratching his chin with the tips of his fingers. After reading, he scanned the workshop, presumably looking for whoever was shown on the paper. Eventually, he pointed an accusing finger in my direction. I looked to my left and right, but to my dismay, I stood alone. The suit moved menacingly towards me. It seemed that I was responsible for some serious transgression. He stood in front of me and consulted the clipboard.

"Bernard James Butler", he inquired.

"Yes," I replied sheepishly. Before I could ask what, I was being accused of, he continued.

"You failed O level Physics last year". It was a damning statement, but I couldn't deny it, and my best subject too.

"Yes, but I can explain". I had no idea this was such a serious offence.

"Never mind that. You have maths and tech drawing, don't you?".

"Yes".

"Would you be prepared to do evening classes and retake physics?".

"I would". It seemed like the only response open to me.

"If that is the case, you can join the Ordinary National Certificate (ONC) Engineering course today. Would you like to do that?".

"Today, er yes" – anything to get out of this workshop and away from filing this bloody block -.

"Then come with me".

I put my work coat on the bench and picked up my satchel. The rasping stopped; the techs looked up as I was led away with the sure knowledge that the first coffee machine sixpenny piece filer had been apprehended.

I followed the grey suit out into the late morning sunshine. As we walked over to the main building, the man explained the circumstances of my deliverance. The college was running a new trial ONC Engineering course.

The new course was an experiment. The administration intended to mix mechanical and electrical engineering subjects together. They believed that electronics was the future and that mechanical engineers, who traditionally steered away from the mysteries of electricity, should prepare to meet that future. Unfortunately, the bulk of the mechanical engineers in the college didn't share that view. They only got two volunteers to sign on, but three students were needed to get the course approved. While scraping the bottom of the barrel they'd found me. It was a dubious honour, but it was one I was happy to accept.

The joy of Kirchhoff's Network Theory

We went to a classroom on the third floor of the main building. There were no desks in the room, just five lab benches set out one behind the other. The benches had polished hardwood tops, approximately three feet wide and nine feet long, almost the room's width. There was a three-foot clear walkway on each side of the benches to allow the lecturer to prowl the room. Each bench had Bunsen burner gas outlets at their back edge facing the podium and blackboard area at the front of the class. I squirmed as I recognised this was the same room Buzz and I had stolen a polythene bag full of gas and been chased down the corridor by Mr S, the physics teacher.

The bench-tops were about three feet above floor level. This allowed students to stand while conducting experiments. Each bench had five high stools for students to sit and write up their experimental results or take notes during lectures. My compliance with the man in grey must have been anticipated because the lesson was already underway. The other two volunteers were perched on stools on the front bench listening intently. The man in the grey suit introduced me to the lecturer, who fortunately had not previously made my acquaintance. He then excused himself, telling me to visit the front office after lunch to re-register for the ONC course. I nodded to the lecturer, who obviously expected me and took my place on a stool with the other two students.

Kirchhoff's Network Theory was written in chalk at the top of the blackboard that took up most of the wall.

In the middle of the board was an electrical diagram showing an interconnected mesh of resistors and batteries, much more complicated than anything I had encountered in our physics lessons.

Two statements had been written on the left of the diagram:

1. The total current flowing towards a junction equals the total current flowing away from that junction. That is to say, the algebraic sum of the currents flowing into a junction is zero, and

2. In a closed circuit, the sum of the products of the currents and the resistance of each part of the circuit is equal to the resultant e.m.f. in the circuit.

On the board's right, the lecturer was developing some simultaneous equations. My first reaction was panic. This looked like an impossible task. Then, something extraordinary happened. A revelation.

Concentrating on the chalked-up letters and numbers, the elegance of what was being developed on the board became clear. The lecturer laid out a complex set of equations in logical numbered steps. As the answers began to emerge, I was captivated. I can't explain what happened. It may have been a reaction to the mind-numbing boredom of block filing or being in the room with two strangers and a teacher with no other distractions. Or, it might have been a confluence of what I had learned to date, a sort of enlightenment. Whatever the reason, fate had once again intervened. I had a light bulb in my head moment, and from that day for the next four years, I would lead a double life. One life was the daily chore of working in a factory and being trained to operate as a cog in the industrial machine. The other life took me into the mysterious world of Newton's calculus and the secret life of the electron. My training as an engineering ninja had begun.

I re-registered for the ONC course in Mathematics, Applied Mechanics, Engineering Drawing and Electrical Engineering, and I signed up for physics evening classes.

Over the next two years, as well as mechanical engineering, I learned about electromagnetic waves, Maxwell's equations, the permeability of free space, dialectics, resonant frequency, cathode rays, diodes, valves and transistors.

Against all odds, fate had intervened and put me on a path that would define my future. I didn't plan it. I had nothing to do with it. Sometimes you just have to go along with the puppeteer. Things looked good, but there was a dark cloud of my own making looming on the horizon.

Back in the factory

The first year of my apprenticeship was the worst. I wasn't allowed to operate any lathes, mills, and grinding machines for the first few months. I had to stand next to a turner named Eric McMinn and watch everything he did on the big Colchester lathe. Eric was a patient man. He tolerated and answered my incessant questions. Occasionally, once he was sure I was responsible enough, he let me carry out some of the more straightforward tasks on the lathe.

Erik and I talked a lot about different things to pass the time. However, all I can remember about those conversations is that Eric was divorced. He told me that he left work early one day because he wasn't feeling well. When he got home, he found his wife in bed with another man. That was the end of Erik's marriage. I felt sorry for Erik; he was a nice man and didn't deserve that. But then, what did I know? It was none of my business.

After that, I'd often have to sit in an isolated part of the factory, cutting endless discs from mild steel bars on a band saw. This was a mind-numbing task. You couldn't sit by the saw and read a book,

or you would get into trouble with the foreman or charge-hand who were always on the prowl.
There was one saving grace. The factory still had a Tannoy system that used to play the radio programme Music While You Work to entertain the workers during the dark days of World War Two. Now it played BBC's Light Programme and, thankfully, pop music on Radio One after the first of September 1967.
Gradually, work became more interesting. After shadowing various skilled men on different machines, I eventually learned to operate capstan lathes, centre lathes, milling machines and grinders. First, I learned to machine simple cylinders and blocks and drilled precision holes in plates. Gradually, I became a competent machinist, and the jobs became more complicated and interesting. However, I hated standing at a machine all day in a factory.

On Smoking

Starting smoking was the stupidest thing I did in my life. Correction, it was one of the stupidest things I did; there were others of some merit.
When I was five years old, my dad caught me smoking one of his discarded roll-ups. He sat me down, rolled a fat cigarette and made me smoke it down to a butt. He didn't think I'd do it, but I did. When I finished it, my eyes were streaming, I was choking, and I threw up. From that day, through school until my early teens, I never touched another cigarette.

However, when I was nearly eighteen, all that changed. It may have been partly to relieve the boredom of being stuck in a factory all day. However, advertising was undoubtedly the primary influence in that folly. There were a lot of cigarette advertisements in the media, on billboards and on TV. They were shown before films and during intermissions in cinemas. Footballers would light up for a rejuvenating puff at half-time. Athletic hikers would stop for a refreshing drag by crystal clear streams. Some ads even showed people smoking while water skiing.

These ads never presented pulmonary embolisms, deep vein thrombosis, heart disease, and lung cancer as smoking benefits. No, smoking was a relaxing, healthy pastime to be enjoyed by everyone.

Cinemas had ashtrays in them. It used to amaze me how a flickering cone of light could make it from the projection room through clouds of smoke and still make an image on the screen.

One of my dad's workmates gave him the Sunday Telegraph supplement every week. The Telegraph magazine was a high-quality colour production with many well-written articles on current affairs, history, science, and the arts. My dad was a Daily Mirror man; he was also an avid reader, so he always brought the magazine home. I found it fascinating reading too.

There was one ad that appeared every week. For some obscure reason, this ad always grabbed my attention. It was a full-page colour spread for 'Three Castles' cigarettes. It showed a green pack of cigarettes with a lovely picture on the front. In the bottom right corner of the cigarette pack, there was a wooden crate on a dock marked WD & HO Wills. Bristol. On top of the crate with his legs outstretched and his back against a wall sat a very relaxed looking sailor, arms folded, puffing on a cigarette. In front of the sailor were stacked three large wooden barrels forming a triangle presumably filled with tobacco. On the round face of each cask in gold was a symbol showing three castles. An old sailing ship could be seen behind the barrels tied to the dock. The picture presented a fascinatingly serene scene for a packet of cigarettes.

One Friday evening, after receiving the little brown envelope that contained my wages of about three-pound notes and some loose change, I walked into the newsagents in the quadrant in Dunstable. I scanned the shelves and bought a pack of Wills' Three Castles' and a box of matches.

When I got home, I went to my bedroom. I sat on my bed in the same position as the sailor on the box, legs outstretched, back against the wall. I removed one of the cigarettes from the green flat pack, popped it between my lips and lit up. I had a little choke for the first couple of puffs, but I persisted.

After a while, I took the smoke into my lungs and boy did it give me a buzz. It was a real soothing experience after a frustrating day at work.

A little over four shillings a pack was a big chunk out of my apprenticeship pay. I'd smoke one, occasionally two cigarettes a day, always by myself, to relax without being disturbed. It was a very enjoyable experience.

After a while, I started experimenting with other brands. 'Passing Clouds' was another Wills product. They were a little more expensive, but they came in a beautiful flip top pink flat pack of two rows of ten. The pack's centre showed a small square coloured picture of a cavalier relaxed in a high-backed chair blowing out a cloud of smoke. These cigarettes were even more sophisticated because, unlike other cigarettes, instead of being round, they were oval shaped. Very cool.

I figured that as I only smoked one pack a week, I might as well buy the best. I tried Gold Flake, Capstan Full Strength, Dunhill International, St Moritz, Rothmans, and 555 State express. I also tested the more obscure foreign, or at least foreign sounding brands such as Sobranie Black Russian, Sobranie Cocktail, Du Maurier, Gauloises, Gitanes and Disque Bleu. I tried American cigarettes popular in the UK like Pall Mall, Camel, and Lucky Strike. For a long time, I kept to just one pack of twenty cigarettes a week. However, smoking is a progressive addiction. After about six months, I smoked every day: I didn't smoke that many, maybe three or four a day, but every day. Eventually, I started rolling my own because I couldn't afford tailor-made on my wage. My mum helped out and often bought me a pack of ten Woodbines or a half-ounce pack of Old Holborn or Golden Virginia, which I could stretch out for a week. If I were desperate, I could bum a Players Weights or a roll-up from my dad. Uncle Billy was always good for a Capstan Full Strength. After lunch at Robin's house on Fridays, Mrs Beagarie would treat us to an Embassy tipped with our cup of tea. If I could have carried on with just three cigarettes a day, I would probably still smoke. However, it doesn't work like that. When I finished my apprenticeship and earned more money, sometimes I smoked a twenty pack a day. I often tried giving up, but my resolve never lasted for long. Finally, in 1982, I managed to quit altogether. Just as hard was quitting Nicorette gum. I spent more on nicotine replacement chewing gum than I'd been spending on cigarettes.

On 1 March 1967, the double A-side single "Strawberry Fields Forever" and "Penny Lane" went to number 2 on the UK charts. The single didn't get to number one because, as a double A-side single, each side took half the sales. Even with overall higher sales, the Beatles stayed at number 2 behind Engelbert Humperdinck's "Release Me".

Bloody Engelbert, can you believe that!

Still, I couldn't be too vocal because Engelbert was Mrs Beagarie's favourite, and she was kind enough to give me lunch every Friday.

The songs were different from anything the group had done before and because they didn't make number 1, the UK press predicted the immediate demise of the Beatles. What a load of tossers.

The songs were nothing like anything the Beatles had released before.

They were nothing like anyone had released before. They were brilliant, and little did we know what was coming next.

After a lifetime, I still have old friends from my childhood in Brogborough. We're scattered around the world now, but we get to see each other surprisingly often. On a few occasions, we've all been in the UK at the same time. Then we managed to get together for a reunion. I have known these friends forever. They have always been in my life. However, there is only one I can clearly remember meeting for the first time. I must have been about four years old, and I was sitting on the front step of our house, 32 Highfield Crescent. It was a bright warm day, possibly in the late spring or summer. Directly across the street at number 25, a little girl was sitting on her doorstep in the sunshine. I'd never seen this little girl before. Her family must have only recently moved onto the estate. I decided to take a closer look, so I walked across the road and up the path to her house. I sat on the low wall that separated the neighbour's path from hers. I said hello, and she smiled at me. She was pretty with tight blond curls like Shirley Temple. An attractive lady with a friendly face came to the door. The lady said hello to me, and in an unusual accent told the girl she had to go in for her lunch. That was the first time I met Erika from the Polish family that lived across the street.

Since then, we have always been friends. That is why what happened later was so surprising. Or maybe it wasn't.

I had a complicated relationship with various girls until after I started my apprenticeship. It must have been the autumn of 1966, sometime around the end of October or early November. It was probably a Saturday or Sunday because it was late afternoon and still light when a group of us from the estate took a stroll along the Salford road. The weather was mild for the time of year. Shortly before sunset, we started to make our way back home. Erika and I were lagging behind the rest, deep in conversation. The two of us always seemed to end up together when we were out with our friends. Then the strangest thing happened.

Without a word, in the fading light with the others well ahead of us, we stopped, wrapped our arms around each other and kissed. It must have been building for some time. Then suddenly, we moved from being just good friends to being in love. I'm sure many people saw this coming for a long time, but it came as a surprise to me. I guess I was always preoccupied or just slow.

So began a three-year love affair. Loving, turbulent, painful but always exciting and full of little adventures. We were two kids from Brogborough with a dormant desire for greater things. In that, she was and remains a special friend.

For a while, I was the Mod with the smart, well dressed, beautiful girl on the back of my scooter. Erika and I were the epitome of Mod culture.

Then disaster. The clutch on my Vespa broke. I can't remember where it happened. Possibly it was one of those painful events in life that the ego erases. That would have been the case if I were all dressed up in my good gear and had to push the bloody machine for miles home. An embarrassment too great for any self-respecting Mod to bear.

I couldn't afford to get the clutch repaired on my apprentice wages. I was now a Mod without a scooter. On the bright side, I still had the girl.

The most pressing problem was that I now had a 32-mile daily round trip to work. I had no vehicle to get me there and back and no practical alternative public transport.

Fortunately, Junction 13 of the M1 motorway was a little over half a mile from my house, a ten-minute walk. For the next three and a quarter years, wind, sleet, snow, rain or sunshine every morning, I thumbed a lift up the motorway to Luton. I caught the bus from the stop close to junction 11 to the Quadrant in Dunstable and then walked a mile up London Road to Headley's factory in Southfields Road. After work, I made the exact reverse journey to get home. Sometimes, in the evening, if the guys weren't working overtime, I'd get a lift to the motorway from someone in the factory who lived in Luton.

Getting to work in the mornings generally wasn't a problem. Before too long, I had regular lifts with people who travelled to work in Luton. Getting home in the evenings could be a real bitch, though. I still had a large group of regular lifts, but often they had already gone home before I got to the motorway. Bad weather nights with rain, fog or snow were the worst. There were times when I waited four or five hours, freezing cold and soaking wet, before someone took pity on me and gave me a lift. My mum would be distraught on those occasions when I finally walked into the house.

Some mornings when the weather was foul, I'd be drenched before I got to the motorway. My feet would be soaked because I had holes in the soles of my working shoes, and I couldn't afford to buy new ones.

Sometimes, on clear, bright mornings during those hard days, I'd look up to see a long contrail with a silver glint at its tip travelling high up east to west against a clear blue sky. The early morning London to New York flight, and I'd say to myself.

"I'll be on that one day" I meant it; I really did, and I'd sing to myself, Eight Miles High by the Byrds. One day I'd take that big silver bird to America.

On the bright side, as Otis Redding put it.

I've got sunshine on a cloudy day.

When it's cold outside, I've got the month of May.

I guess you'd say, what can make me feel this way?"

My girl, my girl, my girl. Talkin' 'bout my girl.

Erika was the light of my life.

That wasn't the only time that music got me through stormy seas.

The soldier's return

The most eventful things in life can happen by chance.

It was early 1967. I'd walked up to Brogborough from the M1 after hitching a lift from work in Dunstable. I'd passed the first few houses on Highfield Crescent when someone shouted, 'Bernard'.

When I looked around, Ray Papworth was on the front steps of his parents' house. I hadn't seen Ray since 1962 when he'd left Grammar school. At fifteen and a half, he'd gone off to join the British Army as a Junior Leader. We'd known each other since we were kids, often up to no good with his cousin Roger. I was a few years younger than them, and I tagged along because I didn't know better. They tolerated me because I was gullible, small, and could get into places they couldn't, like small windows in Army Cadet huts.

Ray had been a daredevil when we were kids. I remembered the time when he almost lost his leg and his life going down old Brogborough hill on a foot-steered, plank, and pram wheeled trolley. That old hill is long gone. Nestled between the new A421 and the Bedford road, it is now overgrown and hidden by trees. In the old days, it was a formidable barrier with its steep slope that Lorries had to change into first gear to climb.

But Ray wasn't all gung-ho. He taught me to play chess on the front step of my house shortly before he left for Harrogate and the army.

I went back, and we sat on his garden wall in the evening sun and talked. He told me he finished his training in 1965 and was posted to Germany, but he wasn't doing the type of soldiering he'd joined the army for. A friend told him about a unit he might be interested in joining. He wrote out an application, but his Officer in Command rejected it. The next application he posted directly. This got him into trouble because the army likes things to go through the proper channels. Nevertheless, in April 1966, he was assigned to 22 SAS Signals Troop Hereford on 3 months' probation.

After that, every time Ray came up to see his parents, we'd go out drinking. I learned a lot about the tough world he inhabited. Not everything, just snippets. There were a lot of grey areas that were never talked about.

To tell the truth, on that day when we reconnected, I'd never heard of the SAS. Not many civilians had. However, all that changed on 5 May 1980 when the SAS spectacularly emerged from the shadows on live TV to break the Iranian Embassy siege in South Kensington. By then, I'd been enlightened. I'd already had a beer at the Sergeants' Mess. It was there I saw the plaque from the USA's Delta Force thanking 22 SAS for their training.

Also, once I was invited by Ray to the New Year's Eve curry dinner at Bradbury Lines, Hereford. I'm not bragging, it's just I'm fortunate and it's true. Well maybe I am bragging. Why not?

A rumble at Brogborough club

The telling of the following incident requires some background information.

We used to have regular Saturday night dances at Brogborough club. These dances were mainly attended by teenagers and a little older because they always had a local rock band playing. Generally, they were fun, a gathering of friends from around the area. Except on nights when the Flitwick Rockers had nothing better to do. Flitwick was a village with a big motorbike community about seven miles away. Like most folks individually, they were alright. I got on well with some of them. However, when they arrived en masse, you could count on trouble. Us Brogborough boys were a pretty easy-going lot, so when the Flitwick Rockers came, it was like a hoard of Vikings descending on Lindisfarne. More times than not, a fight broke out. Even if it didn't, their numbers alone were intimidating, and the resulting tensions spoilt the evening.

Like the Philistines, the Flitwick boys had their own Goliath in the form of a guy called Arnold. Arnold was built like the proverbial 'brick shit house'. We referred to him as Bull Neck, but not to his face for obvious reasons. Whenever they turned up, the Flitwick lot ruined the dance.

It was one evening, sometime in the spring of 1967. Mary Irvine, her boyfriend John Carol, Erika and I were standing in the small entrance cubicle that led from the car park to the dance hall. The small booth was meant for a ticket collector if there was a paid event. The dance was free, so the cubicle was empty except for us four. I don't remember the exact date, but we'd just returned from the wedding reception of our friends Paddy Clifford and Dorothea(Dot) Bjeletić. The dance hall was crammed full, so we were debating whether to go in or not. Three Flitwick boys arrived and stood talking loudly on the car park side of the cubicle. They knew we were inside, but they kept opening the double doors and letting them swing back into the booth. When we complained, they swung the doors harder until one of the doors hit Mary.

With the hall full of their mates, they were just looking to start a fight. Like being confronted by cyborgs, "resistance was futile", so we decided to go home. As we left the cubicle, the three big guys outside jostled and shouted abuse after us before going into the dance.

I'm no warrior; I'm not built for it. I prefer to talk my way out of tricky situations. However, I snapped and turned to go back into the dance hall on that occasion. It was stupid, but then these things happen.

A friend, Nicky Pottle, came out of the club's main entrance and read the situation immediately. He bundled me up the path and across the road and told me to go home. As I followed the others up the street, a volcano started building inside me. By the time I reached my house, I was ready to explode. I'd never experienced anything like it before. I asked Erika to go home and waited for my dad, who was returning after taking the dog for a walk up the street. As soon as my dad saw me, he knew there was a problem.

"What's wrong?" he asked.

"It's that Flitwick lot." I replied, "They spoil everything. I'm just fed up with it."

"Do you want to do something about it?"

"Yes. I do" I couldn't believe I'd said it, not to my dad anyway. There was only one outcome now.

"Wait here while I put the dog in the house," he said calmly.

Like the Earp brothers on their way to the OK Corral, the two of us marched back down the street to the club.

We walked through the swing doors and stood surveying the dance hall. Johnny Irvine, the club manager, was behind the bar at the far end of the room serving drinks. Straight away, he knew something was up. The ex-Royal Marine Commando strode over to see what was brewing.

"What's the problem, Jim?" he asked my dad, who referred him to me.

I pointed to the gang of three standing in the middle of the dance floor.

"They bloody swung the door and hit Mary with it," I told him. Irvine was Mary's uncle or cousin; I can't remember which. That was enough. He jabbed his arm out in their direction with a spread thumb and two fingers indicating three. When he got their attention, he turned his hand palm up and beckoned them over. It was an instruction, not a request. They came over with their mates moving in behind them.

When they got to him, Irvine asked me. "Are these the ones?"

I nodded, and he gestured to dad and me... "Take them outside, Jim. I'll make sure this lot don't bother you."

Irvine stood square in the doorway, arms folded, facing down the mob.

I'm not an aggressive person. I'd rather walk or talk my way out of trouble. What happened next was totally out of character.

As we stepped into the car park, I looked sideways at the three now on our right side. They were all bigger than my dad and me. The smaller of the three was almost at my shoulder. He had a smirk on his face, as did his two mates. Why not? There were three of them and their mates.

I can't explain what happened next. There must have been a thought process, but it was too fast to register. Maybe it was some fight or flight, auto survival response. Either way, it was out of my control. I turned sideways and whacked my fist into the guy's jaw as hard as possible. He went down. At that moment, my dad came past me. He punched the next guy in the solar plexus as hard as a steam hammer. My dad floored him with head butt right on the nose as he crumpled.

Dad then stepped in front of the next bloke and looked up at him.

I thought - Oh, no, dad. He's just too big.

Then the strangest thing happened. The giant towering over my dad ran across the car park and locked himself in a car. Like a pit bull trying to get to him, my dad followed.

Irvine did his job. No one came out through the door. However, people started falling out of the windows of the dance hall onto the gravel of the car park.

A youth ran over to my dad, who was still trying to get to the giant in the car and punched him in the back of his head. My dad turned, they stared at each other for a moment, then my dad kicked him in the crotch, and he crumpled to the floor. In a matter of seconds, my dad had disposed of three blokes. No one bothered him after that.

Then I staggered back from a punch in the face. My opponent was back on his feet, and he was really pissed off with me. We traded punches around the car park like a couple of cavemen whack, whack, whack. Too late, I realised taking on the smaller of the three was probably not my best option. For sure, I'd slowed him down, but he was tough, tougher than me. A funny thing, I didn't feel any pain from the punches, so I just kept going. I had no idea how he was feeling, but I was tiring. I noticed my back was getting close to the car park wall. Late as it was, Spud Taylor's judo lessons came to mind. If I could do a stomach throw, he'd go over me and hit the brick wall head-first.

I grabbed his lapels and rolled backwards with my feet on his stomach. However, I didn't realise how much this fighting business took it out of you. He was heavier, or I was weaker than I'd expected. As he came over, I didn't have the strength to straighten my legs and my knees folded. He ended up on top of me. I'd just broken one of the cardinal rules. 'Don't let your opponent get on top of you'.

He hit me a couple of times, but I'm a sensible fellow. I just put my hands up and said, "OK, mate, I've had enough".

He must have had enough, too, because he stopped immediately. We both got to our feet, and someone made us shake hands. It was over.

I may have lost the physical side of that fight, but I'd won morally, and I wasn't ashamed of my effort. However, as a regular pass time, I wouldn't recommend it.

There were two notable things about that incident.

One, I was never bothered by the Flitwick boys again. In fact, one of them pulled me out of the fray while they were beating up my mates in another time and place.

And two, unbeknown to me, my future wife was one of the spectators of that shameful event.

The next day was a big day in Brogborough. Mr Davis, the father of my mate Des, who lived up the top street, had arranged a special event at the club. Mr Davis had been in the entertainment business. He still put on the occasional performance for the locals. His signature event was being buried alive in a coffin. He'd be lowered into a grave, covered with earth and left. A few hours later, they'd come and dig him up. I don't know if he put himself into a trance or not, but he sure must have had faith in his burial party, who retired to the pub to pass the time. Even now, the thought of it makes me shudder.

For obvious reasons on this occasion, Mr Davis was not performing himself. Through his old connections, to boost Brogborough CIU club's waning finances, he'd arrange a performance involving a stripper.

The proposed event caused quite a stir because it was planned for a Sunday lunchtime when, according to some, people should be at or returning from church. Other than us Catholics, I didn't know any other devout churchgoing Christians on the estate. Father Golston had nothing to say on the subject, but the local Anglican church was up in arms. It was highly immoral. The law was clear on Sunday drinking, but there was no by-law covering strippers, so nothing could be done to stop it.

I got dressed and checked myself in the mirror. I looked like I'd done a couple of rounds with Muhammad Ali. Two black eyes puffed up nose and cheeks and a few cuts and bruises.

Apart from what I looked like; I had no intention of going to church that Sunday. Before last night's entertainment, my mates and I had arranged to meet at the club.

My dad usually went to the club on Sundays at 12:30 after church. He didn't see the need to change the habit because of some stripper. Anyway, he was proud of me and wanted to buy me a pint.

Curtains fluttered as we walked down the street. The more "curious" estate residents covertly spied from the shadows to see who dared to go for a drink that Sunday.

When we got to the club, a crowd had already gathered outside. There were a couple women's rights fanatics with placards, but generally they were a mixed bag from the estate, glad of the distraction from a typical dull Sunday. My cousin Anna was waiting to see what all the fuss was about with some friends.

The local press arrived, but they were too late to catch the stripper who was in the club preparing for her act. Desperate for a photo, the press photographer took a picture of my cousin Anna's legs from the hem of her short skirt to her shoes. When the image appeared in the paper titled 'The legs of the stripper', my aunty Mary was furious. She demanded compensation for the defamation of her daughter's character. Of course, an anonymous pair of legs would never stand up in court. Nevertheless, that was our first experience of fake news.

I was apprehensive when I entered the club. As it was, I got a round of applause for the previous night's quixotic gallantry. However, the greatest accolade was when Irvine gave me the first pint on the house.

The club was packed with a lot of strangers. We paid our entrance and pushed our way into the dance hall at the appointed time. Fold up chairs were set out in orderly rows with a central aisle.

There was a three-yard gap between the stage and the first row. A single chair in this gap was the only prop. It was going to be very close-up and personal. After the performance, the hall would be reconfigured for that night's bingo session.

As the current local hero, Irvine suggested a stranger in the front row move. The man was less than happy, but Irvine could be persuasive, and I was given the vacated seat. I'd rather have been in a less prominent position.

Mr Davis went into the little cubicle on the right side of the stage. A short while later, an attractive, well-dressed woman in her mid-thirties came out of the booth. I don't know what everyone was expecting, but this wasn't it.

Following a "Good morning, boys" and some saucy banter, the music started. She began her exotic dance, first shedding her long coat, then rolling down and discarding her elbow-length silk gloves. She moved up and down the centre aisle. After getting one of the audience to unzip her, she slipped off one, then the other shoulder strap and slowly wiggled her way out of her dress. She was dressed in a pearl necklace, bra, panties, suspenders, black stockings and stilettos. She undid her bra and let it fall to the floor, momentarily covering herself with crossed arms. She slowly uncrossed her arms with whistles and whoops from the crowd, revealing a large pair of breasts with no tassels. Then she sat on the chair, slipped off her shoes and, one by one, stretched out her long legs and rolled down and discarded her stockings, followed by the suspender belt.

After gyrating around the floor a while longer, she removed her panties, swirled them around her head and threw them into the cheering horde.

She stood completely naked except for her pearl necklace and a tiny G-String. But it wasn't over. With my battered face, I stood out from the crowd. I just knew what was going to happen next. I might even have been set up. She came over and sat on my lap, put an arm around my neck and stroked my hair. It was OK having a large pair of breasts jiggling around under my chin. However, not knowing what she might do next, I was relieved when she got off my lap. She took a bow to great applause from the audience and disappeared into the cubicle.

And that was the end of Brogborough club's claim to fame. The place never turned into a den of iniquity. Sundays returned to early lunchtime closing and Bingo in the evening. Mr Davis went back to occasionally being buried alive.

However, if the church and other guardians of the nation's morals thought that was the end of the matter, they were wrong. On 26 September the following year, The Theatres Act became law. It abolished stage censorship, and the next day the American hippy musical Hair opened in London. With nudity, blasphemy and sexually explicit language, the moral decline of Great Britain had begun.

Sometime in early May, we were invited to a party in the house of Erika's friend Tiggie from Wolverton. Tiggie was nice enough, but she probably thought Erika could do better than a poor apprentice like me, which was true. Sometime during the evening, we had a row. I can't remember what it was about, but Erika went off to join Tiggie in another part of the house. I ended up sleeping on the floor with some other stopovers. Sometimes I'm just too stubborn for my own good. I couldn't find Erika the following day, so I walked to Wolverton station to get the train to Bletchley and home. I was angry as I walked onto the platform and sat on a bench where a person had a transistor radio. The radio started playing "Waterloo Sunset" by the Kinks. It was the first time I'd heard it.

The song was brilliant, but it created a melancholic mood that ingrained that moment into my memory. I still feel a certain sadness to this day if I hear that song, but I still love it. I can plot my life by the music in the charts at the time, and that was the weekend I lost my girlfriend to a boy from Wolverton. That was painful.

The following week without a girlfriend, I was moping around in Brogborough Club when my friend Kenny Yates came in. The club was dead, so Kenny asked if I'd like to drive to Marston and look for signs of life.

We got into Kenny's red mini. After starting the engine, the car was filled with the organ introduction to "A Whiter Shade of Pale" by Procol Harum. Neither of us had heard it before. Its impact was so profound we sat and listened to the end before driving off.

There were only two names in the logbook of that mini. One was Kenny's, the other was the previous owner, a notorious lady called Christine Margaret Keeler.

The 19-year-old Miss Keeler had been sexually involved with the British Cabinet minister, John Profumo, and the Soviet naval attaché, Yevgeny Ivanov, both at the same time. During the East-West Cold War of the sixties, this caused a political incident. By the time the scandal broke, Ivanov had been recalled to Moscow. Profumo first denied the affair but later resigned when the truth came out.

If only that car could have talked.

I was still feeling sorry for myself when I bumped into Linda, the college receptionist, by the coffee machine while on day release at Dunstable College.
Linda was a pretty girl about the same age as me. She was friendly, and we always got on well. She said she was having a party on Saturday night and asked me to go. I was unattached, at a loose end, so I happily thanked her for the invitation. On Saturday evening, I hitched a lift up the M1 to Dunstable and found Linda's house.
There weren't that many people at the party, and by midnight everyone had gone home. This left Linda and me alone on the sofa. What could I do? We started kissing, and Linda asked me if I would like to stay the night.
Sleepover with Linda or walk to the M1 and try to hitch a lift home in the early hours? Not much of a contest for an 18-year-old boy. I thought my luck had changed.
At that moment, the door opened and in breezed Linda's older sister, who'd been up the California dance hall. Linda told her I was staying over because I had a long way to go home. Linda's sister looked directly at me and said.
"That's fine. But don't think you're sleeping with my sister".
That was the end of that amorous adventure, and I was consigned to the sofa.
At least in the morning, Linda's guardian angel was kind enough to cook me breakfast before she sent me packing.

Shortly after, missing Erika terribly, I put my pride to one side, knocked on her front door, and asked her to go back with me, which she did.

1967 was a year of change as far as music was concerned. The formation of Cream in 1966 by Clapton, Bruce and Baker started the era of the Supergroup. An example of this development was when Steve Winwood left the Spencer Davis Group to form Traffic. When Cream disbanded, he went on to join Clapton and Baker in Blind Faith.

By the middle of the year, the psychedelic wave was well established, and most of the well-known bands were into it. However, an existing supergroup had, as usual, pre-empted, or to be more precise, started this musical revolution.

The single Penny Lane/Strawberry Fields Forever by the Beatles had gone to number 2 in the charts in March, and we had no idea what they had in store for us next.

On 26 May, the Beatles released Sgt Pepper's Lonely Hearts Club Band.

Eight days later, it was Number 1 on the UK album charts, and it stayed there for 27 weeks.

Erika had another friend at Texas Instruments called Steph. Steph had a boyfriend, Mike Fields. Mike's dad was the golf pro at Dunstable, and Mike was the golf pro at Biddenham near Bedford. Mike was a rally car enthusiast and had a navy-blue convertible Triumph Vitesse. It was a sleek machine styled by the famous Italian designer Giovanni Michelotti. Some evenings, Mike and

Steph would pick us up from Brogborough, and we'd drive to Ashridge park with a picnic and a portable record player.
We'd lay on our backs, staring at a star-filled summer sky. Sipping wine or Strongbow cider listening to "Lucy in the sky with diamonds", "With a Little Help from My Friends", and the other fantastic songs. It was bloody magic.

Hitch-Hiking to Ireland

Living in Brogborough without transport, hitch-hiking became a way of life. I hadn't been back to Rosslare for a couple of years, and I had the urge to reconnect with my Irish roots.
Erika and I had been together for about eight months. Except for our short breakup, it was the longest I'd ever been with a girl, so I asked her if she'd like to go to Ireland.
Being constantly short of cash, I couldn't afford the rail fare. The only way was to hitch-hike from Brogborough to Fishguard in Wales to catch the ferry, a road journey of about 270 miles. We'd never hitched that far before. Erika agreed, and we planned for our adventure.
I wrote to granddad Boyce in Colville Street and asked if I could stay with him, and I wrote to my auntie Emma, who lived on the other side of the street and asked if Erika could stay with her and Uncle Richie.
The replies came back positive, so we were all set to go.
Early on Saturday morning of 15 July 1967, we took the train from Ridgmont to Bletchley with a small amount of luggage. We got off

at Fenny Stratford and climbed the steps at the end of the station to the A5 Watling Street.

I had two weeks of holiday money and a small bonus in my pocket.

It was a beautiful sunny day, and I was on the open road hitch-hiking to Ireland with my girl.

After a six-week run, Procol Harum's 'A Whiter Shade Of Pale' had been knocked off number 1 in the charts by The Beatles with 'All You Need is Love'. With not a care in the world, this was the 1960's at its best.

At around ten o'clock, we crossed the road and took up a position on the railway bridge. The first vehicle that came up the hill was a motorcycle and sidecar. The driver wore an unbuckled leather flying helmet, goggles, and a fleece-lined flying jacket. With a silk scarf flapping from his neck, he was a manifestation of Biggles. Light-heartedly we smiled and stuck out our thumbs. To our surprise, he pulled up beside us.

"Where are you off to?"

"Ireland".

"I'm heading for Oxford. Hop on"

Erika settled in the sidecar with the luggage, and I got on the pillion behind the driver. The motorbike spluttered off under load, and off we went. Other than a few shouted exchanges, there wasn't much opportunity for conversation. After passing through Buckingham and Bicester, we were dropped off at a large roundabout outside of Oxford after little more than an hour. Like a fighter ace, our unknown benefactor roared off in a cloud of blue smoke.

Before long, with a puff of air brakes, a BP petrol tanker pulled up beside us. The driver stretched across the cab and pushed open the passenger door.

"Where are you going?"

"Ireland"

"It's your lucky day. I'm going to Cardiff."

We hoiked our baggage up onto the double passenger seat and climbed on board the huge vehicle. I guess BP would have taken a dim view of him picking up hitchhikers.

With the windows down and a breeze blowing through the cab, we sped on through green country roads in summer sunshine. The tanker driver, probably in his mid-forties, was an interesting man who chatted easily to us about his life. He'd been a soldier. A Chindit, part of the British Army's Long Range Penetration Group in Burma. The group was initially under the command of Brigadier Orde Charles Wingate before he was killed in an air crash. The Chindits fought in Burma, attacking Japanese troops, bases and communications deep behind enemy lines.

I'd seen a couple of Hollywood films about the Burma campaign; Objective, Burma! and Merrill's Marauders, but they were typical 'how the Americans won the war' movies. There was the film Bridge on the River Kwai about allied PoWs building the Burma Railway, which the driver told us was fictitious. The soldiers I knew generally didn't talk about the war. However, because the Chindits were part of what was known as the forgotten army, I think the tanker driver just wanted to educate us. However, what he told us wasn't all 'for king and country' stuff. He spoke about malaria, dysentery, and the lack of food. How the jungle didn't care whether you were Japanese, British, or anyone else. The jungle treated everyone the same.

He said they were constantly on the move to evade the enemy. Sometimes, the British troops would have to shoot their own sick or wounded to stop them from falling into the hands of the Japanese. He said the Japanese were brutal, that they staved, beat and even used prisoners for bayonet practice.

He told us a story about a wounded soldier slumped against a tree who asked his friend to light him up a cigarette. The wounded soldier took a puff and then tapped the side of his head with his finger.

"When I've finished this, just put one in there, mate". It was that matter of fact. He never said if he'd done it himself, but I did wonder.

After the war, the tanker driver married an Indian girl and brought her back to the UK. They had two children and then returned to India, but both the children died from a tropical disease, so they came back to live in Cardiff.

By about one-thirty, we'd reached the river Severn suspension bridge. Before crossing it, we pulled into the service station, where the tanker driver treated us to lunch.

Soon we were flying above the broad Seven estuary into Wales across the new bridge that had been open for less than a year.

Before four in the afternoon, we stopped on the outskirts of Cardiff. We thanked the tanker driver, climbed down from the cab with our luggage and waved him off as he turned for home. As the tanker disappeared in the traffic, I thought he had suffered all that less than twenty-five years earlier, when he was not much older than me. Poor as I was, what a blessed life I was living.

It took a couple more lifts to get from Cardiff to Swansea, where we were picked up by a Welsh family with two children. We crammed into the back of the car with the two kids who interrogated us relentlessly all the way to Carmarthen.

Outside of Carmarthen, we got a lift with a young guy driving a brand-new red Lotus Elan Plus 2 convertible. Plus 2 was optimistic. Erika sat in the front like a film star while I crammed in the back with the luggage, and my legs stretched sideways across the child seats. Nevertheless, speeding through the green hedge and tree-lined country road was exhilarating in the Welsh evening sunlight with warm wind tousling our hair. The young man, not much older than me, explained how he'd managed to get this luxury sports car. He'd inherited shares in the Channel Tunnel Company. Between 1964 and 65, a geological survey was carried out. The British and French governments agreed to go ahead with the project. His shares went up in value, so he sold them and bought the car. It might not have been a very sensible reinvestment of his money, but it sure was fun.

He dropped us off on the country road, pointed us in the right direction and disappeared towards Haverfordwest.

There wasn't much traffic on the road, but eventually, our final lift of the day came by. The builder's truck was full of dusty scaffolding, planks, and a cement mixer tied down with rope.

"Fishguard?" shouted a friendly Welsh voice, and we climbed into the cab.

After a half-hour drive, just before eight-thirty as the sun was setting, the builder obligingly dropped us off at the harbour.

With a wisp of smoke drifting from her funnel and the soft whir of machinery from within, the British Railways ferry St David was already tied up against the dock at the terminal.

We had travelled 270 miles in ten and a quarter hours. Including a short lunch break and the delays between lifts, we'd achieved an average speed of a little over 26 miles an hour, which was fantastic.

Six hours before St David sailed for Rosslare, we bought our tickets and made ourselves uncomfortable on the platform's hard bench.

A little after ten-thirty, the first boat-train pulled into the station. People piled out onto the platform, and we joined them as they made their way to board the ferry. We showed our tickets to the sailor on the boarding way, who double-clicked what looked like a stopwatch to count us on board.

Gratefully we flopped into a couple of padded seats with more comfort than the hard station bench.

Every day for almost a year, I'd stood in the bus stop queue with the same people waiting for the Luton bus into Dunstable. Barely a good morning had passed between us. The English are reserved like that. Now, amongst the banter of these Irish travellers, we were being constantly questioned about our entire history. The Irish are unreserved like that. It's not being nosey; it's called conversation.

Soon a guitar struck up a chord, the instrumentalist was joined by a flautist, and before long, an impromptu band of strangers was in full flow. Occasionally someone shouted a request or came forward to give a rendition. The passenger space was soon filled with everything from sad refrains, pop songs, jigs, and Irish patriotic ballads or, to be more exact, rebel songs.

A little after two in the morning, the ship shuddered and moved away from the dock. We passed the Strumble Head lighthouse and headed westward into the St George's Channel.

The bar was open, and the singing continued. The sea was not particularly rough, but inevitably, the boat's gentle rocking was too much for some passengers. Seasickness is contagious. Except for the hardcore travellers with low tables full of pints of Guinness, Smithwick's and tumblers of Jameson's and Paddy, the singing died off.

As the morning sun rose behind the ferry, Erika and I went out on deck. It was good to get away from the stale smoke-filled air, the smell of spilt beer, and the nauseating effects of passengers' kinetosis.

Outside in the fresh sea air, we could clearly see the Tuskar Rock Lighthouse off the port bow.

Gradually, in morning twilight, the grey strip of the Irish coastline came into view. That first sight of Ireland never failed to fill me with emotion. I was born in England, and I'm forever grateful for that. Still, soon I'd be with my relations and my grandfathers in a country with a history of asymmetric warfare and an alternative

outlook on life. Those two parts of me are not mutually exclusive. They are intertwined and make me who I am.
Around 5:30 in the morning, St David berthed in Rosslare Harbour against the pier, with the squat red lighthouse at its end. My great grandfather, John Boyce, was instrumental in building that pier in the early 1900's. My grandfather, Ben Boyce, had worked on this pier as a crane driver most of his working life. Rosslare was more than a holiday destination. It was my roots.

In 1922 Ireland seceded from the UK and became the Irish Free State. After that, they became two independent countries.
However, when travelling between these two countries, you never had to show any identification. There was no passport control. I didn't have a passport in 1967, nor did Erika. However, you did have to go through customs. Ireland was a very Catholic country in those days. In particular, Irish customs officers would confiscate contraceptives and subversive literature like Playboy magazines. British customs were more interested in spirits, cigarettes and cigarette lighters which were cheaper in Ireland. And woe betide anyone caught smuggling literature relating to the Irish war of independence.
Another odd thing was that the currency of both countries was interchangeable in Ireland. Irish notes were the same size as their UK equivalent, but they had different colours and graphics. The denomination of the notes was also the same 10's, £1, £5, and £10. Likewise, the Irish pound was made up of twenty shillings. Each

shilling was worth 12 pence. Like the British pound, the Irish pound had 240 pence.
The coinage was the same 1/2d, 1d, 3d, 6d, 1s, 2s and 2/6d (two shillings and sixpence, or a half-crown), where d stood for the Latin word denarius, which indicated a penny.
Generally, the coins were the same size and weight. However, being a republic, the obverse of Irish coins didn't show the head of a British monarch. Instead, they showed the symbol of Ireland, the Brian Boru harp. Except the coins had to show the harp in mirror-image because, in 1862, the original harp symbol was registered as a trademark by Guinness.

We were on the cliff top by the Harbour View Hotel, heading for 1170 Colville Street by seven o'clock.
The front of my grandfather's terraced bungalow hadn't changed. The small front garden needed weeding. Neither granddad nor my uncle Ben were much into gardening. However, the thing I loved about that garden was the lovely, fragrant, pink and white honeysuckle bush to the right of the front door. It was still there, and already an early morning long-tongued bumblebee was hovering, flitting between its flowers collecting nectar.
We walked up the short path and knocked on the front door, which was opened by one of the people I loved most in the world, my grandfather Ben Boyce. He was a tall man, but he didn't look as big as I'd remembered him. He was in his mid-seventies, getting smaller in old age while I'd been getting bigger. He wore a white shirt with the sleeves rolled up above the elbow. His dark, high

waisted trousers were held up with a thick, brown, brass buckle belt.

He still had his hair and a pair of eyebrows so straight you could put a spirit level on them.

He'd probably been reading the paper because he looked at us over the top of his reading glasses perched on the end of his long Boyce nose.

His lips were pinched and slightly sunken because he'd forgotten to put his teeth in. Like many old folk, he didn't like wearing his dentures unless he had to. He looked old, but he still had that smile and a sparkle in his eyes.

After breakfast, I took Erika across the street to number 1177 to meet auntie Emma and uncle Richi, the Siggins side of my family. Auntie Emma. had prepared a bedroom for Erika, so I left her there to settle in and have a nap. We'd been on the go for 24 hours without sleep by then.

I have no idea why Colville Street had house numbers in the thousands because it had less than 20 houses.

Back at 1170, I dozed off in the back bedroom, in the same brass bed that I woke up in and saw my granddad for the first-time years ago.

When I got up, Uncle Ben, my mum's youngest brother, had come in from a morning's fishing. Uncle Ben was a big man in his early forties. He was a heavy smoker and only smoked untipped cigarettes like Major, Capstan, and Players. He liked a drink and spent most of his free time in the Railway Social Club supping pints of Smithwick's red ale. The men-only bar in the club was at the top of the road across Goulding street. Another bar on the other side of the club had a dance floor and stage for family and social events.

Uncle Ben preferred the relative quiet of the bar where he could chat or not, depending on his inclination, with his mates. Unlike UK pubs and clubs, there were no distractions like game machines, one-armed bandits or televisions. The bar was for the serious business of drinking and talking.

In the afternoon, there was the 'Holy Hour' when, by law, the shutters came down, and no drinks were served. Before that, the clients would fill their tables with pints to get them through the 60 minutes before the shutters went up again. A great advantage for Uncle Ben was the bar was less than 100 yards from home. He liked his drink, but he was never aggressive. He'd just go home to his bed if he had too much.

Uncle Ben had a couple of relationships with local women. They'd been well-meaning ladies intent on saving Uncle Ben from himself. However, their attempts to remould him met with little success, and they moved on to more malleable subjects. Uncle Ben was a man of the sea. He didn't take to relaxing at home with his feet up in front of the fire. He was very different from my granddad, who never drank at all.

I introduced Erika to my wonderful aunt Betty and uncle Tommy Boyce. They lived in the house behind granddad in Jameson Street with my cousins Marggie, Jimmy and Bernard.

Uncle Tommy was my mum's first cousin, so he was really my first cousin, once removed. That made auntie Betty my second cousin by marriage. All that was too complicated, so we settled for uncle and auntie.

I loved my auntie, Betty. She was a stout, busty, loud, no-nonsense Welsh lady. Generally, she was always in good form unless you got on the wrong side of her, and then you might get a good tongue lashing, but all in good heart. In contrast, Uncle Tommy was a small quiet man. I loved being with auntie Betty. When we were young, and all the cousins got together, it was always love and bedlam around auntie Betty's house.

Later we visited grandad Butler and his daughter, auntie Mai who lived on the back road to Kilrane. Granddad James Butler had been a soldier in the British Army in World War 1. He fought at Gallipoli, after which he was transferred to Ypres in Belgium. He was blinded with trachoma and put on a hospital ship to the UK a few days before the battle of Passchendaele. He was blind for the rest of his life but was trained as a basket maker by the St Dunstan's organisation. His house, Ozier Lodge, was named after the long willow shoots used in basket making.

My dad's sister, Mai, lived with my granddad. Mai had been the winner of the Irish 25-mile National Cycling Championship in 1945. She'd given up cycling and was now running her own cafe.

Erika and I spent our time walking the miles of sand to Carnsore Point and beyond and having picnics on the beach. We took the train from old Kilrane station, on the clifftop where the line comes up from the harbour. Sometimes, we got off a few miles down the track at the small seaside resort of Rosslare Strand. With 300 more hours of sunshine each year than anywhere else, the 'Strand' was famous for being the "sunniest spot in Ireland". It also had more shops, hotels, cafes and restaurants than Rosslare Harbour.

A couple of times, we carried on to the county town of Wexford. The town was full of shops with statuettes, pictures and keyrings of Irish leprechauns, banshees and fairies. There was also an abundance of religious artefacts like the Sacred Heart of Jesus, Crucifixes, Rosary beads, the Virgin Mary and various saints, especially St Patrick.

With the miscellany dedicated to the late John Fitzgerald Kennedy, it seemed he too had been elevated to sainthood.

The assassinated President of the United States; Kennedy's ancestors were Wexford people from New Ross, just 20 miles west of the county town.

Erika was taken with the Claddagh rings, the traditional Irish gold rings representing love, loyalty, and friendship. The head of the ring depicts two hands holding a heart under a crown. The hands represent friendship, the heart represents love, and the crown represents loyalty. I should have bought Erika a Claddagh ring, but being a poor apprentice, I couldn't afford to. Erika worked for Texas Instruments in Bedford, so she bought one herself.

Auntie Mai's cafe was called 'The Butler Arms'. It was situated on top of the cliff where the Dublin Road came up from the harbour. The cafe had a little shop that sold soft drinks, sweets and ice cream. It also had a couple of guest bedrooms that auntie Mai expanded upon each year. She was always in trouble with the council over that. In front of the cafe, she had an Esso petrol pump. It was an excellent spot for people to have an early breakfast, fill up their car, and buy stuff to keep the kids quiet on the journey before heading off into Ireland. The place was quite chaotic at times. The problem was that the cafe was invariably understaffed. Auntie Mai had to rotate between cook, waitress, washer up, shop assistant, petrol pump attendant, housemaid and cleaner.

It was not uncommon for her to leave the kitchen while cooking breakfast, go fill up a car with petrol, sell something from the shop, and return to the kitchen. She'd finish cooking and then serve four Irish breakfasts in the cafe.

A full Irish breakfast with tea, bread and butter cost six old shillings (6/-. Steak and chips ten shillings 10/-, and fried fillet of plaice and chips (on Fridays and Fast Days) five shillings and sixpence 5/6. There was no wine, but a glass of brown sherry cost three shillings 3/-.

We would go to the cafe and help out clearing tables and doing a bit of washing up. For that, Auntie Mai would give us breakfast or lunch or let us cook something for ourselves.

One day while we were helping out, a young local kid, about ten years old, turned up at the cafe. He had a bucket with two black lobsters in seawater. They weren't too big as lobsters go, a little over a foot long, but they were alive, kicking, and fresh out of the sea. Auntie Mai wouldn't buy them. Unbeknown to his father, she said the kid sometimes rowed out in the dory, pulled up his dad's pots, and sold the lobsters for extra pocket money. However, as

Erika had never eaten freshly caught lobster, Mai said we could buy them and boil them up in the kitchen after the lunch period. The boy wanted a pound for the two, but we got the pair for ten shillings after a bit of haggling. We transferred the lobsters to a large saucepan, half-filled it with water and put it in the kitchen sink. When the lunch customers had gone, I left Erika in the kitchen to boil the lobsters while I cleaned the tables and swept the dining room floor.

There was a screech from the kitchen, and I rushed in to find Erika fighting to keep the lid on the saucepan. Black claws kept forcing up the lid as the lobsters attempted to escape from the water, gradually heating up on the gas hob.

"No! You have to boil the water first. Then drop them in to kill them".

I suppose I should have been a bit more specific about boiling them.

We took the pot off the stove and carefully transferred two extremely pissed off nephropidaes with claws snapping into another pan. We brought the big pan to the boil and dropped living lobster in. After that experience, no one can tell me that lobsters are not sentient creatures.

We let the now bright red lobsters cool off, made up a picnic hamper and headed for the beach. It was pure opulence. Sunshine and an empty golden beach to ourselves. We broke open the lobsters and ate the soft white meat with fresh bread and Irish red lemonade.

Erika had treated me to a packet of five long thin Schimmelpenninck cigars. After the meal, I lit one up and lay back on the sand to smoke it.

Until that time, I'd never had a problem with lobster or any marine crustaceans. Uncle Ben often brought great crabs and lobsters to grandad's house for breakfast after a night out fishing. I loved them, but everything changed that day on the beach. By the time I'd smoked half of the cigar, I started to get a headache. I had to close my eyes to keep out the sunlight. The next thing, I rolled over away from Erika and vomited into the sand. Then I was sure I was going to die. My stomach cramped, and I was sick again. I was ill and weak, and it took some time before I could stand. With my head pounding, Erika had to help me off the beach. Climbing the 99 steps to the Harbour View Hotel was slow torture. Eventually, we got back to grandad Boyce's house, and that's how that day ended. I went to bed and didn't get up again until the following day. It took another full day before I felt any way near human.

I'd always eaten lobster, crab, scampi, shrimp and prawns. I loved them, but I could never face eating lobster again from that day.

It took me a long time to realise that most times when I was sick at the weekends, it wasn't due to drinking too much. I eventually found that I was always ill after a Chinese takeaway if the meal included prawns. I was fine if I stuck to boiled or egg fried rice and a meat dish.

After some experimentation and near-death experiences, I concluded that I had developed an extreme allergy to crustaceans of any sort. The odd thing was that I could still eat mussels, cockles, and other clams.

So much for vindictive crustaceans.

Apart from the lobster incident, it was a great holiday in Ireland. Too soon it came to an end. On the last night we sat on the bench on the cliff top looking down at the harbour. The ferry was tied against the wharf waiting for the Dublin train, its lights shimmered across the dark water.

There wasn't much difference between the English and the Irish. However, Ireland had a much smaller population. Consequently the Irish had a natural tendency for friendliness that extended to complete strangers. For the average English person an impromptu conversation with someone you didn't know could be a painful experience. For the Irish, interrogating a stranger was simply a pleasant way to pass the time.

I don't know what Erika had been expecting on this holiday, but the Irish, especially those in Rosslare, seemed to have had a profound effect on her. That night she sobbed on my shoulder because we were leaving Erin's isle in the morning.

29 July 1967. The following morning we had time to do the rounds and say goodbye to family and friends before heading for the harbour. At 11:45am the ferry moved off the dock, past the red lighthouse at the end of the pier and set a course for Wales.

Around four in the afternoon we were outside of Fishguard hitch-hiking home. The return journey had not been considered in the plan. There was no way we were going to make it back home before nightfall. We had a large AA map, and we were flexible with the lifts offered. As long as they were in a general easterly direction, we took whatever came our way. By nine in the evening we were dropped off in Stratford-upon-Avon. We'd travelled about 200 miles in five hours. An average speed of 40 mph was good, but the sun had almost set. It was getting dark, and we still had seventy miles to go. We had to find somewhere to stay for the night. There was no shortage of bed and breakfast places in William Shakespeare's hometown, the problem was we didn't have enough cash on us. I had some money left from the holiday, but my financial planning had not included board and lodging on the trip home. Credit cards had been introduced into the UK the year before, but they were a novelty, on my wages I couldn't get one anyway.

Fortunately, Erika had a good job, a bank account and a cheque book. There were no cheque guarantee cards then, but she could save the day if we found a place that would accept a bank authorisation slip. Surprisingly, we soon found somewhere willing to take a cheque. However, it cost more than necessary. The 1960's, no nonsense, English landlady would not let us share a room.

The following morning after a good English breakfast we set off for home. It was beautiful being driven through the Warwickshire country roads that sunny Sunday morning. We'd never seen so many picturesque old Tudor houses. They had steep pitched roofs, ornate brick doorways and chimneys, and exposed black wood framework in filled with red brick or cream coloured stucco. The houses had well-kept road and riverside gardens ablaze with

colour. Eliminate the cars, the speed and the paved roads and you could easily have been back in Elizabethan England.
By early afternoon we were back in Brogborough. Our Irish adventure and first holiday together over.

The Summer of Love

1967 saw the "Summer of Love". Hippie music, hallucinogenic drugs, free-love and anti-Vietnam war sentiment from America took root in the UK. During Saturday 26 to Monday 28 August, the Summer bank holiday, a "Festival of the Flower Children" was scheduled at Woburn Abbey, a few miles from Brogborough. Tens of thousands of hippies, pseudo-hippies and other curiosities were expected to descend on the village of Woburn from the UK and all parts of Europe. Erika and I, having both worked at Woburn Abbey, knew this was going to be a chaotic event with queues for overpriced food and drink and overused and unpleasant toilet facilities. We decided not to go and took a road trip instead. On Saturday morning we took the train into Bedford, walked up to the A6, the old London to Carlisle road, and around 10 in the morning started thumbing it to Preston to see Erika's Polish grandmother. This might not seem as exotic as attending a 'hippy fest,' but the weather was fantastic, and we had an incredible feeling of joy as we hit the open road for the second time that month.
I can't remember why we didn't use the M1 motorway which was less than a mile from home. The M1 would have taken us most of the way to Preston. I guess the A6 offered a much prettier and

adventurous route. It did, and in bright sunshine, we travelled through beautiful English countryside passing through towns and villages on the way.

Somewhere before Leicester we left the A6 heading towards Stoke-on-Trent. We skirted Manchester and on to Preston.

Shamefully, I can't remember any of the good people who stopped and picked us up on that trip. However, I do remember the joy and overwhelming feeling of freedom. Most of all, I remember the music. BBC Radio 1 wasn't due to come on the air until September. Until then Pirate radio filled the gap. Due to new UK Government legislation, Radio London stopped broadcasting on the afternoon of 14 August. However, Radio Caroline vowed to stay on the air, and it did until 3 March 1968 when it was boarded and seized.

In August 67, pop music played on regardless of the government's efforts. My most nostalgic musical memories of that trip are:

Hole in in my shoe by Traffic,

Excerpt from a Teenage Opera by Mark Wirtz,

Let's Go to San Francisco by the Flowerpot Men,

If you're going to San Francisco (Be Sure To Wear Some Flowers In Your Hair) by Scott McKenzie, and Itchycoo Park by The Small Faces.

There were more great records at that time, but with a movement towards the psychedelic, these are the songs that stick in my mind.

There was only one dark side to that trip. As we passed near Cannock, I saw a signpost to Cannock Chase. Only four days earlier the body of a child, a young girl, had been found there. Over the last twenty months the bodies of three young girls had been discovered in that wooded area. All three had been raped and strangled and the killer was still on the loose. Summer of Love or not, there was a sinister side to humanity that was here to stay.

We arrived in the Lancashire town of Preston, on the river Ribble, around 4 in the afternoon. Preston was a post cotton industry town, nevertheless, it seemed like a vibrant place and not what I'd expected.

Erika's gran had a man living with her in the house. I didn't know what the relationship was, and I didn't ask. He'd been decorating before we arrived, and the house was heavy with the smell of fresh paint. It wasn't an unpleasant smell, I actually found it quite atmospheric, and still recall it as a pleasant memory.

Erika's gran was a lovely lady. She gave us a warm welcome and fed us. We may have gone out for a drink that evening, but after all these years I can't remember.

I do remember we got up early the next morning and after breakfast we accompanied Erika's babcia (grandmother) to church. Preston must have had a big Polish population. The church was packed with Polish families. The priest was Polish and the whole of the Mass was conducted in Polish. I didn't understand a word. The sermon was a long-drawn-out affair, reminiscent of the services I'd been to with my granddad and parents in Kilrane Church in Ireland. To me the priest seemed to be lambasting the congregation about something. Eventually it ended and we streamed out amidst an unintelligible chatter. We could have been in Warsaw.

After lunch we put on the radio. The news that came over from the BBC was unexpected.
"The Beatles' manager, Brian Epstein, has been found dead at his Belgravia home in London. It is not yet clear how he died. Friends found his body in bed after his housekeeper raised the alarm."
Like the Kennedy assassination, it was one of those "Where were you when" moments in my life.

On Monday, after an early lunch, we said our goodbyes and made our way, in glorious August weather, to what must have been a section of the uncompleted M6. From there we hitched a lift to Stoke-on-Trent. Then we made our way across the country east to the M1 close to Leicester. We arrived at M1 Junction 13 about seven in the evening.
The slip roads on both sides of the motorway were crammed with hippies trying to hitch a ride home. A few were staring into the sky, arms outstretched trying to pull down passing clouds. They were high on something stronger than Woodbines, or at least putting on a good show of hippieness. However, the majority of them looked less than euphoric.
No alcohol was sold at the festival, only tea and ice cream. Hot dogs were over a pound each, and a couple of hundred coppers patrolled the venue in search of illegal substances. This crowd bore no resemblance to the gentle creatures from San Francisco we'd seen on TV. Even with washable transfers on their cheeks, headbands and a few flowers in their hair, it was obvious that

English hippie culture had some way to go. And that was on a good weekend, most times it was pouring down with rain in the UK.

By August 1967, the pirate radio stations were doomed. One by one 'The Marine Broadcasting Offences Act' was putting them out of business.

To forestall a full youth rebellion the government, in the form of the BBC, introduced a new pop music radio channel.

With great anticipation, on 30 September we all tuned in. The first full pop record we heard on Radio 1 was 'Flowers in the Rain' by The Move. The record was actually number 2 in the charts that week, but fortunately, the BBC was wise enough not to play the Number 1, 'The Last Waltz' by Engelbert Humperdinck. Bloody Engelbert again.

Expelled from Dunstable College

Back at work in September 1967, I'd completed the first year of my apprenticeship. Until I was conditioned to it, I found being shut up in a factory all day a struggle. To overcome the mind ache, I decided to learn as much as I could about the skills of machining and shaping metal. Which, of course, was the whole object of the apprenticeship. I worked out the quickest and most efficient way to complete the machining of the boring large batch jobs that apprentices were often given. It was always a challenge to get the job done as fast as possible to get onto more interesting work. However, I learned a hard lesson. The better you are at doing something, the more likely you will get more of the same. I hated the work. It was mind-numbing but a good unofficial introduction to ergonomics.

I finished the first year of the experimental ONC Mechanical/Electrical Engineering course with good marks, and I passed O Level Physics, a requirement to stay on the course. The physics teacher was the same man who'd taught me while I was in full-time education at Dunstable College, and I'd failed. In truth, that was my own fault. The tutor had no control, the class was a riot, and I went along with it. This time I'd been determined to pass. I'd decided to study at home instead of attending the evening classes.

I retook the physics examination in May 1967 and passed. In August, I went to the college to sign on for the second and final year of the ONC course. When the administrator looked at the class list, he said I wasn't on it.

"You can't sign into this course".

"Why not?" I asked, "I passed the exams".

"It's your physics," he responded.

"But I passed physics!".

"Yes, you did. But, look at this" The man held up my report.

For physics, it said, "Class attendance, ZERO".

"If you're studying at this college, you're supposed to attend the classes. You should have a minimum attendance of 60%."

It was ridiculous. I'd passed my exams, and I was being expelled. I almost said I didn't go to the classes because the teacher was a pratt, but I thought better of it. No matter how much I bleated, I was out.

'Oh shit', I thought, 'How am I going to explain this to Roe Wilson, the foreman?' So I didn't.

The next evening after work, I hitched a lift from Dunstable up the M1 to junction 13 and from there to Bedford. At Mander College, I presented my end of term report and signed on for the second year ONC course. The administrator thought it was very enterprising to cross the established engineering boundaries and mix disciplines.

That I'd passed physics without attending classes added kudos to my application. The man arranged for me to continue with a mixed Mechanical and Electrical ONC. By replacing Thermodynamics with Electrical Engineering, I was back in business.

I told Roe Wilson I'd signed on at Bedford because it was more convenient and closer to home. Which it was, I didn't have to wait around in Dunstable after work for evening classes.

The factory in Dunstable was 42 Km from Mander. Evening classes started at 19:00, so I had two hours after work to get to Bedford. If I hitched a quick lift up the M1, I could stop off at home for something to eat. If I was late, I thumbed it from the M1 at Brogborough straight into Bedford. Most evenings, things went well. However, it was sometimes difficult to get a lift on rainy, foggy or snowy winter evenings. I'd often squelch into college late and sit through the lesson cold and wet. After class, still damp, I had to thumb it 16Km home. One winter night, I got picked up in Kempston by auntie Mary's husband, uncle Steven, coming home from a bingo session in Bedford. The fog was so thick I was lucky he recognised me, or so I thought. Somewhere near Stewartby, we were involved in an accident. Fortunately, no one was seriously hurt. Uncle Steven ran into the back of the other car, but he insisted that the other driver had caused the accident. Once the argument about whose fault it was subsided, we got home without further incident.

The full day-release at college was better for me. One of the British Telecom guys studying electronics had a car and passed Brogborough, so I generally got a ride into college and home again with him in the evening.

Until then, I could only talk about electronics with the two mechanical engineers at Dunstable college who were novices like myself. The Electrical Engineering class at Mander had twenty students, all working for electrical or electronic companies. Suddenly I had others willing to help me with some of the concepts I found difficult to grasp, and I gained more insight into the mysterious world of the electron.

During this time, I often talked to Johnny Roland from the grocery shop in Brogborough. Johnny was Peggy Wolsey's husband. I don't know why everyone called her Peggy Wolsey when she was really Peggy Roland. Maybe it was because her dad was a founding director of the Marston Valley Brick Company, and it was in deference to him.

Anyway, intentionally or not, it subordinated Johnny's role in the shop. This was unfair because Johnny was an intelligent man; we had many interesting conversations. He'd always shown interest in what I was doing, especially my model making as a kid.

One time he gave me a balsa wood kit of a German ME109. It had been a Christmas present for his son Terry. However, Terry operated on a different heavenly plane and had no interest in building Nazi flying machines. Eventually, Terry went to America to further his study of theology. I was about 11 at the time, and it was the most complicated model I'd ever built. I cut the pieces out with a scalpel, stuck them together and covered the skeleton with doped tissue paper. It flew with a rubber band powered propeller. However, it never flew again after I modified it to take a small electric motor and a 9-volt battery. I had a lot to learn about power to weight ratio.

Either way, Johnny was impressed with my efforts. As well as groceries, Johnny and Peggy's shop sold magazines and newspapers.

Before their massive manufacturing plant on Manton Lane, Bedford's came online, Texas Instruments (TI) operated out of a small building in Dallas Road Kempston. A TI engineer ordered a professional electronics magazine from the shop, which he always picked up on a Thursday. The magazine came into the shop on a Monday. Knowing my current interest in electronics, Johnny would let me keep the magazine until Wednesday evening after gaining a pledge from me to treat it with the utmost care. I treated the document as a sacred script. Studying the mysterious symbols, diagrams and equations that at the time meant nothing to me, I resolved that one day I would master that mystical art.

I continued this mechanical-electrical double life, but now I wanted to become an electronics engineer.

The power of resonance

Working on production machines all day was frustrating because I didn't want to continue on that career path when my apprenticeship finished.

Around November, while reading a local newspaper, I came across a classified ad for a trainee position with an electronics company in Dunstable. On impulse, I phoned them.

With a sense of loyalty to Headley's plus a profound fear of the shop foreman, I said I could only attend an interview outside working hours. They must have been desperate. The following evening I had an interview in an industrial unit not much bigger than a double garage across the road from the Halfway House pub.

The interviewer explained that the company made microwave devices for satellite communications, spacecraft, radar and other military applications. I told him I was very interested in electronics.

I thought the interview was going well because the devices he showed me had a lot of machined parts. However, I think he was trying to let me down gently before he eased me out of the office.

Like Roe Wilson during my interview at Headley's, he prepared the killer question that would sort the men from the boys.

"We are really looking for someone who already has experience in this field of electronics," he said dismissively.

In truth, I had no experience in electronics. I didn't even own a soldering iron.

Then he unleashed it.

"Can you explain resonant frequency in a capacitive-inductive circuit?"

I looked at him for a moment, dumbstruck. He probably thought I was clueless, but I was thinking. I'd done resonance theory at Mander only the previous week. It was absolutely fascinating.

I composed myself.

"Well." I replied, "At resonance, the inductive and capacitive reactance are equal. Therefore, two times Pi times the frequency times the inductance equals one over two times Pi times the frequency times the capacitance. If you manipulate that formula, the resonant frequency is the reciprocal of two times Pi times the square root of the inductance times the capacitance".

He pushed over a piece of paper and a pencil. I wrote down the reactance values and manipulated the formula to show the resonant frequency.

For a moment, he was the one who didn't speak, then.

"That is absolutely correct".

The interview took a turn for the better. I left with a job offer of three times my current pay.

The following morning I walked confidently into Roe Wilson's office and told him I was handing in my notice. He put his hands behind his head, leaned back in his chair, and yawned.

"And where do you think you're going?" he demanded.

When I told him, he said caustically, "I know him. He's always messing around in his garage with bits of wire. He'll never get anywhere".

He went on to tell me I was far better off sticking to real engineering instead of fiddling with a soldering iron and ended with.

"You're bound to this company by a legal contract until you've finished your apprenticeship. You're not going anywhere."

And that was the end of that conversation.

Over the following years, Microwave Associates Ltd expanded into a massive factory and office complex along Poynters Road in Dunstable. So much for Roe Wilson's business projection.

I have to say, though, Roe Wilson probably did me a favour. Over the years, I learned that there was a different approach between electronic and mechanical product development. If your first prototype circuit doesn't work in electronics, you can cut tracks and add a few more components until it works the way you want. In mechanical engineering development, if you get the design wrong, you generally end up with a very expensive heap of scrap metal. Consequently, mechanical engineers have to take a more measured approach to design and development.

That said, continuing at Headley's left me in dire straits financially. To survive, I was totally reliant on the charity of my mum and dad. Well, mainly my mum. Something had to be done.

The rise and fall of the Beagarie-Butler condom sales empire.

I wasn't starving, but my financial situation was desperate. Robin's wasn't that good either. To overcome our poverty, we devised a cunning business plan. Someone in Robin's family, I think it was his brother-in-law, worked at the London Rubber company. He could get gross boxes of condoms for half the street value. Each box had 48 packets of 3 for a total cost of 7 Pounds and 10 Shillings. At that time, condoms were sold retail for 3 Shillings 9 Pence (3/9p) for a pack of three. If we sold our condoms for 2 Shillings 10pence (2s/10p), 25% below the street value, we'd make a profit of 3 Pounds 16 Shillings and 8 Pence on every gross we sold. That was equivalent to more than a week's wages to split between us. The start-up cost for the first gross was big money, but we scraped it together and went into business. After the first weeks' trading in the factory, we'd sold over half our stock. We intended to plough the profits back into the business, buy more condoms and expand onto the street. The only problem was that if my Irish Catholic mother found out that I was selling contraceptives, I'd be excommunicated and condemned to burn in hell. I'd have been better off selling drugs.

However, this was a great start to our venture. Before we left work on Friday, we put our remaining stock and our takings into the tool cupboard by Robin's milling machine.

Unbeknownst to us, there was a cloud on our horizon. Roe Wilson had been keeping a watchful eye on us. As soon as we got into work the following Monday morning, we were called into the foreman's office. He opened his desk drawer and placed our Durex Gossamer box, with the remains of our stock and our takings, onto his desk.

"What's this?" he asked.

Robin and I stood in silence, looking at each other for a moment.

Surely, he knew what they were.

"They're condoms," we told him.

"I know what they are. What are condoms and this money doing in your cupboard?".

We told him it was a little business on the side to help with our finances.

He gave us a proper dressing down.

"Your indentures explicitly forbid you from engaging in any other trade or business while employed as apprentices with this company".

He told us to take our stock and money away at the end of the day.

And to never run a business inside or out of the factory again.

God! they were only condoms. Maybe he was a Catholic too.

So that was the end of the Beagarie-Butler, short-lived condom sales empire.

If Roe Wilson thought that was the end of the matter, he was mistaken. Headley's apprentices were heading into a winter of discontent.

There was another apprentice in the factory named Dave Goss. Dave was about six feet tall. His front teeth were a prominent

feature, resembling Bernie Winters, part of the comedy act Mike and Bernie Winters, who were popular on TV then.
Dave was a gentle giant, but you wouldn't want to upset him. He worked evenings and weekends in the Chinese restaurant on West Street to make up his wages. He was the only English guy I ever knew who worked as a waiter in a Chinese restaurant. Dave trained with the staff in martial arts. If the foreman knew he was involved in some extracurricular activity in contravention of his contract, he never confronted Dave about it.
Dave joined our workers' revolution giving us credibility and a united front.
We learned from the other apprentices at college that they were earning twice, sometimes three times more money than we were. We prepared our case and decided on a day and time to present our grievances. Monday morning was ruled out. In fact, first thing on any morning was not a good idea. We decided that late morning would be the most conducive time towards the end of the week.
We chose Thursday morning at midday. I don't like confrontations, and I spent an anxious morning waiting before we went into action.
At the appointed hour, the three of us left our machines, walked to the foreman's office and knocked on the door. Dave, being the tallest, was pushed in first. We stood in front of the foreman's desk in silence. With all our preparation, we'd not allocated a spokesman.
Roe Wilson looked up, perplexed. "Well?"

I can't remember who started first, but we eventually got out what we had to say. We presented our grievances, conscious not to make it sound like a set of demands.

With no union to contend with, Roe Wilson had an authoritarian approach to management. He didn't tolerate being dictated to, especially by three apprentices.

However, he listened without throwing us out of his office on this occasion. The office had all-around glass windows so the foreman could watch the shop floor. That's probably how he got wise to our illicit condom trade. Now the roles were reversed. Work came to a halt as the intrigued workers watched the drama unfolding in the office.

At the end of the meeting, nothing was decided. Our foreman simply told us he would see what he could do and summarily dismissed the three of us from his presence. Like a Musketeer who'd just survived an inquisition with the cardinal, a wave of elation swept over me as I left the office. However, as the euphoria subsided, I realised I was uncomfortable dealing with authority. It was something I was going to have to deal with.

Nothing happened for a week or so, then we were summoned into the office.

We stood before the foreman, waiting to be reprimanded like a group of naughty schoolboys. To our surprise, Roe told us he'd worked out a deal where we would get extra money each week as a bonus. However, the bonus was not a guaranteed payment; there were strings attached. It was conditional on timekeeping, work performance and general attitude. It could be withdrawn for gross misconduct, which I took as a euphemism for asking for another pay rise.

It was a pittance, but we accepted. As Roe pointed out. We'd freely signed the documents of our enslavement that set our wages for the period of servitude. Of course, Roe Wilson didn't put it in those words.

Don't get me wrong. I was extremely grateful to Headley's, and to Roe Wilson, for that matter, for employing me, but it was hard living on less than four pounds a week even in the 1960's.

And so my lot improved slightly. Because I was good at technical drawing, the owner of Headley's, Mr Brown, gave me the occasional drawing job to do in my own time and paid me cash in hand. That was something between Mr Brown and me, who probably didn't want it to look like favouritism. Roe Wilson undoubtedly took it as a breach of the blessed contract of indenture, but then Mr Brown was his boss.

Racecourse clairvoyant

Sometimes, a machinist from Luton named Tom Drew would give me a lift to the M1 motorway on his way home if he weren't working overtime. One evening he stopped off at the bookies in Church Street to put a one shilling bet on three horses. He said he would let me choose one horse just for a laugh, and if it won, I could have half the winnings. He showed me the board for a race starting at Kempton Park in a few minutes.

I didn't know anything about racehorses, but one horse caught my eye as I looked down the list.

"Prince of Verona," I said.

I've loved Shakespeare ever since seeing the Merchant of Venice in Shaftesbury Avenue London on a trip from Fulbrook School.

"Thirty-Three to one! That hasn't got a chance in hell of winning," said Tom.

"You said to choose a horse. That's the one, so back it".

Tom shrugged and, against his better judgement, he put the bet on.

The radio in the shop crackled to life as the race started. There was no mention of our horse until just before the end of the race.

"And here comes Prince of Verona."

Tom and I jumped up and down, hugging each other in excitement.

The commentary continued.

"It's Prince of Verona challenging now. Prince of Verona, Prince of Verona. Yes! At the line by a head, it's Prince of Verona".

Tom looked at me in disbelief. He went up to collect his winnings, and true to his word, he paid me sixteen shillings and sixpence.

The following day at work, I was famous. Tom extolled my prowess as a tipster. At tea break, I was confronted with a newspaper to pick the winners for that afternoon's race meetings. I protested, but I was forced to choose the winners. I had no clue. I just went down the list, circling in pencil anything that took my fancy. At lunchtime, someone went down town with a pile of money and put on everyone's bets. In the afternoon, a transistor radio on low and away from the foreman's office kept track of the results. Not one horse came good. Everyone lost their money. I went from hero to zero and thus ended my career as a racecourse clairvoyant.

Christmas 1967 saw the Beatles at number one on the UK charts. Not even Engelbert could keep them off it.

From 1963 to 67, they topped the Christmas chart four times with "I Want to Hold Your Hand", "I Feel Fine", and the double A-sided "Day Tripper/We Can Work It Out", now they'd done it again with "Hello, Goodbye".

In 1966 Tom Jones took the Christmas top spot with "Green, Green Grass of Home" To be fair, Tom and probably most other artists wouldn't have made it if the Fab Four had released a song that December. The Beatles were that good.

Christmas Eve was great in Brogborough. Erika lived across the street from me with her two younger brothers and sister. Erika's mum, Lily, was separated and lived with Johnny Falk, also Polish. Old Falky was a stern fellow, very proud and easily offended. Still, you'd be sure to get some Polish sausage and a couple of large glasses of cherry vodka on Christmas Eve. There was always a dance at Brogborough Club, where you could kiss all the girls under the mistletoe.

However, what I liked best was Boxing Day. The ex-Royal Marine Commando, the club manager, Johnny Irvine, would be his usual smiling self. Unfortunately, Johnny suffered a lot from asthma, so he wasn't always in the best of spirits. He could be a cantankerous old sod, but under that persona beat a heart of gold. He was the go-to guy if you were in trouble.

The bar counter would be full of Black Velvets. Well, Guinness and cider, I never saw much champagne in Brogborough. Pint glasses filled with black beer topped off with what looked like shaving foam. We all wore slightly yellow creamy moustaches after the first swig. The girls, and us boys too, would be drinking vodka and lime shots, no ice, of course. I can't remember what lime cordial they used, but you could travel the world and never find that taste again.

Boxing Day was a gathering of the clan, a chance to catch up with all those faces that had flown the coop and were back in Brogborough to have Christmas with their parents. All the usual suspects, and if it was a good year, Norman Stewart came back from University with his own unique brand of intellectual humour.

The Monkees, Daydream Believer, drifting out of the Jukebox, barely audible over the chatter. 'Oh, I could hide 'neath the wings. Of the bluebird as she sings. The six o'clock alarm would never ring...........'.

The air was so thick with cigarette and cigar smoke that it made your eyes run. Standing room only and still people pushing through the swing doors.

Going home pissed, my god, whoever thought of separating Brogborough estate from a Working Men's Club by a main M1 feeder road. Some bloody xenophobes, I suppose. Still, we survived despite the odds.

On a sombre note, as 1967 drifted into a new year, Vietnam had already turned into a TV war.

In February 1968, the execution of a Vietcong soldier, Nguyễn Văn Lém, was shown on television during the evening news. It wasn't broadcast live, but being filmed in Saigon a day earlier, it was as good as.

I watched as a Vietnamese man in a flak jacket raised his arm. In his hand, he held a revolver. As the gun came up to the temple of a man in an open-neck, tartan-patterned shirt on the right of the screen, he pulled the trigger. The man in the tartan-patterned shirt crumpled to the ground. He sat momentarily, then slumped sideways onto the road with a small fountain of blood spurting from the side of his head.

I watched the casual taking of one man's life on a far-off street in Saigon. I'd never seen anything like that before. It wasn't Hollywood. It was real.

The motion film and Eddie Adams' photo of the moment the bullet entered Lém's head were broadcast worldwide. That black and white photograph and one of the young Vietnamese girl Phan Thi Kim Phuc running down a road naked after a napalm attack on her village became the two defining images of that war for me.

My sister's wedding, saved by Granddad Butler's death

The first half of 1968 didn't start well. On Saturday, 16 March, my sister Ellen was getting married to Gary Fisher from Lidlington. Ellen was always highly strung, and to my shame, I'd always exploited that when we were kids and wound her up remorselessly.

However, this time it was none of my doing. The problem was our dad, and his brother Tommy had patched up their differences after the terrible bloody fight they'd had in our house on Christmas Eve 1964. The three Butler brothers Stephen, Tommy and my dad, would all be at the wedding. If everything went as usual, it would only end one way after a few drinks. Tommy was the youngest, and for whatever reason, on past form, he was the one likely to kick it all off. My sister was living in dread during her own wedding ceremony. It wasn't fair, but unfortunately, that's the way it was.

In the end, our grandfather James Butler, who wasn't at the wedding, resolved my sister's problem.

The reception was in the hall in Brogborough Club. Shortly after everyone sat down to eat, Johnny Irvine walked up to the top table and whispered in my dad's ear. Johnny had just received a phone call from Ireland. On the day of my sister's wedding, granddad Butler in Rosslare was killed in a road accident.

The brothers headed for Bletchley to make travel arrangements to go to Ireland.

With that sad news, my sister sighed with relief, and her wedding reception went off without further incident.

Shortly after that, there was more bad news from Rosslare. On 24 March, Aer Lingus Flight 712 crashed while travelling from Cork to London, killing all 61 passengers and crew. The plane came down in the sea off Tuskar Rock lighthouse, some six miles from the Harbour.

A search by the Royal Navy, Rosslare RNLI Lifeboat, the Irish Air Corps, Aer Lingus and Private Planes, and Local Fishing Vessels recovered only fourteen bodies.

With no internet in those days, the staff of Rosslare Harbour post office worked continuous shifts for three days and nights handling calls regarding the crash.

To this day, controversy surrounds the incident because the cause of the crash was never clearly identified.

Then on 4 April, the American civil rights activist Martin Luther King Jr was shot dead in Memphis, Tennessee, by James Earl Ray.

Two months later, on 5 June, Robert F. Kennedy, brother of the late President John F. Kennedy, was shot and killed by Sirhan Sirhan in the Ambassador Hotel in Los Angeles.

With the assassination of JFK in 1963 followed by these two murders, it really seemed as if the dream was over.

2001 A space Odyssey

They were the negative things at the start of 1968. However, an unlikely thing had a profound impact on me at the time - a film.

On 15 May 1968, the Stanley Kubrick film 2001, a Space Odyssey was released in the UK. I saw it previewed on the TV, and I wanted to go and see it. However, my ONC examinations were coming up, and after being thrown out of Dunstable, I didn't want to suffer the same fate at Mander College Bedford. I had to pass Mathematics, Applied Mechanics, Engineering Drawing, and Electrical Engineering to get onto the Higher National Certificate course.

Unfortunately, the film opened at the Granada in Bedford in the middle of my exams.

Fortunately, the film was still showing in Bletchley when the exams were over. At midday one Saturday in early June, after working overtime at Headley's, I hitched a lift from Dunstable along the A5 to Bletchley. I'd arranged to meet Erika, who'd taken the train from Ridgmont, on the steps of the Studio Cinema.

From Richard Strauss' powerful symphonic opening music" Thus Spoke Zarathustra" to the final scene of the 'Star Child' looking from space to Earth, I was blown away.

The film followed the ascent of man from the arrival of an alien monolith amongst a prehistoric tribe of humans on the African veldt to the reappearance of the monolith on the moon in modern times. The story then went forward on a trip to Jupiter and beyond. The transition of millions of years of human evolution was symbolised by an ape tossing a crude bone weapon into the air, turning into an orbiting spacecraft as it fell back to Earth.

In 1968 it showed mobile phones, miniature video cameras, the artificial gravity of a rotating space wheel, zero gravity scenes, Graphical User Interfaces and a misguided Artificial Intelligence computer called HAL.

The film was faithful to physics, from the velcro soled shoes to the floating pen in the space shuttle to the instruction for a zero-gravity toilet. Unlike other science fiction movies of the time, it included communication delays caused by the finite speed of light.

Kubrick added music to fill the silence where sound cannot travel in the vacuum of space. It was pure magic to use Johann Strauss'

Blue Danube to portray the waltz between the rotating space wheel and the Earth shuttle as it manoeuvred to dock.

Leaving the dimness of that cinema into the outside light, I passed through a doorway into the future. Newton's three laws of motion, the law of universal gravitation, the conservation of momentum, Maxwell's Equations and Kirchhoff's laws, all I was studying had real meaning. That was when I understood what it really meant to be an engineer. Despite working as a machinist all day, I now appreciated what I was learning and what the assembly of the parts I was making meant for the first time.

Headley's worked for all the major UK aircraft companies Hawker Siddeley, Westland Helicopters, Dowty, Roll-Royce Aero Engines, and the more recent British Aircraft Corporation that comprised most of the remaining UK aircraft manufacturers. I'd machined parts for the Concorde supersonic airliner, whose maiden flight was scheduled for the following year. My problem was I never got to see the final product. We were just a cog in the machine. Practical knowledge backed by theory meant I'd have a saleable talent when I finished my time as an apprentice. Well, provided I passed my exams. I was committed. Engineering was no longer just a job; it was the future. I might even go and work for NASA.

But the film did more than just galvanise me. It opened a new window on classical music. As a kid, I'd always been into things like Holst's Planet Suite, especially Mars God of War, Grieg's Hall of the Mountain King, and Tchaikovsky's 1812 Overture. All that stuff you could fight battles too. Strauss was for pansies.

Thanks to the genius of Kubrick, my ears were opened. I shouldn't have been surprised at this transformation. Eleanor Rigby, Penny Lane, Strawberry Fields and the album Sgt Pepper's Lonely Hearts Club Band, beyond the words, were all orchestral masterpieces.

After this, we bought an LP of Strauss waltz music and one of the opera De Flaydemouse. I'd spend hours in Erika's house with her and her mum, having Viennese music nights playing the LPs on their home record player.

I was so taken by the music I whistled it continuously until I didn't know I was doing it.

One day, I walked into the foreman's office at Headley's to get some more work. Oblivious, I was whistling the lively part of the opening of De Flaydemouse.

"Do you know that tune?" Roe Wilson demanded.

Christ, I thought, I'm in for a bollocking for whistling.

"It's Die Fledermaus by Johann Strauss", I replied.

He looked at me strangely, slowly nodding in agreement. Bloody hell, he was impressed.

"I'm a member of the Dunstable Amateur Operatic Society," he said. "We're performing that at the end of the month in the Civic Hall. Would you like some tickets?" Not sure if that was a request or an order but intrigued to see my shop foreman as an opera singer, I said yes.

At the end of the month, Erika, Lily and I got dressed up for a night at the opera. By then, Erika had a driving license, so we took Johnny Falk's car, a purple Ford Zephyr, I think it was, and headed for Dunstable.

I still remember the subdued chatter and the magic sound of the orchestra tuning up as we took our seats in the Civic Hall. As the orchestra burst into the overture, live in an acoustic hall, the impact was something far beyond a recording. It was a special night.
If I listen to Strauss now, I think of Lily who has passed, Christmas Eves in Brogborough, smokey coal fires, Polish cherry vodka, kielbasa garlic sausage, and seeing my old foreman dressed as a footman in knee-length breeches wearing a period wig.

Overland to San Sebastian

Sunday 21 July to Sunday 4 August.
The package holiday business was only just starting in the 1960's. Some of my more affluent friends from school went to the continent every year with their parents or took an educational cruise on the school ship Nevasa. That was really posh.
My family always went to Ireland for the summer, which was great because we had family there and didn't have to pay for hotels. One year we went to Jaywick Sands; my dad's friend in the brickyard had a chalet there and let my dad have it cheap.
In June 1968, things were looking up. My ONC exams were over. I had a new positive attitude towards work. A small bonus due to the benevolence of my foreman meant I had some money in my Trustee Bank Book. It was time to think about the summer holidays, and it was time to spread our wings.

Erika and I took the train and went to the travel agent, Frames Tours, on the high street in Bedford. That's where my dad went to order our train and boat tickets to Rosslare. Long haul holidays with flights and hotels to Switzerland, Spain, Italy, and Greece were outside our budget.

However, the girl at Frames showed us some "less expensive" options. That's sales speak for "cheap".

One of these offered a holiday in San Sebastian, Spain. The package included transport from London and ten nights in a hotel with full board for £29.10s (yes! twenty-nine pounds ten shillings) each.

We asked our mate Mary Irvine, who lived in our street, and her current boyfriend John Carol from Bletchley to come with us. Teenagers going off unsupervised to the continent was somewhat too modern for my Irish mum and dad. But we didn't care, it was the sixties, and we were off on an adventure.

We all had to get passports. In those days, that was a simple matter because there was a thing called the British Visitor's Passport. This was a basic travel document that you could get from the Post Office. You only had to present your birth certificate or another valid form of identification.

It was intended for holiday visits to European countries for stays of no more than three months, and it was valid for one year only.

The document was a single buff-coloured card with two creases dividing it into three sections. When folded over each other, the sections formed a booklet with the Royal Coat of Arms on the front. Unfolded, the inside left section had details about the holder; the middle section held the holder's photograph glued on and over stamped by the Post Office; the left area was for country entry and exit stamps.

I can't remember how much it cost, but I doubt it was more than a few shillings. It was a simple document in an uncomplicated world and very easy to obtain. For obvious security reasons, it was scrapped in 1996.

The Friday evening before the holiday, I left work with my pay and holiday bonus in my pocket. I went to Woolworth and bought a bottle of Imperial Leather aftershave and a pair of wire-framed polaroid sunglasses, cool. I popped into the chemist and bought a pack of Sylvasun tablets, a new product advertised to prevent sunburn. With auburn hair and a typical Irish complexion, I burned easily. I hated sun cream, so tablets were a great option for me.

On Sunday morning, 21 July, my suitcase was packed, and I was ready to go. I had my tickets, £20 worth of Thomas Cook travellers' cheques and one thousand Spanish Pesetas in 100 Peseta notes from Frames.

Before midday, John Carol arrived in Brogborough in a 'Water Eaton Taxis' cab from Bletchley. Erika, Mary and I said our goodbyes, loaded our cases and set off for London. By 2 O'clock, we were unloading our gear outside Victoria Air Terminal in Buckingham Palace Road, between London Victoria railway station and Victoria coach station.

While we were paying the driver, a young London Bobby came over and told our taxi driver to remove the 'Water Eaton Taxis' sign on the top of his cab. The driver tried to explain that he'd just come in from outside of London to drop us off and would be returning directly to Bletchley. The young policeman was having none of it. Only licensed Hackney carriages were allowed to operate in London.

It sounds ridiculous today, but we left our poor driver unscrewing the sign from the top of his cab. Fortunately, the overzealous young constable didn't issue him a parking ticket while he did it.

We entered an impressive, curved, 5 story Art Deco building with a central tall clock tower and a "Wings Above The World" sculpture over its entrance.

We checked in our suitcases which we didn't see again until we arrived at our destination.

First-time international travellers, we were early. We had a four-hour wait until our departure time. At about six in the evening, we were shepherded onto our coach and set off out of London.

Either the coach driver had a drink problem, or we were running early because we pulled into a country pub just after seven, somewhere past Maidstone. Either way, sitting in an English pub garden in the warm evening sunshine, sipping a pint of bitter, was a pleasant start to our continental adventure.

We arrived at Lydd Airport at about eight-thirty. Airport was something of an exaggeration. It was, in reality, a rebranded Spitfire wartime station with a hanger, a control tower, and a passenger reception shed.

By nine-thirty, we were sitting in a twin-engine Handley Page Herald, ready for a quick hop across the Channel. Amazingly, during the twenty-minute flight, they ran a duty-free service. I bought a bottle of Haig's Dimple whisky and two hundred Benson and Hedges for about £3. This was the life.

Landing in Boulogne-Sur-Mer, we quickly cleared customs and passport control and headed into the French countryside. It was the first time I'd been in a foreign country travelling on the 'wrong' side of the road.

We reached Paris after midnight. It seemed that part of our travel itinerary was a city tour. However, after passing Notre Dame and the same two old French guys drinking pastis outside a street cafe three times, we realised our driver was lost. We eventually exited Paris early Monday morning, heading south.

From what we'd paid for the holiday, I doubt if the French coach company were making much money out of us. The driver must have been told to keep the fuel consumption down because he never went above 50mph. This was OK by me because the other traffic seemed to be driven by La Mans 24-hour racers with a death wish. I couldn't help noticing that scrap yards piled high with all types of seriously damaged vehicles were situated at regular intervals along our route.

Somewhere past Poitiers, the driver stopped at a cafe. Breakfast was included in the trip. That was just as well because none of us had any French Francs, only Pounds or Spanish Pesetas. It was a simple meal of coffee, a roll with butter and jam. The milky coffee came in huge cups like soup bowls. It was the best I'd ever tasted, utterly different from anything I'd ever had in England. Now, it really felt like we were on the 'continent'.

After breakfast, we pressed on south. Mary and John were in the seat in front of Erika and me. Behind us was a man about forty with a son of about ten. His overweight wife sat in the seat on the other side of the aisle. The man was chain-smoking untipped Senior Service, which was OK because almost everyone on the bus was smoking. However, he was continually complaining. When we uncapped our duty-free and started partying, the complaints got worse. When Mary began laughing, Mary had a very distinctive laugh; he demanded we keep the noise down. We tried to comply, but it degenerated into hand over mouth sniggering, which just infuriated the man more. We didn't care; we were on holiday.

By mid-afternoon, we'd passed the city of Bordeaux and were travelling on a straight road through mile upon mile of pine forest.

Mid-afternoon, we pulled into a large roadside restaurant for another scheduled stop. The place was very basic, with long trestle tables to accommodate mass holiday traffic. The meal was just bread and pâté, potato crisps, apricots and wine.

We were well into the south of France now, and the weather was noticeably warmer.

Travelling on dusty roads in late afternoon sunshine, not close enough to glimpse the sea, we passed Biarritz off to the west. Shortly after, we arrived at the Spanish border.

After clearing passport control, we finally arrived outside Hotel Juana in San Sebastian at about six in the evening. It had been a long trip with little sleep in the uncomfortable coach, but we weren't tired; we were excited. We were in Spain.

The four-story hotel was in a quiet street not far from the seafront. The facade was old, built of sandstone block with decorative stone and wrought iron fenced balconies with tall wooden framed windows. It was an impressive piece of architecture, as were the other buildings in the street and surrounding area. The place had a solid well-kept feel about it. With trees, hanging flower baskets and well-swept litter-free streets. There was an air of prosperity, not at all like the impression given in England of a poor, backward country stuck somewhere in the late 19th century.

Everyone piled off the bus, retrieved their luggage, climbed the few steps and entered through the large arched doorway into the hotel. After handing over our passports, we were taken to the second floor to our rooms.

In Franco's puritanical Spain, the girls were shown to their room at one end of the corridor. John and I were taken a suitable distance away. Our accommodation comprised two rooms because we were sharing with a Canadian man and his seventeen-year-old son who were doing a tour of Europe. It wasn't ideal because you had to pass through one room to get to the other. There were no en-suite facilities, and the toilets and shower rooms were at the end of the corridor. The situation was quickly resolved when the girls arrived and swapped rooms with the Canadians.

After travelling for eighteen hours, we needed to freshen up. A little after seven, we were washed, changed and out on the street, ready to explore.

We made our way onto a busy thoroughfare and headed across the road towards the seafront.

Then, only an hour after our arrival, we fell afoul of the Spanish police. We'd almost reached the pavement on the other side of the street when we heard a shrill whistle. Striding towards us, waving his hand, came an irate policeman in a flat peaked cap. He continued blowing the whistle until he reached us, at which time it fell from his mouth and dangled on a string around his neck. He began castigating us, but we stared blankly, not understanding what he was saying. Soon he realised we were brainless foreign holidaymakers. Even though we were only a couple of steps from the pavement, he shepherded us back across the street to where we'd just come from. He pointed to a group of people waiting to cross at traffic lights further down the road. Gagging Mary from further discussion with the policeman on the absurdity of Jaywalking laws that didn't exist in England, we thanked him politely and made our way to the traffic lights under his fierce glare.

After a quick reconnoitre of the area, we returned to the hotel.

After dinner, we were back on the street. Across from the hotel, there was an old taberna. It looked very traditional and a bit out of place against the grander architecture in the area. We decided to take a look. With no apparent designated crossing points, we reckoned it was safe to directly cross the street.

Nevertheless, we felt it only prudent to keep an eye out for the policeman as we did so. The old place was dimly lit. You could barely see the bar at the far side of the room through a haze of black cigarette tobacco and cigar smoke. The din from the chatter coming from the closely packed tables made it difficult to hear ourselves speaking. Down the right side of the room, there was a row of about six wooden doors, which were individual toilet cubicles that opened directly into the bar.

Not noticing that the other clients called over waiters when they wanted service, we made our way between the crowded tables to the counter. The bar staff, none of whom spoke English, tolerated this indiscretion once they realised, we were extranjeros.

The girls wanted port and lemon and thus started our first cultural interchange.

"Port and Lemon, please".

"Qué?"

We leaned across the bar and shouted above the noise, the standard English method of communication when dealing with foreigners who don't understand them.

"PORT AND LEMON PLEASE"

"QUÉ?"

This repeated dialogue continued for a while, but we were getting nowhere.

John and I walked down the bar, searching the bottles on the shelves until we found what we were looking for.

"THERE, LOOK, PORT." we pointed excitedly.

The barman came down, retrieved the black bottle from the shelf and studied the label.
"AH!" he said with a smile "OPORTO"
It might well have been oporto, but the label definitely said port.
With that linguistic misunderstanding resolved, we used the same method to identify the lemon mixer.
My order wasn't quite so tricky. I'd recently read Ian Fleming's Casino Royale and Moon Raker, so being in my Bond phase, I ordered a Vodka-Martini.
Behind the bar set into the wall was a row of heaven oak doored iceboxes. The barman opened one and went to fill a tall tumbler with ice. Coming from Brogborough, I wasn't used to having ice in my drinks. It certainly wasn't mentioned in the Bond books, so I indicated that I didn't want the ice by waving my hand. The barman put the tumble on the counter and half-filled it with vodka. Then, before I could stop him, he topped up the tall glass with Martini Rosso. I guess he wasn't into James Bond. Nonetheless, it tasted fine to me.
We found a table. Amidst the chatter of humanity, glasses and soda syphons clicked as waiters moved in and out of the tables.
Rows of Jamón Serrano pigs' legs hung above the bar. After a few days, if they weren't fully cured, they would be in an atmosphere filled with smoke from the smouldering black tobacco Ducado and Celta cigarettes.
It was my first experience of the beautiful characteristic smell of old Spain at its best, something almost impossible to find now in an ever protected and sanitised world.

After a few more drinks, we paid the bill of 100 Pesetas, about ten shillings, and went in search of the sea. I was a little wobbly from three tall vodka Martinis when we left the bar.

We got to the seafront a little before sundown. San Sebastian was beautiful. A city of elegant, imposing architecture with a backdrop of mountains against an azure sky. The city was built around La Concha bay that must have been a mile across. On either side of the entrance to the bay, there was a prominent green wooded hill. Between these hills, set like a jewel in blue water, was the island of Santa Clara.

Below the promenade where we were standing, there was a broad golden beach. The beach ran for more than a mile around the whole length of the lower curve of the bay.

We joined the throng on the promenade. The wide pedestrian walkway around the bay was full of people strolling in the warm evening air. It wasn't the number of people that caught my attention; it was the composition of the groups. There were individual married couples. Small family groups of father, mother and a few children. Extended family groups including children, parents, grandparents and great grandparents with walking sticks or being pushed in wheelchairs. There were groups of teenage boys and separate groups of girls.

Noticeably missing from the scene were young couples walking hand in hand, periodically stopping to kiss. In their place were courting couples walking, slightly separated, followed by a chaperone, an old lady with a head shawl dressed in black.

Occasionally you'd see these threesomes on a bench, the youngsters in conversation, their minder crocheting by their side. People were elegantly dressed as if out for a special occasion. This communal human activity was repeated each evening in San Sebastian. It wasn't a special event; it was the norm.

I'd never seen anything like it in England, not on the riverside embankment in Bedford and certainly not on the streets of Brogborough.

However, this tranquil scene was soon disturbed by a foreigner, a little worse for drink and desperate for a pee. With no public toilets to be seen, unable to speak the language to find one, he'd half-concealed himself in a bush to relieve himself.

I felt a hand on my shoulder and craned my neck to see who it was. At first, I thought it might be the policeman. Fortunately, it was a well-dressed man in his fifties who proceeded to give me the Spanish equivalent of a good bollocking. I couldn't turn around because I'd already started and couldn't stop. Again, having no understanding of local culture, I'd shamed my nation and myself. If jaywalking was a traffic violation, then peeing in public was probably a capital offence. Finished, I zipped up, endured a tongue lashing and was lucky not to find myself in a Franco-era cell awaiting trial. Guilty until proven innocent. That would have been an ignominious end to our first day in Spain.

I still remember that incident with an amount of shame, but I had no other choice under the circumstances.

I had my worst hangover the next day since the Christmas Eve rum and black incident. I spent an uncomfortable morning with a throbbing head on the beach with the others. With the resilience of youth, by late morning, I was feeling much better, but I was thinking, stuff James Bond and his Vodka Martinis.

The beach was packed. It highlighted another difference between the UK and Spain at that time. Except for Benidorm, which had special permission from Franco to develop the tourist industry, the bikini was banned in public. Ladies had to wear full bathing costumes that did not show too much flesh. Post-1975, the Generalissimo would turn in his grave.

A man selling drinks from an icebox wandered along the beach shouting "FANTA, COCA-COLA" in a gravelly voice.

I'd never heard of Fanta, so I called him over and bought a bottle. It was a pleasant orange coloured drink with a different flavour than the Corona or Hubbly Bubbly we had at home.

You couldn't buy it in England at the time, and it wasn't until years later I discovered why.

During the Second World War, the American government banned the export of Coca Cola syrup to its subsidiary in Germany. In response, the Germans developed their own drink called Fanta. It's no wonder it wasn't on sale in the UK. 1968 was still too early for the British to tolerate a soft drink invented in Nazi Germany.

It was too hot to sit on the beach by midday, so, suitably dressed, we took a stroll west along the promenade. At one point, coming towards us was a military-looking man. He was dressed in a very smart, well-pressed greenie-blue uniform. His traditional three-sided, shiny black Tricornio hat looked incongruous, almost comical to a British observer. However, the holstered pistol strapped to his hip and the black 9mm machine pistol hanging from his neck across his chest discouraged any act of disrespect. We had been warned not to mess with the Guardia Civil. A cursory glance gave him all the information he needed to know about us, and he continued his patrol.

We walked on until a rocky outcrop blocked further progress. The hill rose at a steep angle from the promenade, but it was scalable, so we decided to climb it to get a better view of the bay. John scrambled up first with me in tow. The girls followed at a more sedate pace.

When we were about twenty metres up the slope, John became interested in a football-sized boulder protruding from the shale. I came up beside him.

"What are you doing," I asked

"Let's make a splash", he replied.

Before I could stop him, he wiggled the rock free and let it roll. A couple of metres apart, Erika and Mary were coming up behind us. Mary saw it first, froze and screamed as it passed between the two girls.

Accelerating, the boulder careered down the slope, bouncing and throwing up shingle as it went until it hit the top of the low retaining wall at the base of the hill. With its accumulated energy, it bounced to the right. Rising in a high arc, it passed close to some people walking on the promenade before crashing with an almighty splash into the sea.

"What the fuck were you thinking, John?" I shouted.

A man in the group below recognised the language and said simply "Inglés" before shepherding his group to safety.

We'd been in the country less than 24 hours, and we'd already been involved in three incidents that could have ended up in an extended stay at the local police station. However, jaywalking or peeing up a tree was nothing compared to that last event. Thinking about the possible consequences of that boulder incident still makes me squirm. But as the Bard says, "all's well that ends well".

We weren't involved in further serious episodes, at least not until the final day we left for home.

We settled into our stay; the city was beautiful, as was the weather. Having put aside our nefarious activities, we found the people extremely friendly and helpful. Drinks were cheap, provided you didn't drink Scotch which was extremely expensive. There was none of that British one-sixth of a gill nonsense that delivered a thimble full of alcohol from an optic. In Spain, they slapped a long glass on the counter and poured the stuff straight out of the bottle until the glass was half full.

A local fizzy lemon drink was as sharp as a razor. I can't remember its name, but it was fantastic mixed with gin or vodka. The local beer came in brown bottles with a lion's head label embossed in white paint. It was excellent and cheap, costing less than a tonic water.

We did a few touristy things like a conducted tour of the shops. This started with a visit to a bodega for a liqueur tasting session to loosen up everyone's wallets. One night we signed on for a meal in a cellar restaurant combined with an exhibition of flamenco dance and Spanish guitar music. We passed on a trip to learn the art of bullfighting with baby bulls at a ranch that bred Toro Bravos. Just as well when we saw the would-be toreros return to the hotel battered and bruised.

One day, Mary said we should hire a boat and visit the island of Santa Clara. We agreed on the condition that she did the rowing. We made a picnic lunch, and to her credit, Mary rowed all four of us unassisted the half a kilometre across the bay to the island.
Leaving the boat bobbing in the clear water tied to a small jetty, we made our way up a winding track to the lighthouse and picnic area at the island's summit. Other than a bar by the jetty and a tiny beach that disappeared with the rising tide, there wasn't much to do on Santa Clara island. However, sitting under a warm sun in a clear blue sky, drinking wine with cheese and bread, with a spectacular view across the bay to the elegant city and mountains beyond, it was well worth the trip. It was a far cry from the grey skies, sulphurous air and the constant clack clacking of the cable trucks bringing clay from the pits to the brick kilns in Brogborough. We returned to the city in the early evening, this time John and I taking turns rowing.
One evening sitting outside a cafe at the fishing wharf on the east side of the bay, we ordered some sardines. The lady owner of the cafe walked across the dock and haggled for a while with a fisherman. She returned with a small basket of fish. A few minutes later, she came to our table with a plate of one-foot-long fried

sardines and a punnet of bread. They were nothing like the tiny things crammed into a tin with tomato sauce that we were used to. Apart from my grandfather's home in Rosslare, I'd never tasted fish like them. They were so good.

Another endearing memory of that time is of the two waiters who befriended us one evening in a local bar. They were genuinely interested in us and England. Strange as it seems, in those Franco days, you could pretty well do what you liked if you stayed within the moral code and kept out of politics. These waiters, and many others, worked freelance. For them, the bureaucracy was lax by today's standards. Each morning they'd assemble outside the aquarium in the old town, where bar owners would employ them on a daily basis depending on their expected workload. It seemed there wasn't much you didn't celebrate in the local bar in Spain with weddings, Christenings, confirmations, funerals, and birthdays.

It was a self-regulating system. Bar owners chose the best waiters, if the waiters didn't like the owners, they didn't take the job, and each had to offer fair service for fair working conditions. If a waiter wanted a day off, he simply didn't turn up at the aquarium.

If we made the 20-minute walk to the aquarium early enough, the waiters would tell us what bars they were working in that day. If we went to those bars, we got the first drink free.

One evening, we met the waiters in the square previously known as 'Plaza de la Constitución' with some of their friends. The square was renamed 'Plaza del 18 de julio' after the date of the 1936 coup d'etat that precipitated the Spanish Civil War that ultimately put

Franco in power. I guess the Basque people didn't think much of that because after Franco's death in 1975, the name reverted to 'Plaza de la Constitución'.

The plaza was fantastic, the epitome of old Spain. About 15 by 30 yards in size, each side of the square was made of sandstone arches. Behind the arches were covered pedestrian walkways with shops, bars, and restaurants. Above the arches were three levels of apartments with decorative wrought iron fenced balconies facing into the square. Each balcony was numbered because the plaza doubled as a bullring. What looked like apartments were actually the spectator boxes that were hired out for the bullfight.

The square was heaving with people. Erika and I became separated. By the time we were reunited, she'd received a marriage proposal from one of the waiter's friends. I should have been angry, but I couldn't really blame him.

We had a great time with the waiters, but they were often reluctant to talk about certain things in public. Towards the end of the holiday, we invited them back to our hotel for a farewell drink. In the privacy of our rooms, they talked freely. They didn't like Franco or his regime. It might have been alright for the old conservatives, but for the young, it was suffocating, especially in light of the cultural revolution going on in northern Europe.

It was clear that some young Basques were resentful. Something that soon became blatantly apparent.

Friday, 2 August, was our last night in San Sebastian before returning home. Unbeknown to us, that evening, an ETA (Basque nationalist) hit squad lay in wait outside the home of Melitón Manzanas in Irun, 13 miles east of San Sebastian. Manzanas was the commander of Franco's political police in San Sebastian. The ETA gunmen shot him seven times outside his house as he returned home from work.

It was ETA's first planned assassination. Franco's government declared a 'state of exception' throughout the Basque province. Late Saturday morning, when we were leaving for home, our coach was stopped at the French border. We were all taken off the bus to be identified by some very touchy, heavily armed Guardia Civil before being allowed to continue our journey. It was a dramatic finale to our Spanish holiday for kids from Brogborough, where an unarmed constable rode around the village on a bicycle.

We had an uneventful journey through France until we got to Paris that night. The son of the Senior Service, chain-smoking, serial complainer, took ill with stomach cramps.

We did our second tour of Paris, looking for a hospital. We eventually stopped outside an austere gothic building where the unfortunate youth was taken off the bus by his parents with our driver as interpreter. We waited for over an hour until the complainer and his family finally emerged from the building. The son, now cured of his malady, the family got back on the bus with little sympathy from their fellow travellers. The driver fired up the engine, and we were on our way.

We left Boulogne-Sur-Mer at daybreak on Sunday 4 August and arrived back at Lydd to the last bit of excitement of that holiday. As we circled the airfield, we could see a large bulldozer parked in the

middle of the airport's single runway. Undeterred, the pilot made a bumpy landing on the grass, passing a few yards from the stationary earth mover.
Back at Victoria, we took the tube to Euston, the train to Bletchley, and arrived home in Brogborough a little after lunchtime.
That holiday started a love affair with Spain that would eventually lead to the most fantastic journey of my life.

Shortly after returning from holiday, I received my exam results from Mander College. I passed all four subjects Mathematics, Applied Mechanics, Engineering Drawing and Electrical Engineering. With my newly acquired ONC, I enrolled on the two-year Higher National Certificate (HNC) course that started in September. I had to drop electrical engineering and concentrate solely on Mechanical and Production Technology. It was a shame. I wanted to enrol on the HNC Electronics course, but there was no way I could slip that past the ever-vigilant foreman, Mr Roe Wilson. Poverty-stricken as I was, at least now I had a little kudos. I was on my way to becoming a real engineer.

Back to college and Liberal studies

In September, I was back at college. With the entire day at college, Thursday was the brightest part of my week. Manipulating formulas and getting answers to complex problems may not seem like fun to some, but I loved it. There was a freedom of expression that you couldn't get working on a machine all day in a factory.

There are countless theories and formulas in engineering, and most of these involve Newton's integral and differential calculus. I have always loved mathematics. Well, ever since Fulbrook school days when I had similar feelings for Mrs Welch, our maths teacher. Engineering also requires a lot of practical hands-on stuff because it has tangible outputs like bridges, ships, dams, cars, aeroplanes, engines, spacecraft and intricate mechanisms. Anything from the manufacture of a needle to a massive moon rocket, so sometimes you have to put on a boiler suit and get your hands dirty. There's nothing wrong with that.

In Britain, at least when I was at college, the word engineer was used loosely. Anyone in a boiler suit carrying a shifting spanner called themselves an engineer. Ask them about Castigliano's theorem of strain energy bending' or 'Fourier transform vibration analysis', or the simple question of the difference between mass and weight. You'd be confronted with the 1000-yard stare. I'm not trying to be elitist. It's just when you've had to cram your head with all that stuff; it's annoying. You wouldn't ask your butcher to take your appendix out. Likewise don't look for an engineer, especially me, to de-bone a carcass.

Maybe I'm too sensitive, but in places like Germany, France and Spain, the title Engineer is protected by law.

This attitude about engineers extended to college. It seemed that the authorities thought we were a lot of rough diamonds that needed polishing. In some respects, they were right. Engineers tended to be down to earth pragmatists who spoke their minds.

Therefore, we were obliged to attend a weekly class called Liberal Studies to supplement our technical training. The idea was to give us a foundation in the humanities, arts and social sciences and integrate us into society. However, I never saw one of those students attend an engineering class. Nevertheless, it was a good idea.

One task was to read and discuss Orwell's Animal Farm (which I'd already read) and '1984' which I hadn't. Another time each week, one student had to present a non-engineering topic, followed by a discussion or debate on the subject. The topics chosen by the students were diverse, ranging from the supernatural and the existence of ghosts to the Roman occupation of Britain, Pike fishing, and Canaletto.

By then, I had a lot of interests, Strauss, art, all things military, girls!

My slot was at the end of October. I wanted to talk about something controversial, but I was having trouble finding a topic. Then out of the blue, a subject presented itself.

On 5 October, a civil rights march was planned in Londonderry, Northern Ireland. The Government banned the march, but the civil rights activists went ahead with it. The Royal Ulster Constabulary (RUC) baton-charged the crowd, and over 100 people were injured.

One of my dad's Sunday newspaper magazines from a friend in the brickyard ran an article on the incident. The civil rights marchers were made up of Catholics who wanted equal rights and Irish Nationalists who wanted the reunification of Ireland. They demanded an end to discrimination in housing allocation and jobs, especially government jobs. They wanted one man, one vote. Only householders could vote. If you had more than one house, you had more than one vote in local elections, whereas all adults had a vote on the British mainland. They wanted an end to gerrymandering, the manipulation of electoral boundaries that reduced Catholic voting power even in areas where they had a majority. They wanted reform of the RUC police force, which was 90% Protestant. They wanted the repeal of the Special Powers Act that allowed police to search without a warrant, arrest and imprison people without charge or trial, ban any assemblies or parades, and ban any publication.

A civil rights campaign in the UK was controversial enough for me. The article also presented wider implications that included the antiquated voting system on the UK mainland.

I asked my dad what he knew about the subject. He was a confirmed Anglophile who loved living in England, but what he told me pretty well agreed with the newspaper article.

To stir things up a bit, I titled my talk "Why Britain is not a democratic country". I didn't really believe that, but I didn't have to if I wanted to start a debate. I spent time in the Bedford library verifying my facts.

On the day of the presentation, I was nervous. I hated public speaking and still do. I knew there'd be a backlash and regretted not choosing a more mundane subject. But it was too late to change.

I started by saying, the British - first past the post - voting system was not equitable. A Member of Parliament (MP) could be elected with less than 51% of the vote. If four candidates contested a seat, an MP could be elected with as little as 28% of the vote (28%, 24%, 24%, 24%).

I continued that because the number of voters in each electoral seat varied, a party could come to power with a majority of seats but a minority of the popular vote. It could and did happen.

Then I came to The House of Lords. The Lords are involved in debating, amending laws, and checking the actions of the Government. However, unlike the US Senate, The Lords are unelected and unaccountable to the UK electorate.

As an example of how things can go wrong in the British form of democracy, I cited the current civil rights grievances in Northern Ireland.

I'd expected to start a debate, but I hadn't anticipated how partisan people could be about their own national system of Government.

In short, I got pilloried.

Regardless of the argument I had presented, I was told in no uncertain terms that all these grievances could be resolved with a referendum. Although, in 1968, a national referendum had never been held in the UK. In addition to that, only Parliament could call a referendum, and because of Parliamentary Sovereignty, the government had no obligation to comply with the wishes of the electorate following a referendum.

The result was a right barney. I learned that one person's perception of a logical argument, in this case, mine, can differ vastly from someone else's. Also, you should not expect logic where human emotion is concerned. Unlike engineering, you could not apply a common formula that works for all in politics. In the end, we all remained friends.

However, no one saw the coming storm in Ireland, not even me.

I think it was sometime in late November when Erika and I fell out again. It wasn't that we had a volatile relationship; on the contrary, we generally got on great. It's just that these things happen when you're young.

Nevertheless, it was always a depressing time for me. It didn't take long before another boyfriend came calling, and living on the opposite side of the street, I couldn't miss the comings and goings. What made it worse this time was that my other good friend Mary, who lived just three houses up from Erika, started going out with a boy from Luton way. As the two girls were best friends. The two of them were off out together all the time, So to me, it seemed I'd lost two friends at the same time.

There was only one thing I could think of to ease the pain. I took the train to Bedford, had a haircut, went to Burtons, and ordered a new bottle green, made to measure suit, which cost about fifteen pounds. It took less than half an hour to get measured up. I returned to the shop two weeks later, and the suit fitted perfectly. No way could I afford to pay for the suit in one go. I made the first payment and walked out with the suit and Burton's twelve-monthly instalment payment card.

As usual, when I was at a loose end, I began spending weekends down at Marston Club and started a relationship with a blond girl called Pat.

Apollo 8 moon orbit

During that time, the late President Kennedy's dream of "landing a man on the Moon and returning him safely to Earth" was close to becoming a reality. On Christmas Eve 1968, the crew of Apollo 8 went into lunar orbit. The crew became the first humans to leave Earth and reach another celestial body. It was an orbital encounter, but there was no moon landing.

That same night my friend Ambrose Cashin (the younger brother of Richard, the shredded wheat box helmeted knight) and I went to the Marston Club dance. After the dance, we took our girlfriends home and then walked along the B557 Bedford road back to Brogborough.

Earlier in the evening, it had snowed. The surrounding landscape of trees, hedgerows and the rooftops of the few houses on that lonely road were covered by a sparkling white blanket. But for the double tracks made by the few vehicles that had passed since the fall, it would have been difficult to negotiate the road blanketed in six inches of snow. Fortunately, the clear black sky was filled with twinkling stars and a bright golden half-moon.

Walking side by side, in our own tyre track, a little drunk and emitting clouds of frozen breath, we chatted happily on our long trudge home.

Suddenly, overcome with emotion, like a stage actor, I threw up my open left hand at the moon.

"Just look at that, Ambrose." I exclaimed, "Can you believe it? Tonight, for the first time in human history, three men from here on earth are in orbit around the moon".

I rambled on about, "If only Galileo and Newton were here to see it".

Ambrose didn't respond. I looked to my right. The track was empty. Ambrose was gone.

Fifty yards behind me, Ambrose was lying flat on his back, across the tracks in the snow. In the distance, a pair of headlights were heading in our direction.

I ran back along the tyre track. When I reached him, I was relieved to see two plumes of white mist puffing from his nostrils. As I grabbed him by his lapels, his eyes opened.

"Hi Bernie", he slurred ", I fell asleep".

I pulled him up, and we stepped back into the snow on the side of the road. Shortly after, an empty coach whizzed by and disappeared into the night.

Three-quarters of an hour later, we arrived in Brogborough. It was well past midnight, it was a white Christmas, man had gone to the moon, and 'Lily the Pink' by The Scaffold was number one in the charts. Life was OK.

It may have been the season of goodwill, but the war dragged on in Vietnam as we drifted from Christmas towards the New Year. 1968 had been the war's deadliest year. It saw the death of over sixteen and a half thousand American troops. Opposing the Americans, the People's Army of Vietnam and the Viet Cong had lost around two hundred thousand killed. Still, they showed no signs of giving up. Some say the average age of the American soldiers fighting in Vietnam was 19; others say it was older. Whatever the age, I was 19 years old in 1968 and happy to be living in Britain with no conscription for National Service. I was glad I didn't have to go off and kill or get killed in some foreign land fighting people I didn't know. Some of my friends like Ray, Frank and Morris had joined the British Army, but they did it because they wanted to, not because some politicians said they had to.

Sometime in January 1969, Ray drove up from Hereford. You never knew when he'd turn up in Brogborough. He was away a lot. Sometimes he'd tell me where he'd been, like when he was in Canada or winter training in Norway. Other times you might as well try to get blood from a stone. In the end, I stopped asking. What he did tell me this time was he had a girlfriend. As far as I remember correctly, she was a trainee teacher. I think they met in the Bunch of Grapes pub, which was a favourite haunt for SAS troopers then before the world changed and that sort of association became a security issue. She was a Welsh girl called Pat, Patricia, the same name as Ray's sister. I hadn't met her then, but I soon would. She wasn't very big, but you wouldn't want to upset her.

I soon learned that if she ever said: "I beg your pardon" or "Excuse me", that wasn't to be taken as politeness. It meant you should think very carefully about what you were about to say next, or you were setting yourself up for a verbal lashing.

Woe betides anyone who said anything derogatory about Wales, "God's own country". However, we soon became good friends. You knew where you stood with Pat, and so did Ray, for that matter.

Ray's sister Pat was also in the Army. Ray had come to pick his sister up from Mill Hill Barracks on this occasion.

While Ray and I were having a beer in the club, Irvine overheard we were going to London, so he gave me some money to buy records for the youth club that was held in the dance hall.

After picking up Ray's sister and a New Zealand girl, who was also in the British Army, we went into Mill Hill to find a record shop.

All I can remember buying was 'Fox on the Run' by Manfred Mann and 'Albatross' by Fleetwood Mac, both of which were in the charts. I also bought an LP by Sonny Terry and Brownie McGhee, an American guitar and harmonica Blues duo.

We got back from Mill Hill on the M1 with Papworth driving like Sterling Moss in about 30 minutes. Ray had no problem taking a calculated risk even after the trolley accident on Brogborough hill that almost killed him. There was a maximum speed limit on the M1 of 70mph since before 1967, but there were no radar traps or speed cameras. In those days, the police had to follow you to log your speed. If you keep your wits about, you could avoid getting caught. However, one serious problem was the lack of central and side crash barriers on the motorway. A high-speed blowout could result in a roll down an embankment or a cross over into the oncoming traffic. I saw that happen one morning when I was on the slip road hitching a lift to work. A woman in a red E-Type Jaguar came thundering under the bridge heading south. She had a front-wheel blowout and spun across the central reservation, facing the wrong direction on the north going lanes. Immediately, a Bedford van screeched to a stop on the southbound fast lane. Two men jumped out, attached a chain to the back of the van, ran across the road and fixed the chain to the woman's car. They leapt back into the van and dragged the E-Type, with the stunned woman still in it, across the central reservation onto the southbound hard shoulder. There wasn't the volume of traffic in those days. Even so, the woman was lucky that the recovery happened so fast during a lull in the flow of vehicles in both directions. I'd never seen anything done so professionally in my life. It was heroic. I guess the two guys would be prosecuted if they tried that today.

Regardless, we got back to Brogborough in one piece.

In February, Erika and I got back together again. Amen Corner were number 1 in the charts with "If Paradise Is Half as Nice", which felt entirely appropriate. To celebrate, Erika got dressed up. I put my new suit on, and we walked down the middle path through the brickyard to the Bedford Arms pub by the side of Ridgmont station. It was a cold dark winter night, it was either that or Brogborough club, but we didn't want company.

A few days later, one evening sitting at the bottom of the stairs in my house, we decided to get engaged. Not a very logical decision on my wages. About half an hour after she went home, Erika was back sobbing. The idea hadn't gone down well at home. I can't remember the reason for the disruption. Maybe Johnny Falk, being head of the household, thought I should have asked his permission, or possibly Lily, Erika's mum, thought we were just too young. Either way, it all blew over, and we went ahead with it. We even had an engagement party at our house. To be honest, it was more symbolic than anything. We didn't actually start planning a wedding, and things just went on as usual.

During the spring, Ray came up to Brogborough a couple of times with Pat. We all got on well together, and when Erika and I told them we planned to go to Ireland for our summer holidays, they asked if they could tag along.

Considering what happened on the island of Ireland and on the UK mainland over the following 30 years, it seems incongruous now that in the late 1960's, you would think of going on holiday to the Republic of Ireland with someone in the British Army, let alone a soldier from the SAS. However, it was a different time. The lull before that horrible storm kicked off.

Letters were exchanged. Auntie Mae said Ray and I could stay at the Butler Arms Cafe and arranged lodgings for the girls in a B&B on the clifftop off St Martin's Road.

On 13 July, a relative of Ray's drove us to Bletchley station, where we took the train to Euston. London was experiencing a heatwave. With a temperature of 88ºF (31ºC), it was sweltering in the underground when we took the 20-minute tube journey to Paddington. But it was great, real holiday weather. I just loved that part of the journey. The underground with its unique smells, full of characters, buskers and fellow travellers, the train's roar coming out of the tunnel pushing a wave of air in front of it. The theatre and cinema poster ads: 'The Mousetrap' by Agatha Christie was still running at Ambassadors Theatre from its opening in 1952. Oh, Calcutta was billed to open at the Roundhouse at the end of the month; The film The Italian Job with Michael Caine was finishing a run in Leicester Square.

Then up the escalator to Paddington, bustling as usual with passengers coming off and running for trains and lines of taxis picking up and dropping off fares.

We found an outside table at a pub close to our platform, sat down with some cold Heineken lagers and watched the world go by. Time Is Tight by Booker T & the MGs drifted out from the pub's music system.

Soon, we were on our way on a long train with corridor carriages and a dining car heading for Fishguard and the ferry to Rosslare.

In Rosslare, the Butler Arms cafe was, as usual, a building site. Aunty Mae was again in conflict with the local council for illegal building. That was not unusual; this time, she was extending the back of the cafe with extra bedrooms and a toilet and shower room to take advantage of the B&B business that was starting to boom in Rosslare. Ray and I got a bedroom each, but I think the building project probably had a restraining order slapped on it. Neither of the bedrooms was finished, the walls were not plastered, and there were no tiles on the floor. However, they did have lighting with a switch by the door and a bulb hanging from the ceiling. Wires were sticking out from the walls that we steered clear of. The toilet-shower room was in the same condition, but at least the toilet and shower were functional. Most importantly, auntie Mae had managed to get a couple of beds set up for our visit.

Having already been deployed to some godforsaken parts of the world, Ray did not have any complaints. As for me, it was just somewhere to sleep, and I was grateful to my auntie Mae for putting us up.

This was all typical of my aunty. She had these grand ideas and, with such enthusiasm, often set to work before obtaining the correct paperwork or first assessing the funds and resources required to complete the project.

Auntie Mae often seemed stern. She was not. She was just always preoccupied with running the cafe, petrol station, and any other business venture that had taken her fancy.

Mae had a heart of gold, and one thing you could be sure of was a good Irish breakfast of sausage, bacon, black pudding, beans, fried eggs, toast and a large pot of tea in the mornings.

In the meantime, Pat and Erika settled into a more tranquil setting overlooking the sea at the other end of the village.

The weather was fantastic most of the time, with bright sunny days well above average temperatures, sometimes as high as 82ºF (28ºC). In Ireland, that was a tropical heatwave.

We spent our days on the beach having picnics and walking south until the beach ran out near Carnsore Point. Other times we took the train north the short distance to Rosslare Strand and had our picnic mixing with the tourists on the beach there.

We'd visit my granddad Ben Boyce and uncle Ben in the evenings at 1170 Colville Street. We'd have a supper of bread, cheese, ham, and Erin dried soup cooked in grandad's kitchen on his paraffin primus stove. After that, we'd spend the night in the Harbour View Hotel drinking and shooting the breeze with my friend Brendan Walsh, the RNLI lifeboat volunteer. Sometimes we had a drink in the bar of the Great Southern Hotel on the clifftop close to auntie Mae's cafe. On one occasion, we spent the evening in the lounge of the Railway Social Club on St Martin's Road with my Welsh auntie Betty and uncle Tommy Boyce.

One evening we indulged ourselves and took the train into Wexford. In the Talbot Hotel, we had a steak dinner and dessert, followed by proper Irish coffees.

Before catching the last train back to Rosslare, we finished the night with Irish Mist liqueurs, a blend of Irish whiskey, heather, clover honey and aromatic herbs.

Another day we took the train to Wicklow. We did some shopping for food, then walked out of the town, found a track and followed it until we came to a field that ended by a rocky cliff overlooking the Irish Sea. Another picnic in glorious sunshine. After lunch, Ray disappeared. A little later, we heard a shout. Carefully approaching the edge, we saw him perched on a tooth of rock projecting from the side of the cliff. I'm not good with heights and looking down on the scene made me nauseous. After being ordered up by Pat, we went back to the safety of the field. A moment later, a hand appeared on the grass, and Ray pulled himself up from the abyss. It never ceases to amaze me what people do for fun, which is a contradiction when you hear what I have to say next.

One morning at about ten o'clock, towards the end of the holiday, Ray and I walked along the clifftop from auntie Mae's to meet the girls at their B&B. As we reached the end of the cliff path, the heavens opened, and it poured with rain. It took us by surprise because until then the weather had been so good. The rain was so bad that we took shelter in the bar of the Harbour View Hotel and ordered two pints of Harp lager to drink until the weather cleared, but the rain continued. The girls found us during a short break in the weather, around lunchtime. By then, Ray and I were settled in for the afternoon. We weren't going anywhere. The girls had a drink but gave up on the weather, and the two of us, for the day. They returned to their lodgings to catch up on their holiday reading.

Ray and I were pretty far gone at about ten that night, having been on the pop for twelve hours. Having exhausted almost every subject under the sun, we decided it was time to try to find our way home.

Halfway along the cliff path, I remembered the old gun emplacement. In the light of an almost full moon, I pointed to a section of flat concrete that was partially buried in the cliff twenty feet below. Inexplicably, with bravado resulting from too much Harp lager, I slid down the steep slope and stood on top of the man-made shelf. I called Ray down, but sensibly he declined, so I did a little jig to show that the roof was stable. It was then that I stepped backwards over the edge. I rolled down the wet grass of the precipice until I hit the road at the bottom. It took me a while to realise where I was and what had happened. No bones broken, I walked up the hill to meet Ray, where the path joined the road at the top of the cliff.

It's said the effects of gravity can be grave! I was lucky, but I wasn't the only one feeling the effects of gravity that week. A few days earlier, Apollo 11 reached the moon. On Sunday, 20 July, a man walked on the lunar surface for the first time. The dream of the late President Kennedy had come true. By strange coincidence, not only was Kennedy of Irish descent but so were the three astronauts on that mission to the moon.

Neil Armstrong, Apollo 11's Mission Commander and the first man to walk on the moon, was proud of his Ulster heritage. Buzz Aldrin, who followed Armstrong down the ladder and into history, had his roots in Co. Fermanagh. Orbiting in the Command Module was the namesake of one of Ireland's most famous heroes, Michael Collins, whose grandfather, Jeremiah Collins, emigrated to the US in 1860 from Dunmanway in Co. Cork. Even the first American to orbit the earth, John Glenn, his great grandparents were David Glenn from Londonderry and Nancy Ann Dunlap from Monaghan.

It was true; the Irish did get everywhere. Now they were on the bloody moon.

Nine days before the moon landing, David Bowie released his single "Space Oddity", and just for the record, You've guessed it. Bowie's great grandparents on his mother's side were Irish immigrants who settled in Manchester.

On Sunday, 27 July, our holiday in Ireland came to an end. Ray and I settled up with auntie Mae. She charged us a token fee of seven shillings and sixpence each for the two weeks. Before we left for the harbour, she gave me back the three half-crowns I'd given her.

While we were getting ready to leave for the ferry, the news came through that the SAS soldier Tom McClean had arrived in Blacksod Bay, Ireland, by boat from Newfoundland, Canada. McClean was the first man to row the Atlantic ocean single-handed from west to east. And you might know it. After being abandoned as a baby, McClean began life as an orphan at the Bethany Home in Dublin.

We sailed back to Fishguard on the St David, but there was one more little adventure before the end of that holiday.

To save some money, we agreed that if Ray bought two discounted return train tickets using his army ID, I'd give Pat my tick and use one of the cheaper tickets. Ray said if anyone asked, I should say I was in the Royal Marines and went off to get the tickets. We were well on our way when the ticket man slid back the compartment door. After checking Ray's ID and perforating the others' tickets, he came to me. He looked at it, then back at me when I handed him my ticket.

"Can I see your ID please?" he asked.

"I'm in the Royal Marines", I replied stupidly. I was such a terrible liar. I did have very short-cropped hair, but the flaw in my new persona was that I didn't have a neck that started at the ears and finished at the width of my shoulders.

"So, where's your ID?" he insisted.

"I don't have it with me," I replied.

"Then how did you buy this ticket?" he demanded.

I didn't know what else to do, so I pointed at Ray.

"He bought it," I said lamely.

He went back to Ray and began haranguing him about buying two tickets on one ID. Supposedly, it shouldn't have happened. I don't know what story Ray had given the ticket office in Fishguard.

Ray asked the ticket inspector if they could continue the discussion out in the corridor. They stepped outside, slid the door shut, and moved out of view. A few minutes later, Ray came back into the compartment. The ticket inspector stood in the doorway.

"Alright," he said, "I'll let it go this time. But don't do it again".

I thought he was talking to me, but I couldn't make eye contact. I held my head slightly lowered, looking suitably chastened.

That over, Ray sat down. When I looked at him, he just shrugged.

I didn't know what was said in the corridor, and I didn't ask. Knowing Ray, it would have been a quiet affair. An apology, an explanation and finally, an appeal to the ticket inspector's better nature because of the problems it would cause if the matter were taken further. As we disembarked at Paddington, the ticket inspector was leaning out of a train door window halfway along the platform. He smiled, raised his hand, and wished us "Good luck" when we passed. We acknowledged him and walked on with renewed belief in humanity. I was happy I wasn't facing a court appearance relating to some 18th-century law regarding impersonating a member of HM Armed Forces and, being Irish, a deportation order to Australia.

We were young, what do you expect?

On 12 August, sixteen days after we returned from holiday, rioting broke out in Londonderry, Northern Ireland, in the Battle of the Bogside. Between 13 and 17 August, sectarian rioting spread across the province, and police used CS gas on rioters for the first time in the UK. The Taoiseach of the Republic of Ireland, Jack Lynch, made a speech requesting a United Nations peacekeeping force.

On 14 August, British troops were deployed to restore law and order on the streets of the UK for the first time since the General Strike of 1926.

This was the first significant confrontation of The Troubles. This conflict killed 3,532 people and maimed countless others from all sides over the next thirty years.

It was ironic. My presentation about British democracy during Liberal Studies at college the year before did not seem so tongue in cheek now.

And Now for Something Completely Different.

On the night of 26 October, I returned home from Brogborough Club. Everyone was in bed. When I turned on the TV, I was confronted with an Army Sergeant teaching a group of men to defend themselves against an assailant armed with fresh fruit, like bananas and strawberries. One man in the group kept asking, in a Welsh accent, how to protect himself against a man with a pointed stick. This was followed by a sketch about some secret service agent in a bookshop that gradually filled up with various undercover dentists.

The show ended with some rousing military marching tune and a cartoon with a big shoeless foot coming down from the sky and crushing someone. It was all quite bizarre but strangely funny. I had never seen anything like it before. I had just watched the end of the fourth episode of Monty Python's Flying Circus. Once more, life would never be the same again.

Chapter 11

Into the Unknown

Sometime around February 1970, Erika and I finished again. This time it was different. We weren't getting back together. She was working at Texas Instruments (TI) in Bedford. She was doing well there; she'd moved from the quality control lab to time and motion study.

I suppose it was inevitable. TI was a big company with a lot of staff. We'd got engaged, but I was as broke as ever. The prospect of getting married was pretty dim, and we were too young anyway. She wasn't a girl any more. She was a woman, and women needed commitment. I was happy to go aimlessly along with the status quo. Understandably, she wasn't.

I should have seen it coming. A chap from TI with a Mark II Ford Cortina started picking her up and bringing her home from work. I suppose that relationship blossomed while we were drifting apart. Even so, it was a jolt when the final break came. It's strange, though; it's difficult to distinguish between a broken heart and wounded pride. Either way, it was one of the most painful periods of my life.

Nevertheless, that jolt was probably the best thing that could have happened to me. I was in a rut at work, just going with the flow from day to day. I couldn't do much about that. But that was coming to an end. In September, I would finish my apprenticeship, and then I'd have the freedom to choose a new path. Mr Maxfield, who owned Hillmax Engineering in Luton, always picked me up when he saw me thumbing to and from work. He seemed to see something in me of which I was unaware. He told me to contact him when I finished my apprenticeship.

After three years, Erika and I were finished, but life is a strange and wonderful thing. Once the bitterness receded, we became the best of friends. Along with Mary and Ray, that friendship has lasted a lifetime. The thing I missed most about being with Erika was the laughter. Sometimes, for no apparent reason, we'd burst into hysterical laughter that was self-perpetuating and physically painful.

After the breakup, I reconnected with many old friends, especially Stephen and Hanns Pauli. They lived two doors down at number 28 Highfield Crescent. Their father had been a young German Afrika Korps soldier, captured while fighting in the western desert. Like thirty thousand other German POWs, Mr Pauli never went home. At the end of the war, he stayed in Brogborough and married the daughter of the local farmer Mr Bevington. I can't remember Mr Pauli; he must have died around the time Hanns was born when they lived on the farm. My dad said he died from a stomach problem he'd contracted in the desert.

I also became good friends with Valerie from Brogborough and her husband, Stevie Devine, from Belfast.

Val's maiden name was Cox; she had an older sister called Marion and two brothers, Colin and Ken.

Ken was married to a girl from up north called Josie. They lived up the top street, and for a while, Billy Brindle, a boy about my age, who may have been Josie's brother, lived there too. I didn't actually know Josie, but I saw her often as a kid because she used the side path, past the two trees where we played, to take the train to Bletchley, where she worked. Josie Cox was always immaculately dressed. I thought she was rather posh, so I never spoke to her other than saying hello when she passed. I wish I had now because I couldn't have been more wrong. In 1987 Josie, the schoolteacher, became Josephine Cox, the author. Her books about working-class life were drawn from her own tough upbringing in a mill house in Blackburn, Lancashire. She wrote over 60 novels selling 20m copies before her death in July 2020, aged 82.

Having been dumped by my girlfriend, the first part of 1970 was a period of adjustment for me. That sounds very resolute, as if I were immersed in some deep planning for my future. It wasn't like that at all. In fact, it was all subliminal. A little voice whispering in my head driven by uncertainty and probably a feeling of inferiority. My apprenticeship didn't finish until September, but that was out of my hands. I'd completed three years, so it was only right that I finish it. I had my final Higher National Engineering exams coming up, so I had to double down and prepare for them. That had to be fitted in around a pastime of chasing girls. I was always short of cash, and I hated being continually poverty-stricken; it was a consideration in everything I did.

For example, in the early spring of 1970, my friend Phil Ramsden from Bedford was marrying Pauline, one of the Coleman girls from Brogborough. Phil and I became good friends when I was on the final ONC course at Mander College, and Pauline and Phil met at a party at my house.

On the wedding day, I was chatting with a group of Phil's mates outside the church when a British racing green MG B GT arrived and parked in the church grounds. We didn't take much notice until the doors opened.

"Bloody hell," someone said. "Look at that.

The conversation stopped, and we watched in silence as two tall blondes in long open leather coats, miniskirts and long boots got out of the car and walked towards the church.

They couldn't have missed our dumb, drop-jaw expressions as they strode in synchronisation, side by side like two catwalk models toward us.

Just as they passed us going into the church, the driver looked directly at me and said.

"Hi Bernard, how are you?"

"Oh er. Good, thanks". I replied, stunned.

As they disappeared into the church, all eyes turned to me.

"Who's she?"

I raised my hands and shrugged in amazement. "I have no idea".

"Well, she certainly knows you".

After the service at the reception in the Bedford Arms by Ridgmont railway station, I sidled up to Pauline. Inclining my head towards the girl, I whispered. "Who's she, and how does she know me?"

"That's Sharon", Pauline replied. "She was on the same course as me at Mander".

Pauline had day release at Mander on the same day as me. I often saw her in the cafeteria at a table with other girls. I'd always go up and say hello. Still, so much for my power of observation. With my head full of formulae, I'd never noticed Sharon.

After the meal, armed with her name, I made it my business to talk to Sharon as if we were old pals. Later Sharon said she had to take her friend to Bletchley station to catch the train and asked me if I'd like to come along. Would I.

To the envy of the other unattached males, I followed the two girls out of the reception. Looking back, I shrugged helplessly. Someone had to do it.

We dropped her friend at the station. I changed from the discomfort of what passes for a back seat in a 2+2 sports car to the front bucket seat next to Sharon.

I thought we were returning to the reception. However, before turning to the Bedford Arms, on the road to Brogborough, she said she was going clubbing in Bedford and asked if I'd go with her.

Bloody hell. I've just been picked up by a rich girl in a sports car.

And there was the problem. Broke, as usual, a ten-shilling note and loose change in my pocket wouldn't get me far where she wanted to go. I could have told her the truth, but I was too embarrassed, so I lied. I told her I intended to go back to the wedding reception. Obviously, she had other plans for me and wasn't very happy with that idea. Nevertheless, she dropped me opposite Brogborough CIU Club and drove off on my insistence.

I went into the club and bought a pint of Whitbread Trophy bitter for one shilling and ten pence to drown my sorrows. What a missed opportunity.

Irvine was behind the bar. When I told him the sad story, he said sympathetically.

"You bloody idiot. Why didn't you come in here and tell me. I would have GIVEN YOU a fiver just to hear the end of the story".

I could imagine Sharon driving home that evening also thinking, 'What a bloody idiot'. She probably thought I was gay, not that that term was in everyday use in those days. I would have liked to have seen the end of the story if I'd had Irvine's fiver. That's life.

As a postscript to my sorry tale, there is a sadder one.

During the reception, I talked with Phil's brother Ronnie. I knew Ronnie had been in the Parachute Regiment and had been involved in the British intervention in Anguilla in March 1969. What I didn't know was he'd recently passed selection and joined the SAS regiment. I asked him if he knew my friend Ray. He said he'd seen him in Hereford, but he didn't know him. Less than two years after that conversation, Ronnie was dead. On 9 March 1972, Ronnie was shot and killed while leading an SAS patrol in Dhofar in Oman. He was 26 years old.

Apollo 13: 11 to 17 April 1970.

It must have been the morning of 14 April. I was having a cup of tea and a slice of toast before going to work when the news broke over the radio that the Apollo 13 moon mission, launched on 11

April, was in trouble. During the night of the 14th (UK time), the Service Module (SM) oxygen tank blew out, venting its contents into space. It wasn't Commander Jim Lovell, played by Tom Hanks in the film, who said, "Houston, we have a problem". The Command Module (CM) pilot Jack Swigert said the fateful words, and those words were actually, "Houston, we've had a problem". Because the three-man crew were too occupied investigating a bang to contact Huston Control.

Low on oxygen and electricity, the crew transferred to the Lunar Module (LM), which acted as a lifeboat to loop around the moon for the return trip to earth.

For the next four days, along with millions of others, I was obsessed with the news and the efforts of the NASA scientists and engineers to save the crew. What we didn't know at the time was such an eventuality had been anticipated and covered in the simulator as part of crew training. However, simulation was one thing, reality was another. The greatest unforeseen danger requiring an impromptu solution was the build-up of carbon dioxide in the LM that threatened to asphyxiate the crew. The LM was designed to support two men on the moon for two days; now, it had to support three men for four days.

On 17 April, millions worldwide watched the crew of Apollo 13 splashdown safely.

Apollo 13 would have been the third moon landing, but already the public had lost interest in the USA-Soviet space race. Due to a lack of public interest and the diversion of funding to the Skylab programme, moon missions after Apollo 17 were cancelled.

Loss of public interest or not, I was still thinking about trying to get a job with NASA.

Apollo 13 wasn't the only drama in April 1970. On the day Apollo 13 arrived safely back from the moon, Paul McCartney released his first solo album 'McCartney'.

On 10 April, instead of holding a promotional interview with the press, McCartney issued a 'self-interview' that included a list of questions to which he'd provided answers.

Some answers were ambiguous, but one was very clear; the song writing partnership of Lennon and McCartney was over. The press read this as an announcement that the Beatles were no more. True or not, the message spread worldwide that the Beatles had officially broken up.

A lot of people were devastated. It was a sad time for me and others like me who'd experienced the music revolution of the sixties. However, a lot of people had already seen it coming.

The previous year, Paul McCartney had married Linda Eastman, and John Lennon had married Yoko Ono. Many blamed the wives for the breakup of the song writing team, but I doubt that. By the time of the breakup, all four Beatles were married. They were individuals who'd stopped playing live concerts together years earlier. They'd grown up.

Nevertheless, it was the end of an era, but it wasn't the end of the music. My God, it still creates a buzz today.

And so I drifted on into the summer. For most of that time, the song Wand'rin' Star by Lee Marvin was on the charts. It was played a lot, and it certainly fit my mood, "Wheels are made for rollin, mules are made to pack". I wanted to get away, but I still had my exams and that bloody apprenticeship to finish.

That's not to say I didn't have some fun times hanging out with my friends from Brogborough. Most weekends, we went dancing; sometimes, this was followed by a take-away and a trip to the ten-pin bowling alley in Bedford. We also had a lot of parties where we drank far too much alcohol.

One time, Tommy Cashin, Ambrose's brother, had a party in the garage at the bottom of his garden. That night Hanns and Stephen had a disagreement. Hanns pushed Stephen, who exited through the side of the garage. In the asbestos side wall, Stephen's outline of the garage looked like something out of a Tom and Jerry cartoon. I became acquainted with a girl with her leg in plaster the same night. That proved to be a logistical challenge.

We all joined the Brogborough Bowls Club. To the annoyance of the more serious players, we spent many genteel evenings playing on the superbly kept green, drinking and laughing into the fading summer light.

After my exams were over, I was walking through town when I saw that the Army Recruitment Centre in Bedford had a recruitment drive for the Royal Engineers. It certainly looked like an interesting life, so I went in to check it out.

The work covered a whole range of technical skills; the Engineers seemed to do everything. However, the massive advertising photos and the promotional films appeared to over-emphasise soldiers crawling around in the mud with metal rods probing for land mines. You would probably have to do that under enemy fire as well. That may have been some people's idea of an exciting and fulfilling occupation, but it wasn't my idea of engineering.

I took a handful of brochures and left, never to return. Thinking about it now, those recruitment guys were pretty clever. The advertising images saved a lot of time by sorting out the wimps at the start.

On Saturday, 11 July, I was moping around the house, feeling sorry for myself and wondering what I would do when my apprenticeship ended in September. I still had this fantasy about going to work for NASA when I passed my exams. Assuming I passed.

My dad, an ardent socialist, was reading the tabloid Daily Mirror, a working-class newspaper that suited his political views. I grabbed the paper when he eventually put it down to go for his Saturday morning pint in the CIU Club. I needed something to lift my mood, so I turned to the Perishers, a cartoon strip about a gang of kids and their dog Boot, who lived a surreal childhood, not unlike my own. It was time for their summer holidays at the seaside when Boot would peer down into his favourite rock pool. To the crabs at the bottom of the pool, this was the annual visitation of the - eyeballs in the sky. A mystical event in the mundane lives of the crabs.

Eventually, I worked my way to the classified ads at the back of the paper.

Two large ads caught my eye. One was for Flight Engineers for British Overseas Airways Corporation (BOAC). The other was for Junior Engineer Officers for the British India Steam Navigation Company Ltd (BI)). Both ads presented the prospect of good wages and travel for qualified engineers. There was hope for my salvation.

The following Monday, I posted a letter to BI and BOAC for a job application form. On Friday 17 July, I finished work for my summer holidays. On the same day, I received a job application from BI.

The BI job application came with other papers about joining the British Merchant Navy. This venture began to look like a big step into the unknown, so I decided to visit the British Shipping Federation (BSF) to get more information. On Monday, 20 July, I thumbed it down the M1 to London with a BSF pamphlet in hand. After dropping me off outside Swiss Cottage underground station, my lift disappeared into the morning traffic. I took the tube to Aldgate. I walked in the drizzle down Leman Street and under the railway bridge from Aldgate underground. Dock Street was lined with yellow brick Georgian style buildings with a large, spired church halfway down the street. The whole area looked run down. However, it wasn't difficult to imagine seeing tall-masted sailing ships between the buildings offloading rum, tea and spices from the glory days of the old St Katharine Docks.

I found the British Shipping Federation building. The downstairs area was filled with the bustle and chatter of merchant seamen, deckhands, ratings and stewards signing up for ships and dealing with paperwork. The second floor was reserved for officers, so I took the stairs. The whole place was a no-nonsense affair. People were there for a reason, pointing at pieces of paper, questioning and arguing with officials. I felt entirely out of place among these tough-looking characters who knew exactly what they were there for and what they wanted.

It was an unpleasant experience, a glimpse into a world I had no knowledge of. I was a novice getting in the way. I was out of my depth.

I picked up some literature lying around and made my escape without talking to anyone. Back on the street, I was relieved to be in more familiar surroundings. I made my way back under the railway bridge and stopped off in the Brown Bear pub. I bought a pint of bitter and read through pamphlets I'd recovered.

I read through the Shipping Federations booklet - Your Safety Aboard Ship. There was a myriad of dangers on a ship other than its sinking.

Ladders, decks, staging's, holds, hatch-covers, ropes, engine room plates and handrails, gauge glass covers, boiler blowbacks, tools and loose parts, cold chisels, hand tools, cargo, smoking, or just lifting things. There were even crankcase explosions. All these had the potential to cause severe injury or death. In fact, the possibility of being killed at sea was significantly greater than in any other industry. As long as the Russians didn't invade Western Europe, it might be safer to join the Royal Engineers and go around poking for mines with a pointed stick.

Suitably forewarned, I drank up, took the tube to Kings Cross and caught the evening coach, the cheapest way to get back to Bedford.

After my experience at the Shipping Federation office in London's dock area, I took a few days to consider what I was doing. By Thursday night, I'd made up my mind.
Friday, 24 July, I hitched a lift to Bedford in a van full of workmen. I felt a bit of a prat, having been over heavy on the Old Spice aftershave that morning. But they didn't rib me too much about it. In the machine in Woolworth's, I paid three old shillings (15p decimal) for the photos I needed to send with my application form to BI.
I had lunch at the Chinese restaurant in Midland Road, soup, chicken chop suey, and ice cream for five old shillings and sixpence (28p decimal). After lunch, it was pouring down with rain, so I ran 150 yards to the Empire cinema on the corner of Allhallows with my coat over my head. I spent the afternoon in the dry watching the Harold Robbins film 'Stiletto 'and the B movie called 'A time for Giving'. Fortunately, it had stopped raining when I came out of the cinema. I walked to Kempston and hitched a lift to Brogborough.

That evening I met Pat and Ray in the club. They'd come up from Hereford for the wedding of Ray's cousin Linda from Salford. Ray was away a lot, but I got to see him when he reappeared in Brogborough to visit his parents. That evening he seemed a little distant. I even made a note in my diary about it. Years later, I realised that the day before, on 23 July, there had been a British inspired coup d'etat in Oman. Oman was a small country on the south-eastern coast of the Arabian Peninsula at the mouth of the Persian Gulf. The ruler Said bin Taimur had been deposed and replaced by his son, Qaboos bin Said. If that news had been on the TV, I didn't see it, and I can't remember it being front-page news in the papers.

From the mid to early 1960's, Britain had been quietly involved in a war in the Southern Omani province of Dhofar against communist rebels, supported by China and the Soviet Union, who opposed the rule of the Sultan.

Compared to the war raging in Vietnam, this was a very small war. However, if the communists had won in Oman, they'd have controlled the oil flow through the Strait of Hormuz. In that respect, the mountain and desert war of Oman was as significant as what was happening in Indochina.

On Saturday night, Val's brother Collin Cox took Val and a group of us down to Marston Club dance. On the way to the van, Erika passed us with her new boyfriend in a jag. That was a dent in my pride, but there was not much I could do about it. However, in life, you just never know what is around the corner.

The usual Marston girls were at the dance. They were a good crowd, but I knew them all, and I didn't feel very sociable, so I decided I'd get drunk on pints of Double Diamond mixed with Gold Label barley wine. The dance hall began to fill, and I started a conversation with a guy standing next to me, which for some reason, was about the price of drinks in Spain. I noticed two girls standing a little way off that I'd not seen before. The taller of the two caught my eye. She was very attractive with long black hair

and dressed in a long-sleeved blue cardigan, short sleeveless jacket and short black skirt.
I had to raise my voice over the music from the band.
"Wow, look at those two. You wouldn't take the small one so I can dance with the taller one?" I asked my new friend.
"Hardly," he replied. "That's my sister and her mate".
Another stranger standing right behind me heard what I said above the din and tapped me on the shoulder.
"I'll do it. I fancy the little one". He said.
I danced with the tall one, her name was Joy, from Flitwick, but she had a boyfriend. Still, I felt reckless, and we ended up sitting in the corner of the hall, talking and kissing for the rest of the evening.
However, with previous experience of the dangers of love triangles, when I walked her to her brother's car to go home, I didn't make a date to see her again.
Afterwards, I sat on the wall with the rest of the gang, waiting for the taxi to take us home to Brogborough. The taxi cost fourteen shillings (70p decimal. 10p each).
Sunday evening was Bingo Night in Brogborough club, all the gang were going, but bingo wasn't my scene. I caught the United Counties double-decker bus from the shops to Marston. The service only operated at weekends. I saw the guy who'd helped me split the girls up the night before sitting with the little girl he'd danced with. I saw a girl with short hair sitting with them in the dim light, but I didn't recognise her, so I went into the bar and bought a beer.

When I came back into the dance hall, I realised the girl next to the couple was Joy. She looked fabulous. Her hair looked short because it was gathered at the back. She was wearing a white blouse, high waisted black pants with outside fly buttons, and a knee-length snakeskin jacket trimmed at the bottom with long thongs.

We spent most of the night snogging in the corner. Before her brother took her home, she said she could not see me during the week because of her boyfriend, but she would come to the dance next Saturday.

Walking back through the graveyard to the main road, I felt pretty high. At the same time, I wondered what the hell I was doing. What if Joy's fella was a boxer like Jillian Brook's old boyfriend. Fuck! What if it was Jillian Brook's old boyfriend, Jack Peters? He might not be so gallant this time.

"Not you again". WHACK. He'd bloody kill me, but I didn't give a damn. I didn't care. It was worth the risk.

When I got to the main road, I got picked up by the local homosexual. Well, picked up is the wrong expression; he gave me a lift. He said he was off to a party in Bletchley, and would I like to come along, but I declined the offer. I had other things on my mind.

I filled in my application form for BISNCo (BI) the following morning, but I did not post it. I took one more day to reconsider what the hell I was doing.

On Tuesday, 28 July, having made up my mind, I posted the application form to British India Steam Navigation Company Ltd, P&O Building, Leadenhall Street, London EC3.

On Saturday 1 August, mum woke me with a letter from BI.
Before I opened it, I thought it was going to be one of those 'Dear Mr Butler, we are sorry to inform you that on this occasion blah blah blah.
To my surprise, it read.
"Dear Mr Butler,
We refer to your recent application for a position with this Company as a Junior Engineer Officer, and now have pleasure in offering you an interview.
We require you to attend this office for an interview at 2 p.m. on 10 August 1970, and accommodation for the night of 10 August has been reserved for you. You will also be required to attend this office on 11 August for further interview. You should bring with you a recent Chest X-Ray certificate, if available, and also relevant testimonials and certificates in support of your application.
All reasonable expenses will be refunded to you on request, and we should be grateful if you would acknowledge receipt of this letter, confirming that you will attend the interview.
Yours faithfully,
for BRITISH INDIA STEAM NAVIGATION COMPANY LIMITED
K,W,M. Paul
Engineering Recruitment and Training Officer.

Bugger me, I thought, this is really serious.
In the evening at the club, I saw Steve and Hanns, who'd just come back from their holiday in Butlins. We got a taxi to the Marston club dance. Joy was there; after the dance, I split from the gang and

paid Ray Anderson from Brogborough ten shillings to take us to Flitwick. Joy and I sat in the back, French kissing all the way. She told me she wouldn't see me until next Friday as she was going to Clacton for the weekend.

Monday, 3 August, back to work after the summer holidays, I decided to tell the foreman of my intention to join the Merchant Navy as a Junior Engineer Officer. I was nervous because I thought he'd go ballistic, but I was amazed at his attitude. He said it was a good idea as I would be wasting my time if I continued working at the firm with my qualifications. That was prophetic, considering I was still waiting for my exam results. He also saw no problem taking two days off work for the interview in London. I would have taken time off anyway, but it was nice there was no conflict about it. Maybe he was just glad to see the back of me.

On Thursday, 6 August, I got home from work to find a letter from the college waiting for me. It was my examination results.

I passed all subjects: Mechanical Technology, Properties of Materials, Manufacturing Technology, and Machine Tools.

Mum gave me a pack of 10 Embassy cigarettes, and dad gave me five shillings to go and celebrate in the club. It wasn't much for two years of study, but it was more than I usually had on a Thursday before payday.

I met Ray in the club, up from Hereford to see his parents. We had a few drinks and a long chat about computers. I studied Computer Numerical Control (CNC) for my HNC. One of the questions in my exam was on programming an 8-bit punched paper tape to control a milling machine, so I knew something about the subject. Ray seemed to know a lot about it. I didn't know what the army was up to, but I got the impression that the SAS was more than just a covert killing machine.

Friday morning started badly. I had a row with mum because I didn't have any clean underpants. The one she gave me was scorched from being under the grill where she'd frantically tried to dry it. I eventually found an old pair that was a bit tatty but clean. I feel ashamed now because my mum was trying to get ready to go to work too. She had to take that job to get me through college and support me through my apprenticeship. What an ungrateful pratt I was.

Things improved in the evening after work. I got dressed, and in a new pair of underpants, I took the train to Millbrook and walked to Marston club. When I met Joy, the first thing I asked was, "What happened to my postcard from Clacton."

She opened her handbag and gave it to me, saying she couldn't find a stamp. It was a good night with a lot of laughter. After the dance, Joy and her friend, Reita, were getting a lift home with a friend's dad. When he came out of the club, he started moaning because we were leaning against his car.

Unwisely, a little tipsy, the girls burst out laughing, so he got in the car and roared off without them. I gave Joy my coat because they had to walk five miles to Flitwick. I walked back to Brogborough in just a short-sleeved shirt.

I saw Joy again at the club over the weekend. We didn't get on very well, and after the Sunday night dance, we finished. In truth, she dumped me. I couldn't blame her; there was not much future in having a boyfriend roaming around on the other side of the world.

On 10 August, I couldn't take the risk of thumbing it up the M1 to London. There was no way I could miss this interview. I walked through the brickyard and caught the 07:27 morning train from Ridgmont to Bedford St John's. Erika was on the train. We sat and talked, and I told her I was off to London for an interview.

As the train travelled through the Bedfordshire countryside, I peered out of the rain-streaked window at places familiar, the many brick factories along the side of the track. Chimneys spewing sulphurous smoke into the atmosphere spread so far that Sweden had made an official complaint about the acid rain it caused to fall on that pristine country. The lunar landscape of working clay pits, the massive excavators shifting thousands of tons of Oxford clay to feed the brick factories. Old worked out clay pits, now landfill sites, the domain of flocks of large white scavenging seagulls. I should have been elated at the prospect of leaving all this behind, but I wasn't. There was an uncomfortable knot in my stomach.

We stopped at Millbrook railway station from where many times I'd made the half-mile walk down the straight country road to Marston club. The place where I'd met so many girls had my first kiss and the place that led to the awkward loss of my virginity. The track between Millbrook and Stewartby Station where we'd ride our bikes to the London Brick Company swimming pool in the summer. Or, if we went by train, we'd put pennies on the track and deface the coins of the realm.

From Bedford, St John's, Erika and I walked up the street past the Phoenix, the Clarence, then to the Kings Arms, all old watering holes with my college mates. I stopped for a moment and looked into Brightmans' Toy shop's window, where I'd bought my long-barrelled Davy Crocket rifle as a kid. The same shop where my parents bought the BSA Star Rider bicycles for my sister and me.

We passed Mander College, where I'd spent my days of freedom from Headley's studying engineering. We crossed the bridge over the Ouse into the town centre. Erika wished me luck and headed off in the rain to Texas Instruments. I caught the 8:50 bus to London. We often took that bus, especially when going to the Motor Show in Earls Court. As the coach travelled through the grey morning, I thought how surreal it was that friends turn into lovers, then into strangers, then back into friends.

When the bus arrived at Kings Cross at 11:00. I took the tube to Aldgate and walked the short distance to Leadenhall Street.

It was still pouring with rain, and as usual, my feet were wet. I couldn't believe I was going for a job that paid up to £4000 a year, and I had holes in the bottom of my shoes.

I was early, so I popped down the stairs below pavement level to the Underwriter pub for a pint of McEwan's Export and a sandwich and dried out.

The P&O Building, 122 Leadenhall Street, was an impressive, rectangular but featureless, 15 story glass and steel structure. I registered at the reception at 13:30. Before taking the lift to the interview floor, I spent some time looking around the BI exhibition room with its large model boats and photographs showing the company's history. The company was originally formed in 1856 as the Calcutta and Burma Steam Navigation Company, a year before the Indian Rebellion. Two years later, the Government of India Act of 1858 led to the British Crown taking direct control of India from the East India Company. The Calcutta and Burma Company evolved into the British India Steam Navigation Company four years later. It was born a child of the British Raj, and from the exhibition's tone, it still was.

I needed that time to calm my nerves. This was a far cry from the Shipping Federation. The building wreaked of old imperial wealth, and I felt entirely out of place as an officer candidate.

There were ten applicants. The first thing we had to do was a timed aptitude test. This included General Science, Arithmetic, Mathematics, Vocabulary, Understanding of Mechanics and Electrics, Manipulation of Shapes, and Verbal Communication.

Following the aptitude test, a man named Mr Paul introduced the company, followed by a Q&A session. By then, the first interview day was over.

We were taken by minibus to Anchor House, in Barking Road, Canning Town, a hotel for seamen run by the Apostleship of the Sea.

I went to the hotel restaurant with a Glaswegian called Gordon Monro, who I'd become friends with during the interview. We had soup, steak, chips and peas; ice cream and apricots; and coffee. Whatever the interview result, at least I'd had a good meal out in London.

We had a few beers in the hotel bar, and then four of us, all BISNCo interviewees, went to the dance hall, where there was a discotheque and another bar. Gordon and I had a dance with a few girls, but the other two blokes weren't interested and just sat on the perimeter talking all night. The girls were amiable and chatty but obviously vetted by the Apostleship of the Sea. They were there to put us on the path to righteousness. It was all reminiscent of the film 'Guys and Dolls' where Jean Simmons played sister Sarah Brown at the Save a Soul Mission. They weren't having much luck with Gordon and me. Nevertheless, it was a pleasant evening.

When the disco finished, we left the hotel, bought some fish and chips and ate them on the street. Back at the hotel, I shared a room with a Mr Bill Swan. About my age, he'd also been for an interview. Mr Swan lay in bed with a crate of Watney's pale ale, so I helped him out. We sat up talking, smoking and drinking Mr Swan's beer most of the night.

I woke up sometime in the early hours, not knowing where I was until I realised, I was lying on the hotel bedroom floor. I swore and got back into bed.

The following morning Bill told me I fell out of bed somewhat hard and lay there for an hour before coming to.

Gordon popped his head in to say goodbye before going for his primary interview, one of the first of the day. My interview wasn't until later, so I got up, showered, dressed, and had a fried breakfast in the hotel. After that, I found a chemist and bought some Alka Seltzer as I felt a little delicate.

At 12:30, I had my interview, part of which was a little chat with the psychologist. The only thing I can remember about that interview was one of the psychologist's questions,

" Do you ever think that someone is following you?".

"No, I don't. If I'm in a crowd, people are obviously behind me, but I wouldn't say they were following me".

It may have been a killer question, but I thought it was a strange thing to ask someone who intended to work on a ship.

I didn't understand that question's significance until one night months later, in the middle of the Indian Ocean. While walking alone in the long propeller shaft tunnel away from the buzz of machinery, I stopped and looked back over my shoulder because I could sense someone behind me.

My work experience was precision, not heavy engineering. Consequently, when I caught the bus back to Bedford, I didn't feel things had gone that well at the interview.

Wednesday and Thursday were a drag, and I wished I'd never told anyone that I was going for a job as an officer in the Merchant Navy.

A letter was waiting for me when I got home on Thursday evening.

I thought that was quick; it didn't take BI long to write me off. But when I opened it, it said that if I passed my medical, I had the job. I was so excited I went up to my auntie Mary's to give her the news. Coming back home, Erika was on her way to the phone box to call her boyfriend. Instead, she took me to the club and bought me a drink to celebrate when I told her the news.

The following days were a tsunami of emotions that ranged from exhilaration to second thoughts about the whole adventure. The standard contract for a BI officer was Eastern Service. This meant I wouldn't return to the UK for two and a half years. That was OK because the tax-free starting wage was £1,500 a year. With no costs for food and accommodation and duty-free spirits and cigarettes, I would be better off than I'd ever been in my life. You could say, rich beyond my wildest dreams. However, I started to have second thoughts.

It seems stupid now, but one of my most serious worries was that all the girls I knew would be married with kids when I returned from two and a half years of Eastern Services. At the age of 24, I'd be an old man. The bloody arrogance of youth. It was the same when I walked out of the cinema after seeing 2001 A Space Odyssey. In 2001 I'd be 52 years old, and my life would be over. I can't believe it now, but these were real considerations then.

However, the other voice inside my head said, "The world is full of possibilities. Life's not over until you're dead. Then it's over for good. Roll the dice, take a chance. Otherwise, you'll go through the rest of your life asking - What if?"

For days I went around with these two conflicting versions of Bernie Butler competing inside my head.

On Wednesday, 19 August, I took the train to Woburn Sands and then the bus to my GP's surgery in Woburn. Dr Currie (an appropriate name considering where I was going) checked my ears, eyes, heart, lungs, kidneys and liver. When I told him why I needed the medical, he gave me some advice about living in the tropics.

Never take ice in your drink because it can be made from local unsanitary water.

Never drink still bottled water for the same reason.

Only drink branded fizzy water, and make sure you remove the top yourself.

Never eat salads because they will be washed in local water.

Eat only food that is prepared and cooked in front of you.

Medical done, he sent me to Bedford for a chest X-Ray.

When I got my pay packet on Friday, I was astonished to find the company had paid me for the Wednesday I'd taken off for my medical. I was 21 years old, and it was the last year of my apprenticeship. After National Insurance and tax deductions from my wages, I was left with £10 - 19s - 4p a week.

Now that I knew what I'd be doing after my apprenticeship, the days began to drag. I was still filled with dread about the future. I spent hours lying in bed, hands behind my head, staring at the ceiling, fretting about the unknown. Finally, I concluded that I had let my world shrink to a sixteen-mile radius around Brogborough. My life consisted of travelling to and from Dunstable each day. Much of my time was spent standing in the rain, trying to thumb a lift. All this to be chained to a machine all day in a factory for a pittance. Occasionally, I'd take a trip to Bedford. My free time was spent in an even smaller world oscillating between the Working Men's Clubs of Brogborough and Marston. I spent most of that time drinking too much and having transient relationships with girls because I wouldn't commit. I was wasting time, time that was not recoverable. Most of my friends said they'd give their right arm for the opportunity, yet I was still uncertain. I wondered how they'd cope as one-armed sailors.

The following Thursday evening, I got a lift home from work with Mr Maxfield, the owner of Hillmax Engineering in Luton. I'd not seen him for some time. I told him I was going to work for the British India Steam Navigation Company as a Junior Officer on an Eastern Service contract. When he dropped me off at junction 13, he gave me his private address and asked me to contact him in two and a half years when I got back to England.

I hadn't realised it then, but when he'd picked me up thumbing it to or from work, I was being interviewed. A three-year interview. He knew more about me than any job application could tell him. He knew more about me than I did myself.

On Friday, 28 August, I received my wages plus one week's pay for the outstanding holiday I would take in the coming week.

That week wasn't very eventful. Monday was a Bank Holiday; my friend Des Davis picked me up and took me to the stock car racing at Brafield. I'd never been to a stock car race before. It was nice of Des to do that, but I didn't actually enjoy it. A load of old bangers racing around a track and smashing into each other against the roar of a demented crowd was not my idea of fun.

It reminded me of 'Into the Arena', an old book I'd read. One that my dad had brought back from a jumble sale. It was about gladiators fighting to the death and charioteers entertaining the citizens of old Rome to distract them from their humdrum lives. In that respect, humanity hadn't moved on much.

On Tuesday, I thumbed it to Dunstable for a dental check-up, took the bus to Luton and went to the cinema. El Condor with Lee Van Cleef and gratuitous violence was about as enjoyable as the stock car race. Roger Ebert's review for the Chicago Sun-Times put it this way: "Lee Van Cleef's last words in El Condor are, 'What am I doing here?' Amen, brother" My sentiments exactly.

Wednesday, I was in the cinema again in Bedford watching - The Battle of Britain - about Britain's stand against Nazi oppression. I especially enjoyed the bit with Susannah York in stockings and suspenders.

Thursday, my pre-sea documents arrived from BI. I took the bundle of papers to the Club and read through them with Johnny Irvine over three pints of Tartan bitter.

That evening my cousin Bernadette came down from Derby. The previous year she and her husband Collin emigrated to South Africa. Collin was a civil engineer. Six months after their arrival, Collin was killed in a site accident when a crane collapsed. Bernadette came home with Collin's ashes which she buried in the cemetery of St Mary's, Father Golston's church in Woburn Sands. Bernadette was a hairdresser, but she couldn't go back to that mundane life after the tragedy, so she got a job in a hospital.

We went for a drink at the Oak in Woburn Sands with auntie Mary, uncle Steven, my cousin Anna and Anna's boyfriend, Trevor. Later we went on to the Fir Tree on the Woburn road.

It's strange how the mind hangs on to seemingly insignificant fragments of memory. The jukebox started playing The Last Waltz by Engelbert Humperdinck. Bernadette got up and went to the ladies. Auntie Mary, tipsily sentimental, leaned over and whispered that Bernadette and Collin had an attachment to that song. When Bernadette returned, I mentioned the comment to her.
She looked at me, puzzled. "I hate that record", she replied.
The weekend seemed to drag on.

On Monday, 7 September, my dad had to go to Dunstable to sign off my apprenticeship documents. I still had a day off work because of the previous week's bank holiday, and I had a yellow fever vaccination appointment in London.
At 07:00, I was on the M1 slip road Junction 13, thumbing it to London. I got a lift with a man in an Alfa Romeo. At 08:30, he dropped me off by Big Ben at the north end of the Palace of Westminster, the UK Parliament.
On that bright warm morning, it was a pleasure walking past Buckingham Palace, up Constitution Hill to the Wellington Arch at Hyde Park Corner and along Park Lane by the side of Hyde Park. London looked beautiful in the sunshine as I passed through arcades of trees and all the wealth and trappings of post-Imperial Britain. I arrived at the Yellow Fever Clinic, Great Cumberland Place, at 09:30 and was vaccinated almost immediately. After that, I went to the Board of Trade to apply for my British Seaman's Card.

That done, I had lunch in a restaurant in Chinatown, then walked to the Odeon in Leicester Square and watched Michael Caine in the film Too Late the Hero.
Waiting to go home on the bus at Kings Cross station, an old tramp started shouting. He was ranting about getting rid of all the Germans. I think he was talking about the British Royal Family because he told everyone he was the real King of England. London certainly was an exciting place.

I received my first week's pay packet as a skilled man on Friday. £21 - 10s on top and £15 - 15s after tax and National Insurance deductions. That still didn't seem like much money after four years of poverty as an apprentice. After paying 15 shillings for passport photos, then putting away £2 for my passport and giving my mum £4 for board, there wasn't much left. I had to borrow £30 from my dad to put toward the cost of my uniform, tropical gear and engine-room clothes.
On Saturday I decided to go to London to get my uniform. Except for one thing, that trip turned out to be a complete waste of time because when I got to the Miller and Rayner shop, it was closed.
The good thing was that I bumped into Lorraine Hopkinson in Bletchley railway station, coming off a train from Northampton. God, how that girl had broken my heart at school, I loved her, and she wouldn't even look at me. Now she greeted me like an old lost friend. She was no longer a girl, though. She was a really beautiful woman. She sat and talked with me as I waited for my train. I told her I was an officer in the British Merchant Navy (well, I soon

would be). She told me she was going to join the WRAFs, and immediately I had a vision of her in place of Susannah York in that bedroom scene from The Battle of Britain. I should be so lucky.
Yet another of life's strange coincidences, I wouldn't have met Lorraine at the station if it hadn't rained that morning. I waited until the rain stopped before going to catch a later train. It was a brief encounter that brightened my day, but I kicked myself on the way to London because I didn't try to make a date with her. I didn't know where she lived, and I would probably never see her again.
On Monday 14 September, my friend Mary Irvine, now Mrs Christian, gave birth to a little girl, Maxine. It was hard to believe all the fun we'd had together as kids and teenagers. Now Mary was married with a baby and living somewhere else. Soon I'd be gone too. We weren't kids anymore. We were all spreading our wings and flying the coop.

On Tuesday, I was up at 07:45. I caught the train to Woburn Sands and then the bus to Woburn. Back in Dr Currie's surgery, I had more vaccinations. Over the last few days, my International Health Certificate booklet had gone from empty to stamps for smallpox, yellow fever, typhoid, typhus and cholera. Wherever I was off to, it wasn't going to be healthy.
From Woburn, I thumbed a lift back to Woburn Sands. I caught the train to Bletchley and took a train to London. I queued in a long line downstairs at the Shipping Federation to pick up my pale blue Discharge Book. I also collected my British Seaman's Card. It wasn't a card at all; it was more like a red passport. The official

handed it over and told me to look after it. He said it was a government document, and for a British seaman in a foreign land, it was more important than my passport. The book had a photograph of me with cropped hair. The number R890373 on a board across my chest made me look like a suspect in a police filing cabinet. The same photo was in the discharge book.

I walked from Dock Street to Miller Rayner's shop at 110 Fenchurch Street to collect my Junior Engineer Officer's uniform, tropical whites and working gear. The list included:

1 Blue uniform with Company's buttons and braid

1 Uniform peaked cap with Company's badge and white plastic cover

1 Pair epaulettes with Company's brade

3 Pair white shorts

6 White boiler suits

2 Pairs of black socks

3 Pairs of white shirts collars attached

1 White mess jacket

1 Black bow tie

3 White uniform short-sleeved shirts collars attached

1 Black tie

1 Pair of black uniform shoes

1 Pair of white uniform shoes

1 Pair of heavy engine room shoes

3 Pairs of long white stockings

1 Cummerbund black

1 Expanding fibre suitcase

I was a bit perturbed about wearing white stockings. Fortunately, they turned out to be long white socks to go with the tropical white uniform. As for the cummerbund, a broad black sash worn around the waist with the short white mess jacket, I had no clue; I had to look it up in the dictionary beforehand. It was as if I were travelling back to the time of the Indian Raj.

The whole purchase cost £91 - 3s - 8p. I had a £50 credit note from the BI and the £30 I'd borrowed from my dad. I left the shop owing Miller Rayner £11 - 3 - 8p. Now I was not only short of cash, but I was also £41 - 3 - 8p in dept. Nevertheless, now an officer and presumably a gentleman, they put everything in the expanding suitcase and let me take it from the shop to drag it home on the train. The only things missing were my blue serge uniform jacket and trousers that would be delivered later by post.

With all the previous days' vaccinations, travelling and dragging that suitcase home, I felt too exhausted to go to work, so I stayed in bed most of the following day. Consequently, when I got my pay on Friday, it was only £12.

Friday evening, I was having a beer with my friend Bob Ellis from Marston in the Bedford Arms by Ridgmont railway station when Lorraine Hopkinson walked into the pub.

I couldn't believe it, I'd not seen her since I'd left school, and now we'd crossed paths twice in six days. It seemed like fate. The problem was she was accompanied by one of the Bailey boys from Lidlington, who was six feet something tall and built like a rugby player. I admit I experienced a little heart flutter, but I wasn't stupid enough to make my feelings obvious. I looked sideways down the bar, smiled nonchalantly, and raised a hand in acknowledgement.

"It's dead in here", complained Bob. "Let's go up the club".

Passing the couple on our way out, I remarked casually.

"We're off to the dance at Brogborough club".

Shortly before closing time Lorraine and her partner came into the club. This time I struck up a conversation with them. The bell for last orders sounded, and while her friend was at the bar, Lorraine took a biro from her handbag. She wrote 2493 on the back of my hand. When I got home, I wrote the telephone number on a piece of paper.

Saturday, Hanns came round, and we went fishing down one of the old, abandoned clay pits. It was scorching, and we didn't catch anything, but I wasn't concerned. I had other things on my mind. In one week, I would soon finish my job at Headley's. Any time after that, I could be called up by BI. How would it look if I were laid up in hospital having been brutalised by one, if not both, of the Bailey brothers?

Best to just forget about Lorraine.

On Sunday and on Monday at work, I ran the same argument over in my head. It was settled. No way was I going to risk my career over some girl; it would be absolutely stupid, totally irresponsible. At 7 o'clock Monday evening, I walked to the telephone box and called Lorraine. At eight twenty, I caught the train. Lorraine was waiting for me at Aspley Guise station.

It was a beautiful warm summer evening. We strolled up the hill through that pretty English village of green hedges, trees and flower gardens past the old Saxon church. Then we walked down the hill to the square passing the high red brick wall at the back of Aspley House, where the Sturdee family let us swim in their pool during the school summer holidays.
Lorraine and I spent the evening in the Bell pub. We sat in a corner and talked and talked. At closing time, the publican let us stay in our corner, and we carried on talking until 11:30pm. I walked Lorraine home to where she lived, close to the railway station. We kissed for a while on the back doorstep of her mother's house. I asked her to come to the going away party I was having on Saturday, and we made a date to see each other on Friday night.
After all these years, I'd gone out with Lorraine Hopkinson. I walked the two and a half miles home with not a care in the world and no thought about the Bailey boys until a car pulled up beside me on that dark road.
No, I'm only joking. I got home safe and sound before one in the morning.

A paid escort.

Early in the evening of 24 September, a small red GPO van stopped outside my house with a special delivery. The package contained an immaculately pressed navy-blue worsted serge British Merchant Navy uniform jacket and trousers. The bottom of each sleeve of the jacket had a gold braid ring with a purple trim denoting the rank of a Junior Engineer Officer.

I took the parcel upstairs, put on a clean white shirt, a black tie, the uniform jacket and trousers and my new black shoes. Then, I put on the peaked cap with the company badge embroidered in gold and coloured thread showing Britannia holding a trident and an oval Union Jack shield, standing beside a lion, all enclosed in a cluster of olive leaves. I went downstairs and presented myself to my parents and sister. They were very impressed. Just then, my sister's friend Betty came into the house.

"Oh Bernard, you look absolutely wonderful. Take me to the Club dressed in your uniform", she said.

I was appalled. "Goodness Betty! I'm an officer in the British Merchant Navy now. I couldn't think of doing that; it's highly irregular to go parading around ashore in uniform".

"Oh please," she pleaded. "Please".

"No, absolutely not. I couldn't. It's just not done", I replied.

"I'll pay you ten shillings", she said

"TEN SHILLINGS!" I was shocked. "OK, Betty, but you buy the drinks".

Betty beamed with joy, got her purse out and put a new crisp ten-shilling note into my hand. She whisked me out the door, linked her arm in mine and marched me down the street to the CIU Working Men's Club.

We entered the Club, and Betty proudly walked me up to the bar. Johnny Irvine was serving behind the counter. When the ex-Royal Marine Commando saw me, he closed his eyes and shook his head

a couple of times. When he opened his eyes again, he looked straight at me.
"Butler, what the fuck do you look like? This is Bedfordshire; the nearest sea is ninety miles away".
I leaned over and whispered in his ear, "She paid me ten shillings to bring her out".
"You bloody whore!".
True to her word Betty bought the drinks. Halfway through the evening, Johnnie Roland from the corner shop came in. He was impressed and bought me a drink, then asked me to go over to the shop with him so he could show me off to his wife, Peggy. I thought about asking him for a fee, but I thought better of it with Irvine standing by.

Friday, 25 September 1970, was my last day of work with Headley's Engineering. On Fridays, I'd generally go to Mrs Beagarie's for lunch, but on this day, Robin, Dave Goss, the other apprentice, and some others from work took me down to the pub for a drink. They bought me quite a few gin and tonics, and we laughed about happenings over the last four years.
Back at the factory at 3pm, the machinists, the inspectors and the foreman walked out of the workshop. Not knowing what was happening, I followed them into the work's canteen. No one said anything to me when I walked in, so I went and sat in my usual seat and waited to see what was going on. Mr Brown walked in with the office staff, and when everyone was seated or standing around the walls, he started to make a speech. Which, to my

amazement, was about me. When he finished, he asked me to come forward. He presented me with a box containing an expensive silver Ronson gas lighter and a card. Everyone had contributed towards the lighter. On the front of the card was a cartoon of a ship, 'SS Fun' with the caption 'Going Places?'.

Everyone from Headley's had signed the card under the message, 'WISHING YOU ALL THE BEST FOR THE FUTURE'. I was overwhelmed. I didn't know what to say and kept muttering, "It's too much, it's too much.

After the ceremony, Mr Brown took me into his office. He gave me an envelope containing a cheque for five guineas and a handwritten letter.

The letter said he was pleased I was joining his old service, and he had no doubt I would be a Chief Engineer one day. He wished me every success in the future.

All the ladies in the office kissed me farewell before I went and said my goodbyes to everyone in the factory. I left work early. After four years, I should have been happy getting out of that factory, but I wasn't. I can't explain my feelings, but I was sad, I had a lot of friends there, and it was the end of part of my life.

In the evening, my mood lifted. I caught the train to Aspley Guise and spent the evening with Lorraine again, talking all night in the Bell. It was a dark night as I walked back to Brogborough, but I'd walked and cycled that road so many times that I knew it well.

With only a sliver of light from the waning moon, I was a happy man walking home on that warm English summer's night under a clear star-filled sky.

When I got home, my mum was still up. She gave me an envelope posted through the door during the evening. It was a card from Erika letting me know she couldn't come to my going away party. Understandable, I suppose. It would have been awkward, us going out together for so long, especially if she brought the new boyfriend.

On Saturday morning, I got a lift into Bedford with Uncle Steve. The first thing I did was go to Standards, the stationary shop on Midland Road. I wanted to see Mrs Frost who worked there to ask her to tell her son Chris and his mate Andrew, two friends of mine from college, to come to my party. I went to Safeways, bought some drinks for the party, and then took the train home.

Back in Brogborough, I went to the club before lunch. Ray White, a few years older than me, lived up the end of my street towards my auntie Mary's. He was in the club buying crates of drinks because he was having a party at his house that same evening. He was with the boyfriend of his wife's sister, a girl named Stephanie, who came from Flitwick.

Here the story gets a little involved, and you're probably going to think what a convoluted life I led, and you'd probably be right. However, you have to understand this was a very emotional part of my life. I was a young man leaving my home and family and heading off into the unknown. I was leaving behind all the girls I'd ever known and loved and some I'd never even met. It was a psychological trauma for this young man, a very difficult period in my life. That's my excuse anyway.

One night months before, Ambrose and I were standing outside Marston club after a dance when two lovely young ladies came out. To cut a long story short, we had a laugh and ended up in a snogging session before their lift came to take them home. It was all very light-hearted, just a brief encounter of no real consequence, or so I thought. Following that meeting, I often bumped into one of the girls, Stephanie (Steph), because her sister had married Ray White from Brogborough. I soon realised Steph had a steady boyfriend. She must have broken up with him for a while on the occasion we'd met. It seemed I had a gift for meeting girls with relationship problems. The thing was, every time we met, I had this electric feeling of attraction toward her. I could tell the feeling was mutual because whenever we were in the same vicinity, if I didn't go to her, she would come to me, and we'd chat easily in each other's company, just small talk. To others, it may have seemed a very innocent flirtation. I can't speak for Steph, but for me, every time we met, there was a sort of unresolved sexual attraction, something difficult to explain. The reason I tell you this will become apparent later.

At 7pm, I walked down to Ridgmont station to meet Lorraine off the train. We went to the club because I'd arranged to meet everyone there to start things off. Many friends from Headley's turned up, as did my friends from college, including Phil Ramsden and Pauline. All the Brogborough gang were there. My friend Buzz came with his girlfriend Lynn, they gave me a leather wallet as a going-away present. They couldn't stay because Buzz was a guitarist in a band and had a gig that night.

At 9pm we went back to my house for the party proper. My friend Mary Irvine came with her husband Bill; I still hadn't gotten used to her being Mrs Christian. Soon the house was packed and filled with chatter and the thud of music. Around midnight, Steph and her friend Maggie arrived by themselves. They'd come to say goodbye; it was wonderful. They were there for well over an hour and had no intention of leaving until Ray White's cousin Linda arrived to take them back. It turned out that the party at Ray White's house was for Steph's 21st birthday, and her absence had been noticed.

At 2pm Sunday morning, my cousin Anna's boyfriend, Trev, took Lorraine and me to Aspley Guise. I kissed Lorraine goodbye on the back doorstep of her house. She said she'd enjoyed the last week with me. I told her it had been great for me, too. It really had. I kissed her again and said I'd see her in 1973.

Back to Brogborough, most people had left and gone home, but there was still a hardcore of revellers enjoying themselves. However, we were almost out of alcohol, and the night was coming to an end.

That's when Johnny Irvine poked his head around the door.

"Have you lot run out of drink yet?" he shouted against the chatter and the beat of 'All Right Now' by Free coming from the record player.

"Yes," we yelled back.

"Well, I know where there's plenty," he replied. "Follow me".

A line of insatiable drunks followed Irvine up the street to Ray White's house. There was lots of drink there, but the party had run out of people. A few individuals were sitting around talking quietly. I asked someone where Steph was, and they said she'd gone to bed. Music was playing, but it was low and slow, so I walked over to where Steph's friend Maggie was sitting in conversation with an older woman. Maggie looked up and smiled.

In a slightly slurred voice, I asked her,

"Would you please honour me with a dance?"

Maggie accepted. My arms around her waist, hers around my neck, and our foreheads touching, we smooched around in a small circle. Eventually, we slumped into a large leather armchair. With Maggie sitting sideways across my lap, we kissed each other until we fell asleep. Sometime during the early morning, I woke up. Maggie was sleeping with her head on my shoulder, breathing softly in my ear. A couple of people were asleep on the sofa, and to my surprise, Steph's boyfriend was sleeping alone in the armchair beside us.

"Come with me", I whispered into Maggie's ear.

We went into the kitchen and closed the door. I kissed her and said,

"You are so beautiful, Maggie."

"You're not fooling anybody," she replied with a wistful smile.

I knew what she meant. Women can be so perceptive at times. Nevertheless, she let me unzip the back of her dress, pull it down to her hips and take off her bra.

It was still dark in the room when we went back to sleep in the armchair.

Maggie had to leave early in the morning for a family event at home. Steph drove her back to Flitwick with her sister Sue and I tagged along.

Steph's boyfriend had gone to bed when we returned to Brogborough. The house was empty. I helped Sue and Steph clear up the mess. After putting the place into a semblance of order, Sue disappeared. She may have gone back to bed, I don't know, but she left Steph and me alone together.

And there it was again, that strange old feeling. I didn't really know her, yet I felt so comfortable when I was with her. She looked at me, and her eyes penetrated my soul. When she said, "I'll miss you when you go away", I couldn't help myself. I took her in my arms and kissed her, and she responded.

I remember thinking, - I'm in love with this girl, and it's the wrong time and the wrong place.

Life was suddenly very complicated.

I don't know how long we were there like that, but, corny as they might be, the words of the old Platters song had it right - In the morning mist. Two lovers kissed, and the world stood still.

I had to leave before everyone got up. My feelings were an open book, and I didn't want to leave a mess in my wake as I sailed off into the sunset.

Steph straightened me up, smoothed out my hair, kissed me and sent me home with a cardboard box full of beer.

I dropped the box off at home and then went across the street to Mr and Mrs Irvine's house to see Mary, Bill and the new baby,

Maxine. I stayed there for a few hours. When I got back home, mum said that Ray White's wife's sister had come to see me while I was out and dropped off some bottles of spirits leftover from the party. My mum had no clue. It made me wonder what would have happened if that meeting had taken place.

I got washed up and changed and then fell asleep in the chair for the rest of the afternoon. I woke up in the evening with Val Cox standing over me, telling me to get up because all the gang were going to the Marston club Sunday dance. I told her I was too tired, but Val wouldn't have it. She dragged me out and squeezed me into her brother Collin's van with the rest of the gang. I was dead on my feet, but I managed to do the rounds and say goodbye to everyone.

On Monday evening, I was in Brogborough club with my friends when Steph, her boyfriend, Sue, and Ray White walked in. I went and sat and talked to Steph for a while as if we were just old friends. I had to fight the urge to put out my hand and touch her. Occasionally there was a pause in the conversation, and we just looked at each other. When they left, Steph came over to say goodbye. It was a painful parting, but that wasn't the end of it.

When the club closed, I sat on the wall talking with Hanns and Steven under the streetlamp outside their house. A car came down the street and pulled up in front of us. The window rolled down. Steph sat in the passenger seat next to her boyfriend. I walked over, thanked them both for the party and the leftover alcohol and told them to look after each other. I wanted to say more to Steph, I wanted to kiss her, but I couldn't. It was hard to believe no one had picked up on the situation, especially the boyfriend. But when I

walked back to the wall, Hanns looked at me with a wry smile and said,
"Butler, you old dog".
If you think my account of the last 48 hours was an old man's machinations, I can tell you I transposed the account almost word for word from the diary I kept at that time.
I never saw Steph again after that weekend. I bumped into her sister some years later. Sue told me Steph had married her boyfriend, and they had emigrated. If I ever think about her, which is not so often now, I have no regrets, just fond memories. Thinking 'What if' is a pointless exercise. It's just a game people play inside their heads. The Butler coat of arms motto reads - Comme je trouve. Which means "I take and make life as I find it". Love and life are a continuous flow of uncertainties with infinite possibilities. A moment's hesitation, bending to tie a shoelace, can change the future. When an event happens, all other possibilities disappear, and the wheel is in spin again.
When I eventually found the woman I would love for the rest of my life, it came in familiar surroundings, but it was a completely unexpected event.

After the weekend's events, the following day was an anti-climax. Wednesday evening, Erika came around to say goodbye in case she didn't see me again before I went away. I showed her my uniform, but she never offered to pay me to take her out in it. Because she'd missed the party, I invited her out for a drink at the club. Walking down the street, she gave me a present of a gold Papermate biro.

Bob Ellis came into the club with Erika's younger sister Regina, who Bob was going with. We went to the Rose and Crown at Wootton in Bob's car. Bob's dad was there with Johnny Irvine, and they kept buying us drinks all night. When the pub shut, we went looking for something to eat, then Bob drove us to his boss's house. I admit it felt awkward arriving at a stranger's house at eleven o'clock at night with a Chinese takeaway. We got back to Brogborough at about one in the morning. Erika invited me in for a coffee, and we talked and talked. At about two in the morning, we promised we wouldn't forget each other, and I went home.

Mum woke me the following morning with two letters. One was a card from Erika; inside, she'd written:

"Wherever you may be and whatever you may do.

Your first order. Take care of yourself."

Erika (Ned).

The (Ned) was because that's what I called her. Don't ask me why because I don't know.

Life is a strange and wonderful thing. Now that the heartache and the bitterness had receded, we were once more best friends. Along with Mary and Ray, that friendship has lasted a lifetime.

The second letter was from BI with instructions for me to go to Liverpool for a shipboard firefighting course. I found it surprising that shipboard firefighting was being taught at Speke airport.

Only two things of interest happened before I went to Liverpool. First, on Saturday, a cheque book arrived in the post. BI had opened a Midland Bank account for me in Jersey in the Channel Islands as I was on a two and a half year tax-free Eastern Service contract. The problem was, I wasn't in the far east. Because of the tax implications, I didn't know if I had any wages in my account or if I was able to draw on it if I did. As usual, I still had a severe cash flow problem. Two things you can't avoid in life are death and taxes.

The second thing was my cousin Bernadette came down from Derby to see me before I went away.

On Saturday evening, Bernadette, her younger sister Anna, Anna's boyfriend Trev and I went to the California Ballroom on the Whipsnade Road, Dunstable. The Cali, as it was known, was one of the county's premier venues for top pop groups during the 1960's and 70's. All the big names performed there on a Saturday night. This Saturday, the California was hosting Hot Chocolate. In August, the group had their first hit - Love is Life - and the song was still on the charts. It's one of those songs that puts me right back in the moment every time I hear it.

We arrived shortly before the main event and were fortunate to find a space in the car park next to a large van.

After the show, we realised we'd parked next to the group's van, which was being loaded after the gig. We talked for a while with Errol Brown, who was leaning out of the window. He was a really nice guy and invited us to a party in London, Islington, I think it was. That was too far for us, so we declined the invitation. Before they left, Anna got their autographs, and we ended up in the Key Club on West Street until two in the morning.

Firefighting in Liverpool.

On Monday, 5 October 1970, I took a train from Bletchley and arrived late afternoon in Liverpool. It was a short walk from Lime Street station to Hardman Road, where BI had booked me into Atlantic House Seaman's Mission Hotel. Bill Swan, who I'd met at the BI interview in London, arrived shortly after me.

In those days, pubs closed early, but in Liverpool, you could become a club member and drink all night. For two shillings and sixpence each, Bill and I became members of the Indiana Club. There, we met two young ladies who agreed to accompany us to our hotel for a nightcap. Unfortunately, back at Atlantic House, our interpretation of the hotel's mission statement, "To meet the spiritual, physical and emotional needs of seafarers", was fundamentally different from that of the night porter. Gentlemen that we were, we walked the ladies' home and returned to the hotel at 3:30 in the morning.

Tuesday, we met another BI recruit on the course called Collin. Bill and I were a little jaded, but fortunately, the day was devoted to orientation and theory with nothing physical.

During the day, we covered: Risk management, the fire triangle, sources of ignition, flammable materials, detectors and alarm systems, types of fires and suitable extinguishers, fire suppression and extinguishing systems, shipboard firefighting specific methods and hazards, and situational awareness and emergency escape routes. It was a lot to take in.

After class and looking forward to going to the Indiana club, we were unexpectedly introduced to what, for firemen, passes as humour. The instructors took us outside to the practical training facility, a large steel chamber like a ship's bridge with two rooms downstairs connected by steel ladders and trap doors to the rooms above. We were shepherded into the chamber to have a look round. While chatting amiably, two sulphurous smoke canisters fell to the floor behind us, and the steel door clanked shut. The door opened after a suitable period, and twelve coughing, spluttering, eyes streaming, disorientated trainees gasped their way out. The two instructors stood outside; arms folded with looks of amused disdain. It seemed we had not absorbed all we could have from the first day's study. We'd been especially remiss in the final section on Situational Awareness and Emergency Escape Routes.

Wednesday morning, we returned to Speke airport with a suitably heightened awareness of our sociopath instructors.

We had lectures and films on types of extinguishers, their uses and maintenance. After lunch, we were divided into two six-man teams with water extinguishers. The idea was to put out multiple Class A wood, paper and textiles fires by holding our breath for short periods in the smoke-filled chambers before being relieved by a team member.

"Don't worry, I've got this", said a salvage diver on our team. "I can hold my breath for three minutes".

We watched in admiration as he stepped heroically into the smoke and flame. The instructors did nothing to stop him. The metabolic effects of battling a fire with a heavy water-filled extinguisher are a little different from reclining at the bottom of a swimming pool. In under two minutes, out of air, he gasped in the smoke-filled atmosphere and dropped like a stone. The instructors dragged him out and revived him. They told us that it was a good demonstration of what teamwork was NOT and that ego wasn't a helpful tool for firefighting. A man has to know his limitations.

We put out other types of fires with the appropriate extinguishers. We finished using a bellows contraption connected to a face mask by a flexible air pipe to work in high smoke environments.

Back at the hotel that evening, Bill received a message that he was required to join the company's educational cruise ship Nevasa in Liverpool that Sunday. The lucky sod, he had a new ship and a new uniform to impress all those St Trinian sixth form schoolgirls as well. We celebrated his good fortune and went out clubbing.

Thursday morning was again devoted to theory with films on High Expansion Foams and Dry Powder for fighting class B petrol, diesel, alcohol, solvents and paint fires. We were introduced to the Breathing Apparatus (BA) Set. Colin and I teamed up using BA sets to put out small oil fires in the lower bridge chamber in the afternoon. It was tough, but we were pleased with our efforts when we finished.

It was our last night together, and we planned to go to the Grafton Ballroom. However, I was once again out of cash. When we finished training, I went to find a Midland Bank before it closed to try out my new cheque book. The bank cashier had to phone Jersey, who said there was no money in the account. I said I was desperate, I had to get home, and I didn't have the fare. That was a lie; I'd bought a return ticket in Bletchley. While I waited, Jersey phoned BI in London. After a delay, BI returned the call to Jersey, and then Jersey phoned Liverpool. BI had agreed to cover a £5 cheque. I was all set for a night out in Liverpool. Later, my first Midland Bank statement entry showed I was £5 overdrawn. It had taken four long-distance phone calls to get that money, and the bank charges. Well, they were zero. How times have changed.

Bill, Colin and I took a taxi to the Grafton Ballroom. Bill, the sensible fellow, left early; he had a ship to catch. Collin and I got picked up by two pretty Liverpool girls. My girl's name was Pat; we got on really great. We shared pictures we had taken together in a photo booth, and Pat wrote her address on the back of my two and told me to keep in touch.

After dancing the night away, we took the girls home in a taxi to Maria road. When Colin and I got back to the Atlantic House, it was five in the morning. Little did we know what was in store for us during the last training day.

We were given an ominous warning at the start of our final day. The instructor advised us it would be a good idea to pay particular attention to the day's class. We saw an oil fire raging in an open tank in the drill area during the lesson. When the lecture finished, we went outside. An instructor with protective clothing and a face mask held a long pole with a metal container the size of a bean can at the end of it. Another fireman filled the can with water. With the trainees at a safe distance, the instructor tipped the water into the blazing oil with the pole at full length.

A fireball four metres across erupted like the mushroom cloud of an atomic bomb from the oil tank. The instructor put down the pole, took off the mask and said.

"Gentlemen, I hope you were paying attention this morning because you are now going to put out some heavy-oil fires with water. Do I have a volunteer to take the first team in?"

We stood heads down in silence, avoiding eye contact. No one stepped forward.

I felt a hand on my back give a gentle push, and I involuntarily took one step forward.

"Well done, Mr Butler". Grinning, Colin followed me as the backup man.

With our BA sets on, and the water hose nozzle set to conical atomised mist spray, an instructor opened the steel door of the bridge structure. Black smoke poured out. Even with Colin behind, it was an effort to drag the hose forward into the room. The instructor closed the door behind us with the hose in the gully. Nothing could have prepared us for what followed. We were in total blackness, we couldn't see the fire, not even a faint glow. I was disorientated and paralysed. Collin's taps tap on my helmet and his hand pushing on my shoulder broke the trance. We went down into a crouch, trying to remember the lesson. I took off my glove and put my hand, palm forward, through the cone of water, then swung left and right until I felt the hot spot. I tugged on the hose, and we moved forward. We stopped, repeated the procedure, and moved on in total blackness every few feet. All I could hear was the loud rasping of my own breath inside my helmet.

Not until we stepped over a low metal obstruction did, I realise we were crouching in the oil tank with the fire extinguished.
There was another fire to deal with upstairs. Blindly we felt our way down the wall to find the metal ladder. When I gripped the rung of the ladder, I could feel the heat of the metal through my gloves. Even with the two of us, it was a struggle to climb with the hose. I'd forgotten about controlled breathing, and my heart was pounding. I was breathing hard, too hard. In the blackness, we struggled through the trapdoor, and as we found and started on the fire, my - air low alarm - went off. With the alarm whistling in my ear, we started back down the ladder. Still blind, we worked our way around the wall, trying to find the door out. The hose or the lifeline was snagged. Exercise or not, I panicked; I needed more training to handle this. That's when an instructor, who must have been in with us all the time, stepped in. He untangled the mess and dragged us to the door. Despite the ignominious ending, we walked out of that chamber exhilarated, with a new respect for firefighters but not ready to sign up as one. Masks off, we gave a verbal report, and two of our teammates went in and finished the job.
Colin, Bill and I rushed back to the hotel, picked up our cases, and went straight to Lime Street Station. We took the same train out and exchanged addresses at Crew before going our separate ways. Even though we all worked for BI, we never met each other again.
I am forever grateful to the Speke Fire Brigade. Despite my youthful desire to pursue other interests, they taught me valuable life lessons. Whenever I hear 'Band of Gold' by Freda Payne or

'Montego Bay' by Bobby Bloom, I am reminded of a night at the Grafton Ballroom and a Liverpool girl called Pat.

I can't remember the exact date now, but I had to go to Bedford Town Hall. It was something to do with registering my vaccinations and International Health Certificate.

When I got back home, my mum said that two soldiers in a Land Rover had arrived at the house looking for me while I was in Bedford. They'd told her I'd been requisitioned by MOD and transferred for duties with the army. They'd gone off, and I had to wait until they returned to pick me up. I was packed and ready to go, but I didn't understand what this was all about. I vaguely recalled seeing framed photographs of the army's Landing Ship Logistics (LSLs) Sir Galahad and Sir Tristram from my interview in London. BI staff had crewed these ships, but I thought that contract had finished.

Nonetheless, the only thing I could think of was that I'd been transferred as a BI officer to the Royal Fleet Auxiliary. It was feasible, but I didn't like it. It didn't fit with my exotic plans of sailing around the far east. There was nothing for it; I had to wait and see what fate had in store for me.

When the two soldiers returned, one of them started giving me some implausible story about being transferred to the army's Corps of Royal Electrical and Mechanical Engineers (REME). Once I recovered from the initial shock, I realised something suspicious was going on. One of the soldiers stood with his arms folded, looking stern. The other one was still talking, but now I wasn't

listening. He looked vaguely familiar. I hadn't seen him for about ten years, but finally, I recognised my cousin from Birkenhead.
"Jimmy Greenslade, you arsehole."
They were both in the REME and had been to Kempston Barracks probably to pick up some equipment for repair. On the way, Jimmy had decided to drop in for a cup of tea at his auntie Win's, where he and my mum had cooked up this ruse, and I'd almost fallen for it.

By Thursday, 15 October, I felt like a charlatan. It had been almost three weeks since my going away party, and I was still in Brogborough. I was in limbo, stuck in a no-man's-land between leaving and staying.
"Haven't you gone yet?" was the usual greeting I received when I met people in the street. It was getting embarrassing. All that was about to change.
At seven o'clock on Friday morning, there was a knock on the front door. I ran downstairs. Standing on the doorstep was a uniformed postman in a peaked cap. The postman handed me a brown telegram envelope and a clipboard for a signature. I signed the form, and he drove off into the morning mist in his little red Austin van. The air was sulphurous from the smoke of the brickyard chimneys held down by a grey overcast sky.
I opened the envelope and removed a buff-coloured Post Office Telegram form with white strips of single line telex paper pasted to it. The message strips read.

+FH129 6.2 LONDON TELEX PRIORITY 28

PRIORITY BUTLER 32 HIGHFIELD CRESCENT

BROGBOROUGH =

REPORT BOAC AIRTERMINAL VICTORIA TO COLLECT

TICKET AT 1425 HOURS DEPART LONDON AIRPORT

FLIGHT BA720 16:15HOURS 16OCT FOR CHANDPARA

KARACHI ACKNOWLEDGE BY TELEPHONE.

"Shit! That's today!"

"Mum, I've got a ship". I shouted up the stairs.

She came down, tying up her dressing gown.

"I'm flying to Karachi, mum. KARACHI" I exclaimed.

"You must have some breakfast before you go". Oh! My Irish mother.

My gear was packed and ready in the expandable fibre suitcase and a small grip bag.

I didn't have much time. I ran to the phone box by the shops and booked a taxi. Then, I went to the brickyard to tell my dad, who told his foreman and then came back home to change his clothes.

Shortly after getting back to the house, there was a knock on the door.

Dina Humphries was standing on the front step, the other girl who broke my heart in my last years at Fulbrook school. The object of my unrequited love, she had shown no interest in me.

What was she doing here?

How did she know I was leaving?

Then it clicked. Her family was related to the owners of Sibley's' Taxis in Aspley Guise. She was probably helping out. Today, by some strange twist of fate, she was my driver.
"Where are you going, Bernard?" she asked when she saw my luggage. At least she remembered my name.
"I'm flying to Karachi this afternoon, Dina. I'm an officer in the British Merchant Navy," I replied casually.
She was impressed.' Too late now, Dina' I thought.
I imagined it like an old silent movie. She, the back of her hand to her forehead, her other arm outstretched, a look of inconsolable remorse on her face. Me, a shrug of indifference before striding off to do my duty.
Dina dropped us off at Bletchley railway station. On the platform, not much was said. Mum sat in silence, and dad displayed a masculine stoicism reserved for these occasions. As the train departed for London, I hung out of the carriage window shamefully unmoved by my poor mother, who was weeping uncontrollably as she waved goodbye. For me, it was a great adventure.
The attendant handed me an envelope when I booked my luggage in at Victoria Air Terminal on Buckingham Palace Road. The envelope contained an air ticket and a message from BI.
The Karachi trip was cancelled, and I was booked into a hotel for the night. I was now flying to Bombay in the morning. The ticket had cost BI one hundred and nineteen pounds eighteen shillings. As a skilled man working for Headley's, that would have been roughly six weeks' wages.

I asked if I could leave my case. The attendant flipped up the countertop and dragged it in. He put it on a rack amongst hundreds of other cases, duffle bags, backpacks and taped-up cardboard boxes. He gave me a baggage receipt and told me the case would go on to Heathrow for the morning flight. I wouldn't see it again until I landed in Bombay. It seems incongruous now; there were no X-Ray scanners, security searches or sniffer dogs, just rows of luggage and packages.

A night alone in London, contemplating an uncertain future, was not what I'd wanted. My euphoria ebbed, and I had a troubled night.

I was back at Buckingham Palace Road at nine on Saturday morning to check-in for the flight. With just my grip bag and a one-way ticket to Bombay, I caught the transfer coach to the airport.

In the departure lounge at Heathrow, I bought a litre bottle of Smirnoff Blue label vodka and two-hundred 555 State Express cigarettes. I mailed one postcard to Pat, the girl I'd met in Liverpool, one to Lorraine, and one to my mum and dad. Apart from some loose change, I had just one £5 note safety-pinned into the inside pocket of my Burton suit jacket.

At a quarter to eleven, I was settled in a large comfortable starboard window seat of a British Overseas Airways Corporation (BOAC) Vickers VC10 Super. The plane was less than half full.

At 11 am, with its four Rolls-Royce Conway turbofans roaring at the rear of the fuselage, 'The Queen of the Sky's' accelerated forward and lifted off the runway.

Before long, we'd crossed the English Channel. Leaving my home far behind, the plane headed east to India.

Sitting alone with just the soft whine of the engines, I put my head back against the seat, closed my eyes and thought.

"What the hell have I done now".

......

The stewardess' voice shook me out of my reverie.

"The drinks are complimentary, sir. Would you like one?"

"Oh, yes please! I'll have a gin and tonic, thank you".

THE END

I don't think so!

Epilogue

Primarily this is a book about childhood, adolescence and coming of age.

However, the story reflects another history.

Britain's need to rebuild after the devastation of World War Two brought industrial growth, high employment, and new affluence. Like many others, the post-war boom brought my father from Ireland to the brick fields of Bedfordshire looking for work. The world couldn't get enough bricks, and the factories worked twenty-four hours a day. People earned and spent more on cars, holidays, entertainment and consumer goods. We always had a large cabinet radio in our house. However, the things we now take for granted, like a refrigerator, television, washing machine, and vacuum cleaner, didn't materialise until later. Most of these appliances arrived following a knock on the door by a travelling salesman. One thing we never had was a telephone.

The old school were shocked by the drop in moral standards. In 1960, the Crown's obscenity case against D. H. Lawrence's novel, Lady Chatterley's Lover, was squashed. In 1961 the sexual liberation of women began when the contraceptive pill became available on the NHS. This was followed by the 1967 Abortion Act legalising the termination of pregnancies under 28 weeks. The same year saw the introduction of the Sexual Offences Act, decriminalising homosexual activity between men over 21 years of age.

Religion became generally less important, and church attendance began to drop. Mind you, with my mum at the helm on Sundays, that didn't apply in our house.

In the late 1950's, my dad bought one of the first televisions in Brogborough. By 1961, three-quarters of the homes in Britain had one. By the decade's end, there were 12 million colour TVs in the country.

In 1962 the communications satellite Telstar initiated live TV transmission across the world. However, in November 1963, when President Kennedy was assassinated, it happened in its downtime.

In 1964 the BBC began broadcasting Top of The Pops on Thursday nights. One of the greatest innovations of the 20th century. At the same time, we had day-long pop music from the offshore Pirate Radio ships, which lasted until they were banned in 1967. To pacify the populous and forestall a revolution, the government gave us BBC Radio 1.

In 1964 Harold Wilson's Labour government came to power. More university places, polytechnics and technical colleges became available. This gave working-class youth, like me, access to further education. Whether we used it wisely or not was another matter. Nevertheless, it had a significant impact on my life.

In 1966 the country watched TV as England defeated Germany and won the World Cup, an achievement yet to be repeated.

In August 1969, sixty-six years after the Wright brothers' first 12-second manned flight, a human walked on the moon.

The Beatles changed music forever and led the British invasion of America, followed by the Rolling Stones, The Kinks, The Who, The Animals and others.

The Vietnam war became an almost live TV event. A reality show to watch during evening teatime.

All this, along with a general distrust of government after the Profumo affair, youth fashion, mobility, and increased spending power (me excluded), made the 1950's and 60s a special time to grow up in Britain.

*****

It's hard to believe that the events in this book happened over fifty years ago. Time indeed is a thief. Today in Brogborough, all traces of the brickyard, the old oak tree Merry England, the middle path and the corn field it bisected are long gone. In their place, the ground is covered by a clean and tidy industrial park. The side path is still there, winding its way through the industrial buildings to Ridgmont railway station as it did through the old brickworks. I wonder how long it has been since any kid from the village entered the mysterious world of the green tunnel beside the path. The Two Trees are gone, felled years ago by Dutch Elm disease.

The time when I could walk the streets of Brogborough and name every person who lived in each house is just a memory. Brogborough is now an estate of private homes and mainly strangers to me. The houses are more personalised than they used to be and there are many more trees than I remember. The village hall now stands where old Horris used to mix his cement, and Mr Cook did his carpentry and maintenance work. I'm glad the estate still has a heart to replace the old CIU Club that is gone and replaced by private houses.

There have been times when back in the UK, I parked outside 32 Highfield Crescent, looked up at the big-bedroom window and thought. "Wow, that's where I was born". But it's just a place of ghosts now.

The ghosts that formed my character and prepared me for the world. I am forever grateful to that little place on a south-facing hill in Bedfordshire and the characters that contributed to a magical childhood.

One of the things I've learned in life is that nothing stays the same.

*****

Some people think they are the masters of their own destiny. They believe success is due to talent, hard work, self-motivation, drive, and a plan. Indeed it is difficult to imagine success without those things. I have put in my share of time and effort. However, whatever success I've had in life has come through a lot of luck. My tech drawing teacher seeing more in me than a draughtsman. A chance meeting with Sue Brown in the students' common room. Having the answer to the foreman's killer question. The college finding me at the bottom of the barrel when it was looking for one more student to launch a special engineering course. Getting the job in electronics because I knew the formula for resonance which I'd learned only the week before at college. My foreman blocking me from taking that job in electronics and making me complete my apprenticeship in mechanical engineering because

I was legally bound to. Becoming an officer with British India because I'd finished my training and was qualified in mechanical engineering. Going off to sail the seas on tramp steamers before they were confined to history, replaced by container ships, bulk carriers and supertankers. None of these links in fortune's chain of events was of my making. Yet they were all fundamental to what happened next.

Is moving to a Mediterranean island aged 36 with my wife and children a sign of success? If it is, I can tell you it only resulted from a chance conversation one evening in a car park in Bovingdon. But that's another story.

We are all subject to the butterfly effect. Every day, small random events determine our destiny. My point is that life is like a journey in a time machine. Go back and change one insignificant thing; it will change your final destination and even determine your time in this world.

Would I go back and change anything in my life if I had the chance?

No, not one thing.

For now, I'll take a break, rest a while, and catch up on all those household jobs I've neglected over the last year.

After that, I'll start on Ocean Tramp in a month or so.

Acknowledgments

To my friends, without whom I would have had little to write about. I hope you're not upset about appearing in this book. You're in this book because I care about you all. You have enriched my life, for that I thank you. We will all be dust and forgotten soon enough. I want our grandkids to know the characters we were and are.

To our descendants who follow. To a great extent this book was inspired by and written for you, so you have some idea where you came from. Even though we may never meet, our love is always with you. Look on old people kindly because you're not the only ones that have had to go through all this stuff.

Finally, to Phillip Witcomb, my publisher, thank you for your encouragement and belief that I could turn my short stories into a book. Three books, time permitting.

Thanks for the laughs, mate. There's never a dull moment when we get together. Even when we argue totally opposing views it's always fun.

Printed in Poland
by Amazon Fulfillment
Poland Sp. z o.o., Wrocław
20 November 2023

da4e88b5-7cba-4a28-90e4-199dee819031R01